# THE EPISTLE OF PAUL TO THE GALATIANS.

BY

OTTO SCHMOLLER, PH. DR.

*TRANSLATED FROM THE GERMAN,*

BY

C. C. STARBUCK, A. M.

*EDITED, WITH ADDITIONS,*

BY

M. B. RIDDLE, D.D.

*Wipf & Stock*
PUBLISHERS
*Eugene, Oregon*

Wipf and Stock Publishers
199 W 8th Ave, Suite 3
Eugene, OR 97401

The Epistle of Paul to the Galatians
an Exegetical and Doctrinal Commentary
By Schmoller, Otto
ISBN 13: 978-1-55635-409-0
ISBN 10: 1-55635-409-6
Publication date 4/6/2007
Previously published by Charles Scribner, 1871

# EDITOR'S PREFACE TO THE SEVENTH VOLUME.

This volume of the American edition of Lange's *Biblework*, being the seventh of the New Testament Division, embraces the following Epistles of St. Paul:

GALATIANS. By OTTO SCHMOLLER, Ph. D., of Urach, Würtemberg. Translated by C. C. STARBUCK, A. M., with additions by M. B. RIDDLE, D. D.

EPHESIANS AND COLOSSIANS. By KARL BRAUNE, D. D., General Superintendent of Altenburg, Saxony. Translated, enlarged and edited by M. B. RIDDLE, D. D.

PHILIPPIANS. By Dr. BRAUNE. Edited, with additions, by Prof. HACKETT, D. D., formerly of Newton Centre, now of the Theological Seminary at Rochester, N. Y.

The Epistle to the Ephesians had been originally assigned to Prof. Dr. HITCHCOCK, of Union Theological Seminary, New York, but, much to the regret of the general editor, Dr. H. was obliged to abandon the task on account of illness. This interruption and the absence of Dr. Riddle in Germany have caused some delay in the publication of the volume.

The translation was prepared from the last editions of the original. The additions were made with constant reference to the best German as well as English and American commentators, especially to ALFORD, ELLICOTT, LIGHTFOOT, EADIE and HODGE. Dr. EADIE's work on the Galatians appeared after this part of the volume was in type. Dr. SCHENKEL's commentaries on the Ephesians, Philippians and Colossians (1862, 2d ed., 1867),—originally a part of the *Biblework*, but replaced since, for reasons connected with the theological change of the author, by those of Dr. BRAUNE—were also consulted throughout. BRAUNE is an able, careful, concise, sound and judicious exegete. Special attention was paid to the enlargement of the Textual and Exegetical departments. Where the translators differ from the German authors, the reasons are generally given.

Upon the whole, the additions amount to about one third of the volume, and will commend themselves to the judgment of competent readers as a valuable improvement.

The New Testament part of this laborious work is now drawing to a close. The Commentaries on the Gospel of John, and on Revelation will complete it. The former is far advanced and, if the Lord spare the health and strength of the general editor, will be finished during the coming winter.* The commentary on Revelation has not yet appeared in German, but may be expected in a few months, and will be immediately taken in hand. The last part will also contain a complete and careful Index of all the volumes on the New Testament. The Old Testament is progressing more slowly, yet as fast as the nature of the work will admit.

*New York*, 10 *Bible House*, *Aug.* 24*th*, 1870. PHILIP SCHAFF.

---

* In reply to the many inquiries concerning the issue of the volume on John, I beg leave to say that the delay has been occasioned in great part by the death of my dear friend, Dr. Yeomans, to whom it had been originally assigned, and who left his unfinished translation to me as a sacred legacy. I am progressing with the revision and the numerous additions as fast as the multiplicity of my engagements and constant interruptions will at all permit, and I am desirous to make the commentary as full and satisfactory to English readers as I can.

# EDITOR'S PREFACE TO THE SEVENTH VOLUME.

This volume of the American edition of Lange's *Biblework*, being the seventh of the New Testament Division, embraces the following Epistles of St. Paul:

GALATIANS. By OTTO SCHMOLLER, Ph. D., of Urach, Würtemberg. Translated by C. C. STARBUCK, A. M., with additions by M. B. RIDDLE, D. D.

EPHESIANS AND COLOSSIANS. By KARL BRAUNE, D. D., General Superintendent of Altenburg, Saxony. Translated, enlarged and edited by M. B. RIDDLE, D. D.

PHILIPPIANS. By Dr. BRAUNE. Edited, with additions, by Prof. HACKETT, D. D., formerly of Newton Centre, now of the Theological Seminary at Rochester, N. Y.

The Epistle to the Ephesians had been originally assigned to Prof. Dr. HITCHCOCK, of Union Theological Seminary, New York, but, much to the regret of the general editor, Dr. H. was obliged to abandon the task on account of illness. This interruption and the absence of Dr. Riddle in Germany have caused some delay in the publication of the volume.

The translation was prepared from the last editions of the original. The additions were made with constant reference to the best German as well as English and American commentators, especially to ALFORD, ELLICOTT, LIGHTFOOT, EADIE and HODGE. Dr. EADIE's work on the Galatians appeared after this part of the volume was in type. Dr. SCHENKEL's commentaries on the Ephesians, Philippians and Colossians (1862, 2d ed., 1867),—originally a part of the *Biblework*, but replaced since, for reasons connected with the theological change of the author, by those of Dr. BRAUNE—were also consulted throughout. BRAUNE is an able, careful, concise, sound and judicious exegete. Special attention was paid to the enlargement of the Textual and Exegetical departments. Where the translators differ from the German authors, the reasons are generally given.

Upon the whole, the additions amount to about one third of the volume, and will commend themselves to the judgment of competent readers as a valuable improvement.

The New Testament part of this laborious work is now drawing to a close. The Commentaries on the Gospel of John, and on Revelation will complete it. The former is far advanced and, if the Lord spare the health and strength of the general editor, will be finished during the coming winter.* The commentary on Revelation has not yet appeared in German, but may be expected in a few months, and will be immediately taken in hand. The last part will also contain a complete and careful Index of all the volumes on the New Testament. The Old Testament is progressing more slowly, yet as fast as the nature of the work will admit.

*New York*, 10 *Bible House*, *Aug*. 24*th*, 1870. PHILIP SCHAFF.

* In reply to the many inquiries concerning the issue of the volume on John, I beg leave to say that the delay has been occasioned in great part by the death of my dear friend, Dr. Yeomans, to whom it had been originally assigned, and who left his unfinished translation to me as a sacred legacy. I am progressing with the revision and the numerous additions as fast as the multiplicity of my engagements and constant interruptions will at all permit, and I am desirous to make the commentary as full and satisfactory to English readers as I can.

THE

# EPISTLE OF PAUL TO THE GALATIANS.

---

## INTRODUCTION.

### § 1. THE RECIPIENTS OF THE EPISTLE.

The recipients of the Epistle are αἱ ἐκκλησίαι τῆς Γαλατίας, the churches of Galatia.

The district of Galatia in Asia Minor owes its name and origin to the immigration of the tribes of the Trocmi, Tolistobogii and Tectosages, included by ancient writers under the generic name of Galatians, Gauls or Celts. These left their abode on the Rhine in the third century B. C., and after having made desolating incursions into Macedonia and Greece, they founded in Thrace the kingdom of Thyle, whence they forced their way into Asia Minor under the leaders Leonorius and Lutarius. Here they received from the Bithynian king Nicomedes, a part of Phrygia as a reward for services rendered in war. [LIGHTFOOT intimates that this movement across the Hellespont was connected with the final repulse, given at Delphi (B. C. 279) to the Celtic invasion of Greece. A considerable force that had refused to take part in this expedition was joined by a remnant of the repulsed army, and under the leaders above named forced their way through Thrace to the Hellespont, across which they were soon attracted by the fertility of Asia Minor. They overran a large extent of territory, but their power was finally curbed by the Pergamene prince Attalus the First (about B. C. 230). See the authorities quoted in his *Introd. Galatians*, pp. 5, 6.—R.] As they mixed with the Greeks and spoke the Greek language too, they were also called *Gallograeci*, and their territory, *Gallograecia*, Γαλλογραικία. They are described as a valiant and liberty-loving people, who, from their fondness for fighting, could readily be hired as mercenaries, and were dreaded as soldiers, far and wide. But in the year B. C. 189, they were subjected to the Roman power by Consul Cneius Manlius Vulso; retaining, however, their ancient federative constitution under their own Tetrarchs, who finally bore the title of Kings. From this time forth they devoted themselves more and more to the arts of peace, and made their country one of the most flourishing in existence. Through the favor of Antony and Augustus towards their last king, Amyntas, Pisidia and parts of Lycaonia and Pamphylia were added to his dominions. After the death of Amyntas, Galatia thus enlarged became a Roman province.

JEROME, who spent some time in Gaul and also in Galatia, remarks (*Proleg. in libr. II., ep. ad. Gal.*) that the language of the Galatians was identical with that of the Treviri; this is the chief ground for the opinion that the Galatians were not Celts, but Germans. The name, Galatians, Gauls, is not against this; for this designation is to be explained from the usage of the third century B. C., when the Romans as yet included the Germans under the name of Gauls. Since, however, the nationality of the Treviri themselves is a matter of dispute, that of the Galatians cannot be certainly thus determined. The supposition that one tribe of the Galatians, the Tectosages (MEYER), were Germans, while the other two were Gauls, is inconsistent with Strabo's remark, that the three tribes had the same manners and the same language; and as a native of the neighboring Cappadocia, he must have been accurately informed on this point. We can at all events adduce in favor of their German origin the names of the leaders, Leonorius (comp. Leonhardt, Leonore) and Lutharius, that is, Lothar, and also their polity as described by Strabo, according to which their princes, and not their priests, dispensed justice, this being, according to CÆSAR (*Bell. Gall. VI.* 13), a chief distinction between the Gauls and Germans (WIESELER). Tradition relates also, that an army of crusaders was struck with astonishment at hearing all at once, in this region, the Bavarian dialect.

[WIESELER and OLSHAUSEN advocate the Teutonic origin, at which Luther hints in his warning to the Germans against like inconstancy (*Com. Gal.* i. 6). MEYER suggests the mixed origin mentioned above, while Thierry, and other French writers (including the Emperor Napoleon III. *Cesar. II.* p. 2), claim this settlement of Celts as an evidence of Gallic enterprise. English writers generally advocate the Celtic origin. The matter is ably discussed by LIGHTFOOT, *Galatians, Dissert. I. p.* 235 *sq.*: "Were the Galatians Celts or Teutons?" He maintains that they were Celts, arguing both from the authority of classical writers, and from the philological data furnished by the proper names which remain. But the most convincing argument is drawn from the character of the people. "They are described by the ancient writers as a frank, warlike, impetuous, intelligent and impressible, but unsteady, ostentatious and vain people, strongly resembling the cognate French" (SCHAFF). That their peculiarities were more akin to those of the ancient Gauls and modern Celtic races, than to those of the Teutonic race, ancient or modern, is very evident. Luther might have spared his rebuke about "inconstancy," could he have foretold modern history. LIGHTFOOT (*Introd.* pp. 1–17) speaks of the tough vitality of national character, so strongly marked in the Celts, which is shown also by the Galatians in Asia Minor; the similar *fickle* temperament (i. 6; iii. 1), and even hints that the vices rebuked in this epistle are not foreign to the distinctive character of the Celts, e. g.: v. 21, "drunkenness and revellings;" vi. 6, 7, niggardliness in alms giving; v. 26, "vain glory;" v. 15, "bite and devour one another." Certainly the tendency of the Galatians in religion was toward superstitious ritualism (iii. 3), not to mysticism as among their neighbors, the Phrygians, and to-day the Celtic people have the same tendency. It is worthy of note, if the Celtic extraction be admitted, that those Epistles (*Galatians* and *Romans*) which assail most plainly the errors of legalism and ritualism, should have been addressed to Celtic and Latin readers. The progress of ethnographic science seems to favor the view that the Galatians were Celts. Comp. CONYBEARE and HOWSON: *Life and Epistle of St. Paul, I. p.* 243 *sq.*—R.]

The opinion, that we are to regard, not the Galatians proper, but inhabitants of the district added under King Amyntas, Lycaonians (especially the christians of Derbe and Lystra), and Pisidians, as the recipients of our Epistle, is altogether untenable, owing its rise to hypotheses about the time of its composition.

The recipients of the Epistle are more particularly, the Christian congregations, *αἱ ἐκκλησίαι* of Galatia. There were therefore several Christian churches in this district—perhaps in the chief places, Ancyra, Tavium and Pessinus, according to a missionary principle observed by the Apostle (WIESELER). In the book of Acts also no places are mentioned. In one other passage these churches are spoken of in the same way (1 Cor. xvi. 1). The passages, 2 Tim. iv. 10; 1 Pet. i. 1, also presuppose Christians in Galatia. These churches were founded by Paul himself. This appears indisputably from our Epistle, i. 6–8; iv. 13 sq., and is confirmed by the narrative in the Acts. According to this he came hither for the first time soon after the apostolic council, Acts xvi. 6. He must then have preached the gospel there, and founded churches; for although this is not expressly stated, it is to be assumed, since, at the visit mentioned in Acts xviii. 23, he was already employed in "strengthening" the churches there. A second visit of the Apostle to Galatia is also indicated in our Epistle, especially iv. 13 (comp. *ad. loc.*). The first one is more particularly described as having been occasioned by bodily weakness, which had constrained him to delay in Galatia, and given him opportunity to preach the gospel there. This visit, therefore, cannot well coincide with that mentioned in Acts xviii. 23.

These churches were undoubtedly chiefly composed of Gentile Christians, as is clear from our Epistle, partly from the passages of general reference, i. 16; ii. 9, in which Paul takes pains to prove to the Galatians his vocation as Apostle to the Gentiles, partly and especially from iv. 8, where the readers, as a whole, are designated as having been idolaters, and from v. 2, 3; vi. 12, 13, according to which they were as yet uncircumcised. Unquestionably there was also in Galatia a Jewish population, perhaps a numerous one (comp. Josephus, Ant. 12, 3, 4; 16, 6, 2), and so there may have been Jewish Christians also in the churches. But we cannot draw a certain conclusion from the ἡμεῖς in passages which refer especially to Jewish Christians, as iii. 23–25; iv. 3; for we cannot decidedly affirm that here Paul includes the readers also in the first person. The abrupt transition from the first to the second person in iii. 25, 26; iv. 5, 6, might rather favor the opposite conclusion, namely, that he has reference to the readers only in the second part of these passages where he treats of the Christian state, and not in what precedes, respecting the condition of a Jew. [It is by no means certain that the use of the first person in the passages cited involves an exclusive reference to "the condition of a Jew." See EXEG. NOTES, iv. 3.—R.] Nor is the fact that acquaintance with the Old Testament is presupposed in the arguments of the epistle, a convincing proof. For all evangelical preaching rested on the Old Testament Scripture. Besides this, thorough discussion of the Old Testament was here demanded by the subject of the epistle. For the churches were wrought upon by Judaizing false teachers, who endeavored to lead them back to an Old Testament position; as they had doubtless been already sufficiently instructed by these teachers in the Old Testament, on this account alone Paul was obliged to enter on the discussion of the Old Testament, and out of it to refute them; to open up to them a still deeper and juster understanding of the Old Testament economy. Only so could they be delivered from an authority pretending a support from the Old Testament. The supposition that the Galatian Christians had formerly been in great part proselytes, is therefore unnecessary. [SCHAFF: The congregations of Galatia were, like all the churches founded by Paul, of a mixed, yet predominantly Gentile Christian character.—R.]

## § 2. OCCASION OF THE EPISTLE.

The spiritual state of these Galatian churches, at first a matter of joy, had been sadly disturbed by certain unnamed persons, who, to be sure, were Christians, but of Judaizing or pharisaistic tendencies. These, it is plain, had come from abroad, and perhaps were emissaries from Palestine. They were hardly proselytes. Such a conclusion does not follow from v. 12; vi. 13. They set themselves in direct opposition to the Christian view, which had, till then, prevailed in the church; and, moreover, directed their polemics expressly against Paul, as the first promulgator of this view. To the persuasion which had taken root through him, that justification and salvation are to be attained alone through faith in Christ, by grace, they opposed the assertion that certain works of the law, especially the observance of the Jewish festivals, and the receiving of circumcision, were necessary to salvation. From prudential motives, they did not require the observance of the whole law. In order to gain entrance for this view, diametrically opposed as it was to the doctrine of Paul, they sought to undermine the consideration in which the Galatians held him, by denying to him the apostolic dignity, and by appealing, in opposition, to the authority of the senior Apostles, especially James, Peter and John, as the true pillars of the church, to whom Paul, as they represented, stood in opposition, while they proceeded in concurrence with them. Nay, they appear to have even imputed to Paul the *inconsistency* of sometimes himself preaching circumcision among the Jews, v. 11; and would have it, therefore, that his doctrine of the freedom of believers from the law proceeded only from unworthy complaisance towards the Gentiles. (Comp. i. 10.)

How long these false teachers had been working in the church cannot be precisely determined; yet we see from i. 9; v. 3; iv. 16, that Paul, on his second visit, had already spoken against this Judaizing error; chiefly, we may suppose, by way of warning and precautionary instruction, as the danger was yet only imminent, although the inclination to yield was already present. Matters came to an actual leading astray only after the departure of the Apostle. For from the impression which the Epistle makes, we must conclude that he has now, for the first time, to deal with the church after its actual fall into error. This falling away, however, must have made surprisingly rapid progress, as unmistakably appears from the tone of the Epistle; comp. also i. 6: *οὕτω ταχέως*.

As just remarked, the false teachers actually succeeded in finding entrance and seducing the churches. How far can only be partially determined. At all events, we must not underrate their success. From the whole tenor of the Epistle from the earnestness with which Paul speaks (e. g. i. 6; iii. i. 3; iv. 12, 19, 20; v. 1 sq. 7), from his thorough handling of the question of his own doctrinal position, and of the question respecting his apostolic authority, as also from the allusion to the division that had arisen in the church (chaps. v. and vi.), it is sufficiently clear that the Judaizing *view*, at least, had already completely got the upper hand, and especially that the consideration enjoyed by the Apostle was already a good deal shaken. (Comp. the peculiarly full exposition of this question in the Epistle.) On the other hand, the apostasy from the principle of justifying faith was as yet by no means complete, but only incipient. (Comp. e. g. i. 6; iv. 9, 17, 21.) Especially the practical observance of Judaism was only in its beginnings. The observance of the Jewish days and times had commenced, but "to the chief requirement of the false teachers, obedience to which would first render the apostasy from evangelical Christianity complete, namely the receiving of circumcision, they had as yet yielded no compliance, in any numbers worth speaking of, since the circumcision of the readers is mentioned as something still impending." On the other hand, we cannot, from the "little leaven," (v. 2), draw the inference of a falling away as yet insignificant, since this expression rather refers to the small number of their corrupters, or rather to the fact that a deviation from evangelical truth in one point or a few points may easily work great mischief.

This condition of the Galatian churches has evidently been speedily reported to the Apostle; for, as yet, all is in the bud; he has still good hope of the Galatians, that all will come right again; he deals with them throughout as having but just set foot on the downward path, and feels himself to be still standing in close connection with them, notwithstanding that, on their side, some estrangement may have already taken place, inasmuch as the personal consideration of the apostle itself had been so directly impugned. Yet he does not appear to have received his intelligence so very soon, but that he speaks of their already having begun to observe days, and months, and times, and years. Though we cannot, of course, from this last expression, draw the inference of their having been already a year in this condition, yet the Judaizing usage in this respect must have already, in some measure, obtained prevalence. Such intelligence is it which gives the Apostle occasion for the writing of our Epistle to the Galatians.

[LIGHTFOOT: "The fragmentary notices of its subsequent career reflect some light on the temper and disposition of the Galatian church in St. Paul's day. Asia Minor was the nursery of heresy, and, of all the Asiatic churches, it was no where so rife as in Galatia. The Galatian capital was the stronghold of the Montanist revival, which lingered on for more than two centuries, splitting into diverse sects, each distinguished by some fantastic gesture or minute ritual observance. Here too were to be found Ophites, Manichæans, sectarians of all kinds. Hence during the great controversies of the fourth century issued two successive bishops (Marcellus and Basilius), who disturbed the peace of the Church, the one on the side of Sabellian, the other of Arian error. A Christian father of this period (GREGORY NAZ.), denounces 'the folly of the Galatians, who abound in many impious denominations.'" Still both in the Diocletian persecution and against Julian, who personally attempted the restoration of heathenism in Galatia, the Christians bore themselves with fortitude and constancy.—R.]

### § 3. TIME AND PLACE OF COMPOSITION: GENUINENESS.

It is evident that Paul composed the Epistle immediately after he had received the unpleasing intelligence, for it is written under the fresh, immediate impression of it, as appears by the troubled style, full of astonishment and strong feeling. If the opinion given above is correct, that Paul himself, in his letter, intimates having made a second visit to Galatia (comp. especially iv. 13), the Epistle was, of course, written after this; and, therefore, if the second visit is the one mentioned, Acts xviii. 23, about A. D. 55 or 56. As Paul, after laboring the second time in Galatia, went to Ephesus, and remained there three years, it is most natural to suppose that he wrote the Epistle in Ephesus. The common subscription says, ἐγράφη ἀπὸ Ῥώμης, and several fathers favor this view, but it has arisen only out of a misunderstanding of iv. 20; vi. 2, and especially of vi. 17.

[Time and place are linked together; the two most probable opinions are: 1. That it was written from Ephesus, A. D. 54–57 (Acts xix. 1–10). 2. From Corinth, A. D. 57–58 (Acts

xx. 3). If 1. be adopted, then it was written before the Epistles to the Corinthians; if 2., then subsequently. 1. is held by as more probable among others by MEYER, LANGE, SCHAFF (*History of the apostolic church, p.* 282), REUSS (*Gesch. der heil. Schriften des N. T.* 4th ed. p. 73), ALFORD, ELLICOTT, DAVIDSON, TURNER; 2. by DE WETTE, CONYBEARE, BLEEK, and by LIGHTFOOT most decidedly. STANLEY and JOWETT, leave the question undetermined, while WORDSWORTH dates it as early as A. D. 53, before Paul's second visit from Corinth, during his first visit there. (See his *Introd.* to *Gal.*) As the first named is the view generally received, it will be proper to state more fully the arguments of LIGHTFOOT. 1. The resemblance to the Second Epistle to the Corinthians, and that to the Romans, between which he would place it, its affinity in tone of feeling to the former, and in thought to the latter. 2. This order best accords with the history of Paul's personal sufferings and the progress of his controversy with the Judaizers, as shown in the fulness of doctrinal statement against their views. 3. This date explains one or two allusions more satisfactorily, as vi. 1, against severe treatment, the evil effects of which he may have witnessed at Corinth; vi. 7: "Be not deceived," *etc.*, referring to their illiberality in response to the "orders to the churches of Galatia," mentioned 1 Cor. xvi. 1. See LIGHTFOOT, pp. 36–56. The question is one of probabilities, yet, as respects internal evidence, it may be remarked that the strong emotion of the Galatian Epistle renders it more probable that it was written speedily after the news of their error had come to the Apostle, while the calmer, more didactic setting of the same truth in the Epistle to the Romans indicates the lapse of a considerable interval between the two. Hence, the earlier date, from Ephesus, is to be preferred, and until lately was generally allowed by the best commentators. The view of WORDSWORTH, assigning a yet earlier date, involves a somewhat forced intepretation of iv. 13, 14, and, while ingeniously supported, rests too entirely upon hypotheses respecting Paul's course in dealing with an erring church.—R.]

Although the apostolic fathers contain no trace even measurably certain, and Justin's writings only a probable trace of the Epistle, its genuineness is nevertheless so firmly established, that it has never yet been doubted. It is supported partly by external, and partly by internal testimony. As to the former, the Epistle is already in use by the Gnostic Valentine (IREN. *Adv. hær.* 3: 3.) and by his disciple THEODOTUS (*Exc. ap. Clem. Alex.* c. 53*); and by MARCION about the middle of the second century, who has it in his canon as the first of the Pauline epistles, and draws his chief arguments from it to prove the other apostles Judaizers (*Epiph. hær*, 42: 9); it is known to Tatian (JEROME, *Comm. in Gal.* 6); it is found on the testimony of the elder Peshito in the Syrian church; and according to the CANON of MURATORI, composed in 170, it is found in the church of the Occident; towards the end of the second century, it is used by the fathers IRENÆUS [*Adv. hær.* III. 7, 2—R.], CLEM. ALEX. [*Strom.* III. p. 468—R.] and TERTULLIAN [*De Præscript. hær.* c. 6—R.]; and, finally, it is reckoned by EUSEBIUS among the Homologoumena. Yet stronger is the thoroughly Pauline character and style of the Epistle. The Tübingen school, far from denying its genuineness, uses it rather as the great lever of its criticism upon the writings whose genuineness this school impugns. The sole exception to this universal consent is BRUNO BAUR (*Kritik der Paulin. Br.*, 1*ste Abtheilung*, 1850), who has discovered in the author a compiler, that fabricated the Epistle out of that to the Romans and the two to the Corinthians. His imaginary proof, however, is so utterly without foundation, or scientific worth, that it bears its refutation on its face (WIESELER, MEYER).

## § 4. OBJECT, STYLE AND COURSE OF THOUGHT OF THE EPISTLE.

As implied in the occasion of writing indicated above, the Apostle intended by this, his Epistle, to destroy the influence which the Judaizing teachers, with their legal doctrine, had gained in the Galatian churches, and to bring anew to general acknowledgment, in the first place his apostolic authority, and next, on this basis, the gospel preached by him of the sinner's justification through faith, and of the freedom of the believer from the law. His essential aim is, to bring back the misled Galatians into the right path, as he also cherishes the strong hope, that he shall succeed in this. To this end he exhorts them most earnestly to a return, and supports this ad-

* ["Where Gal. iii. 19, 20 is quoted: but the date and authorship of these excerpts are uncertain" (LIGHTFOOT).—R.]

monition by a careful demonstration of the perversity of that which the false teachers have brought in the way.

Inasmuch, therefore, as the Epistle has as its object, on the one hand, the combatting of an intriguing attempt, that had succeeded but too well, to destroy a work which had had a fair beginning, and at the same time, the combatting of a general doctrine of error, which overturned the evangelical foundation; and on the other hand the bringing back of a beloved church, which had erred from the truth, and the firm establishment of a momentous fundamental truth of the gospel, it is easy to explain the style of strong feeling which the Apostle on the whole maintains. Especially may we thus explain the sharp earnestness with which ever and anon he breaks forth against the false teachers; the zeal of love pervaded by sadness, with which he seeks to persuade the readers of their error, and to make clear the matter to them in the most varied aspects; while with all this personal reference he does not shrink from going into the most thorough exposition of that which had been brought into doubt.

In treating a writing of such a kind, nothing is more mistaken than the desire to dispose it according to scholastic rules. It is true, the thought moves in thoroughly close connection, and a steady and clear progress is found, but the whole is a living growth, where one thing grows out of the other in the most immediate connection. With all the steadiness of the progress of thought, there prevails also a freedom of movement, and all pedantic analysis does violence to this mighty gush of thought.

As usual, Paul begins his Epistle with an ADDRESS and SALUTATION (i. 1–5), except that even here, agreeably to the purpose of the Epistle he emphasizes his apostolate in a very peculiar manner, i. 1, and brings into prominence the significance of the atoning death of Christ (i. 4). Then entering at once upon the matter, he sets forth the *occasion of the Epistle*, by expressing his astonishment at the speedy entrance which false teachers had found into the Galatian churches; and against every one, who preaches another gospel than that which he had brought them, denounces the Anathema—a severity which he justifies by reference to his duty as a servant of Christ (i. 6–10). There follows now:

I. The clearly marked FIRST CHIEF DIVISION of the Epistle (I. 4—II. 21)—*a detailed demonstration of his full apostolic dignity, and thereby of the full authority of his evangelical preaching.* Although the polemical reference is not distinctly announced, this is of course in definite opposition to the attacks of his opposers. Because this was the point of departure, the base of operations for the legal doctrine, he accordingly refutes these attacks first and before all, in order to have a foundation for what follows. For only by re-establishing his apostolic consideration, could he hope to destroy the influence which the false teachers and their legal doctrine had won and to convince his readers of the truth of his own preaching. The proof Paul conducts in the following manner. He shows,

(1), How he had received his commission to preach the gospel from God and Christ Himself, through special revelation, and not otherwise, as from the senior Apostles; how he could not possibly have received it from these, since for a long time he had only come once into hasty communication with them (vers. 11–24).

(2), That during a later interview in Jerusalem with the senior Apostles, having reference to doctrine, the latter by no means assumed any authority over him, or uttered any censure of his course; that on the contrary, while he, in opposition to the false brethren, most decidedly upheld the evangelical truth, it was precisely by the "pillars" of the church, the Apostles James, Peter and John that he was acknowledged as an Apostle of equal authority, and the preaching among the Gentiles left to him by a free and friendly agreement (ii. 1–10).

(3), That when Peter, although himself fully committed to the freer view respecting the Mosaic law, yet from fear of man had once deviated from it, he had not hesitated publicly to rebuke him, and to lay before him in the most definite manner the principles of his preaching among the Gentile Christians, in order to guard against these being led astray (ii. 11, 26). With Chap. iii. Paul passes over:

II. to a new section, the HEART of the whole Epistle. In this, *he sets himself in complete opposition to the legal tendency itself*, or to the opinion of a *necessity of the observance of the law to the attainment of salvation*, which, in opposition to the evangelical view inculcated by him, had found entrance, by means of the false teachers, among the Galatians. In this part, doctrine, complaint, and admonition alternate with one another (III. 1—VI. 10).

A. He begins (iii. 1–5) by expressing astonishment at the opposition into which they thus come with their own *experience* in the receiving of the Spirit, and then:

B. For the first time passes into a *doctrinal exposition,* namely,

1. To the proof of the principle, that through *works of the law,* Salvation (Justification, Blessedness, Inheritance) is *not to be obtained, but through Faith alone.* (iii. 6–18). The proof of this he finds in the Scripture, partly in the testimony of the Scripture concerning the justification of Abraham through faith, partly in the promise given to Abraham, that in him all the Gentiles shall be *blessed;* which promise finds its fulfilment only through faith in Christ, since the law intead of a blessing, brings a curse, while Christ has become a curse, in order to redeem us from that curse (iii. 6–14). The principle to be proved is, moreover, indicated even by the *relation of time* between the law and the covenant of promise. According to a fundamental principle of law, universally valid, the law, as given much later, could not annul the promise, that is, works of law could not be subsequently made a condition of attaining the inheritance, after it had been first promised as a gift (iii. 15–18). Paul, however, does not content himself with this demonstration, which, in relation to the law, afforded a merely negative result, nor indeed could the readers content themselves with it, since the *fact* of the law was not thereby explained. He therefore passes now:

2. To the *Law itself,* and its *relation to* the *covenant of promise,* and shows, (positively), *what significance attaches to the law, in order therefrom to demonstrate, definitely and positively the freedom of Christians from the same* (iii. 19; iv. 7).

*a*) The law had its sufficient end, one having an important reference even to the attainment of salvation. This end, however, was only preparatory, namely, to prepare the way, as a schoolmaster to bring us to Christ.

*b*) But from this itself appears the merely transitory significance of the law: with the coming in of faith, the way forwhich it was to prepare, this ceases; believers are now all, without distinction, God's children, and so heirs (iii. 25–29). That is, remarks Paul more definitely still:

*c*) God's children and heirs (as were the children of Israel), might, it is true (after the analogy of human relations), be placed in servitude under the law, during their state of minority, but with the sending of the Son of God the stated majority, and with it the full position of children and heirs, has come in, which finds its realization in fact through the Spirit's inward witness of adoption (iv. 1–7). With this, the didactic exposition is, in its main part completed, and the Apostle's painful sense of the contrast in which the present behavior of the Galatians stands to the freedom from the law, which has fallen to the portion of Christians and therefore to them also, forces him again:

C. To a *lamentation* over this behavior of theirs. He presents before them the inconceivable retrogression which they make, and also, in painfully agitated language, the equally groundless personal estrangement, which had sprung up between themselves and him, through the selfish intrigues of the false teachers (iv. 8–18).

D. His complaint, pervaded by the motherly wish for a restoration of misguided children to the right way,* unconsciously passes over once more into *instruction,* into a *confirmation* of what had been taught concerning the freedom of Christians, from the *Scripture* narrative of the two sons of Abraham, Ishmael and Isaac, by means of an interpretation referring these to the Jewish and the Christian churches (iv. 19–31).

E. This gives so much the better right to utter the *admonition* to stand fast in this freedom from the law; an admonition which is at once strengthened by a *threatening* reference to the *dangerous consequences* of a return to the law, even in the one point of circumcision: that thus they lost Christ in whom alone that faith which works by love is efficacious (v. 1–6).

F. This admonition and warning now suggesting the thought how much lies at stake, pass over again into *complaint,* through which, however, hopefulness is visible, the complaint taking rather the form of accusation against their false guides (v. 7–12).

G. But so much the more urgently is the *admonition* again pressed, in the form of an exhor-

*[Vers. 19, 20, containing this motherly wish, seem to belong more properly to the preceding section, and are thus joined by most commentators. The illustration or allegory (vers. 21–30) then forms a section by itself.—R.]

tation (supplementing that under E.), instead of returning to the law, as if faith were insufficient, to accredit their faith, in a right understanding of the freedom bestowed on believers, by a serving *love*, through a walk in the *Spirit*, which is the best fulfilling of the law. This admonition is given *a*) more in general, and with reference to the principle on which it rests, namely, the opposition between Flesh and Spirit; *b*) with a special inculcation of the duty of love in several particular relations, for which the churches may have given occasion (v. 25—vi. 10).

VI. 11-18. Paul adds a CONCLUSION written with his own hand.* In this with a few strokes he portrays himself in opposition to the false teachers, and opposes to their shrinking from persecution his own joy in the cross of Christ, through which he has become a new man. Wishing then a blessing on all who walk according to the principles laid down by him, he alludes to the marks of the Lord Jesus in his body, and begs that henceforth no man may trouble him, closing with the accustomed benediction.

[Subjoined is the satisfactory summary of DR. SCHAFF, published as a part of a projected commentary:

The object of the Epistle was both apologetic and polemic. It is a personal and a doctrinal self-defence, and a refutation of the Judaizing heresy. To this are added appropriate exhortations.

The first part, chap. i. 1—ii. 14, is historical and personal, giving a resumé of the Apostle's career, partly confirmatory, partly supplementary to the narrative of the Acts, and justifying his office and authority from the direct call of Christ, the revelation of the gospel doctrine made to him, and the testimony of the other Apostles during the Council of Jerusalem.

In the second or doctrinal part, chap. ii. 15—iv. 31, he defends his teaching, the free gospel of Christianity, in opposition to the slavish and carnal legalism of his opponents.

In the third or practical part, chaps. v. vi., he exhorts the Galatians to hold fast to the evangelical liberty without abusing it, to study love, unity and other Christian virtues, and concludes with a benediction.

Comp. the able analysis of LIGHTFOOT, which may be roughly sketched as a division into three sections of two chapters each: the first couplet *Personal*, the second *Doctrinal*, the third *Hortatory*.—R.]

## § 5. VALUE AND SIGNIFICANCE OF THE EPISTLE.

The high doctrinal importance of our Epistle needs no proof. It is the *Magna Charta* of the freedom of a Christian man. A spirit of holy zeal for the freedom which the Christian has through his faith, and for the Christian's right thereto, breathes through the whole. Hereby is the freedom which we have in Christ, established for all time; and against all attempts to induce it to make a law, or any outward performances, the condition of salvation, the Christian commonwealth can always oppose our Epistle as its charter of manumission. Our Reformers, therefore, in contending against the yoke, which the papacy, in the course of time, had again laid on the Christian conscience, supported themselves chiefly on our Epistle, and the nearly related Epistle to the Romans: and "through the famous exposition of its doctrinal contents rendered by Luther, has it become for ever part and parcel of the church of the Reformation." WIESELER.

A more particular comparison presents the doctrine of justification by faith, and not by works of the law, as, it is true, developed in the Epistle to the Romans with greater fulness, "according to its essence and its effects, in contrast with the corruption of sin;" in our Epistle it is brought forward rather as a means of proving the freedom of Christians from the obligation of observing the law. In this direction, then, are we to look for the peculiar significance of our Epistle: in the firm establishment of the high and holy right which Christians have to this freedom through their faith, in the demonstration of the dignity which faith in Christ bestows, so that our Epistle might be called not only the Christian's deed of manumission, but also his patent of nobility. At the same time the relation of law and promise, of religious childhood and maturity, from which this freedom results, are so clearly exhibited, in a profound and noble interpretation of the history of salvation, as to give a sure and immovable basis for all more special exposition.

* [On the disputed point whether the whole letter or only this conclusion was written by Paul's own hand, see notes on vi. 11.—R.]

But decidedly as the Apostle enters the lists to combat for the freedom of a Christian man, he is just as far from overlooking its ethical character, so that in our Epistle, both the dogmatical and the ethical features, essential to the idea of evangelical freedom, are contained.

While our Epistle is thus, first and chiefly, of high, abiding worth for Christian *doctrine*, it is moreover, important for the *history* of the church, through the valuable communications which it gives in chaps. i. and ii., respecting the history of the Apostle, and of the beginnings of Christianity generally. Considering the indisputable genuineness of the Epistle, these accounts, as being statements of the Apostle himself, are peculiarly valuable; and, although it is true that they have been abused by negative criticism of a destructive tendency, for the construction of its own system, yet the unprejudiced Church historian will, on the other hand, use them only the more effectively, as a sure starting point, with which what is elsewhere related respecting the state of things in early Christianity connects itself, and with which it unites itself to form a harmonious whole.

[SCHAFF: "The Epistle is polemical, impetuous and overpowering; and yet tender, affectionate and warning in tone. It strikes like lightning every projecting point that approaches its path, and yet undelayed by these zigzag deflexions, instantaneously attains the goal. Every verse breathes the spirit of the great and free Apostle of the Gentiles. His earnestness and mildness, his severity and love, his vehemence and tenderness, his depth and simplicity, his commanding authority and sincere humility, are here vividly brought before us in fresh and bold outlines." A half barbarous people, like the Galatians, known for their simplicity and impressibility, would be likely to listen to both of these methods of address; to be won by his fatherly pleading, as well as over-awed by his apostolic rebukes and denunciations (ALFORD).

LUTHER said of it, "The Epistle to the Galatians is my Epistle; I have betrothed myself to it; it is my wife." And he might well thus speak of "his most efficient engine in overthrowing the mass of error which time had piled on the simple foundations of the gospel." "In this epistle we have to this day the divine right and divine seal of genuine Protestantism against Romanism as far as this is a revival of Judaism, and denies to the Christian man that liberty 'wherewith Christ hath made us free.' But it is also, at the same time, an earnest protest against all pseudo-protestantism, which would abuse the evangelical freedom and pervert it into carnal license" (SCHAFF).

Besides furnishing the keenest weapons for the Reformers in their struggle for liberty within the camp, it is now of like value in the war of defence against assailants from without. This Epistle affords the refutation of that rationalistic view, which claims that the earliest form of Christianity was a modified Judaism, but that the distinctive features of our Christianity were added by Paul, which distinctive features prevailed after a long struggle between the Apostles and their antagonistic doctrines. True we here see the mutual jealousy of the Jew and Gentile converts, and are told of personal but temporary disagreement between Paul and Peter, yet are also shown the true relation between Paul and the Twelve; in fact, both the narrative and argument of the Epistle lose their point, if any such continued antagonism be admitted. See LIGHTFOOT, *Introd. p.* 58.—R.]

## § 6. LITERATURE.

Of Antiquity—The well-known works of CHRYSOSTOM, THEODORET, ŒCUMENIUS, THEOPHYLACT, JEROME, AMBROSIASTER (Hilary), AUGUSTINE, PELAGIUS, CLAUDIUS of Turin. Of the time of the Reformation—The classical exposition of LUTHER: 1. *In epistolam Pauli ad Galatas commentarius (minor) primum anno* 1519 *excusus, anno* 1523 *ab auctore recognitus.* 2. *In epist. Pauli ad Gal. Commentarius (major) ex prælectionibus Dr. M. Lutheri collectus a M. Georg. Rorario, a Luthero recognitus et castigatus, primum anno* 1535 *Viteb. excusus.* Translated into German by Justus Menius; published separately, among others, by J. G. Walch, 1737; a new impression in 1856, by G. Schlawitz. (This detailed exposition is used in the present commentary).* Also, CALVIN: *In Novi Testamenti epist. commentarii.*

*[Schmoller uses Luther's Commentary so largely in the Homiletical department of this work, that it almost requires an apology. Which apology may be made in the words of JOHN BUNYAN: "This methinks I must let fall before all men, I do prefer this book of Martin Luther upon the Galatians, excepting the Holy Bible, before all books that ever I have seen, as most fit for a wounded conscience."—R.]

Among modern commentators, besides WINER, RÜCKERT, USTERI, SCHOTT, DE WETTE, BAUMGARTEN-CRUSIUS, the most noteworthy are, MEYER, *Kritisch-exeg. Handbuch über den Brief an die Galater* [4th ed., 1862.—R.]; EWALD: *Die Sendschreiben des Apostels Paulus*, 1857; WIESELER: *Commentar über den Brief Pauli an die Galater. Mit besonderer Rücksicht auf die Lehre und Geschichte des Apostels*, 1859.—JATHO: *Pauli Brief an die Galater, nach seinem inneren Gedankengang*, 1856.—HOLSTEN: *Inhalt und Gedankengang des Briefs an die Galater*, Rostock, 1859.—VON HOFMANN: *Die heilige Schrift Neuen Testamentes*, 2 Thl. 1 Abth. *Brief an die Galater*, 1863.—DE WETTE: *Kurzgefasstes exegetisches Handbuch*, II. 3, *Briefe an die Galater und Thessalonicher*, 3. Aufl. ed. Dr. Möller, 1864.

[G. W. MATTHIAS: *Der Galaterbrief griechish und deutsch, nebst einer Erklärung seiner schwierigeren Stellen*, etc., Cassel, 1865.—R.]

For the practical exposition of the epistle, besides STARKE's *Bibelwerk;* BENGEL, *Gnomon;* RIEGER, *Betrachtungen über das Neue Testament;* M. F. ROOS, a contemporary of these, *Kurze Auslegung des Briefs St. Pauli an die Galater*, 1786 (a small, but admirable tractate); in this century: F. MÜLLER, formerly pastor at Wandsbeck, *Brief Pauli an die Galater, in Bibelstunden erklärt*, 1853; ANACKER, the same, 1856; TWELE, *Galaterbrief in Predigten ausgelegt*, 1858; A. FRANZ: *Die Rechtfertigung durch den Glauben, Homiletische Auslegung der Ep. St. Pauli an die Galater*, 1860; and HEUBNER, *Praktische Erklarung des Neuen Testaments.* B. 3. 1858.

[For a full list and notices of patristic commentaries, see LIGHTFOOT, p. 223 sq.

Luther's commentary was translated into English, and published under the approval of the Bishop of London, 1575. So highly esteemed was this work that there are but few early English commentaries. We may notice, however, THOMAS LUSHINGTON: *Commentary on the Galatians*, London, 1650. JAMES FERGUSON, Edinburgh, 1659.

Of later works, the following are prominent:

J. A. HALDANE: *Commentary.* 1848.

JOHN BROWN: *An exposition of the Epistle of Paul the Apostle to the Galatians.* Edinburgh, 1853.

C. J. ELLICOTT: *A Commentary, critical and grammatical, of the Epistle to the Gal., with a revised translation.* London, 1853. 3d edition, 1863. The first commentary of this lucid, exact, and scholarly author, whose translation has been largely used in the emendations of the English text in the present work.

B. JOWETT: *The Epistle of St. Paul to the Galatians and Romans, with critical notes and illustrations.* London, 1856.

SAMUEL H. TURNER: *The Epistle to the Galatians in Greek and English, with an analysis and exegetical commentary.* New York, 1856.

H. T. J. BAGGE: *The Epistle of St. Paul to the Galatians, with a revised text and commentary.* London, 1857.

J. B. LIGHTFOOT: *St. Paul's Epistle to the Galatians. A revised text with introduction, notes and dissertations.* London, 1865. Exceedingly valuable, on account of its full discussion of difficult questions. The frequent citations from this work are made from the Second Edition. 1866.

The American Editor of Lange's Commentary, PHILIP SCHAFF, D. D., has published an Introduction and comments on chaps. i., ii., as a specimen of a projected popular commentary on the New Testament. Mercersburg Review, Jan., 1861. Most of the material there presented is incorporated here.

*The History of the Apostolic Church* of the same author treats of many questions belonging to the exposition of this Epistle. So CONYBEARE and HOWSON, *Life and Epistles of St. Paul.* The works of ALFORD, WORDSWORTH, BURKITT, HENRY, and others (for full list, see General Introduction to New Testament, LANGE's *Comm. Matthew*), include comments on this Epistle. The reader is also referred to the Introduction to the Pauline Epistles in the volume on the Epistle to the Romans.—R.]

THE

# EPISTLE OF PAUL TO THE GALATIANS.*

## **Introduction:** ADDRESS AND SALUTATION (WITH BENEDICTION).

### CHAPTER I. 1–5.

1 Paul, an apostle, (not [apostle not][1] of men, neither by [through, *διά*] man, but
by [through] Jesus Christ, and God the Father, who raised him from the dead;)
2 [omit parenthesis] And all the brethren which [who] are with me, unto the churches
3 of Galatia: [.] Grace *be* to you, and peace, from God the Father, and *from* our[2]
4 Lord Jesus Christ, Who gave himself for[3] our sins, that he might deliver us from
5 this present evil world, according to the will of God and our Father: To whom *be*
glory for ever and ever. Amen.

* [TITLE: Rec. ἡ πρὸς Γαλάτας ἐπιστολὴ Παύλου. Elz. Παύλου τοῦ ἀποστόλου ἡ πρὸς Γαλάτας ἐπιστολή. ℵ. A. B. K., Lachmann, Tischendorf and most editors, πρὸς Γαλάτας.—R.]

[1] Ver. 1.—[The comma after "apostle," and the parenthesis are better omitted, since the clauses immediately following "Apostle" are most closely connected with it, and the idea so far from being parenthetical is one of the most prominent in the whole Epistle. "Of" is changed to "from" by Ellicott, while he retains "by" as a sufficiently exact translation of διά.—R.]

[2] Ver. 3.—ℵ. inserts ἡμῶν after πατρός, omitting it after κυρίου. [This reading is an alteration to conform with other salutations (Meyer). That of Rec. is undoubtedly correct. So all modern editors.—R.]

[3] Ver. 4.—Περί (instead of ὑπέρ. Rec.) is found in most MSS. and in the best MSS. ℵ. also, though ℵ[3]., reads ὑπέρ. [The external authorities are decisive against the reading of the Rec.; περί is adopted by modern editors almost universally.—R.]

### EXEGETICAL AND CRITICAL.

Ver. 1. **Paul, an apostle not of men, neither through man,** *etc.*—His office, Paul says, is not derived from men (ἀπ' ἀνθρώπων), so as to be in itself human, and therefore subservient only to human interests; nor has it even been committed to him through the medium of any man (δι' ἀνθρώπου), in which case it might still be a divine function, although only not directly so. The change of number is only of secondary importance. The general sense: "of human derivation," is better expressed by the indefinite plural; while on the other hand, in denying human mediation, the singular is used with more precision, by Paul, the rather, as having already in mind the definite antithesis "but by Jesus Christ."

This double negation is essentially only a setting forth of the definition of "Apostle." He would be in no event an Apostle, if he had his office, ἀπ' ἀνθρ.; nor yet, if he had it, δι' ἀνθρ. He would then stand only on equal footing with a Timothy and others, in short with all laborers in the gospel, who are inducted into their office by men; he is an Apostle only because called and inducted into his office, **through Jesus Christ**, *etc.* He was therefore placed in his office immediately through Christ, not through a man; for the activity of Ananias in Damascus had been only secondary and subsequent, the beginnings were divine. But, furthermore, he has received his office through Christ from God the Father, so that, as "through Jesus Christ" explains "not through man," so **God the Father** explains "not of men." Yet Paul does not place this θεοῦ πατρ. in express antithesis to ἀπ' ἀνθρ., inasmuch as he does not say ἀπὸ θεοῦ π. There being on the positive side no occasion for so precise a discrimination, he here no longer distinguishes between author and medium: perhaps not without design, in order thus to set his apostleship in a like direct relation, as to Christ, so to God the Father, and thereby to place the dignity of the same so much the more strongly in view. What in the first place constitutes the apostolic office, is the immediate calling through Christ, who is the κύριος ἀποστέλλων (on which account διὰ 'Ι. Χρ. is placed before καὶ πατρός). Christ Himself, certainly, cannot be reduced to the same level with men, if "not of men," *etc.*, is to remain true. And every thought of it is precluded by this very comprehending of Christ with God the Father, as it were, in one conception, under one preposition.

[ELLICOTT neatly paraphrases thus: "Not from men as an ultimate, nor through man as a mediate authority." The second ἀπό which we should expect to find before θεοῦ πατρός has not been omitted without good reason: while the preposition διά admits an extension of meaning that would cover both ideas (MEYER), the Apostle's language, as it stands, is more forcible; the directness of his divine commission is emphasized (LIGHTFOOT), and although an argument for the consubstantiality of the Father and the Son, must not be forced from the passage, "there is something *very* noticeable in this use of a common preposition with both the first and second Persons of the Trinity, by a writer so cumulative, and yet for the most part so exact in his use of prepositions as St. Paul" (ELLICOTT). SCHAFF: "*By* includes here the instrumental and the more remote originating cause.—The immediate coördination of Christ with God the Father, and this in contrast with the preceding *men* and *man*, prove that the Apostle regarded the Saviour as a Divine being."—R.]

Paul here, probably, designates God the Father [*i. e.*, "of Christ,"—R.] as **who raised him from the dead**, simply because through this divine act, namely, the resurrection of Christ, his own immediate vocation through Christ had been made possible (1 Cor. xv. 8). [While it is not necessary to insist on a polemic reference here, as an answer to the reproach that he had not seen Christ (CALVIN), there seems to be an *immediate* reference to the fact that Paul was called by the exalted Christ, not that he claimed a preëminence on this account (AUGUSTINE, ERASMUS, and others), but God having raised Christ from the dead, and Christ having immediately chosen him to be an Apostle, it was fitting that he should give prominence here to that act of God which enabled him also to be an Apostle, a witness of the resurrection.—R.]

This laying claim so expressly to apostolic dignity in the very introduction, stands (as is shown by what follows) in connection with the vital questions of the Epistle, since his equal apostolic rank had been impugned by the Galatian false teachers. In chap. i. 11–ii. *fin.* there follows the detailed proof of this "not through man, but through Jesus Christ," whereby the "not of men" is also indirectly proved. (In other Epistles, where he has not this definite purpose in mind, Paul designates himself more simply, but in substantially the same style as ἀπόστολος or κλητὸς ἀπ. Ἰ. Χρ. διὰ θελήματος θεοῦ.)

Ver. 2. **And all the brethren who are with me.**—Hardly his companions in travel at that time merely, especially helpers in his office (MEYER), but rather all the Christians of his place of residence at that time. This addition has, at all events, the special purpose of adding the authority of others to his own. He wishes the Galatians to understand, that he has on his side all the brethren in the midst of whom he writes, that these have the same opinion of their conduct, and thus indicates that the Galatians, unless they came to another mind, would sever themselves from the great communion of the brethren, who stand and abide upon the foundation of faith which Paul had laid. Of course the Apostle alone wrote the Epistle. He can, however, bring in the brethren as joint authors, so far as they may, after a previous communication of the leading thoughts, or, more probably, after hearing the Epistle itself read, have signified their agreement with it. [The more restricted meaning is allowable (see Phil. iv. 21, 22, where "the brethren which are with me" are distinguished from "all the saints.") The idea of the patristic commentators, that thus additional authority would be given, is incorrect; "the Epistle, being the product of an infallible Apostle, required no such help" (SCHAFF). CALVIN's remark is just, however: "The concurrence of so many godly persons must have had some degree of influence in softening the minds of the Galatians, and preparing them to receive instruction." ELLICOTT: "He adopts the inclusive term to show the unanimity that was felt on the subject of the Epistle; did it mean the whole Christian community we should certainly have expected 'with whom I am' rather than 'who are with me.'"—R.]

**Unto the churches of Galatia.**—The same title, 1 Cor. xvi. 1. There existed there, it seems, therefore, different local congregations, of which each one constituted at least a relatively complete whole, and the Epistle was so far a circular letter. The omission of a phrase of commendation, such as is usually found in the other Epistles of the Apostle, has perhaps its ground in dissatisfaction with the Galatians. Perhaps, however, the omission is in part attributable to the external circumstance, that ἐκκλησίαι, whole congregations, are addressed, hence any such titles as κλητοί, ἅγιοι, would have been less suitable. [The dissatisfaction of the Apostle is so natural and evident a reason for the omission of any commendatory addition to the simple address, that any other explanation is farfetched. ALFORD quotes MEYER as saying that 1 and 2 Thess. present a similar instance, but in the 4th ed. MEYER expressly mentions these Epistles as no exceptions. WORDSWORTH: "a remarkable address in what it does *not*, as well as in what it does say."—R.]

Ver. 3. **Grace be to you—and peace.**—Respecting the Pauline form of salutation, χάρις καὶ εἰρήνη, consult remarks on the other Epistles.—**From God the Father and our Lord,** *etc.* As in ver. 1. Christ and the Father were comprehended under the one preposition διά, without distinction of the Father through an ἀπό, so here the reverse takes place, an evident token how little Paul has in mind a severance of the Divine Persons. Christ is by no means, then, the merely instrumental medium of grace, but, as well as the Father Himself, the Bestower of grace (see DOCTRINAL and ETHICAL notes). Here, however, "God the Father" is placed first; in ver. 1 the order was reversed. There is, moreover, a special reason here for placing "our Lord Jesus Christ" last, namely, that it receives in addition a predicate defining it more closely. Grace and peace, Paul wishes for the Galatians, especially in view of the path of error into which they had been led, and for this very reason with especial allusion to that, which alone secures this grace and this peace, namely, the atoning death of Christ.

**Who gave Himself for us.**—In this clause the Apostle anticipates the other main point which he has to unfold. Instead of regarding the cross of Christ alone as the ground of salvation, the false teachers had influenced the Galatians to seek salvation again in observance of the law. In ver. 1 Paul touches on the personal, here he touches on the doctrinal question, which he afterwards handles. Δόντος ἑαυτόν, "gave *Himself*," nothing less than His own person, which could be fully accomplished only in His death. Περί undefined: "in respect to our sins." The sense, however, clearly appears not only from the following, "that He might deliver us," but also in the very form of the expression, which sets forth an expiatory sacrifice that has been offered, in which Christ was the Offerer and the Offered, the Highpriest and the Sacrifice, in one person (comp. WIESELER's careful investigation of the use of περί, ὑπέρ, ἀντί, in declarations respecting the death of Christ). [ELLICOTT: In its ethical sense, ὑπέρ retains some trace of its local meaning, "bending over to protect," and thus points more immediately to the action, than to the object or circumstance from which the action is supposed to spring. The latter relation is more correctly defined by περί, which is thus more naturally used with the thing, "sins," ὑπέρ with the persons, "sinners." Often, however, in the N. T. the distinction is scarcely appreciable.—R.]

Ver. 4. **That He might deliver us.**—Effect of the expiation accomplished through Christ.—Ἐξαιρεῖσθαι, to tear away from a power. The evil world is viewed as possessor by force, as a tyrant, who brings destruction, and in whose power we are by nature. This deliverance Paul doubtless understands in a double sense, as a making free from the moral corruption of the world, and also as a keeping from the destruction which it thereby brings upon its own at the judgment day. The immediate reference is to the latter, which, however, in view of the ethical character of Christianity, cannot take place without the former, as indeed there can be no doubt that the death of Christ has an ethical intent. It is false, however, to think only of this here.—"Present world" may mean, present or impending age. The latter signification is, however, hardly to be assumed here—contrary to MEYER, who would take it as meaning the evil times which, according to many passages of Scripture, are shortly to precede the second coming of Christ, and on this account are wont elsewhere to be called the last times. But "our phrase, on account of the union of ἐνεστώς with αἰών, is most naturally regarded as parallel with ὁ αἰὼν οὗτος or ὁ νῦν αἰών. The expression ὁ αἰών, since this appears to denote a period of time complete in itself, is nowhere used of the last times, preparatory only, as the pangs of travail, to the αἰὼν μέλλων. Nor, finally, is there in the connection the least reason why Paul should have confined the salutary workings of the redeeming death of Jesus to the last times." (WIESELER). Therefore we must take it as, "the present period of time," in sense the same as ὁ κόσμος, so that the translation "present world," is substantially correct.—"Evil" emphasizes the ethical character of "this world," which is besides included in the very conception of "the present world." It is, equivalent to "ruined by sin," and therefore a deliverance out of it was necessary in the twofold relation given above. [SCHAFF: "The words contain an allusion to the Jewish distinction between 'this world,' and 'the world to come,' or the period before, and the period after the appearance of the Messiah. But the sense of these terms is modified in the N. T., so as to make the *second* coming of Christ the dividing line between the two æons." LIGHTFOOT: "The distinction of time between the two, which is the primary distinction, becomes lost in the moral and spiritual conception." The second adjective πονηρός, emphatically placed, gives prominence to the ethical idea, especially if the better supported order of the Rec., ἐκ τοῦ ἐνεστῶτος αἰῶνος πονηροῦ, be adopted.—R.]

**According to the will of God and our Father.**—It is best to connect this with the whole of ver. 4. It refers the redeeming work as a whole to the gracious will of the Father, and thus cuts off every ground of objection against this work from the legal point of view. The thought of this redemptive counsel of the Father moves him very naturally, then, to the concluding doxology.—In τοῦ θεοῦ καὶ πατρὸς ἡμῶν, ἡμῶν belongs probably only to πατρός. By θεός God is meant to be designated as the God of all alike; by πατήρ, according to His special relation to the Christian. By the prefixed article two predicates are ascribed to the same person. The same who is God is also our Father. [LIGHTFOOT argues from the absence of the article before πατρός, that ἡμῶν belongs to both nouns, but as ELLICOTT well remarks, "πατήρ is anarthrous according to rule." CALVIN, MEYER and most, restrict the pronoun to Father, giving the last words somewhat of a predicative force: "God, who is our Father." It is to be remarked that in vers. 1–3 Paul speaks of "God the Father," *i. e.*, the Father of Christ—but having in this verse spoken of the redemptive act of Christ, and its redeeming design for us he calls God, who has purposed this "our Father."—WORDSWORTH: "Specially our *Father* by the redemption of us His *children* by the blood of His *Son*."—R.]

Ver. 5. **To whom be glory.**—To be taken as optative; for δόξα means Honor, Praise—not Essential Glory, although it is true that the δόξα which should be given to God, rests upon the δόξα which He has. [SCHAFF: "The doxology in this place is likewise an indirect reproof of the Galatians for dividing the glory of our salvation between God and man." It is an affirmation rather than a wish. There can be no reasonable doubt that τοὺς αἰῶνας τῶν αἰώνων here is an expression for eternity.—R.]

## DOCTRINAL AND ETHICAL.

1. *The Apostolate.* a. An essential characteristic of the apostolate was the immediate "call" through Christ, as whose "delegates" the apostles went out into the world with that proclamation of the Gospel, which should lay the foundation of all that followed. Hence the express assertion here (and afterwards the detailed proof) of this immediate calling. For this, if for no other reason, the

office of the Apostles was specifically distinct from all others.* In the office of preacher in these days, there always occurs a "call" δι' ἀνθρώπου. The office, however, is not on this account ἀπ' ἀνθρώπων, nor should any bearer of it thus regard it. It is on the contrary "from" "Jesus Christ and God the Father," is *divina institutio*.

b. In the decision and certainty with which Paul insists upon his apostolic rank, there is implied, on the one hand, a justifiable sense of personal dignity in opposition to all who would question it, and especially to false teachers: "I am an Apostle and nothing less." This personal feeling, however, was certainly counterpoised at once, by the feeling of humility in view of the momentous duties involved, for the discharge of which grace alone could give strength. But, above all, the Apostle lays stress on this his dignity, not in his personal interest, but in the interest of his Lord, and the gospel of his Lord; in order to shield this against the "perverting" (ver. 7) of the false teachers, he is forced to lay this emphasis on the fact that he is really an Apostle of Christ, and therefore was such in his preaching of the gospel.

c. The care with which he proves his fundamental authority and capacity for preaching the gospel, is a pledge to us of the soundness of this preaching. The Christian church has, therefore, in this foundation laid by the Apostle, a standard for all time by which to prove doctrine.

d. That Christ has been raised, and now lives, is the fundamental truth, which to the Apostle stands immovably firm, and on which rests, for Paul, the certainty of his calling, and for him and the other Apostles the vigor and joyfulness of their labor in their vocation. For the Apostles were in a special sense to be witnesses of the resurrection of Jesus, and to be persuaded of it by a personal beholding of the Risen One. It was only because the risen Jesus had appeared to him, that Paul was an Apostle.

2. *The brethren.* This strong emphasizing of his particular vocation (or office) does not imply the least prejudice to his brotherly relation toward other Christians, who have no such vocation. Far from it. Paul not only mentions them in immediate connection with himself, including himself and them in the same salutation, but even treats them as fellow-writers, hence as those who, together with him, impart instruction and admonition, thus strengthening the weight of his own words by their concurrence. He is only called to preach what, as the substance of his faith, is the substance of theirs also; and he wishes to bring back his erring readers to the same faith in which these, his companions, stand and have remained firm. [Their concurrence could add nothing to the real authority of his apostolic teaching, but might aid in establishing that authority among the Galatians. Yet the Apostle seems fond of thus associating others of lower rank with himself in his Epistles.—R.] Here is a hint for the behavior of office-bearers towards other Christians now as well; in personal conduct, to regard and treat them as "brethren," standing on precisely the same footing; to lay claim to no precedence; and in official activity also, while maintaining full consciousness of their own special vocation, and of the authority inherent in it, never to ignore the might which dwells in the personal faith and believing life of the members of the Church, when there is an opportunity of joining them with one's self in exhortation and rebuke.

3. "*Churches*" *still.* Paul, it is true, gives to the Galatian Christians no especial title of honor, "yet he still counts them worthy to be called churches, because, though they were indeed for the most part fallen from the truth in some main points, they had, notwithstanding this, retained many parts of the pure Christian doctrine; he cherishes then the hope that they would still suffer themselves to be brought right again" (STARKE). Hence important doctrinal and ethical defects of a church do not of themselves warrant us in withholding or withdrawing from it the predicate ἐκκλησία. A judgment, whether in any place there is the Church of Christ or not, depends, although largely, yet not in the chief degree, upon subjective character, but in the chief degree stand the objective factors, namely, that *verbum divinum recte docetur*, and *sacramenta recte administrantur*. This, as is well known, is one of Luther's prime principles. In the objective factors, there certainly resides the power (even if latent) to work subjectively.—Yet it cannot therefore be denied that there may be, notwithstanding, a subjective character of the congregation as respects doctrine and morals, where the predicate ἐκκλησία ceases to be applicable; we cannot, however, pronounce a judgment thereon, but must leave this to the searcher of hearts, so far as it is not a question of *scandalous* offences in the case of individuals.

4. *God and Christ.* Both in ver. 1 and in ver. 3, Christ is placed in the closest connection with God the Father; and in ver. 3 in such a way that Grace and Peace are invoked in the same manner from God the Father, and from Christ. From this appears, in immediate certainty, the eminent, godlike position of Christ. For the highest and best things, those which are needful for all men, proceed from Him, as much as from the Father. As respects grace, as much depends on His dispositions towards us, as on those of the Father. As

* It is one of the anti-scriptural fancies of the Irvingites to believe, notwithstanding this, in the reappearance of Apostles proper in their churches. WIESELER. [In LIGHTFOOT, p. 92 sq., there is an interesting discussion on "the name and office of an Apostle." He, however, objects to the restriction of the office to the twelve, with only the exception of St. Paul, adducing the apostleship of Barnabas, and implying that "James, the Lord's brother" (ver. 19) was an Apostle, even though not the same as James, the son of Alpheus. This position is not safe, nor is it accordant with the argument of Paul in this Epistle, where he lays so much stress upon the "immediate call." Lightfoot is forced, therefore, to deny the necessity for a call from an outward personal communication with our Lord, though his admission that the having seen Christ was a necessary qualification, is a denial of the perpetuation of the office. It is better to hold that there were but Twelve Apostles, to whom was added, by direct call, Paul the Apostle to the Gentiles—Barnabas and others were "apostolic men." On the relation of Paul to the original *college of apostles*, see SCHAFF, *History of the Apostolic Church*, p. 512 sq., p. 233 sq. His note p. 234 is appropriate here: "The strict hierarchical view, which always looks for an outward, palpable succession, admits no satisfactory explanation of the fact, that the *Apostles* had no share whatever in the ordination of Paul after his conversion (Acts ix. 17), and in his being sent to the Gentiles by the Church of Antioch (xiii. 3). The divine irregularity of his call, and the subsequent independence of his labors, make Paul, so to speak, a prototype of evangelical Protestantism, which has always looked to him as its main authority, as Romanism to Peter."—R.]

Christ is thus placed with the Father on one Divine level, so is the Father, on the other side, placed on the same level with the Son, who, through His Incarnation, has drawn so near to us. LUTHER: "Therefore Paul, in wishing grace and peace not only from God the Father, but also from Jesus Christ, teacheth, first, that we should abstain from the curious searching of the Divine Majesty (for God no man knoweth), and hear Christ, who is in the bosom of the Father, and uttereth to us His will."

5. *Christ's giving Himself.* The expression for the death of Christ is here (ver. 4) so chosen, that it appears as His own free act, while, as is known, there runs parallel to the series of passages which apprehend it thus, another representing it as something decreed by God concerning Christ, representing Christ as burdened with the Father's curse (comp. iii. 13). This designation is here chosen, in order to render prominent and bring home to the hearts of the Galatians the great love of Christ, displayed in His "giving Himself for us." "The giving of Himself consisted of many actions, from the incarnation on, but it applies especially to his atoning death." This "giving Himself"—this morally great act was occasioned by our sins, our moral perversion; a cutting contrast, and yet a necessary nexus between cause and effect!—For its intent was to procure a remedy for our sins, and their ruinous results.

6. *This present evil world.* Through our sins we belong to this present evil world, bear its character, and are in its power, that is, through it and with it are going to destruction. From this destroying might Christ would rescue us, and has rescued us, by His giving Himself for our sins, that is, through the reconciliation thus accomplished for our sins; because we, when reconciled, lie no longer under the judgment of God upon the sinful world, and therefore do not go with it to ruin. Undoubtedly Christ had in view besides, an inward, moral deliverance from the corrupt course of the world; yet this is the secondary aim; the primary is the deliverance from judgment and perdition.—God's acts of grace, according to the Biblical view, are throughout directed, first of all, toward a deliverance from destruction, and consequently to the impartation of a good, of a definite happy destiny, not chiefly to the rehabilitation of certain ethical qualities, of a particular direction of life and will. They are directed thus, in a certain measure, towards an outward end, with which however an inward one is inseparably connected, as the economy of the Spirit, whose work it is to bring forth the corresponding ethical quality, is, although inseparable from that of the Father and the Son, yet distinct from it, presupposing it. The deliverance from the evil world, is, so far as concerns its being won, already accomplished by the sacrifice of Christ. Of course a participation in this is only gained through faith (this is implied in ἡμᾶς, which refers to believers), and is actually perfected only on the coming in of the αἰὼν μέλλων. A certain pledge and a joyful foretaste of it, however, the believer has already in justification, because this is an assurance of the divine grace. As to the rest, the apostolical expectation of the αἰὼν μέλλων as near lies at the foundation of this passage. [Whatever indications there may be elsewhere of "this apostolical expectation," neither the words nor context show any trace of it here, except on the view of MEYER, which refers "present evil world" to the times of danger immediately preceding the second coming of Christ, a view which is not adopted by Schmoller himself, nor by any other commentator of note.—R.]

7. *Redemption according to God's will.* The work of redemption was accomplished "according to the will" of the Father. This indicates the other side in the redeeming work, alluded to under 6, namely, that the death of Christ was also decreed to Him, by God for an expiation, and that Christ's "giving Himself" was accordingly, at the same time an act of obedience to the Father's will, a suffering Himself to be given up. Love to man and obedience to the Father, all in one, was the source of His sacrifice of Himself. This view is in full harmony with the declarations of Christ Himself, especially in John, with the emphasis which He lays on His having been sent, on His doing the will of the Father. There was nothing whatever self-elected in the redeeming work of Christ; it was a God-appointed work.—In this it first finds its firm, immovable foundation, and all scruples as to the availing worth of this self-sacrifice of Christ before God are taken away from the troubled conscience. At the same time, all clinging to such scruples is also condemned, as a striving against the will of God. We *may*, but we also *ought* to believe in the atoning death of Christ; hence especially, we ought not to lessen its significance by a righteousness of works. This will of God is the will that we should be saved, according to which, He willed both the way that should lead to our salvation, Christ's dying on account of our sins, and also the result, our redemption. It was a loving will, but also a will of holy love, condemning sin and forgiving it; the latter only on the foundation of the former, but the former also for the sake of the latter. Because aiming at our salvation it was in any case the will of God our *Father.*

8. *God's honor its end.* As and because the will of God is the origin of the work of redemption, so the honor of God is its aim. That He, His name, be honored, is the purpose and result of redemption. To Him belongeth honor—and that honor forever—for redemption, and such honor will be rendered Him by the Redeemed. The phrase εἰς τοὺς αἰῶν. τ. αἰών. no doubt looks forward to the αἰὼν μέλλων. The expression is, however, thus indefinitely framed, in order, as far as the language admits, to express an eternal duration. There is nothing in this, of course, against the division found elsewhere, into simply two æons, present and future.

## HOMILETICAL AND PRACTICAL.

Ver. 1. STARKE:—To all peculiarly spiritual offices belongs a divine vocation. Every man may take comfort in the consciousness of his office and calling, and also appeal to it when there is need. Let no one deem this pride or boasting. —SPENER:—Christ is the founder of the preacher's office. He is the King in His Kingdom, and so sends whom He will. He is the Chief Shepherd, and therefore all under shepherds must be appointed by Him. He has obtained by His merits the spiritual power needed for the ministry, and has received the Holy Ghost to that end for our sakes. It is He, therefore, who speaks through His servants.—LUTHER:—Wert thou wiser than Solomon and Daniel, yet until thou art called, flee the sacred ministry, as thou wouldst hell and the devil, then wilt thou not spill the word of God to no purpose. If God needs thee, He will know how to call thee. — LANGE:—To be sure of one's divine, although only mediate vocation, is a weighty matter, and gives to the conscience rest, in the office blessing, and to vindication of the same and of the pure doctrine, much joyfulness. —WÜRT. SUMM.:—There is a twofold vocation to the ministry; both are of God, who will have the gospel preached to the end of the world; but some are called of God without means, of which sort are the patriarchs, prophets, apostles; and some through men, although according to God's commandment and ordinance. — RIEGER: — As certainly as every believer shall be taught of God, so that what he has apprehended from human instruction is confirmed in his heart with divine impressions and powerful workings, just so certainly must every teacher have in his conscience a divine seal upon his vocation, although derived through men, and on this account a joyfulness which his hearers cannot impeach.

The apostolate in its high significance; 1. for the founding, 2. for the continuance of the Christian church which must perpetually rest upon the foundation of the apostolic doctrine.—The divine vocation to office: 1. To have it, is under all circumstances needful; 2. To be certain of it, is often important; 3. To appeal to it, may often be right and proper.—How independent (of men), and yet at the same time, how dependent (on God), the preacher of the gospel is and knows himself (may and should know himself) to be!—Even so the Christian generally: he is what he is, not from men (although through men), for not natural descent nor outward fellowship makes him such — but through Jesus Christ and God the Father.—Christian sense of personal worth: 1. its justification, 2. its limits.—All through Jesus Christ! *a*) humbling truth—not through us; *b*) exalting truth — through no less a one than Christ, and thereby through the Highest, God.—[CALVIN:—In the church we ought to listen to God alone, and to Jesus Christ, whom He has appointed to be our teacher. Whoever assumes a right to instruct us, must speak in the name of God or of Christ.—BURKITT:—Behold the peculiar prerogative of St. Paul above the rest of the Apostles; they were called by Christ in the day of His humiliation; but he was called by Christ when sitting at His Father's right hand in heaven. As his call was thus very extraordinary, so his gifts were answerable to his call.—R.]

Ver. 2. WÜRT. SUMM.:—Although the truth of a doctrine does not rest upon the multitude of people, but alone upon God's word, yet, when many support a doctrine founded in God's word, the weak in the faith are noticeably strengthened thereby, because they see that not merely one or two, but many, confess such a doctrine.—SPENER: — Christians are "brethren" to each other; for they have one Heavenly Father, one first-born brother, Christ; one mother, the Christian church; one seed of regeneration, the divine word; one inheritance of eternal life. That is a more intimate and strict brotherhood than the common one among all men.—STARKE:—In names and titles we must give good heed not willingly to commit falsehood, nor attribute to any one, praise that does not belong to him; yet common and authorized titles must be understood not in absolute strictness, but according to common use. —SPENER:—There remains even in a loose crowd a Christian church, even though grave errors, which remove the ground of faith are found there, so long as God's word and the holy sacraments are there and are maintained.

On Vers. 1 and 2. Let us hear, when we begin to waver in the truth: 1. Apostolic doctrine; 2. The testimony of brethren!—Apostolic doctrine and the voice of brethren; an admonition to every church to abide in the evangelical truth.

Ver. 3. RIEGER:—Paul flees in this perplexity to the riches of God in Christ Jesus, and entrusts to the grace and the peace from thence, the restoration of the Galatians also; with this greeting, as with a cordial, he not only refreshes their hearts but quickens himself also to a confidence towards God in Christ.—WÜRT. SUMM.: — We see here where we must begin, when after sin committed we will come to God for grace; namely, not with ourselves, not with our piety! for if we had kept this, we should be already in favor with God, nor even with God Himself out of Christ, for He is to sinners a consuming fire, but alone with Christ, and His bitter passion and death for our sins.—LUTHER: — Paul wishes the Galatians grace and peace, not from the emperor or kings and princes; for these are wont ofttimes to persecute the godly: nor does he wish them grace and peace from the world, for in the world they shall have tribulation; but from God our Father, that is, he wishes them a godly and heavenly peace. —LANGE:—True peace can never exist without grace, for grace is the ground and source of peace; on the other hand there is grace sometimes without peace, especially with the tempted, who may, for awhile fall into great disquietness of soul, and yet remain in God's grace.

Ver. 4. STARKE:—If Christ has for our sakes given His all, ah! should not we surrender ourselves, with all that in us is, to Him? Man! keep thyself from sin, on account of which Christ hath endured so much, lest thou thyself bring to nought for Him this great work, for which He came. — LUTHER:—Mark diligently the word: "for *our*." For therein lies all the virtue, namely, that all which is said concerning us in the Holy Scriptures, in such passages as "for me," "for us," "for our sin," and the like, we should know how to take well in mind, and apply particularly to ourselves, and hold fast thereto by faith. — For thou hast, no doubt, easily brought thyself to believe that Christ, God's Son, was given for St. Peter's, St. Paul's, and other saints' sins, who were worthy of such grace; but, contrariwise it is especially and thoroughly hard, that thou, for thine own person, a poor, unworthy, condemned sinner, shouldst from thine heart certainly believe, hold, and say, that Christ, God's Son was given for thy so many and so great sins, who yet nevertheless hast never yet been worthy of such grace.—Therefore should we well train and prepare our hearts with this utterance and the like utterances of St. Paul, that when the devil hereafter comes and accuses us and says: "See, you are a sinner, therefore you must be damned!" we may meet him and answer, "yea, good devil, for the very reason that you accuse me and will be condemning me for a sinner, for that reason will I be righteous and holy, be not damned, but saved the rather. For in this very thing, that you tell me how I am a poor sinner, and a great one, you give me a sword and weapon in hand wherewith I can mightily overcome you, yea, slay you and put you under my feet with your own arms. For if you can tell me that I am a poor sinner, I can say to you again, that Christ died for sinners."—Count these words of St. Paul as said in earnest, and to be true, and not as a dream, when he says that the world is evil, although many people therein have many noble, beautiful, virtues; and although in outward guise and appearance there is much holiness and brilliant excellence.—To this evil world belongs also all art, wisdom, righteousness, &c., of a godless man. Thy wisdom, which thou hast out of Christ, is a double folly, thy righteousness is a double sin and godlessness, since it knows nothing of the wisdom and righteousness of Christ, and since, over and above this, it darkens, hinders, reviles and persecutes you; wherefore St. Paul may well name the world an evil world; for it is the worst when it will be at the best and most pious. In the religious, wise and learned men, it will be at its most pious and best, and yet it is twice as wicked.

Berlenb. Bible:—Of this present evil world, ordinances of religion form no small part, of which much is instituted whereby men will take one another captive to the spirit of the world. Without religion nevertheless will the world not be; so it dresses up such things as may be congruous with flesh and blood; but true religion burdens and depresses it. Thus the deliverance takes place especially from the Pharisaic leaven.—Starke:—See how availing and certain is our redemption and salvation, because it proceeds from the will of the Father: how can that be unavailing, which has come to pass according to His will.—[Schaff:—God is *our* Father because He is the Father (not simply of Jesus Christ which would place him on a par with us, but) of *our Lord* Jesus Christ.—R.]

Ver. 5. As often as we think on the great work of redemption, we should heartily praise God; and therefore should we often think thereon; that we may be powerfully excited to praise.—To praise God is the best divine service; it is that which must endure unto eternity. Happy he who begins it here, and prepares himself thereby for a blessed eternity. It is a proof that he knows God aright, and has become partaker of His grace, and that he will one day come to the heavenly choirs of angels who praise God.

Jesus' giving Himself to death: 1. Its occasion (our sins); 2. Its purpose (our deliverance therefrom); or: 1. the strongest testimony against us (our sin); 2. the mightiest consolation for us; or: 1. Its great effect (to deliver us from this evil world); 2. Whence it has this effect (as being a satisfying and bearing and thereby a taking away of the divine wrath; 3. in whom it is thus effectual (only in those who are His in faith).—What defends us from being lost with this evil world? 1. Not our own righteousness whereby we only entangle ourselves in this evil world the more, but 2. Christ's sacrificial death alone.—The appropriation of the merits of Christ: 1. Every one needs it on account of his sins; 2. The sinner needs it precisely as sinner.—Jesus Christ the Deliverer out of the power of this present evil world: 1. The world the tyrant in whose power we are; 2. Christ the Deliverer that has appeared.—Evil—the character of this world: 1. Therefore the Christian in this world longs for the world to come; 2. He must however be delivered from this present world, in order to enter the world to come.—Redemption through Christ rests upon the will of God: 1. A rich consolation (against all doubts); 2. An earnest admonition: Whoever lightly esteems the redemption accomplished through Christ, sins thereby against the will of God Himself.—The honor which is due to God for the redemption in Christ.—The praise of God: 1. a fruit of the redeemed state; 2. a proof of the same.—The praise which the redeemed bring to God: 1. begins in time; 2. continues into eternity.

Vers. 3-5. Lisco:—The Apostle's invocation of blessings for his churches: 1. What does it contain? The greatest benefits which are bestowed by God on man. 2. On what is this invocation grounded? a. On the free will offering of Christ. b. On the gracious counsel of God, to redeem us by such offering.—The benediction of the Apostle: 1. A proof his hearty love: even to the unthankful, who through their apostasy have so troubled him, he wishes the best things; 2. A proof of his standing fast in the truth: in direct opposition to them he held fast so much the more definitely the evangelical truth, of redemption through Christ's death alone, and points them to that in contrast with their erroneous opinions.—Right wishing: 1. wishes true benefits; 2. points to the true source of such benefits.—The right behavior toward those who are disposed to depart from the truth: to open the heart fully to them in expressions of desire, full of divine blessing, before closing with and combatting their errors.

Vers. 1-5. The appearance of the Apostle against the Galatians: 1. in the full dignity of his office, at the same time, however, associating the brethren with himself; 2. with the full love of his heart, at the same time conceding nothing of the truth.

**Occasion of the Epistle:** APOSTASY OF THE GALATIANS FROM THE GOSPEL, WHICH PAUL HAD PREACHED TO THEM, TO THE FALSE DOCTRINE OF CERTAIN SEDUCERS, AGAINST WHOM HE THEREFORE UTTERS THE ANATHEMA.

CHAPTER I. 6–10.

6 I marvel that ye are so soon removed [changing over][1] from him that called you
7 into [in or by][2] the grace of Christ[3] unto another [a different][4] gospel: Which is
not another; but there be [except that there are] some that trouble you, and would
8 [θέλοντες, wish to] pervert the gospel of Christ. But though we, or an angel from
heaven, preach [should preach][5] any other gospel unto you[6] than [or contrary to][7]
9 that which we have preached unto you, let him be accursed [anathema]. As we
said before,[8] so say I now again, If any *man* preach any other gospel unto you than
10 [or contrary to] that ye have received, let him be accursed [anathema]. For do I
now persuade [am I now conciliating][9] men, or God? or do I seek to please men?
for [omit for][10] if I yet pleased men, I should not be the [a] servant of Christ.

1 Ver. 6.—[Μετατίθεσθε, middle, not passive, see EXEG. NOTES.—R.]
2 Ver. 6.—[Ἐν cannot mean "into," especially after καλέω.—R.]
3 Ver. 6.—[The many variations, such as the omission of Χρ., the insertion of Ἰησοῦ, the substitution of θεοῦ, all probably sprang from mistaken exegesis, joining Χρ. with καλέσαντος. The reading Χριστοῦ is very well supported and now universally retained.—R.]
4 Ver. 6.—[Ἕτερον, "different in kind," not "another of the same kind" (ἄλλο, ver. 7). So Alford, Ellicott, Wordsworth, Lightfoot.—R.]
5 Ver. 8.—[The periphrasis of the E. V. is necessary to bring out the force of εὐαγγελίζηται, in its reference to εὐαγγέλιον, vers. 6, 7; but the subjunctive must not be overlooked, as marking the different conditional propositions of vers. 8, 9.—R.]
6 Ver. 8.—א. omits ὑμῖν, א3. first adds it.
7 Ver. 8.—[On the meaning of παρά, here and ver. 9. See EXEG. NOTES.—R.]
8 Ver. 9.—א1.: προείρηκα.
9 Ver. 10.—["Persuade" is obviously inapplicable to God. Πείθω here means "to conciliate," "to make friends of." So modern English commentators. The form: "am I," *etc.*, is required by the emphatic ἄρτι (Ellicott).—R.]
10 Ver. 10.—Rec. εἰ γὰρ ἔτι; but γάρ is best omitted. [Rejected on preponderant MSS. authority by all modern editors.—R.]

## EXEGETICAL AND CRITICAL.

Without any thanksgiving for the readers' gifts of grace, as in other Epistles, the Apostle passes immediately from the invocation of a blessing to sharp rebuke which, however, strikes not so much the Galatians themselves as their seducing teaches. Vers. 6–9.

Ver. 6. **I marvel that ye are so soon changing over.**—He finds it strange, since he has expected, and had reason to expect, something different. "So soon" refers rather to the entrance of the apostasy than to its course, as having so rapidly developed itself from its commencement. The latter view suits the connection the less, inasmuch as μετατίθεσθε designates the apostasy as yet in process of development; οὕτω ταχέως, is therefore, we may say, equivalent to—so soon after the last visit of the Apostle. ["So soon" either 1) after conversion, or 2) after his visit, or 3) after the false teachers came; all three may be included, and are true; which is the primary reference cannot be *certainly* determined. In any case in view of the middle force of μετατίθεσθε ("turning renegades," LIGHTFOOT), it is a charge that the change was sudden and one for which they were to blame. SCHAFF: "The Greek implies first that the apostasy was voluntary, hence their own guilt; secondly, that it was not yet completed, and hence might be averted. The passive rendering would transfer the guilt to the false teachers."—R.]

**From him that called you:** most probably from God, who called you on the ground of the grace of Christ, which He has shown in His surrender of Himself to death; not=from Christ, who out of grace has called you. It is true that with the first explanation ἐν χάρ. Χρ. is difficult to render, but in any case it is not to be understood of the state of grace, as if=called you to the possession and enjoyment of grace.—[**By the grace of Christ.**—The E. V. renders ἐν χάριτι, "into the grace," following the Vulgate, but ἐν is here used in its instrumental sense. ALFORD: "Christ's grace is the elementary medium of our 'calling of God;' the sum of all that He has suffered and done for us to bring us to God; — *whereby* we come to the Father, — in which, as its element, the Father's calling of us has place." ELLICOTT: "The *dogmatical* consideration that the grace of Christ, in the sense it here appears used by St. Paul, denotes an active and energizing influence rather than a passive element, seems distinctly to suggest the instrumental sense." Comp. his notes *in loco*.—R.] But it is God Himself who "calls." The reference of καλέσαντος to the Apostle has some support in the fact that he afterwards opposes so expressly his own preaching to that of others, yet must be rejected, as καλεῖν too constantly expresses an activity of God for this interpretation. The apostasy is described, doubtless not undesignedly, as an apostasy from a person, not from a doctrine, that it may appear as ingratitude.—**To a different gospel.** — More exactly: to another kind of gospel = εὐαγγ. παρ' ὃ παρελ. (ver. 9). A *gospel*, either because the Galatians naturally took the doctrine which the false teachers brought them for the Gospel, or primarily in the general sense of Doctrine of Salvation, which the legal doctrine also claimed to be.

Ver. 7. Yet Paul as it were at once corrects himself, and respecting that which he has just named "gospel," denies again that this predicate in fact belongs to it, this false teaching is no gospel, but a subversion of the gospel. This is at all events the sense, if ὃ — the most obvious construction — is referred to the immediately preceding εὐαγγ. = "which other sort of gospel is no other, by the side of that preached by me, except that there are," *etc.* [The more correct reference is to ἕτερον εὐαγγέλιον. So MEYER, ALFORD, ELLICOTT, LIGHTFOOT, and Schmoller himself. See ALFORD's notes *in loco* for a full discussion and objections to the reference below. —R.] The reference however to the whole sentence is possible=which is nothing else (that is, this turning to another gospel) than that you have let yourselves be seduced by such as wish to subvert the gospel.

**There be some that trouble you.**—"Paul is fond of calling his opposers: τινές, *i. e.*, certain well known people, whom one for any reason whatever, in this case out of disparagement, will not designate more nearly." WIESELER.—[WORDSWORTH suggests and defends an ironical meaning: "unless they who are troubling you, are somebody," but this seems forced. LIGHTFOOT paraphrases well: "only in this sense is it another gospel, in that it is an attempt to pervert the one true gospel."—R.] — Ταράσσειν = to disturb the conscience and thereby the feelings by exciting doubts whether the gospel preached to them were the true teaching or not.—**Wish to pervert** = to have the will, to labor for; as the sequel plainly shows, it has not yet come to an actual perversion; μεταστρέφειν= הָפַךְ, *funditus evertere*.—**The gospel of Christ,** probably=gospel respecting Christ, inasmuch as in the first place the gospel treats of Christ generally; especially, however, because the merit of Christ is the chief theme of the true gospel in distinction from the legal teaching. The gospel, of course, could not, in itself, be destroyed, but the evangelical preaching among the Galatians might be, if they received another teaching.

Ver. 8. **But though we—let him be anathema.**—Certain persons wish to destroy the gospel of Christ among you, and bring you another, but (ἀλλά) rather let every one who does that be ἀνάθεμα, instead of passing for an evangelist.—Ἡμεῖς: first and chiefly the Apostle himself, then, however, also the "brethren who are with me," in whose name he likewise writes.—**Angel from heaven**, to be taken together=angel descended from heaven. "If Paul repudiates his own and even angelic authority in the case assumed, as accursed, then every one, without exception (comp. ὅστις ἂν ᾖ, v. 10), is subject to the same curse in the same case." MEYER. — Παρ' ὃ εὐηγγ. ὑμῖν=literally: beyond that, *etc.*, may be equivalent to *praterquam*, or to *contra.* "Formerly dogmatic interest came here into play, the Lutherans, in opposition to tradition, contending for *praterquam*, and the Catholics in defence of it, for *contra.* *Contra*, or more exactly the sense of specific difference, is according to the context the right sense. (See ver. 6. ἕτερον.)" MEYER. [This sense of παρά, "contrary to," is now generally conceded by Protestant commentators. WORDSWORTH and LIGHTFOOT give it the sense of "besides;" the latter arguing from the context that Paul means, his gospel will brook no rival, will suffer no foreign admixture, but, as ELLICOTT remarks: "the Apostle implies throughout the Epistle that the Judaical gospel was in the strict sense of the words an ἕτερον εὐαγγ., and in its very essence opposed to the true gospel." Both ideas may properly be included (ALFORD, SCHAFF).—R.]—Εὐηγγελισάμεθα ὑμῖν: namely, I and my companions at the time of your conversion. Comp. παρελάβ. ver. 9.

**Let him be anathema.**—A translation of חֵרֶם = Dedicated to God without ransom=given over to annihilation, to death, in the Old Testament to bodily, in the New Testament to θάνατος in opposition to ζωή, to eternal death. See in WIESELER a detailed elucidation and refutation of the explanation, "excommunicated." ['Ανάθεμα is the common Hellenistic form of the classical and Attic word ἀνάθημα, which in both forms originally meant "devoted to God." When the two forms were desynonymized, the Hellenistic word naturally took a meaning from the Hebrew (through the LXX.) *in malam partem*, while the Attic form was used in a good sense. Comp. Luke xxi. 5, where only it is found in N. T. This distinction was general, but not universal. Afterwards the common patristic sense of our word undoubtedly was "excommunicated," though sometimes accompanied with distinct execration. It cannot have this meaning here, for "an angel from heaven" is not open to excommunication, nor does N. T. usage favor such a signification. Comp. Rom. ix. 3; 1 Cor. xii. 3. See also TRENCH, *Syn. N. T.* § 5, MEYER, ELLICOTT, LIGHTFOOT.—This passage affords no warrant for ecclesiastical anathemas. Such a practice presupposes the milder meaning, which is incorrect, and as milder, in itself forbids such anathematizing. It is obviously unfair to find in St. Paul's language first, a reason for ecclesiastical "excommunication," and then a warrant for "anathematizing."—R.]

Ver. 9. **As we said before.**—Referring probably to his last visit, not to ver. 8.—The Apostle repeats the curse, which he has pronounced ver. 8, in order to show that he "speaks deliberately." BENGEL. — [Notice that in ver. 8 the Apostle uses ἐάν with the subjunctive: "though we, or an angel, should preach," in ver. 9, εἰ with the indicative: "if any man preach," appending the anathema in both cases. "In the former, a pure hypothesis is put forward, in itself highly improbable; in the latter a fact which had actually occurred and was occurring" (LIGHTFOOT). There is additional force in the change of subject: even Paul or an angel from heaven — did they do so — would be anathema, much more—any man, neither Apostle nor angel—is anathema, having done so.—R.]

Ver. 10. **For am I now conciliating men?**—Explanation (γάρ) of the severity with which he demeans himself towards the false teachers by this repeated ἀνάθεμα. He does it, because he is concerned only for the favor of God, not that of men. It would be natural to understand "now" like ver. 9 of the time of the composition of the epistle. Yet on the other hand this limitation is not quite congruous to the general contents of the verse, it is therefore better to understand it more generally of the time of the Apostle's conversion. [It seems more natural to regard "now" as an emphatic taking up of "now" in ver. 9—"now in what I have said." Paul had not been a man-pleaser before conversion. If he had been charged with it among the Galatians, he was not so NOW in what he had been writing.—R.]—Πείθειν=to win over, to draw to one's side by persuasion, whether directly by words or otherwise; here, in view of the reference to God=to gain for one's self, to win for one's self as a friend.—Ἀρέσκειν: sometimes to please, sometimes to be disposed to please, to live according to the pleasure of; the latter here. "Yet" goes back to the same time with "now." ["Yet," *i. e.*, after my call to the apostleship, and all that has happened to me (SCHAFF). "It is equivalent to 'at this stage, at this late date'" (LIGHTFOOT).—R.]—**I should not be a servant of Christ**=could make no claim to this title. As a true servant of Christ, who dares not act to please men, I must, even though it should not please men, judge with all sharpness and severity respecting those who subvert the gospel. "Servant of Christ" is here doubtless to be taken in its official sense=could make no claim to the name of a teacher. With how much right Paul could say so of himself is shown, *e. g.*, by 2 Cor. xi. 23 sq.

### DOCTRINAL AND ETHICAL.

1. *Apostasy even in the early church.* The glimpse of such scenes of the first Christian Church as our Epistle speaks of, and as are mentioned by anticipation in our section, is instructive. Even in such as had been brought to the faith by a Paul himself, a speedy lapse was possible, and yet he certainly fulfilled his office among them in the right way, and his activity was blessed. Even the best preaching cannot overcome the sinful nature of the human heart. This preserving and making steadfast in the truth, is a work of the Holy Ghost, and it goes on, just as growth is wont to do: through advances and fallings back on account of the opposing might of the flesh, according to the account of the Apostle himself. Chap. v. 17.

2. *The false teachers.* Deflections from evangelical truth, however, are not on this account to be taken lightly; but on the contrary, very gravely, as the language of the Apostle in this passage shows. Paul had full justification in uttering a curse against the false teachers, and thus giving them over to everlasting destruction, in the wickedness they committed with their false teaching; which was a double one—1) against persons: they perplexed their consciences and brought them in danger of losing the salvation of their souls; 2) against the cause: they went about to subvert the gospel of Christ. They made an attack on the sacred rights of believers, and their conduct was therefore worthy of a curse. That this curse does not flow from personal mortification, because they had rejected his teaching, Paul shows plainly by placing himself under the curse, in case he should teach differently. Besides, the anathema is, of course, aimed at this conduct of the false teachers in itself, and this sharp opposition by no means excluded the wish that they might themselves see the error of their way, and themselves come to the knowledge of the evangelical truth. But this was not the place for saying this. He expresses himself with thorough earnestness against the false teachers, only to open the eyes of the Galatians, and to release them from the snares in which they had allowed themselves to be taken. Although in this earnestness he comes in conflict with men, he must do what beseems a servant of Christ: be zealous for Christ and the salvation of His people.

3. *Pleasing men.* What Paul says, ver. 10, appears to be opposite to 1 Cor. x. 33; but in 1 Cor. Paul speaks of things indifferent, in which a man may yield somewhat without wounding his conscience (comp. Rom. xv. 2). Here, however, he means sinful complaisance, where one fashions his doctrine and preaching according to the sense of men, in order thus to gain their favor. He only then is a servant of Christ, who subordinates unconditionally the favor of men to the favor of God, who in His official activity does not seek to make Himself pleasing to men, does not make this his object. When, however, from time to time—for uninterrupted it can never be—the favor of men falls to his lot, he is to receive it from God's hand with thankfulness and humility, as a kind indulgence, which in his manifold conflicts may be of value. That the servant of Christ must be on his guard, not to draw upon himself deservedly the ill-will of the world through pride and self-will; that he is not in carnal temper to fly in the face of men, and hence that he must always examine well whether his zeal is a spiritual one, or is not becoming a carnal one, if it were not such from the beginning, is indeed self-evident, but cannot be carefully enough considered; as in general the theory of the relation of human and divine favor is tolerably simple, but the practice is very difficult.

[4. WORDSWORTH:—Not to please men, be they never so many or great, out of flatness of spirit, so as, for the pleasing of them, either

1) To neglect any part of our duty towards God and Christ; or,
2) To go against our own consciences, by doing any dishonest or unlawful thing; or,
3) To do them harm whom we would please, by confirming them in their errors, flattering them in their sins, humoring them in their peevishness, or but even cherishing their weakness; for weakness, though it may be borne with, yet it must not be cherished.

But then, by yielding to their infirmities for a time, in hope to win them, by patiently expecting their conversion or strengthening, by restoring them with the spirit of meekness, with meekness instructing them that oppose themselves, should we seek to please all men.—R.]

### HOMILETICAL AND PRACTICAL.

Ver. 1. "I marvel:"—is a word of apostolic wisdom.—LUTHER:—St. Paul does not set upon the Galatians with vehement and terrifying words, but speaks in quite fatherly and friendly wise with them; and does not only soften down their fall and error, but excuses them also in a manner, yet so that he nevertheless also punishes them. Therefore, of all sweet and mild words, he could hardly have chosen one more fit than when he says, "I marvel."—RIEGER:—In itself the preservation and perseverance of a man in good is more to be wondered at than when there is a stumbling or falling. But the Apostle says, "I marvel," in order to express to them thereby the confidence of something better, which he has retained on their behalf, and to let them discover something of the hope, in which he stands, of begetting them again through the gospel unto their first faith.

WÜRT. SUMM.:—We are here reminded of our human weakness. We should endeavor to be so assured of divine truth in our own heart, as to be able to persevere therein, though even an angel would persuade us of something else, and the whole world would believe otherwise. Such perseverance is not in our power, however, but must be obtained from God through prayer and through diligent use of the divine word, which alone can make our walk steadfast.

"From him that called you by the grace of Christ unto another gospel."—RIEGER:—A tender description of the good work begun in them. A feeling contrast with the yoke which some would now lay upon their necks.—SPENER:—Whosoever will no longer be saved simply through the grace of God in Christ falls away from the Father and the grace of Christ to another gospel, even though he holds the other articles of faith. For so soon as merit is mixed therewith, it is no more grace.

Apostasy from the truth: 1. how far not to be wondered at; 2. how far to be wondered at. —So soon alienated! 1. a word of grief, true of so many; 2. a warning word, in relation to all.—An apostatizing tendency, or inconstancy a radical fault of the human heart: 1. sluggish and immovable, where it is of moment that it should move and apply itself; 2. so movable and unsteady where it should abide firm.—To turn ourselves from Him who hath called us: 1. so lightly done; 2. weighs yet so heavily.—Another Gospel! is the world's cry; no other! must forever remain our answering testimony.

Ver. 7. SPENER:—The gospel of Christ will not let itself be mixed with the doctrine of works, as if these were necessary to salvation; but as soon as this is done, the gospel is perverted.—HEDINGER:—More taught than God has thought, is to the gospel quite athwart. The false teachers will have Christ's grace, to be sure, but something of their own works therewith. Gross error! Adding more destroys the store.—STARKE:—Where Satan cannot persuade men to open sins, he seeks to perplex their consciences, and pervert the gospel, which is the only means of salvation; in this too he very easily succeeds, because the doctrine of works appears quite agreeable to the reason.

Ver. 8. LUTHER:—It is not in vain that St. Paul sets himself first, and will, first of all, be accursed, if he shows himself herein worthy of it. For all excellent workmen are wont also thus to do, namely, to reprehend their own faults first, for then can they so much the more freely chide and censure the faults of others.—SPENER:—No creature has authority to change anything in the gospel, or to add thereto, of however eminent rank, office, enlightenment, holiness, and miraculous power he may be. Not even the whole Church, nor her teachers, nor her councils and the like. If the change is made, no inquiry is needed; but it is to be reprobated, because it is new and another.—LANGE:—As the blessing coming out of the gospel is the most weighty and noble of all, so is the curse which rests upon the hindering of the blessing through falsifying the gospel, the greatest of all, one which remains forever upon soul and body.

Ver. 10. LUTHER:—We cannot more hotly and bitterly anger the world than by attacking and condemning her wisdom, righteousness, ability, and powers. If we now reject and condemn these highest gifts of the world, that is truly not to behave feigningly to the world, but to strive after hate and ill luck, and, moreover, to get both our hands full of the same. For if we condemn men with all their doings, it can never fail but that we must soon take our chance and bring upon ourselves such scorn and envy that we shall be persecuted, hunted, banished, condemned, and, very likely, even murdered.—SPENER:—The sincerity of a teacher, when men see that his concern is alone to please God, and not men, is a strong ground for believing that his teaching is sound and pure.—HEDINGER:—Just so! Whoever in the church, in the state, in the family, serves men, fears and cowers before men, and, for their sake, bends the right, flatters and fawns, has trifled away his best title—Christ's servant and disciple. A thunder-stroke! Whose ears tingle not, when he hears it?—RIEGER:—O God! preserve all thy servants, that no one, through pride and self-will, may draw persecution upon himself, and fly in the faces of men; but grant also that we may not count persecution, mocking, and contempt as tokens of our having betrayed the truth, but may view them and bear them as the marks in the foreheads of thine approved servants!

The earnestness with which Paul opposes the false teachers: 1. well founded, 2. very significant for us: should (a) withhold us from the reception of any unevangelical doctrine; (b) strengthen us in the certainty that the gospel, which we have, is the true one.—A curse upon him who preaches a false doctrine! 1. A fearfully earnest utterance; 2. yet pressingly needful; 3. instructive for all that are wavering.—Let not every man undertake to be a teacher, but whoever is, let him take heed what he teaches.—The curse which Paul pronounces upon himself, if he should preach another gospel, is a token: 1. how high the gospel stands in his view; 2. how humbly he thinks of himself (viewing himself only as a mere instrument, as a servant, who has to accomplish what his Master has commanded him).—Not the Church above the word, but the word above the Church!—Two earnest questions: 1. Which seekest thou most, man's favor or God's favor? 2. Which is weightier, man's favor or God's favor?—Man's favor or God's favor? Choose: there is no third.—The right union of unsparingness and forbearance in our intercourse with men: an art of difficult attainment.—To be entirely unsparing, and entirely forbearing, each in the right way, is the Christian's duty in dealing with men.—Man's disfavor, compared with God's favor, as insignificant as wholesome, perfects us in humility, and impels us the more to assure ourselves of the favor of God.

*On the whole section.*—LISCO:—The curse of the Apostle against the false apostles: I. Whom it strikes: 1. Necessarily every one, without exception, who changes the blessing of the gospel into mischief, and so out of good prepares for himself death; 2. those also who have deep insight, or other high qualities for serving the kingdom of God, and yet do not preach it purely; 3. even an angel himself, if he could preach another gospel. II. Why must it be uttered? 1. He who preaches the gospel must have a will thereby to serve, not men, but God; 2. through a false gospel men may, indeed, be attracted, but God views it as blasphemy; 3. therefore, he is placed under the curse, who will serve the gospel, and yet doing so as a man-pleaser, is found an unfruitful servant of Christ.

The apostasy of believers: 1. is, alas, sometimes a fact; 2. from what does it proceed? 3. how is it to be remedied?—The Apostle's demeanor: 1. towards the misled: he makes a complaint and charge; but through it all the full tones of compassion and love are heard; 2. towards the misleaders: unsparingly stern even to denouncing a curse.—To fall away from the gospel is bad, but to subvert the gospel is worse.

---

# I.

## TO DESTROY THE INFLUENCE WHICH THE FALSE TEACHERS HAD GAINED IN THE CHURCHES, PAUL REFUTES THEIR ATTACKS UPON HIS APOSTOLIC DIGNITY, AND PROVES THEREBY THE FULL AUTHORITY OF HIS PREACHING.

### CHAPTER I. 11—II. 21.

### 1. To this end he appeals to the fact that he received his commission to declare the Gospel from God and Christ Himself through immediate revelation, not from the senior Apostles.

(CHAP. i. 11–24.)

11 But I certify you [Now I declare unto you],[1] brethren, that the gospel which was
12 preached of [ὑπ', by] me is not after man. For I neither received [For neither did
I receive][2] it of [from] man, neither was I taught *it*, but by [through] the [omit the]
13 revelation of [from][3] Jesus Christ. For ye have [omit have] heard of my conversa-
tion in time past in the Jews' religion [Judaism],[4] how that beyond measure I per-
14 secuted the church of God and wasted [was destroying][5] it: And profited in the
Jews' religion above many my equals [And surpassed in Judaism many of my
age][6] in mine own nation, being more exceedingly zealous of the traditions of my
15 fathers [or my ancestral traditions]. But when it pleased God,[7] who separated me
16 [set me apart][8] from my mother's womb, and called *me* by his grace, To reveal
his Son in [within] me, that I might preach him among the heathen [Gentiles];
17 immediately I conferred not with flesh and blood: Neither went I up [away][9] to
Jerusalem to them which [who] were apostles before me; but I went [went away] into
18 Arabia, and returned again unto Damascus. Then after three years I went up to
Jerusalem to see Peter [to make the acquaintance of Cephas],[10] and abode with
19 him fifteen days. But other of the apostles saw I none [I did not see], save
20 James the Lord's brother. Now the things which I write unto you, behold, be-
21 fore God I lie not. Afterwards I came into the regions of Syria and Cilicia;
22 And [but] was unknown by face unto the churches of Judea which were in Christ:
23 But they had heard only [only they were hearing],[11] That he which persecuted us
in times past [who once persecuted us] now preacheth [is now preaching] the faith
24 which once he destroyed [was destroying]. And they glorified God in me.

[1] Ver. 11.—The *Recepta* γνωρίζω δέ is well attested, adopted by Lachmann and latterly by Tischendorf. [Alford retains γάρ on the authority of B. F. and a few others; δέ is adopted by Wordsworth, Ellicott and Lightfoot, on the authority of ℵ. A. D[23]. K. L. and most versions. "Now I declare unto you" is taken from E. V., 1 Cor. xv. 1, where the Greek is the same.—R.]

[2] Ver. 12.—[Ellicott's rendering given above, is an alteration made to retain the emphasis on "I," and to indicate that the first negative is not strictly correlative to the second. "From" instead of "of," in conformity with modern usage.—R.]

[3] Ver. 12.—[The genitive Ἰησοῦ Χριστοῦ is a subjective genitive. See EXEG. NOTES.—R.]

[4] Ver. 13.—[Ἰουδαϊσμῷ is better rendered literally. So in ver. 14.—R.]

[5] Ver. 13.—[The sense of the imperfect, ἐπόρθουν, is best expressed thus. Schaff renders: "labored to destroy." The same change in ver. 23.—R.]

[6] Ver. 14.—[Schaff thus renders it. The E. V. is unusually unsatisfactory here; the ἅπαξ λεγόμενον, συνηλικιώτας means "contemporaries."—R.]

[7] Ver. 15.—Ὁ Θεός of Rec. is rejected by Tischendorf, and bracketted by Lachmann. ℵ. has the words [so also A. D. K. L., many cursives and versions; retained by Ellicott, Wordsworth. There are paradiplomatic reasons for retaining it, but if a gloss, undoubtedly a correct one.—R.]

[8] Ver. 15.—["Separated" has a local sense not intended here.—R.]

[9] Ver. 17.—Of the two readings ἀνῆλθον (Rec.) and ἀπῆλθον, about equally attested, the second is decidedly preferable on internal grounds. Not only does the latter give a more formal and sharper antithesis; οὐδὲ ἀπῆλθον—ἀλλὰ ἀπῆλθον, but the former betrays itself as a correction from the fact that ἀνέρχομαι or ἀναβαίνω is generally used of the journey to Jerusalem, as in ver. 18. Wieseler. ℵ. has ἀνῆλθον, [adopted by Tischendorf, Wordsworth. B. D. F. have ἀπῆλθον; adopted by Lachmann, Meyer, Wieseler, Alford, Ellicott; Lightfoot is doubtful. "Went away" follows the latter reading.—R.]

[10] Ver. 18.—Instead of Πέτρον (Rec.), Κηφᾶν is to be read, as also in ii. 9, 11, 14. So also ℵ. The Hebrew name was suppressed by the Greek gloss, hence in ii. 7, 8, where Paul himself wrote the Greek name, the variation Κηφᾶς is not found [So all modern editors. Ἱστορῆσαι means more than to see, "to visit, to make the acquaintance of."—R.]

[11] Ver. 23.—[The English text has been amended to bring out the force of the Greek imperfects.—R.]

### EXEGETICAL AND CRITICAL.

Ver. 11. **Now I declare unto you—not after man.**—[Literally: "I make known unto you as respects the gospel, the one preached by me, that it is not according to man."—R.] To the warm burst of feeling succeeds the composed statement of reasons. Accordingly we have the formal γνωρίζω, and the address "brethren," which also shows that Paul, although in the introduction he gives no peculiar title of honor to the Galatian Christians, feels himself to be still standing in the fraternal relation to them. He takes this as his starting point with them, because his aim in what follows is to bring them back and win them again from their error. He first justifies his preceding rebuke by the distinct and formal assurance that his teaching is not of man. Of course this was not something entirely new to the church, yet it had, doubtless, been at first a merely tacit presupposition in connection with the Apostle's preaching, without having been expressly emphasized: hence the γνωρίζω; after it had been called in question, it must be definitely affirmed.

**The gospel which was preached by me** is most naturally referred to the preaching of the gospel among the Galatians, although self-evidently the same declaration was of general validity.—Οὐ κατὰ ἄνθρωπον literally: "not according to man," not after the fashion of man, not man's work. This applies not immediately to its origin, but to its character, which however is especially and primarily conditioned by its origin (ver. 12). The sequel shows the phrase to be nearly equivalent in sense to "scholastic" [*schulmässig*].

Ver. 12. **For neither did I receive it of man, neither was I taught it.**—"Neither did I" = any more than the Twelve. By the denial of any human origin of his gospel he asserts his equal rank with the other Apostles. The sentence receives a simple exposition when compared with ver. 1, which it more closely explains. The first and negative part: "neither did I receive it from man, neither was I taught it," is an explanation of "not of men, neither through man," while the second part, "but through revelation from Jesus Christ," is an explanation of "through Jesus Christ and God the Father," which is afterwards made yet more definite (vers. 15, 16).—[LIGHTFOOT: The idea of the preposition (παρά) is sufficiently wide to include both the ἀπό and διά of ver. 1.—R.]

**Through revelation from Jesus Christ.**—This is commonly explained as merely a giving of instruction respecting the contents of the gospel, and there is then a difficulty as to when Christ gave to Paul this ἀποκάλυψις, discovery. Here Ἰησοῦ Χριστοῦ is taken as *gen. subj.* = the revelation which Jesus Christ gave. MEYER explains it of revelations received soon after the event near Damascus, of which, however, there is no mention in the Acts. Others, with reason, refuse to assume any such revelations, but explain the "revelation" as identical with the actual appearance of Christ on the way to Damascus, through which Paul received certainty of that which is precisely the essence of the gospel, namely, "Jesus the Son of God." They are led to this, moreover, by a just instinct, that it is not the developed contents of that which Paul taught, that is here in question. This explanation, therefore, is quite correct, and Paul's reference here is solely to the fact of that appearance on the way. Yet he has in view chiefly, not a receiving of instruction thereby, but his *call to the apostleship itself*, for this was a call "to preach the gospel" (see also ver. 18), and therefore a "receiving the gospel." The expression, that he had received the gospel through revelation from Jesus Christ, has primarily the simple meaning, that through this he had been called and appointed to preach. In the phrase "through revelation," *etc.*, Ἰησοῦ Χριστοῦ is at all events the *subjective genitive*, for Christ is in any case to be regarded as active in the installation of the Apostle (ver. 1), and hence in his call to preach. As the object of this "revelation" we are to understand not the contents of the gospel, but more simply Christ Himself, hence it is = by Christ's revealing Himself to me.—This view is, it is true, in apparent contradiction to the "taught" immediately preceding, which seems to point to a definitely developed doctrine, but only in apparent contradiction. It is only in the negative that he speaks of "being taught;" in order to deny most entirely the human calling to preach, Paul denies also the "being taught;" he did not, he says, first receive in a course of school instruction, his equipment, authorization and capacity to preach, hence not in a secondary, derived manner, as a scholar (of the Apostles). Over against this human origin, Paul now simply asserts his "revelation from Jesus Christ" which need not be complemented by "taught"—an expression in itself awkward too—but merely by "received."—In what immediately follows it is not "through revelation from Jesus Christ," so much as the negative "neither was I taught it," that is proven. For in vers. 15, 16, where "through revelation" has to be touched, it is mentioned properly only as a historical notice, in order to mark the transition from the first period of his life to the second, hence only in the subordinate clause. From this, however, the conclusion cannot of course be drawn; "I was taught through revelation from Jesus Christ;" for this reason first, that then we should expect a detailed statement of this positive side. But all that was to be said on the positive side, had been said already in the short *δι' ἀποκαλύψεως Ἰησοῦ Χριστοῦ* because here a simple fact only was in question; on the other hand the "received from man" and "taught" could have taken place in many ways and at different times, might have been of long continuance; and on this account the demonstration was needed that there had been no point of time whatever, when such instruction from the senior Apostles (whom he has in mind throughout in "from man"), could have taken place, since at first he has been hostile to Christianity, and after his calling had never lived in intercourse with the senior Apostles, though at the same time he had already preached the gospel. And, he proceeds to say in chap. ii., when afterwards, he was once somewhat longer with them, he then appeared as a fully equal Apostle, and was so acknowledged; hence there could no longer be any talk of his occupying the place of a pupil.

[Since the design of the Apostle in what follows is to prove that his doctrine as well as his apostleship was God-given, that He was "taught of God," it seems more natural to refer "revelation from Jesus Christ," to instruction as well as to calling to the apostleship. WORDSWORTH calls attention to the force of *ἀλλά*, which he considers to be here "except" "save"—"nor was I taught it *except* by revelation." He was *θεοδίδακτος*. And this view is further sustained by the omission of the article before the noun, which is not rendered definite either by the genitive following or by the fact that there was but one revelation (Paul undoubtedly had many). To what instructive revelation does he refer? Undoubtedly to that on the way to Damascus, but not to that exclusively. Nor to any particular revelation soon after his conversion (AQUINAS, MEYER, ELLICOTT, ALFORD, who suggest the sojourn in Arabia, ver. 17, as the probable time), but to the revelation on the way to Damascus as "the fundamental and central illumination," "followed by special revelation" at different periods of his life. Comp. Acts xxii. 17; xxiii. 11; 1 Cor. xi. 13; 2 Cor. xii. 1 sq.; Gal. ii. 2. SCHAFF. Schmoller's view on this point colors his notes on the entire section.—R.]

Ver. 13. **For ye heard of my conversation in time past,** *etc.*—How far this statement is meant to confirm the previous proposition (*γάρ*), has just been indicated. Perhaps, however, he also emphasizes his former Jewish zeal, with particular reference to his Judaistic opposers. He wishes thereby to call attention to the fact that his present anti-Judaistic position does not result from any want of acquaintance with Judaism, but that, on the contrary, it rests upon only too intimate an acquaintance with it.

*Ἰουδαϊσμός*: the word in itself, it is true, signifies nothing more than the Jewish religion; yet Paul, in this connection, evidently throws more meaning into it, joining with it the additional idea: Jewish zealotism. Only thus is a proper meaning given to "surpassed in Judaism" (ver. 14). This again finds its explanation in **how that beyond measure I persecuted,** *etc.* "He was really engaged in the work of destruction, not merely in that of disturbance." MEYER.

Ver. 14. **In mine own nation.**—Literally "race," the people are regarded as a single race, descending from the same ancestor.—**My ancestral traditions**:—not the Pharisaic traditions or the Mosaic law, together with those traditions, but teachings which the fathers of the collective people held (see WIESELER). The phrase: "the traditions of my fathers," in itself, describes only the doctrinal and ritual definitions respecting the Jewish worship which then obtained, though, of course, resting on the Mosaic law as their foundation. But Paul, in calling himself a zealot, who surpassed many of his contemporaries, has undoubtedly in view chiefly his observance of these usages according to the peculiarly strict rule of Pharisaism. [SCHAFF: "The word *παράδοσις*, 'tradition,' which figures so prominently in the Roman Catholic controversy, in the general sense, embraces everything which is taught and handed down, either orally or in writing, or in both ways, from generation to generation; in the particular sense it may be used favorably of the divine doctrine, and even of Christianity itself, as is the case 1 Cor. xi. 2 (E. V. 'ordinances' instead of 'traditions'); 2 Thess. ii. 15; iii. 6, or unfavorably of the human additions to, and perversions of the religion of the Old or New Testament, in which case it is generally more clearly defined as the traditions 'of the elders' or 'of men,' as Matt. xxv. 2; Mark vii. 3, 5, 8; Col. ii. 8. In our passage it means the whole Jewish religion, or mode of worship, divine and human; but in the Pharisaic sense, as opposed to Christianity." LIGHTFOOT'S paraphrase is excellent: "My early education is a proof that I did not receive the gospel from man. I was brought up in a rigid school of ritualism, directly opposed to the liberty of the gospel. I was from age and temper a staunch adherent of the principles of that school. Acting upon them, I relentlessly persecuted the Christian brotherhood. No human agency, therefore, could have brought about the change. It required a direct interposition from God."—R.]

Vers. 15, 16. **But when it pleased God.**—In the interest of his demonstration of the independence of his apostolate, as respects men, he here studiously emphasizes the activity of God in conferring it, going back even to the divine ordination thereto at his very conception. [LIGHTFOOT: "Observe how words are accumulated to tell upon the one point on which he is insisting—the sole agency of God as distinct from his own efforts."—R.]—**From my mother's womb**=when he was yet in his mother's womb, he was already set apart as an Apostle. [SCHAFF: "Comp. Jerem. i. 5; Isa. xlix. 1. The decree of redemption is eternal as God's love and omniscience, but its temporal realization begins in each individual case with the natural birth, and more properly with the gospel-call and the spiritual birth. He refers, however, here more particularly to his call to the *apostleship*, for which he was 'set apart' or destined, 'elected and dedicated by a Divine act. Comp. the same term, Rom. i. 1; Acts xiii. 2."—R.]—His calling followed afterwards near Damascus. In the Acts, Christ's appearance only is mentioned; here Paul takes up the event with a more doctrinal reference, and hence refers this appearance to its first cause, God. This, of course, implies no discrepancy with the narrative of the Acts.—Although appearances favor such a view, "called" does not denote an earlier act, preceding the revelation (ver. 16) which, therefore, refers to subsequent revelations (MEYER). [The aorist participle, καλέσας, in this connection, at first sight, seems to refer to an act prior to the "revelation," not, however, necessarily long before. It does not mean a "calling" in the Divine mind, as some infer from its connection with "set apart;" but most probably the Divine act which, "by means of His grace," resulted immediately in his conversion, when the revelation was made. ELLICOTT: "The *moving* cause of the call was the Divine pleasure; the *mediating* cause, the boundless grace of God; the instrument, the heaven-sent voice" or revelation; the purpose of the setting apart, the call and the revelation alike was, "that I might preach him among the Gentiles." "To reveal" depends on "pleased," not on "called."—R.]

So then "reveal" is only the explanation of the "calling;" more precisely: there is thereby indicated what took place at the calling, namely, the enlightenment and conviction then effected. For this reason also, because the calling comes into mention only as respects its result, he speaks only of revealing "His Son within me." Accordingly Paul, in this passage, indeed, says nothing of having had an outward appearance of Christ. But, that Paul, in the expression, **to reveal his Son within me**, was thinking of a definite, individual fact, which was connected with a definite locality, the city or the neighborhood of the city of Damascus, and not of a purely internal event, appears most clearly from what follows ver. 17, "returned again." "Had the event of his conversion been a purely inward one, his recollection of the locality where it occurred would not, more than twenty years after, have still forced itself so strongly into the foreground that, in describing only the general inner result of that revolution, he would have been constrained at once to think of Damascus." PARET, *Jahrbücher für deutsche Theologie*, 1858. H. 1. Furthermore and principally, the whole proof which Paul here brings for his apostolic parity rests upon the fact that he had really and truly had an appearance of the Risen One. "I have not been called by men, but just as truly as the older Apostles, by Christ Himself to be an Apostle," is his fundamental thought: how could he be thinking on a mere internal event, a vocation by Christ only in spirit? With that, instead of his equality, his difference from the others would have been established. Therefore, if any conclusion is justified, it is this: Paul has here in his eye the event related in the Acts; presupposing, however, the outward occurrence as well known, he avails himself only of that element of it which has pertinence here, namely, that he was inwardly enlightened concerning Christ, that Christ was revealed to his inner eye, to faith. Of his conversion in itself, Paul does not speak here, or only so far as it was a condition of his capacity for the apostleship, as through it the "calling" to be an Apostle became a reality. He dates his calling, therefore, from the moment of his conversion. Therefore, he continues: **that I might preach him among the Gentiles**.—Him whom God has revealed to him as His Son, he was, and is still (therefore the present), to declare as such; this is the gospel which he received "through revelation from Jesus Christ" (ver. 12), this "the gospel which was preached by me" (ver. 11).—Ἐν τοῖς ἔθνεσιν: *among* the Gentile nations, therefore ἐν, not the dative. For Paul preached not merely to the Gentiles, but among the Gentile nations, first to the Jews dwelling among them, and only then to the heathen themselves.

**Immediately I conferred not with flesh and blood**.—Εὐθέως, of course, belongs strictly not to the negative sentence immediately following, but to the affirmative sentence: "went away into Arabia," it does not, however, exclude a brief previous activity in Damascus, since the Apostle was only concerned to prove that he did not go out from Damascus in any other direction than Arabia, and particularly that he did not go to Jerusalem.—"I conferred not," I addressed no communication to flesh and blood, in order to receive instruction and direction—"flesh and blood;" here merely—one clothed with a mortal body, therefore in sense equivalent simply to —Man. The conception is thus strongly expressed, because Man appears here in antithesis with God.

Ver. 17. **Neither went I away to Jerusalem to them who were apostles before me**.—This is the only distinction which he concedes between himself and them.—**Into Arabia**. "This Arabian journey is to be regarded as his first essay of foreign labor, and it is, by εὐθέως, put in connection with the purpose of the divine revelation, that he should preach the gospel among the heathen."—(MEYER). Yet I would not on this account wholly reject the other conjectures that have been offered as to the purpose of this journey, such as seeking protection from the Jews, "severing himself from pressure of the national spirit," and partially also, perhaps to prepare himself in stillness for his work.—This journey into Arabia is not mentioned in the Acts, probably because it was of short duration and therefore perhaps not known to Luke; it is, with most probability, placed in the time of the "many days," Acts ix. 23; the flight from Damascus must therefore be placed at the end of this second visit there. [Two questions arise: 1. as to the *place*; 2. the *object* of this sojourn. 1. Although "the desert region about Damascus" may have been the place (since Justin includes Damascus in Arabia, and Xenophon applies the name to the region beyond the Euphrates, *Anab.* I. 5), yet Paul is always more definite in his geographical statements than most ancient authors, and as in the only other place where Arabia is mentioned in the N. T. (Gal. iv. 25), it must mean the Sinaitic peninsula, it seems decidedly preferable to refer it to that locality in this case. Besides, as LIGHTFOOT well remarks, any other view "deprives this visit of a significance which, on a more probable hypothesis, it possesses in relation to this crisis of St. Paul's life." If iv. 25 refers to "Hagar" as the Arabic name of Sinai, the argument is conclusive, for he was not likely to have heard this name anywhere but on the spot. If it be a mere geographical remark, then it is a very indefinite one, granting that Paul here uses "Arabia" with so extended a signification. 2. "Paul's object in this residence in Arabia, as seems most probable from the context, was not to preach the gospel—but to enjoy a season of undisturbed preparation for his high and holy calling. This period, therefore, belongs more properly to the history of the Apostle's inward life; and this affords the simplest explanation of the silence of the book of Acts respecting it. It was for him a sort of substitute for the three years' personal intercourse with the Lord, enjoyed by the other Apostles" (SCHAFF, *Apostolic Church*, p. 236). This view of the *object* confirms the opinion that the Sinaitic peninsula was the locality. Where Moses and Elijah had been before him, Paul went. "Thus in the wilderness of Sinai, as on the mount of transfiguration, the three dispensations met in one;" Law, Prophecy and Gospel; Moses, Elijah and Paul. Comp. LIGHTFOOT, p. 87 sq.; STANLEY, *Sinai and Palestine*, p. 50.—R.]

Ver. 18. **Then after three years.**—To be reckoned probably from his calling to the apostleship; for he means: I did not go up at once to Jerusalem, but only three years after. This is the first journey of Paul to Jerusalem, Acts ix. 26.—Ἱστορῆσαι K.=in order to become personally acquainted with Cephas, not: in order to obtain instruction from him. The more precise expression is therefore designedly chosen.—**Fifteen days.**—Had it been in itself possible that Paul at this time received instruction, still a course of instruction strictly so called, a schooling under the senior Apostles would not have been possible in so short a time. Hence the length of his stay is expressly mentioned. [Nor does the singling out of Peter prove anything more than his prominence among the Twelve; Paul puts himself on a par with all the Apostles, including Peter.—R.]

Ver. 19. **But other of the apostles I did not see.**—"Apostle" must be taken in the strict sense of the Twelve, since it is precisely his parity with these that Paul wishes to make out. Therefore **James the Lord's brother** is either to be reckoned among the Apostles and identified with James, the son of Alpheus, and so "brother" to be taken in the sense of "cousin;" or "save" (εἰ μή) is to be referred only to "I did not see" =another one of the apostles I did not see, but I saw only James. Grammatically the former is decidedly the less difficult; but the identification with James, the son of Alpheus, is attended with great difficulties. Comp. WIESELER *in loco*. Besides this impression is evidently conveyed, that Paul by the special addition he appends to the name, wishes to distinguish this James from the Apostles, not to include him in their number. For this reason the second interpretation is to be preferred. Although not an Apostle, this James could still be mentioned by Paul, as is done here, along with the Twelve, because he had a standing well-nigh apostolic. Respecting the question how the James mentioned chap. ii. 9, is related to this James, see remarks on that passage. "The notice that at that time Paul only saw Peter and James in Jerusalem, does not conflict with the indefinite τοὺς ἀποστόλους, Acts ix. 27, but authentically defines it." MEYER.

[The interpretation turns upon the much discussed question what is meant by "the brethren of the Lord," for unless this James can be identified with James, the son of Alpheus, he is not an Apostle. The view of LIGHTFOOT, ALFORD and others that he might be an Apostle, and yet not of the Twelve, seems altogether untenable. Only one point is undisputed: This James is the one who was frequently called by the church fathers "bishop of Jerusalem," and also "the Just." Whether he were an Apostle, whether he wrote the general Epistle, whether referred to again in this Epistle, are open questions. Without entering into an extended discussion, it will suffice to mention the leading views and their bearing on this passage, referring the reader to special dissertations. There are three principal theories. That the brethren of the Lord were 1. the sons of Joseph and Mary; 2. the sons of Joseph by a former wife; 3. the cousins of our Lord, either the sons of the Virgin's sister, or the sons of Joseph's brother, *etc.* 1 and 2 are the older views; 3 originated with Jerome.—On this latter theory alone can we identify James, the brother of our Lord, with James, the son of Alpheus, for the other theories imply that Joseph, not Alpheus, was his father. But this theory is with difficulty supported, for not only did it originate in an attempt to justify and thus enjoin virginity in man as well as woman, but it has always been forced to call to its aid mere conjectures. Hence, if it be rejected, our verse means that Paul saw none other of the Apostles, but he did see the Lord's brother. To which view we are in a measure forced also by the statement of John (vii. 5: "neither did his brethren believe in him") after the twelve were chosen. Comp. John vi. 67, where "the twelve" are spoken of. That his brethren were afterwards believers is stated (Acts i. 14, where they are mentioned in distinction from the Apostles); the reason of the so speedy conversion *may* be found in 1 Cor. xv. 7, if "James," of whom "he was seen," be distinguished from "the twelve" (ver. 5) and "all the Apostles" in the same verse.

As between 1 and 2, it may be remarked, that it seems more natural to consider the brethren of our Lord the sons of Mary, were it not for two reasons, first, the instinctive repugnance (Jos. ADD. ALEXANDER) to such a view, and secondly, the fact that the dying Saviour committed His mother to another than these brethren, a strange fact, were they her own sons. Still these are not insuperable objections. The whole question is an open one, and it was only necessary to discuss it here so far as to decide upon the meaning of this particular passage. The reader is referred to LANGE's *Commentary, Matthew*, p. 255 sq., where LANGE defends the modified cousin-theory, and SCHAFF advocates at length the first view stated above. Also to LANGE's *Commentary, James*, p. 9 sq.; SCHAFF, *Monograph on James*, Berlin, 1842; ALFORD, *Prolegomena, Epistle of James*. Comp. the authorities quoted by these writers. The best classification and history of opinions will be found in LIGHTFOOT, *Dissertat.* II., p. 247 sq., which has been freely used in the above remarks. He, however, defends the second theory. As regards this passage, it seems on the whole best to consider this James—1. as *not* identical with the son of Alpheus; 2. as *not* an Apostle. Both points are involved in the exegesis of the passage, but as εἰ μή is susceptible of either interpretation, these results must be reached on other than grammatical grounds. The grounds for the above opinions cannot be stated at length, but may be found in the more extended discussions. —R.]

[WORDSWORTH: "Paul's meeting with Peter and James. Peter cordially received him.—'Fifteen days;' ample time for Peter to have seen what I was, and to have proclaimed me to the world as a deceiver, if the Gospel which I preached was not consistent with his own. Therefore they who cavil at me involve Peter also in the charge of conniving at error and delusion." But thus indicating his respect for Peter and James, "he wisely guards himself against any imputations on the part of his Judaizing adversaries, that he, a new Apostle, was liable to the charge of disparaging the original Apostles of Christ. And he prepares the way for what he is about to say in the next chapter concerning his resistance to St. Peter."—R.]

Ver. 20. **Now the things which I write unto you.**—Ver. 20 contains a solemn asseveration, which has its ground in the importance of the account just given for the Apostle's purpose, namely, to prove his own apostolic dignity.

[Ver. 21. **Into the regions of Syria and Cilicia;**—No mention is made of his going into Syria in the narrative in the Acts, but he is said to have been brought down to Cesarea, and sent forth to Tarsus (in Cilicia), where Barnabas afterwards went to seek him (Acts ix. 30; xi. 25). There is no discrepancy. Paul may have gone to Antioch on his way to Cilicia, or returned that way in his labors before Barnabas came for him; or the expression here may be indefinite, since "Syria and Cilicia" appears in history almost as a generic geographical term, the more important district being mentioned first. Comp. CONY. and HOWSON. I. pp. 104, 105. LANGE's *Comm., Acts*, p. 182.—R.]

Ver. 22. **And I was unknown.**—This remark also belongs to the proof that he had not been a disciple of the Apostles, for had he stood in near connection with them, he could not but have become known to the churches of Judea.—**The churches of Judea**, *i. e.*, outside of Jerusalem. [The phrase **which are in Christ Jesus**, doubtless means "which are incorporated with Him who is the head" (ELLICOTT), yet it is also used to distinguish the bodies of believers from other bodies, of Jews, for example. ALFORD: "By thus showing the spirit with which the churches of Judea were actuated toward him, he marks more strongly the contrast between them and the Galatian Judaizers."—R.]

Ver. 23. **Is now preaching the faith.**—Πίστις here also not=Christian doctrine [it being very doubtful, as ELLICOTT remarks, whether πίστις ever has in the N. T., this more distinctly objective sense, so frequent in ecclesiastical writers. See also the valuable note of LIGHTFOOT, p. 152, sq. on the word "faith."—R.], but= Faith; he preached that men should believe, as well as, of course, what they should believe. Formerly he sought by persecution to hinder men from believing in Christ, that is, he was destroying it; *i. e.*, Faith.

Ver. 24. **In me.**—Paul is not only regarded as the occasion of the praise, but as the foundation on which their faith rested. "With this impression which Paul then made upon the congregations in Judea, the hateful plotting of the Judaizers in Galatia against him stood in striking contrast. Therefore the added clause." MEYER. [ELLICOTT: "The preposition in such cases as the present, points to the object as being, as it were, the *sphere* in which, or the *substratum* on which the action takes place."—R.]

## DOCTRINAL AND ETHICAL.

1. *How Paul was taught.* A right understanding of ver. 12, according to which Paul here denies only that his calling and preparation to be an Apostle (a preacher of the gospel) was through men, is by no means inconsistent with assuming, as in any case is necessary, that Paul learned the historical particulars of the life of Jesus not by immediate intuition, but through the testimony of men, as indeed the Apostle in other passages unhesitatingly expresses the traditional character of his historical knowledge, as in 1 Cor. xv. 1; ix. 14; vii. 10, 25; also xi. 23. Comp. on this the instructive article of PARET, "*Paul and Jesus.*" *Jahrbücher für deutsche Theologie* B. 3, H. 1, 1858. "The passage in the Galatians," remarks PARET, "becomes, in fact, first fairly intelligible by assuming as above. Just because Paul was remitted, in respect to particulars, to the testimony of others, could his opposers make the attempt to represent his whole knowledge and teaching, and ultimately his faith in Jesus itself, as something merely derivative, to construct the whole man, as it were, out of purely external Christian influences, human in immediate origin, and thereby to depress him in the esteem of his churches below the Apostolic elevation, to place him on one level with common Christians, and to dispute his right to make valid decisions in the domain of doctrine and discipline. If his antagonists thus made this one side promi-

nent, in a one-sided, unintelligent way, Paul was constrained, accordingly, to bring the other side forward in the strongest light: to show that it was not from men or through any man that he from a persecutor had become an Apostle, but through Jesus Christ Himself, whom he had seen alive; that his gospel was not a school task got by heart, but rested upon a revelation of Jesus." But according to the representation of the course of events in our chapter, according to which Paul for three years did not come at all, and then came only for a very short time, into contact with the senior Apostles, we must assume that he did not derive even his knowledge of the historical particulars of the life of Jesus from these, but from other Christians; possibly from Ananias. In view of the attack which his apostolic rank suffered, compared with that of the senior Apostles, even this circumstance is of moment to him, although it was not from the beginning precisely the result of design.

[It will appear from the exegetical notes on ver. 12, how labored an effort is required to support the view, that Paul does not intend to assert here that he had learned his gospel through revelation from Jesus Christ. Of course on any theory of inspiration, save that mechanical one, which ignores the human element, it will be admitted that Paul learned the facts of the life and death of Christ from human lips; but that must be a narrow view of the gospel as Paul preached it, which could limit his "being taught it" to such human statements. "Paul does not mean here the outward historical information concerning the life of Christ, but the internal exhibition of Christ to his spiritual sense as the Messiah, and the only and all-sufficient Saviour of the world, and the unfolding of the true import of His death and resurrection; in other words the spiritual communication of the gospel system of saving truth as taught by him in his sermons and Epistles" (Schaff). It is more in accordance both with Paul's argument here, and with the actual phenomena of his history to believe that after the revelation on the way to Damascus there were "subsequent special disclosures of the Spirit, respecting single points of Christian doctrine and practice; for we are to conceive the inspiration of the Apostles in general as not merely an act, done once for all, but a permanent influence and state, varying in strength as occasion required" (Schaff). Ellicott very judiciously remarks: "On the one hand we may reverently presume that all the fundamental truths of the Gospel would be *fully* revealed to St. Paul before he commenced preaching; so, on the other, it might have been ordained, that (in accordance with the laws of our spiritual nature) its deeper mysteries and profounder harmonies should be seen and felt through the practical experiences of his apostolical labors."—R.]

2. *The Revelation from Jesus Christ.* Paul has been called by the Lord Himself to the apostleship, as well as the other Apostles, with the single exception that they were called by the Lord in His state of humiliation, he by the Lord in His state of exaltation; this is the fundamental truth, which stands to the Apostle immovably firm, and on which he founded the whole proof of his apostolic parity. There can therefore be no doubt that he was conscious of an objective appearance of Christ, in the well known occurrence on the way to Damascus, and we have in the decision with which Paul himself in this doctrinal treatise, in opposition to hostilely disposed antagonists, asserts this immediateness of his calling through Christ, the simplest and surest proof for the historical character of the narrative respecting the conversion of Paul contained in the Acts. For, as has been already remarked in the exegesis, we are of course not to think of a merely internal vocation—a calling in spirit. Such a notion would take away from the proof which Paul is setting forth its very ground and foundation. It is true that in it a spiritual operation, an operation of the Spirit of God upon the mind of the Apostle, also took place ("to reveal within me"), but only in consequence of the objective outward appearance of Christ. This itself was, first of all, the deciding and penetrating power; upon it all turned. And very naturally. That Christ had risen and was living, became by means of this at once a certainty to Paul. This, however, involved almost necessarily that total revolution of all his views and of the direction of his life, which followed. For Paul was a man who even previously stood upon the foundation of Israelitish faith, and whose faith in the Messiah was in itself steadfast, and who had even been misled by this to take his hostile position against Jesus and His cause, under the delusion that the dignity of Messiah was claimed for Him presumptuously. So much the more overpowering must the impression of the actual appearance of Christ, who was thereby manifested as risen and exalted to Heaven, have been upon him. This was a sudden collapse of the system held fast with so much zeal, a sudden conviction of the nothingness of that persuasion to which he had so energetically clung, and, moreover, a conviction through fact, against which therefore there was nothing more to object. As it would have been almost incomprehensible if that effect had not followed, which did follow, so on the other hand this effect presupposes the definite cause which is related in the Acts, and indicated by the Apostle himself in this passage. [That the conversion of Paul must necessarily follow the actual appearance of Jesus Christ to him, is not to be assumed in order to establish the fact of such appearance; for as in the narrative prominence is given to the actual revelation *to* Paul, here the stress is laid by the Apostle himself on the other fact, the revelation of Christ *within* him; both facts are essential in accounting for the conversion of Paul, and for Christianity itself.—R.] That the Apostle in this passage by "revelation from Christ," "to reveal His Son within me," means primarily only the external revelation at his conversion is, of course, not inconsistent with his having received subsequent revelations, such as that mentioned in Acts xxii. 17, which, however, as an *εἶναι ἐν ἐκστάσει*, appears to be distinguished from that first fundamental one, or such as are alluded to in 2 Cor. xii., and besides immediately afterwards in this Epistle ii. 2. (Comp. 1 Tim. i. 13).

3. *The calling of Paul.* The conversion of Paul according to his own representation is to be viewed essentially as a call to the apostleship. Although at the same time his conversion was of course for

him personally, of the greatest moment, and undoubtedly the condition of his apostolic activity (comp. 1 Tim. i. 14), yet strictly speaking the appearance on the way to Damascus had as its end the calling to the apostleship as well, and not merely his personal conversion to Christianity. Indeed, according to the Apostle's own conception, the eighth chapter of Acts would be better entitled: The Calling of Paul. In this relation of the event to the whole church—inasmuch as it specially concerned the calling of an Apostle, that which is extraordinary in it, namely, the revelation of Christ finds its explanation. This event appears also as a call to the apostleship according to the representation of the Apostle in Acts ix. 15; xxii. 15; xxvi. 17, that is, it was first made known to Ananias, but in immediate connection with the wonderful scene, so that the purpose of the latter cannot be mistaken, and Paul, before Herod Agrippa, Acts xxvi. 17, could speak of the message which was communicated to him by the mouth of Ananias, as an immediate message of Jesus to himself. The definite direction to preach the gospel among the Gentiles, Paul first received, according to Acts xxii. 21, during his first visit to Jerusalem. Yet even the first commission he received, pointed in a very distinct manner to the Gentiles, so that from the very beginning his call as Apostle of the Gentiles, in distinction from the other Apostles, was firmly established. So far, therefore, Paul is not to be reckoned with them, as thirteenth or indeed as twelfth (if the choice of Matthias be considered a premature one), but he stands beside them, in a certain measure over against them, with a special calling; only in the originality of his apostleship he is not inferior to them, but fully their peer. Comp. ii. 7, 9. Futhermore, the special purpose of his calling stands certainly in a causal connection with the manner of the calling. "The Paul who through so unexpected a mercy of God was brought to the knowledge of His Son, was well fitted for the preaching of the same among the Gentiles, called as they also were out of God's unlooked for mercy" (RIEGER). The very manner of his calling, out of pure grace, passing thus a sentence of condemnation upon the legal position, caused him to know that to the Gentiles also, who are ἄνομοι, the way to salvation of grace must stand open. Comp. also for 2 and 3, LANGE'S *Commentary, Acts*, p. 165 sq.

4. *Paul set apart by God.* Paul cannot regard himself otherwise than as destined by God Himself, even in his mother's womb, for what he now is, separated to the peculiar calling of the apostleship (an analogy, as it were, to the Nazarite's vow, by which the child was dedicated, even from the womb, to be a Nazarite). His life up to his conversion, Paul then of course regards as standing in opposition to this, his divine destination; and therefore a special vocation was necessary. This vocation, however, has its root in the elections and as this, of course, was an entirely free one, founded on no manner of merit (as being entirely precedent to the whole course of his life), the calling, therefore, was a pure act of grace ("by his grace"), on account of the opposition in which the previous life of Paul stood to his destined work. In the connection of this particular passage Paul contemplates his previous life from no other point of view, and certainly therefore does not designate himself as one set apart even from his mother's womb, because he thought that before his conversion he possessed qualities for the sake of which God had called him. It is true his natural gifts and his acquirements of knowledge served to capacitate him for his vocation; and it was doubtless providential that even before his conversion he was the person that he was; and this natural adaptedness itself had its root in the divine destination of the man. And negatively, beyond question, the legal zeal by which Paul was animated, bringing as it did his subsequent evangelical position into so much more decided contrast with it, was advantageous to his apostolic activity, as in general the zeal with which Paul acted—at first, it is true, in the interest of the law, turned afterwards to the good of the gospel. Otherwise, however, his religious character, as a blindly legal, Pharisaical one, resting on the righteousness of works, stood in decided opposition to his destination. "'He has called me,' says the Apostle. But how? For my standing as a Pharisee? For my holy and blameless life? For my admirable works? No; I trow! Still less, then, for my blasphemy against God, my persecution and mad rage. How then? Through his pure grace." LUTHER.—[CALVIN:—He intends to assert that his calling depends on the secret election of God; and that he was ordained an Apostle not because by his own industry he had fitted himself, but because God had counted him worthy to undertake that high office, and because, before he was born, he had been set apart by the secret purpose of God. The Apostle had most explicitly attributed his calling to the free grace of God, when he traced its origin to his separation from the womb. But he repeats the direct statement ("by his grace") both to take away all grounds of boasting by his commendation of Divine grace, and to testify his own gratitude to God.—R.]

5. *Paul's walk in Judaism.* "His former walk Paul calls a walk in Judaism: if it had been a walk in the footsteps of the faith of Abraham, it would have led him to faith in the gospel. It was, therefore, a walk in the Judaism that was tending towards apostasy, that, under pretext of the law, would defend itself against the faith in Christ." RIEGER.—Judaism of course here means the Jewish religion in its then form, when the soul of the Old Covenant, by which it pointed beyond itself, and in general its character of promise, was more or less overlooked. Or at least the legal sense in which the whole divine revelation was then apprehended, took away the right understanding of this character of promise. Hence the incapacity to understand Him in whom the fulfillment came. On this account proficiency in Judaism and persecution of the Christian church could go hand in hand with each other.

6. *Paul's solemn oaths.* The solemn asseverations which Paul more than once utters (in ver. 20; Rom. i. 9; ix. 1; 2 Cor. xi. 31), would of themselves sufficiently show how little the passages, Matt. v. 34 sq., James v. 12 sq., are meant to forbid swearing in itself and totally, and how unwarranted it is to limit lawful oaths to oaths required by the magistrate, while on the other

hand we certainly cannot be too strongly warned against all lightness in the taking of an oath. It must ever, as here, have respect to a weighty matter. [WORDSWORTH from Augustine: "An oath which cometh not from the evil of him who swears, but from the unbelief of him *to* whom he swears, is not against our Lord's precept: 'Swear not.' Our Lord commands that *as far as in us lies* we should not swear; which command is broken by those who have in their mouths an oath as if it were something pleasant in itself. As far as in him lies, the Apostle swears not. He does not catch at an oath with eagerness, but when he swears it is by constraint, through the infirmity or incredulity of those who will not otherwise believe what he says."—R.]

## HOMILETICAL AND PRACTICAL.

Ver. 11. RIEGER:—In the address he has omitted the customary appellations: saints, beloved of God, etc.; after the first rebuke, however, he now adds, as the mollifying ointment, the name of "brethren." What we cannot always do in unimpaired love, may yet be done at times in hope.

Ver. 12. LUTHER (who emphasizes this so expressly in remarking on this passage):—Human teaching, human tradition, though it come down from holy fathers and teachers, from the holy Church herself, is in itself nothing; for in all this there may be error, just because it is human. And hence we must not let any one scare us by appealing to never so great human authorities; over against all this the only concern is, to abide simply by the Word of God.

SPENER:—Such as should be true, enlightened preachers, must have learned the Gospel through revelation from Christ; not immediately, to be sure, but so that, having been instructed by men, Christ's spirit by means of such instruction having become a power in their hearts, they truly have a divine light in their souls, from which they then enlighten others.

The gospel no work of man: 1. as a word of doctrine, not sprung from men, nor taught by men, but by Christ Himself (who brought it Himself and through whom alone His people have it); 2. as a word of comfort, only through Him can we commit ourselves to it; 3. as a word of power, in which there should be no change, from which no departure.

Ver. 13. RIEGER:—Oh, how often and how toilsomely do we gather much that in the right light must be counted harm and dung, and cast from us.—QUESNEL:—A man may make his past sins known out of pride, but also out of humility. Whoever does not boast himself of the same, but humbles himself therefor before God, and willingly bears the shame of them before men, not relying upon himself, makes a good confession, but one not needful to be uttered before every man, as sometimes it would bring more scandal than benefit.—From STARKE:—God is wise, permitting some things to be accomplished even by His enemies, that in His time He will direct to His own honor, to which before they were quite opposed. Paul studied in the law, and in his ancestral institutions, that he might thereby the better withstand the Christians. This afterwards served to enable him to dispute all the better with the Jews in favor of Christianity, as thoroughly understanding their side.

Ver. 14. BERLENB. BIBLE:—Even unconverted men may be exceedingly zealous for ancestral traditions, traditional doctrines.—[Yes, the might of traditions, because received from "my fathers,"—whether from God or no, not being taken into the account,—is often in proportion to the ignorance of real Christianity. How conservative, yet often how contracting and how cruel the zeal for "the traditions of my fathers!" True in every age.—R.]—STARKE:—Good intentions do not of themselves make a thing good before God. Many a one means well in his conduct, and see, he still is doing a sin; yes, out of good intentions the most cruel actions may sometimes arise. Such sins, however, are much less heinous than those which spring from real godlessness and malice.

On vers. 13, 14.—Judaism and the Old Testament are different from one another: 1. the former closes the sense for Christ; 2. the latter opens it.—Persecution of the Church of God 1. takes place so easily in false zeal; 2. is so evil, therefore, take good heed!—When against others, so zealous; when for them, so lukewarm!—Take heed: is not thy progress, in reality, a retrogression?—Zeal for ancestral traditions 1. in itself good, but 2. no proof of a converted heart.—Condemnation of the perverseness of a former walk: 1. It *must* take place within, as a sign of a converted heart; 2. it *may* also become necessary before others, yet so that it is always done in humility.

Ver. 15. WÜRT. SUMM.:—Behold the Fatherly Providence of God, who careth for us and marks out the course of our life from our mother's womb. Think not that God hath passed thee over, and that thou must care for thyself. Fear God and trust Him, for what He has designed for us from our mother's womb will be sure to come, and no one shall divert it from us.—BERLENB. BIBLE:—As Paul here does, so should we look back and behold God from behind, as God says to Moses. God gives preintimations, which are forgotten. But then men should wake up when the work of God is fulfilled, and bethink themselves. His work is nothing uncertain and doubtful, although we cannot constrain others to believe it. Nevertheless we yet ourselves may know well enough how we are to look upon it.

[BUSHNELL:—Every man's life a plan of God. Go to God Himself, and ask for the calling of God; for as certainly as He has a place or calling for you, He will somehow guide you into it. Do you call it success, that you are getting on in a plan of your own? There cannot be a greater delusion.—R.]

Ver. 16. SPENER:—To the rightly profitable administration of the preacher's office, there is needful the revelation of God in us, that we should have a living knowledge of that which we are to declare to others. Without this, the word preached retains, to be sure, its power, if it is left pure and unadulterated; but such people cannot well leave it pure, or set it forth worthily; they understand not to apply it rightly, and destroy much of its power with the hearers.—

BERL. BIBLE:—The true work of God is done within, albeit He uses all manner of means thereto. The hurt is within; therefore, must the enlightenment also have place within. God must come and take away the veil. There needs then a heavenly illumination. This is the crown of conversions, that the Son becomes right plainly known to a man. But there are many veils between, and one after another is taken away, till one comes at last into the knowledge of God and the Son.

RIEGER:—The Son of God is still the pith and kernel of all revelation to be wished for in the heart.—LUTHER:—If the gospel is a revelation of the Son of God, as Paul declares, it is then certain that it does not accuse poor consciences, nor terrify them, but of Christ alone does it teach, who is no law nor work, but our righteousness, wisdom, sanctification, and redemption. —The gospel is a divine word, that comes down from Heaven, and is revealed by the Holy Ghost, yet so that the outward word goes before. For even St. Paul himself first heard the outward word from Heaven: Saul, Saul, why persecutest thou me? Not till then did he have secret and hidden, inner revelations.—Among the Gentiles, therefore, should be preached no law, but the gospel; no Moses, but God's Son; no righteousness of works, but the righteousness of faith. This is the right preaching, whereto the heathen have claim, and which is apt for them. — STARKE:—Paul was chiefly a teacher of the Gentiles, and that of divine purpose. Therefore we act not against God's counsel if we keep especially to Paul's writings (not excluding the other apostolical books), because in these we find most distinctly and most expressly what suits our condition, and is needful for us to know.—[WORDSWORTH:—A striking contrast! He who had been stricken with blindness as a persecutor, has now Christ, the Light of the world, revealed in him as a preacher. He who was himself dark, has become a light to others, a light revealing to them Christ.—R.]

On vers. 15 and 16. The grace of God, as free (without any merit of ours) as it is mighty in working—it can change the hearts so fully, that the man throws himself into the directly opposite course.—It is God, who defines our life's course: therefore, courage!—All depends on this, that the Son of God be revealed in us.—The revelation of Christ in us: 1. wherein it consists; 2. how it is brought to pass (only through God's grace); 3. whereto it helps.—Christ, the marrow 1. of all Christian knowledge, 2. of all Christian testimony.—God reveals His Son in the hearts of believers, that they may preach Him among the Gentiles. The former attains its purpose only in the latter; the latter has its foundation only in the former.—Every Christian, even without a special call to the ministry, is yet called to preach Christ among the heathen, that is he is called to a steady testimony in deed (and more or less also in word), against all heathen living, to call men back from dead idols to serve the living God.

Ver. 16. LUTHER:—Herein the Apostle did right. For it would, indeed, have been a godless thing, if he would have had the divine revelation strengthened by man's counsel, like one who doubted thereon.—STARKE, after the Berlenb. Bible:—Yet the meaning is not, that we may not hear other people's opinion, yet we are not to give it the *præ*, the upper hand, where God has given His testimony. If the will of God is plain, and if the matter is plain in God's word, there is no need to ask other men for counsel. But if the will of God is yet doubtful, we may well ask good friends for advice; only these advisers must be such as possess the fear of God and wisdom. —RIEGER:—Now, as then, the surest course for every one who will find the way of life is, to look alone upon God's commandment, to make the testimonies of the Lord his counsellors, and to hasten thereunto. Without this faithfulness in that which is hidden, the best advice of another may become a temptation and a snare.—HEDINGER:—Much doubting and long considering spoils matters. The good will, which God creates, goes to work and does not stand hesitating long.

Divine guidance and human counsel in their right relation to each other.

Ver. 17 sq. RIEGER:—God foresaw all that would afterwards be brought against Paul, therefore He so ordered his ways that men could not say: he received his authority from the chief Apostles at Jerusalem; nor yet on the other side: he does not presume to go to Jerusalem; he joins himself with no one. God's good Spirit always brings us out into a plain way.

Even the apparently slight, accidental circumstances of our lives stand under God's direction; if we know it not at the time, yet afterwards we do.

[Ver. 18. BURKITT:—Ministers ought to maintain correspondency and familiarity with each other, in token of their harmony. But though this visit was in the most delightful and desirable, yea most profitable company, yet it was but for *fifteen* days. After the *short* time spent in visiting, we must return to our business, and mind, above all things, our ministerial charge.—R.]

Ver. 20. STARKE:—God is a witness of the truth, and a righteous judge of all lies. Can you in all that you say, call on God as the witness of its truth? In all cases this ought to be possible, although it is seldom needful or proper. Ver. 21. It is excellent, when any one, having left his country and his friends, a wicked man, returns back to them again a true child of God. Universities should especially serve this purpose, that those who went to them unconverted youths, should return home converted ones. Ver. 23. It is of God's grace, when from a persecutor and misleader a man becomes a true teacher and confessor. O wonder! Is not that as much as if a dead man were raised to life? And it serves to the praise of the Divine compassion, that the Lord does not destroy His enemies, but wins them over and converts them to his service.—RIEGER:—The glory redounding to God from his conversion has wiped out much of the harm of his former course.

When Jesus, here and there again,
His time of grace declares,
That mercy count as thine own gain,
Which others find as theirs.

2. **In a subsequent conference in the mother church, he had most definitely guarded the Gospel liberty over against the demands of false brethren; while the Apostles had been fully convinced of his divine mission to preach to the Gentiles, and hence in an entirely free and peaceful agreement a division of the field of labor had been decided upon, and the Gentile world committed to him, without any obligation (respecting doctrine) to the mother church.**

(Chap. ii. 1–10.)

1 Then fourteen years after I went up again to Jerusalem with Barnabas, and took
2 Titus with *me* also [also with *me*]. And I went up by revelation, and communi-
cated unto [or laid before] them that [the] gospel which I preach among the Gen-
tiles, but privately to them which were [are] of reputation, lest by any means [per-
3 chance][1] I should run [be running][2] or had [have][3] run, in vain. But neither [not
even] Titus, who was with me, being [though he was][4] a Greek, was compelled to be
4 circumcised: And that because of [the] false brethren unawares [insidiously][5]
brought in, who came in privily [crept in] to spy out our liberty which we have in
5 Christ Jesus, that they might bring us into bondage:[6] To whom we gave place by
subjection [by the submission, *i. e.*, required of us][7] no, not [not even][7] for an hour;
6 that the truth of the gospel might continue with you. But of those who seemed to be
somewhat, [who are of reputation—][8] whatsoever they were, it maketh no matter to
me: God accepteth no man's person: for they who seemed *to be somewhat* in conference
added nothing to me: [—to me those who are of reputation imparted[9] nothing]:
7 But contrariwise, when they saw that the gospel of the uncircumcision was commit-
ted unto me [that I am entrusted with the gospel of the uncircumcision],[10] as *the gos-*
8 *pel* of the circumcision *was* unto Peter [as Peter *with that* of the circumcision]: (For
he that wrought effectually [omit effectually] in [for][11] Peter to [toward] the apostle-
ship of the circumcision, the same [omit the same] was mighty in me [wrought for
9 me also] toward the Gentiles;) And when James, Cephas,[12] and John, who seemed to
be pillars, perceived the grace that was given unto me, they [and became aware of the
grace that was given unto me, James and Cephas and John, who were esteemed as pil-
lars,][13] gave to me and Barnabas the right hands of fellowship; that we *should go*[14] unto
10 the heathen [Gentiles], and they unto the circumcision. Only *they would* that we
should remember the poor; the same which [which very thing][15] I also was for-
ward to do.

[1] Ver. 2.—[On μήπως. See Exegetical Notes.—R.]

[2] Ver. 2.—[This form of the English present undoubtedly gives the better meaning. So Alford, Ellicott, Lightfoot.—R.]

[3] Ver. 2.—["Have" must take the place of "had" for grammatical reasons, "should" being an auxiliary here also.—R.]

[4] Ver. 3.—[The E. V. is literally correct, but does not bring out the reason for his being circumcised, here implied.—R.]

[5] Ver. 4.—[Παρεισάκτους, only here in N. T. It means "insidious," "those foisted in" (Alford, Schaff). It must be rendered adverbially in English.—R.]

[6] Ver. 4.—[The reading of the Rec. καταδουλώσωνται is generally regarded as a correction, since the subjunctive usually follows ἵνα. The future καταδουλώσουσιν is found in ℵ. A. B. C. D. E., and adopted by modern editors.—R.]

Ver. 5.—[Τῇ ὑποταγῇ, a particular submission, that demanded of us.—R.]

[7] Ver. 5.—Οἷς οὐδέ is to be retained with Lachmann, Tischendorf, *etc.* [For this reading there is an immense preponderance of external authority; ℵ. A. B. C. F. K. L. Modern editors all retain it—the omission is easily accounted for. See the extended critical note of Lightfoot on this passage, p. 120 sq.—R.]

[8] Ver. 6.—[Τῶν δοκούντων εἶναί τι. The idea of "seeming to be somewhat," must give place to that of "being deemed somewhat." So Alford, Ellicott, Lightfoot, and most commentators, and E. V. ver. 2. The very strong anacoluthon is rendered more easy by putting ὁποῖοί . . . λαμβάνει, "whatsoever . . . person" in a parenthesis, and placing "to me" in the beginning of the resumptive clause, as indeed is done in the Greek, ἐμοί standing first.—R.]

[9] Ver. 6.—[Προσανέθεντο. Ellicott, "communicated;" Alford, "imparted;" Schaff, "gave no new instruction." See Exeg. Notes.—R.]

[10] Ver. 7—[The structure is altered from the original in the E. V., "I" and "Peter" are the proper subjects of the respective clauses. "Am entrusted with" is a better rendering of πεπίστευμαι, the perfect of permanent state.—R.]

[11] Ver. 8.—[Ἐνεργέω takes ἐν after it, when the meaning is "wrought in;" here it is the simple dative. The E. V. renders the same verb differently in this verse. Literally: "energized," "gave strength to."—R.]

[12] Ver. 9.—D. E. F. G. H. and most of the Fathers have Πέτρος καὶ Ἰάκωβος. An inversion to preserve the precedence of rank. Meyer. [The reading Ἰάκωβος καὶ Κηφᾶς is supported by ℵ. B. C. K. L. and adopted by modern editors generally, on internal as well as external grounds.—R.]

[13] Ver. 9.—[The order of the E. V. is an inversion of the original. The true order, given above, is found in Wickliffe's, Tyndale's, Cranmer's, Bishop's and Rhemish, with a slight variation from the above reading. The participle γνόντες is co-ordinate with ἰδόντες (ver. 7). The whole passage should read thus: "When they saw that I am entrusted with the gospel of the uncircumcision, as Peter with that of the circumcision: (For he that wrought for Peter toward the apostleship of the circumcision, wrought for me also toward the Gentiles;) and became aware of the grace that was given

unto me, James and Cephas and John, who were esteemed as pillars, gave to me and Barnabas the right hands of fellowship."—R.]

14 Ver. 9.—[Ellicott supplies here "should be apostles," which is objectionable on historical and dogmatical grounds. Schaff: "that we should preach the gospel for."—R].

15 Ver. 10.—[῝Ο αὐτὸ τοῦτο, is stronger than "the same which." "Which very thing" (Ellicott). Alford more literally: "Which was the very thing that I also was anxious to do."—R.]

## EXEGETICAL AND CRITICAL.

Ver. 1. **Then fourteen years after.**—Is this to be reckoned from the calling of the Apostle, or from his first journey to Jerusalem (chap. i. 18)? At first view we might incline to the latter opinion. But the period of time mentioned chap. i. 18, is unquestionably to be reckoned from the calling, not from the return to Damascus; it is natural, therefore, to do the same here. His calling is the deciding point of time, and Paul wishes to show what he was doing from that time on, how his apostolical activity has its root in the revelation of Christ then given, and not in human instruction. Besides, if it is acknowledged that Paul here does not mean to enumerate his journeys to Jerusalem in an uninterrupted series, but that the journey to the apostolic council is here meant, there is no purpose served in giving the interval between the two journeys; but it might well be of importance to make known how many years he had already spent in his apostolical office. It would be important to know that, having received it at his calling, he had already been long in the exercise of it, when the other Apostles expressed their concurrence with his doctrine. Comp. also ELWERT, *Programm* on *Galat.* ii. 1–10. The difficult question, which of the Apostle's journeys to Jerusalem, mentioned in the Acts, is here meant, is too extended to be treated in our present space. Besides, it is of more essential importance for the Acts than for our Epistle. For no one doubts the historical character of the journey mentioned in the Epistle. The result of my investigation is that it was no other than the journey to the apostolic council, that it is not that mentioned Acts xi. 30—since he is not giving an unbroken enumeration—nor that mentioned Acts xviii. 21 (against WIESELER).

[Although this question occupies so large a space in most commentaries on this Epistle, the view given above has been so ably defended latterly, and is now so well established, that a synopsis of the argument and a reference to more extended discussions will be sufficient. The point from which Paul reckons, is his conversion, "being a purely subjective epoch" (ELLICOTT). SCHAFF thus states the case: "The Acts mention five journeys after his conversion, *viz.:* 1. ix. 23 (comp. Gal. i. 18), the journey of the year 40, three years after his conversion. 2. xi. 30; xii. 25, the journey during the famine year in 44. 3. xv. 2, the journey to the apostolic council in 50 or 51. 4. xviii. 22, the journey in 54. 5. xxi. 15 (comp. Rom. xv. 25 sq.), the last visit, on which he was made a prisoner and sent to Cæsarea, in 58.

"Of these journeys the first, of course, cannot be meant on account of Gal. i. 18. The second is excluded by the chronological date in ii. 1. For as it took place during the famine of Palestine and in the year in which Herod died, A. D. 44, it would put the conversion of Paul back to the year 30, which is much too early. Some proposed to read four instead of fourteen, but without any critical authority whatever. There is no necessity why Paul should have mentioned this second journey, since it was undertaken simply for the transmission of a collection of the Christians at Antioch for the relief of the brethren in Judea, and not for the purpose of conferring with the Apostles on matters of dispute. In all probability he saw none of them on that occasion, since in that year a persecution raged in which James the elder suffered martyrdom, and Peter was imprisoned. The fifth journey cannot be meant, as it took place after the composition of the Epistle to the Galatians and after the dispersion of the Apostles. Nor can we think of the fourth, which was very short and transient (Acts xviii. 21, 22), leaving no time for such important transactions as are here alluded to; nor was Barnabas with him on that occasion, having separated from Paul some time before (Acts xv. 39).

"We must therefore identify our journey with the third one mentioned in the 15th chapter of Acts. For this took place in 50 or 51, *i. e.*, fourteen years after his conversion (37), and was occasioned by the important controversy on the authority of the law of Moses and the exact relation of the Gentile converts to the Christian church (Acts xv. 2). This visit Paul could not possibly pass over, as it was of the greatest moment to his argument. It is true our passage differs somewhat from the account given by the Acts. But the difference is not irreconcilable. Luke, in keeping with the documentary character of his historical narrative, gives us only the public transactions of the council at Jerusalem; Paul shortly alludes to his personal conference and agreement with the Apostles (ver. 2); both together give us a complete history of that remarkable convention, the first Synod in Christendom, for the settlement of the first doctrinal and practical controversy which agitated the Church." (SCHAFF, *Comm. in loco.*) See also his *Apostolic Church*, p. 245 sq.; CONYB. and HOWSON, Vol. I., p. 227 sq.; MEYER and WORDSWORTH, *in loco;* ALFORD, Vol. II., *Proleg.*, p. 26; and the valuable note of LIGHTFOOT, p. 122 sq. The authorities in support of this view might be multiplied.—R.]

Ver. 2. **And I went up by revelation.**—Not without design, doubtless, does he bring into view the fact that he went up κατὰ ἀποκάλυψιν, and so was again deemed worthy of a special revelation from God. He will also remove every thought of his having been, as it were, obliged to present himself before the Apostles, of their having summoned him before them. **Laid before them the gospel**=that which I preach among the Gentiles, namely, that they are justified by faith.—"Them," probably the whole church of Jerusalem.—**But privately to them which are of reputation.**—Besides having addressed the Christians in Jerusalem generally, he appears to have held separate conferences with those "of reputation." Wieseler's distinction, however, is quite arbitrary; making vers. 3–5 contain the account of his general agreement with the whole church of Jerusalem, and vers. 6–10 the first account of the separate conferences with the Apostles. [ALFORD thinks there was but one conference, making κατ' ἰδίαν δέ limit αὐτοῖς; "when I say 'to them,' I mean privately to those," etc., but the view given above (that of MEYER, ELLICOTT, LIGHTFOOT) is preferable. The general conference is described Acts xv.; "they declared what things God had done with them," (Acts. xv. 4) may refer to these private conferences which probably preceded. The emphasis here is undoubtedly on the private consultations, the result of the public council being already known to the Galatians.—R.] The judgment of "them" [the whole body] is thrown in the background, and he only speaks of "those in reputation," just mentioned; for the fact that he had received *their* acquiescence is what he is opposing to the false teachers. Hence we must regard what is stated in ver. 3, as their judgment also.—Δοκοῦντες, *æstimati*, principal persons. Men of authority; in fact, doubtless, the senior Apostles; especially the three who are named afterwards in ver. 9. He calls them not "Apostles," but δοκοῦντες, "men of repute" because it is as authorities, as those who stood in repute in the Jerusalem church first, but also in the Christian church generally, nay more, were decisive authorities, that they come into consideration. For precisely this is of moment to him, to be able to say to the Galatians that he has been acknowledged by these as an equally authorized Apostle. Of course δοκοῦντες does not in the least imply a disparagement of the Apostles themselves, for it is the church that accords to them this consideration;—the expression conveys a censure upon this estimation in the church only so far as it might imply a failure to recognize his own apostolic dignity. The censures therefore, touched especially this estimation in the sense in which the Apostles were δοκοῦντες for the Galatian false teachers, and in which these turned it to their own account. The censure of this false preference is given prominence in ver. 6, by the addditional phrase "whatsoever they were." Paul cannot intend to dispute in the least that in the right sense the senior Apostles were δοκοῦντες for the Christians. [The force of Paul's expression is weakened by rendering "*were* of reputation," since when he writes, they "*are*" of reputation, hence thus brought into the argument (LIGHTFOOT).—It must be noted also that Paul throughout does not use the word "Apostle." Whether they were Apostles or no, is not evident from anything in the passage, except the mention of James and Cephas and John (ver. 9), and whether that James was either an Apostle or one of the twelve is an open question. Without discussing the point here, it may be suggested that one reason for not calling them "Apostles," was that one of the three "who seemed to be pillars," and "of repute" was not an Apostle, but James the Just, the head of the church at Jerusalem. This will not only explain the omission of the title, but meet subsequent difficulties.—R.]

**Lest perchance I should be running or have run in vain.**—The sense remains essentially the same, whether we take μήπως as a final particle, or=whether perchance. After the thorough exposition of WIESELER, however, the latter is to be preferred. (So also MEYER in 4th ed.) Of course, however, he does not mean to say that he himself was doubtful about it. This would have been in conflict with the whole purpose of his detailed account, and would have represented him as dependent on the Senior Apostles. He wished only, on account of the antagonists of his teaching, to obtain from the Apostles, on whose authority these supported themselves, a confirmation of this teaching, in order to cut off every pretext from his opponents. "Run in vain"=labor to no purpose, *operam perdere.* This would have been the case, if Paul had actually proclaimed a false doctrine, with which the senior Apostles could not agree. The outward success of his preaching is not primarily in view, though we may conclude from ver. 7, 8, 9, that he spoke of this also. Others take μήπως as a final particle, and interpret as follows: in order not *to appear* as one who was running or had run, in vain, as might have been the case, if I had not submitted my gospel to examination, had its harmony with Apostles established; but the idea of "appearing" is extraneous to the passage. [For a clear discussion of the grammatical and exegetical difficulties of this clause, see ELLICOTT, *in loco.* Whatever view be adopted, we must not concede that Paul had any doubt about his Gospel. The conditional μήπως is probably used to indicate respect for those in reputation at Jerusalem. The doubt could only concern the opinion of others, which by being opposed, might render his labors in vain.—R.] In what follows he says that he received the desired acquiescence on the part of the Apostles. He does not however at once declare this, but mentions a special circumstance, which implies it in a striking manner.

Vers. 3. **But not even Titus.**—The sense is clear: οὐδέ points to a thought to be supplied. "I laid frankly before them, how I preach among the Gentiles; not concealing that I do not at all hold them to the keeping of the law, to the receiving of circumcision—and now, according to the representation of the false teachers, it was to be expected that they would appear in opposition to me; but (ἀλλά) so far was this from being the case, so far from declaring this doctrine false [or, connecting it with the last clause, so far from my having run in vain—R.], not even with respect to Titus, a born Gentile, who had come to Jerusalem, to the very mother of the Jewish Christian churches with me, was the demand made that he should be circumcised, though it might readily have been, when Jewish prejudice was so greatly offended by his uncircumcision." Still less did they censure the doctrine of Paul, or demand of him that he should preach the necessity of circumcision among the Gentile Christians as a body. The case has been thoroughly perplexed by bringing in, in direct contradiction to what the words say, the thought, that the Apostles had wished, or even demanded, the circumcision of Titus; but that Paul and Titus had set themselves against their desire. ELWERT justly remarks, *Programm*, p. 10: *Quid enim ineptius dici potest quam illud: tantum abfuit, ut apostoli causam meam improbarent, ut ne Titus quidem illis contraria petentibus obsequeretur?* [The word ἠναγκάσθη seems to imply that there was a demand made for the circumcision of Titus, not by the Apostles, but by the false brethren (ver. 4). Had the idea been merely, that the circumcision was not even demanded, so strong a word would not have been used. There is some force in the suggestion of LIGHTFOOT, that the Apostles recommended Paul to yield as a charitable concession, but convinced at length that he was right, they gave him their support. Still we have not sufficient knowledge of the circumstances to decide whether Paul cites this as an evidence of the Apostles' agreement with him or of his firmness—in all probability it is both. Not even Titus, of whom as a Greek the false brethren made the demand, was required to submit—or whom as a Greek I would not allow to be circumcised, since this would have been a giving up of the whole matter. The preceding context suggests the former, the subsequent context the latter side of the occurrence. On the reasons for the non-circumcision of Titus, and the circumcision of Timothy (Acts xvi. 2), see DOCTRINAL NOTES.—R.]

Ver. 4. **And that because of the false brethren.**—What is to be supplied with "because of the false brethren?" After an examination of all the views presented, it appears to me that we can only say: we do not and cannot know, since Paul has broken off the sentence, and all attempts to fill it out are hazardous, from the danger of introducing foreign matter. The mention of the ψευδάδελφοι is very intelligible. He has already indicated the concurrence of the Apostles by reference to the striking case of Titus, or at least, negatively, that they did not oppose him. But before he says anything definite, positive, respecting this concurrence (ver. 6 sq), he mentions his opposers, who did not concur, who attacked him and his teaching, and had also especially occasioned his journey to Jerusalem. The mention of the false brethren, however, stirs his displeasure, so that he does not complete the thought begun, but first by a brief and fit phrase, describes his opposers, and then falling out of the construction, continues with οἷς, and expresses the thought, which probably he had in mind in mentioning the "false brethren," namely, that he had not in the least yielded to them. In what he did not yield, is not expressed; probably to their demands, in general, respecting the obligation of the Gentile Christians to keep the law. Not till he has first established this negative result does he revert to the action of the δοκοῦντες, and he now relates the positive acknowledgment, which he had from them.—If we seek a complement to διά, three suggest themselves. (1), ἀνέθην—(EWALD, substantially). According to this, as he cannot pass over the remoter cause of his journey, namely, the intrigues of the Pharisees, the same party that had now of late again persecuted him so bitterly, he begins in ver. 4, anew, as it were, the account of this journey.—Ordinarily, however, the complement is sought in the foregoing sentence, because the somewhat abrupt character of this was rather perplexing, and its contents appeared to require the statement of a reason. This view took δέ usually as epexegetical, and therefore supplied (2) οὐκ ἠναγκάσθη, which, in fact, strongly commends itself; simply, however, in the sense: Now, this took place on account of the "false brethren," that is, it was even on account of these, that the Christians in Jerusalem, particularly the Apostles, did not urge it upon him, lest, by yielding to them, the opinion that circumcision was necessary, should receive sanction. This contains the implied thought, that in itself they would not unwillingly have seen him circumcised, but that now, for the sake of principle, they did not press it. But this makes it necessary, first to ascribe to the Jewish Christians in Jerusalem a way of thinking, which is not ascribed to them in this chapter, but expressly limited to individuals, "false brethren," in order afterwards to find it impossible that they should have abstained from all demands for circumcising Titus, *on account of* these "false brethren." Whether the "false brethren" demanded particularly the circumcision of Titus, is not said. On the other hand, if we complete the sentence thus, the sense is inadmissible, that *Paul*, precisely on account of the false brethren, opposed himself to a demand to have Titus circumcised, from whomever it proceeded. This alters the plain meaning of ver. 3; ἠναγκάσθη receives the sense: the constraint, which it was attempted to exercise, was frustrated; and especially οὐδέ, and the implied thought to which it points, is quite neglected. Then we should have this absurdity: "so far were they from disapproving my teaching, that I or Titus did not even yield when his circumcision was demanded." If this demand is referred to the Apostles, the thought is completely inverted (*see* above), but even if it is referred only to the "false brethren," it is none the less impossible. And the case remains the same, if, instead of "he was not compelled," we supply "he was not circumcised," still explaining it, "*I* or *we*, on account of the false brethren, did not consent, when it was desired." Finally, (3) "He was circumcised," is supplied (δέ therefore being taken adversatively), and in its turn defended by ELWERT, *Programm*, with much acuteness. And, in fact, if we must fill out the sentence, I should be most disposed to declare for this. It especially commends itself by the light which it throws both upon ver. 3 and upon ver. 11. For, beyond question, it remains somewhat enigmatical, why he instances so particularly this one fact of refusing to circumcise Titus, hastening to it even before he has spoken, on the positive side, of the reception of his preaching in Jerusalem. The reproach (ver. 11) then remains not altogether intelligible. On the other hand, all is easily explained, if we assume that Titus was then circumcised. That is, many founded upon this the allegation that he commended circumcision. But especially was this circumstance urged, in order to deduce therefrom, that his teaching had been disapproved by the Apostles, and that he had yielded to these. Therefore, he declares at once: It is not even true, as is commonly related, that Titus was constrained to receive circumcision. Titus was circumcised, not upon a requisition of the Apostles, but voluntarily by me, solely on account of the false brethren insidiously brought in, that they might not, making a handle of his being uncircumcised, prepossess the Christians in Jerusalem against me, and dispose them to a resolution unfavorable for the Gentile Christians. "*Quare eandem, quam semper et in omnibus normam secutus, ne quid detrimenti capiat res Christiana, suæ libertatis minime tenax illorum se voluntati submittit, imbecillioribus servit. Neutiquam fratrum irreptitiorum habita ratione hoc fecit, sed eos respiciens, quos, quum fidei infirma ac judicii parum subacti essent, illorum insectationibus objectos videret. Circumcisione Titi permissa insidias hominum malignorum evitavit, animos imbecilliorum sibi conciliavit apostolus.*" ELWERT, p. 13. This interpretation is only apparently in conflict with ver. 5. Nay, ELWERT remarks that only so does τῇ ὑποταγῇ find its true explanation; for that only the following translation is natural: to whom not even for an hour did we yield by the submission: "*obsequium se præstitisse Paulus profitetur, sed non ita præstitisse, ut illis se victum daret vel de jure suo aliquid cederet.*" For he provided that the truth of the Gospel should remain with the Gentile Christians. Of course, he could not yield to the circumstances of the time, without, at the same time, giving a testimony to the evangelical truth, whereby this was maintained in its integrity. This explanation of τῇ ὑποταγῇ, however, awakens some misgiving; could Paul well admit a "ὑποταγή" towards the ψευδάδελφοι? Is not this expression too strong? We are tempted, therefore, even admitting this explanation of διά, *etc.*, to join τῇ ὑποταγῇ to the negation, making Paul say that an εἴκειν τῇ ὑποταγῇ nevertheless did not take place, even if their behavior occasioned him to have Titus circumcised.

[As LIGHTFOOT well remarks: "The counsels of the Apostles of the circumcision are the hidden rock on which the grammar of the sentence is wrecked," but because the grammar is wrecked on this hidden rock, it is not necessary to wreck Paul's facts and arguments and even principles, on a rock so easily avoided as the theory of ELWERT advanced above. In fact, as MEYER remarks, such conduct "would have been unprincipled and wrong." That is an all-sufficient objection. As regards what should be supplied, it is most naturally taken from the preceding verse, to which our verse then refers, δέ being explicative. Whether "he was not compelled," or "he was not circumcised," is open to discussion. The first implies that "those of reputation" did not compel it on this account; the other, that the thing was not done, either because Paul would not thus surrender a principle, or "those of reputation" thought it were best not to do it. As this latter does not imply any definite counsel of the other Apostles—the very point about which there is greatest doubt—it is on the whole safer to adopt it.—R.]

Ψευδάδελφοι (also 2 Cor. xi. 26), comp. ψευδαπόστολοι, ψευδοπροφῆται, are in general, brethren, fellow-Christians, who bear this name unworthily; specifically, because they, on account of their Judaizing opinions, especially on the necessity of circumcision for Christians, are properly still Jews. So WIESELER. Yet this in itself hardly suffices to explain the strong ψευδο (and especially the παρείσακτοι and παρεισῆλθον), but we must add to it their behavior towards the other Christians, the utterly unbrotherly hateful opposition (not shrinking indeed from intrigues and slanders), which they maintained against the freer evangelical views. The complete definition of "false brethren" is given in "spy out," "bring us into bondage;" they do not yet stand in the freedom which there is in Christ; nay, more they wish to deprive others also of it; nay, more, they exercise a system of espionage against these. The false teachers in Galatia were essentially such people, perhaps they were emissaries of those in Jerusalem; and on this account it is with special purpose that their conduct in Jerusalem, and their discomfiture, are mentioned. But the Galatian teachers themselves are not meant here; this would be entirely foreign to the context.—A more particular notice respecting these people is given Acts xv. 5, whatever judgment may be held of the general relation of the present chapter to Acts xv. They were, according to this, persons of the sect of the Pharisees, who, it is true, had come to believe on Jesus, that He was the Christ, but had not given up their Nomism and Ergism, and, therefore, doubtless were so much the more hostile to their former fellow-Pharisee, Paul, on account of his present position, so sharply anti-Pharisaic. Holding fast, as they thus did, essentially, to their Pharisaism, it is easy to understand that their belief in Christ had as yet produced in them few effects of moral transformation. The article describes the persons as the Pharisaical Christians, historically known to the readers; either the particular individuals were known, or, at all events, this sort of people, since the Galatian false teachers were of the same class.

[**Insidiously brought in.**—LIGHTFOOT:—"The metaphor is that of spies or traitors introducing themselves by stealth into the enemy's camp. The camp is the Christian Church. Pharisees at heart, these traitors assume the name and garb of believers." He thus paraphrases: "The agitators, who headed the movement, were no true brethren, no loyal soldiers of Christ. They were spies, who had made their way into the camp of the gospel under false colors, and were striving to undermine our liberty in Christ, to reduce us again to bondage." WORDSWORTH:—"By mentioning these, he clears the holy Apostles from the imputation of being supposed to have been parties to such a requisition, as that Titus, a Gentile, should be compelled to be circumcised."—R.] "What is already indicated in the composite ψευδάδελφοι is, by the predicate παρείσακτοι, interchanging immediately after with παρεισῆλθον, brought forward with especial emphasis. They are called παρείσακτοι, because they have pressed in on one side of the entrance; that is, by a forbidden way, *sc.* into the Christian church, and, therefore, do not properly belong to it. Παρείσακτοι and παρεισῆλθον are doubtless to be applied to these alone, and not to an outward insinuation of themselves into a single church (for instance, that of Antioch), in order there to oppose Paul. Comp. Acts xv."—WIESELER. Of course, they did the latter also; it was closely connected with their having insinuated themselves into the Christian Church. But here, doubtless, the primary reference is only to their appearance in Jerusalem itself. A local interpretation of παρείσακτοι and παρεισῆλθον is the less necessary, as parallel expressions are found: παρεισάγειν, 2 Pet. ii. 1, and παρεισδύειν, Jude 4, where the reference is clearly to the Christian Church in general. **Who crept in to spy out.**—The immediate purpose of their "creeping in" in itself was hardly "to spy out" the liberty of others; but what they did made their coming in (εἰσέρχεσθαι) a "creeping in" (παρεισέρχεσθαι) whose purpose could only be regarded as this "spying out." "The false brethren are thus characterized according to their common dangerousness to Christian liberty, in order to give the reason why Paul could not yield to such false brethren." —WIESELER.

Two things are laid to their charge: first, a "spying out of" **our liberty**;—they lie in ambush for our liberty, spy out in what we show ourselves freemen, turn their notice to that, but with hostile intent; therefore, how widely removed from brotherly love! Then, in the second place, they seek to reënslave the free, *i. e.*, they demand of them to give up their freedom. By the freedom which we have in Christ Jesus is primarily meant freedom from the Mosaic law, from its ritual ordinances, and especially therefore from circumcision. The wider, deeper meaning of this freedom is involved in this, but here, doubtless, not primarily in view. "Our liberty." Whose? Certainly it does refer to Paul merely, but yet primarily only to those who understood the freedom in Christ, and availed themselves of it, and these without exception. But as Paul no doubt vindicates this standing fast in freedom as at least a right of all Christians, and regards the "false brethren" with their views and their conduct as in truth no Christians, the "we," in point of fact, embraces all Christians, the Gentile Christians, of course, and also the Jewish Christians, so far as these were not "false brethren."—**In Jesus Christ**, as being found in him. [SCHAFF:—"In living union with Him who is the end of the law (Rom. x. 4). This is the positive side of freedom."—ELLICOTT:—Not "through Christ," a meaning it may bear, but in the fuller and deeper sense "in Christ."—R.]—**That they might bring us into bondage**:—that is, under the law. On this account, also, the reading καταδουλώσωνται=make us *their* servants, is to be rejected, and καταδουλώσουσιν to be read, which is better attested than the subjunctive—σωσιν.

Ver. 5. **To whom we gave place by the submission, no, not even for an hour.**—Here "we" unquestionably, takes on a more restricted sense=I, Paul, probably also Titus himself, and Barnabas. This narrowing of the sense will appear arbitrary to no one. For here the reference is to a single, definite transaction, where Paul can have in mind only the individuals who had part in it; it is somewhat different with "freedom in Christ." The yielding is still more strongly designated by ὑποταγῇ. (Comp. the different interpretation of ELWERT above, ver. 4.)

This decided refusal to yield had been adequately explained by the foregoing characterization of the pseudo-brethren; it is now given again; **that the truth of the gospel might continue.**—For yielding would have represented Christian freedom as void, and would have overturned the truth of the gospel, on which it is founded.—**With you**; in itself, doubtless, signifying with the Gentile Christians generally—nay, more, with all Christians; but Paul "individualizes the matter, with reference to those to whom he writes." For it concerned him to bring home to them, that even at that time he had guarded the benefit of Christian freedom for them, in order to show in what contradiction their present behavior stood with this fact, since they themselves were now abjuring this benefit.

Ver. 6. **But of those who are of reputation.**—To the pseudo-brethren he now opposes "those of repute." The former he withstood, from the latter he received no instruction implying disapprobation of his teaching. Ver. 6 is an anacoluthon, his language being somewhat disturbed in the thoughts of the presumption and deceit with which the Galatian false teachers had elevated the "δοκοῦντες" above him, and had vindicated the apostolic authority of the former only, denying it to him. He begins as if he would subjoin an οὐδὲν ἔλαβον. But the remark respecting the δοκεῖν εἶναί τι leads him away from this, and he continues with another verb, afterwards resuming δοκοῦντες, and giving at the same time the grounds of the parenthetical statements. EWALD, on the contrary, however, joins οὐδέν μοι διαφέρει with ἀπὸ τῶν δοκ.=compared with these, however high they stood, I am in nothing inferior. It is difficult to justify this grammatically.—"Of repute."—See above, ver. 2. The main idea implied in δοκοῦντες, used absolutely, is here clearly expressed by the addition εἶναί τι=to be something great, to be of some account; with what incidental meaning, see above.—**Whatsoever they were, it maketh no matter to me.**—On the one hand Paul has emphasized the consideration in which the Apostles stood, because it was of moment to him to be able to say, that he had been acknowledged even by these. Yet this might be misunderstood, hence the parenthesis. He emphasizes only for the sake of his readers. To him, on his own account, "it makes no difference in how high authority soever they stood;" as respected him, they did not come into consideration as δοκοῦντες, they asserted no authority: **to me** they **imparted nothing.** This exaltation of individuals=the Apostles, in such a way as to throw the authority of Paul into the shade, rests entirely upon mere human judgment. God's census does not rank them thus: **God accepteth no man's person.**—He makes no such distinction, to Him the senior Apostles are not "of repute" in contrast with Paul; he has chosen Paul to be an Apostle as much as them. And, he continues, I have a right so to speak, for those "of repute" demeaned themselves altogether agreeably to this divine valuation, and did not undertake to instruct me. [The E. V., "in conference added nothing to me," gives the commonly received interpretation of the verb προςανέθεντο: "gave no new or additional instruction." But notwithstanding the authority for such a rendering, it does not seem to be justified by the use of the word (MEYER, ALFORD, ELLICOTT). The idea of imposing burdens is obviously inadmissible.—R.]

It is most simple to refer the ποτέ to the lifetime of Jesus=it signifies nothing to me that they enjoyed the immediate, confidential intercourse of Jesus, while I did not. For it was on this that the Judaizers founded special preëminence which they attributed to the other Apostles over Paul. Others: then in Jerusalem; which is less probable. [The point in question respecting ποτέ is: has it a temporal reference in the sense of *olim*, formerly (either during our Lord's lifetime or then in Jerusalem), or does it simply render ὁποῖοι more general and inclusive, having the force of *cunque*. The latter is classical, but the N. T. usage is disputed. Since it is not said anywhere that these "of repute" were Apostles, who enjoyed immediate intercourse with the Lord, the latter is, on the whole, preferable, as giving a wider signification to δοκοῦντες. "Were" may mean in the past from the time of narration or of the incident narrated; the latter is more probable if ποτέ is taken as referring to intercourse with the Lord during His lifetime.—R.]

Ver. 7. **When they saw that I am entrusted with the gospel of the uncircumcision.**—Naturally, "gospel" of course means here (comp. πεπίστ. and ver. 8) an official activity of the Apostle, therefore not the gospel as to its contents, but the evangelical preaching, τὸ εὐαγγελίζεσθαι, as often. The genitives, "of the uncircumcision," "of the circumcision," are therefore *gen. obj.*=preaching of the gospel among the uncircumcision, or the circumcision; ver. 8 exchanges it for "apostleship of the circumcision," and as εἰς τὰ ἔθνη (vers. 8, 9) shows that the abstracts "uncircumcision," "circumcision," stand for the concretes—Jews, Heathen. That here we are not to suppose two gospels different in character, the Gospel of the Uncircumcision, and the Gospel of the Circumcision, of which the latter maintained the necessity of circumcision, while the former let it drop (BAUR), but only two different circles of hearers of the same gospel, may be regarded as self-evident to the unprejudiced reader.* Peter appears as the representative of the Apostles to the Jews, because he especially had hitherto labored as such. Afterwards, however, the two other Apostles, James and John, are designated, with Peter, as Apostles for the Jews (ver. 9. αὐτοὶ δέ). "That Peter had a Gentile Christian vocation also (Acts xv. 7) is not denied, but *a parte potiori fit denominatio*."—MEYER. The converse applies to Paul. In ver. 9 Barnabas also appears conjointly with him, as Gentile Apostle. [It must be noted that while Paul uses the word "apostleship" in ver. 8, with reference to himself and Peter, he does not use it or anything to the same purport in ver. 9, where James and Barnabas are spoken of. The same is true of the whole passage. There is no evidence of the apostleship of James or Barnabas in this whole Epistle, whatever the probabilities may be. See notes on ver. 9.—R.] "Entrusted;"† Supply: By God through Christ—agreeably to the proof of this affirmation rendered in ver. 8. For from what facts did they perceive what is said in ver. 7 respecting the different mission of each? Primarily from what follows in ver. 8 (γάρ).

Ver. 8. **For he that wrought effectually for Peter.**—From the fact that God had been *operative for Peter* in the one, and for Paul in the other direction, they concluded that God had given to the one the one, and to the other the other *vocation*. How far now was God operative for one and the other?—MEYER, WIESELER:—"He furnished them forth for the apostolic office, with illumination and endowments, gave them the χαρίσματα of an Apostle." (Comp. Acts xv. 12: God did miracles and wonders by them among the Gentiles.) True, it is certainly not merely these endowments themselves that are referred to, but also and especially what they did in virtue of the same, the beginning and result of their activity, wherein God's "working" was recognized. What immediately follows in ver. 9: **and became aware of the grace that was given unto me,** [unfortunately misplaced in E. V.—R.] undoubtedly also refers to the outfit for the apostolic office by means of charisms, yet it is most naturally referred mainly to the success of their preaching. Precisely from this they perceived how highly endowed Paul was. They first inferred his equal apostolic calling from the "grace given," hence the calling itself cannot be meant. [Yet what more natural than that Paul should mean: "they recognize my calling, because they perceive that I was called by grace." The main reference may be to the success, but the perception of the calling through the grace given, is not to be excluded. On the two participles ἰδόντες and γνόντες, LIGHTFOOT says: "the former describes the *apprehension* of the outward tokens of his commission, as evinced by his successful labors; the latter the *conviction* arrived at in consequence that the grace of God was with him."—R.]

Ver. 9. **James and Cephas and John.**—"James." Is this one identical with James the Lord's brother, chap. i. 19? The fact that there the additional appellation is expressly given, while it is lacking here, does not, of course, disprove the identity. Inasmuch as James had already been just mentioned as "the Lord's brother," if the same one is meant this special designation might be omitted here. The main question is: Could the James, whom Paul names in this passage, have been other than an Apostle? And this question we shall always be inclined to answer negatively. In itself it would be very intelligible, that a brother of the Lord converted to the faith, although not an Apostle, might have attained an eminent position in the church of Jerusalem. But, considering how plainly our Epistle itself brings to view the strong emphasis laid by the Jewish Christians on an immediate inauguration into the apostolate by Christ, would it have been probable that such a one, not an Apostle, would have been reckoned by these among the "pillars," "those of reputation?" And if one not an Apostle had enjoyed so eminent an estimation as a "pillar" (James being here placed even before Peter), could they then have so strongly charged upon Paul a want of parity with the senior Apostles? And would he then have found it necessary to prove his equality with such strength of asser-

* [TERTULLIAN; *Non separationem evangelii, nec ut* aliud *alter sed ut* aliis *alter prædicassent.*—R.]

† [Notice the exact use of the perfect πεπίστευμαι, "I have been, I am still entrusted with it."—R.]

tion as he does in Gal. i.? James, the Lord's brother also lacks this parity, and could claim it even less than Paul, since he could not appeal to any immediate revelation and calling [? comp. 1 Cor. xv. 7.—R.], and Paul certainly would not have omitted bringing this forward, thereby to invalidate the reasoning of his opponents. These are substantially WIESELER's arguments. We must then either take James the Lord's brother as identical with James, the son of Alpheus, and therefore himself an Apostle (a view already rejected in commenting on chap. i. 19), or take the James of this passage as a different one, *i. e.* the son of Alpheus and not the Lord's brother. That the James in question occupied a certain official position as chief pastor in the church of Jerusalem is justly inferred from the precedence of his name here and also from ver. 12. This on the other hand accords well with the special prominence given to Peter, vers. 7, 8. In reference to proper apostolic activity, in missionary activity, Peter precedes James.

[We are again confronted with this difficult question respecting James. On the theory of the identity of James Alphaei and James, the Lord's brother, all difficulty vanishes here, as well as in Acts xv., and for this reason it is adopted by many. The view, that there were other Apostles besides the Twelve and Paul, avoids both the other difficulties, but is on other grounds very objectionable. We are to reconcile the view advanced i. 19 (that there were two prominent men named James, one the son of Alpheus and an Apostle, the other James the Lord's brother, who was not an Apostle) with this passage. Which is referred to here? Schmoller, following WIESELER, says, the former, to which view objection must now be made. 1. The James here referred to was the head of the church at Jerusalem. Such a position is ascribed to the Lord's brother, to James the Just; if he cannot be identified with the son of Alpheus, the son of Alpheus is not referred to here. 2. This position over the church of Jerusalem, so obviously implied here, does not necessarily imply that James was an Apostle. For with respect to missionary activity Peter stands first, with respect to the church at Jerusalem this James. Was not missionary work distinctively apostolic work? was not one not an Apostle more likely to be in a permanent position at Jerusalem? 3. Paul does not call these three, Apostles, any more than he calls Barnabas an Apostle. In fact all the way through he uses a term that is indefinite—"of reputation." If he meant Apostles only and wished to show his agreement with the senior Apostles, he would hardly have so carefully avoided saying so.—"Those in repute" were esteemed in Galatia as well as Jerusalem, and he was defending himself against Judaizers, who while denying his apostleship, quoted against him the *mother church* as well as the college of the Apostles. Hence he speaks of "the pillars" of the church then and there, not of Apostles as such, and puts them in the order of precedence in that church, "James and Peter and John." Had all of them been of the Twelve, and as such recognized his apostleship (for these three gave him the right hand of fellowship), how could James' name come first? Any argument proving James to have done this as a distinctively apostolic act proves too much: proves him to be the head of the apostolic college. It is as head of that church, whence the Judaizing influence in Galatia came, that he takes precedence. Therefore we identify this James with the Lord's brother (so in ver. 12).—R.]

**Who were esteemed as pillars**=as supports of the Christian church. Christ, of course, is the foundation. The Christian world is viewed as an οἰκοδομή.

**They gave—the right hands of fellowship.**—In general=They concluded with me and Barnabas an agreement as formal and firm as it was amicable. The more precise sense is given by the preceding context, inasmuch as this agreement was founded upon that. Seeing the coöperation (ἐνεργεῖν) of God rendered to both Peter and Paul, they had become persuaded of the equal *divine* vocation of *each*, of the former to the preaching of the gospel among the Gentiles, of the latter to the preaching of the gospel among the Jews. To this clearly recognized divine will they now rendered obedience by the formation of this compact. Agreeably to this twofold vocation they regulated also the twofold activity; assigning formally to each the field of labor to which, as they had become convinced, he was called. This was, it is true, a division of the work, but in the consciousness that it was a common work of preaching the gospel, one in God, who had only assigned to one this post, and to the other that. Therefore they gave "right hands of *fellowship*." [LIGHTFOOT: "gave pledges." "The outward gesture is lost sight of in this expression, as appears from the fact that the plural is often used of a single person."—R.] It was to be a parallel but a coöperative activity. The assumption of BAUR therefore is entirely untenable, that it had only been a purely *external* compromise, that the senior Apostles after as before had held firmly the necessity of circumcision and the observance of the Mosaic law to salvation; that for the mission to the Gentiles they had tolerated Paul's so widely divergent principles, because they could not prevent them, but that a further, inner bond between Paul's mission to the Gentiles, and their mission to the Jews, did not exist. This would make "gave the right hands of fellowship" signify nothing more than, to come to an agreement and indeed really to an agreement to separate.*

**That we should go unto the Gentiles, and they unto the Circumcision.**—The *purpose* of the words, according to the connection, is doubtless to point out, that in this act the acknowledgment of the parity of Paul, and particularly the approbation of his teaching, was expressed in the strongest manner. So far were the senior Apostles from demanding a change in his teaching, that by this fixed compact they gave a full sanction to it, and declared in the most unequivocal manner, that they held it to be a pure gospel and worthy

*[For a compact survey of the transactions narrated in this section, see SCHAFF, *Apostolic church*, p. 249 sq.—for a valuable note against BAUR's hypotheses, p. 251 sq.—For a very thoughtful and interesting sketch of the relations between Jewish and Gentile Christianity in the first ages of the church, against the advocates of a distinctive Pauline Christianity, the reader is referred to LIGHTFOOT, *Dissertation iii. Paul and the Three*, p. 283 sq.—R.]

to be preached. For otherwise they would not have been able so composedly to make over the Gentile world to Paul as his mission field. To the general purpose of the statement the added clause "only," etc., (ver. 10) also contributes. One wish, to be sure, they had respecting Paul and Barnabas; which, however, related in no way to a change of doctrine, implied no obligation toward the "circumcision," concerning doctrine, but was only an entreaty to remember the poor. But the meaning and purpose of this added clause is not, that this was the only limitation of the separation here coming to light (BAUR). In practice, modifications of this partition of the field of labor arose, especially to Paul, in consequence of the Jews of the dispersion. The partition therefore is to be understood not so much ethnographically as geographically. (Comp. also ver. 10, where "the poor" means poor people in Judea, and, therefore, "circumcision" here in contrast with the Gentile countries is also Judea.)

Ver. 10: **Remember the poor**:—of course by gifts. As to the cause of the poverty of the Christians in Judea there are different conjectures.—**Which very thing.**—Paul studiously brings this forward in order to strengthen the contrast between the Jewish Christian opposition to him, and his approved zeal and affection for the Jewish Christians.

### DOCTRINAL AND ETHICAL.

1. *The significance of this event.* On the significance, with respect to Christian doctrine and the Christian Church, of the proceedings between the Apostle Paul and the Christians in Jerusalem, especially the senior Apostles, since the proceedings themselves are not here detailed, the reader is referred to Acts xv. and to the remarks of Lechler *in loco*, LANGE'S *Comm. Acts*, p. 282 sq. Only this need be said here; by the acknowledgment of the "liberty in Christ Jesus," an emancipation from the old Covenant was for the first time effected; it was authoritatively established that a new Covenant was come, and Christianity was recognized as the absolutely perfect and the universal religion. Even though it was Paul who first brought this truth, in theory and practice, to its just validity, it was not, by any means, merely his own subjective view to such an extent as to make of Christianity something else than what it was, or was meant to be, in itself. This appears in the clearest light from his representation. Doubtless there were not a few who imputed this to him, and, therefore, were passionately hostile to the rise of his influence ("pseudo-brethren"), Jewish Christians, who were as yet more Jews than Christians. Against these Paul had to combat, and to what extent is shown, not only in our Epistle, but also in the Second Epistle to the Corinthians. But precisely those whose voice was most availing ("those of repute"), and who, at the same time, best knew what was Christ's true mind and purpose, frankly concurred with Paul, were one with him, and with them certainly all who had *really* become disciples of Christ, and, in the power of the Holy Ghost, had overcome all Pharisaic leanings, or had never had them. And although they for themselves did not stand upon that point of the "liberty in Christ Jesus" represented by Paul, yet these only needed a setting forth, on the part of Paul, of his preaching among the Gentiles, and of the argument inhering in the fact of its success, to convince them, in the first place of the possibility, in the case of the Gentiles, of being saved through faith in Christ alone. Comp. respecting Peter, Gal. ii. 16; moreover, his course, Acts x., his justification of it, Acts xi.; must not the other Apostles then have been prepared by the latter for the report rendered by Paul, Acts xv.? Therefore, that chapter and Gal. ii., do not at all make the impression that they might still have had an opposite opinion and only now gave it up; and, of course, not the impression that they yet retained their antagonistic opinion, and yielded only externally. And even if they, and with them, the greater part of the Jewish Christians emancipated themselves only partially and gradually from a personal observance of the law, yet with that admission respecting the Gentiles, the principle of Christianity was acknowledged, it was acknowledged that a new Covenant had come, founded upon Christ alone.—There existed a *consensus apostolorum* on this question of principle: shall we have Law and the old Covenant or Christ and the new Covenant? This, thank God, is securely guaranteed, and the *dissensus*, which is said to have arisen between the original Apostles, as contracted Judaizers, and Paul, the man of Progress, is a discovery of modern criticism, which views testimony so plain as that of our chapter, and of Acts xv., only through the glass of its own preconceptions.

2. *Liberty in Christ.* In opposition to the pseudo-brethren, Paul, in the interest of the truth of the gospel, indicates the "liberty in Christ," with the utmost decision, and will not be brought into bondage. On the other hand, where the truth of the gospel is not at stake, Paul scruples not of his own accord to make himself the servant of all, and for the sake of gaining souls (1 Cor. ix. 19, 20) renounces "liberty." The rule herein contained for the conduct of the Christian is clear; he may not bind his conscience by a human ordinance, which passes itself off for a commandment of God, nor permit it to be imposed upon him as a condition of salvation; but he not only may, but ought to, make himself a servant, to bind himself, to make something a duty of conscience to himself, for the sake of a weak brother. But because he does this of free will, in thus "becoming a servant," he most shows his freedom, he does it as freeman, and remains clearly conscious of the distinction between God's commandment and man's ordinance. The rule in itself is clear, but demands much wisdom in its practical applications.

3. [*Titus and Timothy.* The principle just stated can best be illustrated by a reference to the Apostle's conduct in this case of Titus and that of Timothy (Acts xvi. 3) subsequently. WORDSWORTH thus judiciously states the difference: "If Timothy was circumcised (as was probably well known in Galatia), why not Titus? If not Titus, why Timothy? St. Paul replies to this question here: 'But not even he who was with me at *Jerusalem*, being a *Gentile*, was compelled to be circumcised.' I would not consent that he should be circumcised, even at Jerusalem. I do not consent to your

circumcision,—*because* you are *Gentiles*, and because you have embraced the *gospel*, and because it would be to force you backwards, instead of forwards, if I compelled you, or permitted others to compel you, to submit to the Levitical Law. But Timothy's case was very different from yours. As has been well said by Augustine, St. Paul circumcised *Timothy*, in order that Timothy's mother and maternal friends might not imagine that he *detested* circumcision, as if it were an idolatrous thing; for circumcision was from God, but Idolatry is of the Devil. But he did not circumcise *Titus*, lest he should afford a handle to those who alleged that Gentiles, receiving the gospel, could not be served without circumcision; and who deceived the Gentile Christians by imputing such an opinion to St. Paul. He might perhaps have allowed even Titus to receive circumcision, as a thing *indifferent*, and for the sake of peace and charity. But these false brethren did not proffer circumcision as a thing indifferent, but as *necessary*. Observe 1) His *charity*, in circumcising *Timothy* at Lystra, in condescension to the scruples of *weak* brethren. 2) His *courage* in refusing to circumcise *Titus* at *Jerusalem*, in submission to the requisitions of *false* brethren. He would be tender-hearted to the erring, but he would not make the least compromise with error; and he would make no concession to any who would impose their errors on others as terms of communion."—R.]

4. *The importance of Paul's position.* Paul emphasizes so decidedly the fact that the senior Apostles gave him no new instruction, but recognized him as of equal authority, not out of pride, but in order to establish the truth of his preaching of the gospel, and the title by which he exercised the apostleship. He does it in the same spirit as in chap. 1; he declares that he did not receive his gospel from man.—Paul is protesting, in fact, against the beginnings of a Papacy, which the "false brethren" wished to erect by exaggerating the authority of the "Pillar Apostles" (and probably of Peter especially), as something to which a Paul must accommodate himself, as having no commission independently of it. "The authority of the pillars," however, was only a pretext, the rallying word that they used; their own authority was what they sought.—HEUBNER.

[The authority of the "Mother Church" seems, from the drift of Paul's narrative, to have been the rallying cry rather than the authority of Peter, since, in the sentence which establishes the acquiescence of the "pillars," the name of James stands first. The argument gains force as a protest in this view (especially if James were not one of the Twelve). For the essence of Papacy is not the primacy of Peter, that was just such a pretext as the Galatians used, but the infallible authority of a Mother-Church. Therefore, the ground on which Paul stands is the basis for other protests than the famous one of the 16th century, since the insisting upon things indifferent as necessary is not confined to one Pope at Rome, but often issues from a body, claiming like authority.—R.]

5. *Diversity of calling.* Paul and Peter were engaged in the same one gospel, but to each the Lord had assigned a different mission; to the one, that to the Gentiles; to the latter, that to the Jews. Clearly conscious of this, they divided the field of labor between them. This diversity of calling, resting upon diversity of gifts (Charisms), or perhaps diversity in the providential course of previous life, *etc.*, must be carefully considered in the kingdom of God, if anything is to be really accomplished. One may stand fully and firmly upon the ground of evangelical faith, himself have living faith, and yet be by no means qualified for every task in the kingdom of God. In this respect also, the body of Christ has many members, having diverse offices, but coöperating for the same end. It is an organic whole, and hence such an organization as took place on a small scale among the Apostles is entirely admissible. It must, however, be natural, inwardly true, not artificial and merely external, else it were mechanical, not organic.

### HOMILETICAL AND PRACTICAL

Ver. 1. From STARKE:—A preacher must not shrink from toil and labor, when he finds opportunity in his ministry to further the gospel, but neglecting his own convenience, should be ready to offer up all the powers of his body and spirit in the service of God.—RIEGER:—A carefully chosen company; Barnabas, a Jew, one of the first fruits unto Christ, and Titus a born Gentile, not even circumcised, but both one in Christ.—STARKE:—It is an excellent thing when brethren are at one.—This is in the church of God a beginning of Synods, which are rightly retained.

Ver. 2. Let us strive at least for this, that what we do in weighty matters, we may do by God's governance and not after our own will. Conferences which are held concerning the affairs of the kingdom of God, by men who stand in one Spirit, have a great advantage, for thereby there comes to pass a communication of gifts between each other to the common use.—HEDINGER:—To ask men for counsel, must have divine command, will and order, else it helps little in matters of faith, and it is hurtful for man to trust thereon.—RIEGER:—Also as concerns repute with others, a man can receive nothing except it be given him from above. Paul with all that God had bestowed on him, and wrought through him, came into no such general repute. He had to endure continually increasing contradiction against himself. It must, however, have been for him a needful mantle of obscurity.—STARKE:—As all hindrances, that can hinder the fruit of the Gospel must be diligently avoided, and removed out of the way, so also the undeserved suspicion of any.

Paul does not therefore defiantly say, "I know that I preach the right Gospel, let others think of it what they will," but he is concerned for a mutual understanding, for the convincing of others, in the interest of peace and of the cause which they serve in common.—[CALVIN:—What then? Does the word of God fall, when it is unsupported by the testimony of men? No, but a powerful confirmation of faith is yielded, when all the teachers "speak the same thing and there are no divisions among them." Were many as desirous as he to edify the Church, they would take more pains to be agreed among themselves.—WORDSWORTH:—Paul did all that was requisite on his part to *obviate* that very result which, unhappily, manifested itself among the Galatians, *viz.:* the bringing of his doctrine into *public* collision with that of the other Apostles. Also by the mention of the *private* conference, particularly with Peter, he prudently prepares the way for his description of the *public* dispute with Peter at Antioch.—R.]

Ver. 3. SPENER:—In things indifferent we may well, out of love, yield something of our liberty to the good of the weak. But where men would press these upon us as necessary to salvation, and our yielding would have the appearance of bringing the truth of the gospel into jeopardy, we should never yield.—STARKE:—It is wholly contrary to the nature of the gospel to lay on any one a constraint of conscience in things that concern our salvation, for the nature of the gospel is not to constrain, but to beseech, to allure, and to convince. But the spirit of Antichrist binds and constrains the consciences to his ordinances and doctrines of men.

Ver. 4. Even in the best state of the Christian church there are false brethren, who will be taken as right-minded Christians, and are not. Now these are much more dangerous than open enemies of the gospel.—CRAMER:—The true behavior of false teachers. They come not in at the right door; they are sneakers in, and hide themselves behind a false disguise.—HEDINGER:—Legal disciplinarians, who look at the outward cannot endure that others should enjoy liberty, and yet in the Spirit do more than they. Dear Christian! learn once for all, that outward task-work cannot make a living heir of God. The heart! the heart! The heart, from its inmost centre must love, fear, honor God, flee sin, and praise Him, who for thee has died and is risen again.—STARKE:—The main aim of false teachers is only to take us prisoners to deprive us of our liberty in Christ, although they do not confess such an aim in words, but will have the appearance of wishing only to check carnal security and liberty.

Ver. 5. BERLENB. BIBLE:—The world and hypocrites count this for obstinacy. Is that then commendable? is the cry with it. I thought now that Christians should yield, and Paul boasts himself of just the opposite! But we must get the true understanding of the matter from the words that follows: We would not give way thereto in subjection, so as to suffer ourselves to be placed under this order of things. Otherwise a Christian willingly gives way, as Paul also proved when he circumcised Timothy. But when they would have him do it as a matter of conscience he did it not. One may be zealous for true freedom, and yet for love's sake bear with much. If it be not given out for a first step to salvation, love endures all; but faith will suffer no derogation of itself.—In our time many a one thinks on a sudden, that he will be as valorous as Paul, as Luther; but he must first have their spirit. For valor there needs a divine power.—Freedom and Truth must go together, else freedom profits not. Truth is inward, freedom, what one maintains outwardly thereof. They are treasures of two kinds, but springing from the same root. And because I will not suffer men to plant anything false in my heart, I must guard myself without.—From STARKE:—The law is something transient: it is the gospel that is permanent. The gospel too contains the kernel of all the Mosaic ceremonies, the shell only falls away. The shadow recedes when the sun rises.

The liberty which is in Christ: 1. We may renounce it for love's sake; 2. we must not let ourselves be robbed of it—for the truth of the gospel's sake.—The truth of the gospel is above all; may be hazarded at no price.—If the truth of the gospel is at stake, the combat may not be shunned.—[Our freedom, 1. negatively, from the bondage of the law, 2. positively, in Christ Jesus; hence Christian liberty no license.—False brethren the most dangerous enemies to liberty. Weak brethren disturb yet strengthen it; false brethren seek to undermine and destroy it. Because "out of Christ," yet in His camp, they spy out and would betray what we have in Him, our liberty.—What a contrast! the false brethren creeping in to rob others of truth and liberty; Paul our faithful, fearless, yet humble and holy champion for the truth which makes us free (Jno. viii. 32).—R.]

Ver. 6. WURT. SUMM.:—This is Paul's meaning: God looks not on the outward person and standing of a man, so that he should prefer a learned one to an unlearned, a rich man to a poor, a powerful man to a weak, but abides by the rule of His word, namely: "In every nation he that feareth Him, and worketh righteousness, is accepted of Him." In which thing we then should all follow God, and neither for the sake of a person or of any earthly thing, should we retire from the right or from the rule of God's word, but should abide steadfastly by it, even though an emperor, a king or a governor should command otherwise, or though it should cost life or limb.—STARKE:—In matters of faith, the authority of persons and outward prëeminence has no weight, but only the truth of doctrine, which is Christ's and from Christ.—[SCHAFF:—Paul means no disrespect to his colleagues, but even their advantages, he represents as having no weight where the truth of the gospel was concerned. His high sense of independence far from being identical with pride, rested in his humility; it was but the complement to the feeling of his absolute dependence upon God.

"God no respecter of persons." The Galatians were; why else this constant reference to those "of repute?" There is no slight intended to those of repute, but a rebuke to those who in their Christian opinion lean not on God, but on men, men of position, reputation. How many neither false brethren, nor so far gone in error as the bewitched Galatians pin their faith on the δοκοῦντες.—R.]

Ver. 7. STARKE:—The gospel is a Divine deposit and treasure, which is not given to any one for his own, but is only entrusted, so that we must deal with it as pleases Him who has given us such a trust.—SPENER:—God has made wise distribution among His servants; though He calls them in common to all spiritual functions, and none of them is quite free from some; yet He appoints to each in particular his certain part, where and in which he shall serve Him, and for that He fits him out with the needful gifts. Therefore, special blessing attends their labor, when they are where the Lord has set them.

[The gospel treasure, the chosen vessels to which it was entrusted. The adaptation for the field of labor is the gift and trust of God's grace. The preparation of the field, God's providential work. The assignment of the field, God's act, to which the Church but consents, as in the first and weightiest case.—R.]

Ver. 8. SPENER:—All gifts, all power in instruction and success of labor, come from God, who must be effectual with us and in us, if we are to accomplish anything. 1 Cor. iii. 6; 2 Cor. iii. 6. Therefore, to Him belongs all the praise and thanks.—CRAMER:—The holy ministry is not a mere babbling, but a mighty instrument, wherewith God breaks hearts to pieces, as with a hammer, and also a two-edged sword, and a sharp knife, wherewith He cuts out the stony heart.

Ver. 9. STARKE:—We are bound, not only to recognize the grace which God has given to us, and rightly to use the same, but also to recognize that which others have received, and to be helpful that this also may be turned to use.

["James, and Cephas, and John." From WORDSWORTH:—He mentions these by name, because what he says was honorable to them. When he has anything less creditable to record, he spares the names of individuals even of the false brethren. He mentions Peter below, for which, doubtless, there was a necessity. It was providential, too, since some who claim to be the successors of St. Peter profess to be above error and beyond rebuke.—R.]

SPENER:—Although the teachers of the gospel, in respect of their office, are alike, yet there is a distinction between them in respect to gifts; and it is not amiss that, according to such distinction, they should be used for weightier and greater, or for lesser functions, and accordingly should be had in greater or less reputation. [CALVIN:—Even in the Church of God, he who enjoys a larger measure of grace ought, on that account, to receive higher honor. But, in all cases, let the rule be followed: "He that is greatest among you shall be your servant."—R.]—"They gave the right hands of fellowship." ANACKER, *Bibelstunden:*—What a moment must that have been! What a blessed working of the Holy Ghost! What a victory for the good cause of Paul, or rather for the cause of Christ's Gospel itself!

We here see the distinction between true and false union in matters of faith; it would have been false union, if Paul had yielded; that is, had abandoned the sound evangelical ground upon which he stood, and the three senior Apostles had then first recognized him; it was true union when Paul, with decision, maintained the evangelical truth, and the three yet joined fellowship with him, because they were persuaded of the truth, of the divine origin, of his preaching.—Accord in matters of faith: 1. Possible and permitted only where evangelical truth is maintained, and, therefore, Paul's firmness is not to be censured; 2. but this maintained, it is not only beautiful, but a duty; *a*) in the interest of the fulfilment of the commandment of love; *b*) in the interest of the advancement of the cause of God's kingdom.—The willingness of the Apostles to recognize Paul, an example for us; 1. they examined Paul's doctrine first; but 2. so soon as they had persuaded themselves of his Divine mission, they entered into fellowship with him, giving up their particular opinions and scruples.—The one apostolic church, built: 1. not upon the authority of one or another Apostle, but 2. upon the agreement of the same, or rather upon the One Gospel.—The gospel of righteousness through faith in Christ Jesus, the touchstone of true and false Apostles; the former unite in this, in spite of all other differences; the latter not, because they are concerned for themselves, and not for Christ.—ANACKER, *Bibelstunden:*—Did they not then immediately separate themselves again? O, no; they were and remained one in the Lord, but each knew the field into which especially the Lord had sent him, each joyfully accepted his part, and joyfully and humbly left to the other what belonged to him. So should it be among Christians!

Ver. 10. CRAMER:—It is a part of the holy ministry to have an eye to the poor and to the distribution of alms.—ANACKER, *Bibelstunden:*—With respect to the poor no division should occur; but in all the various spheres and callings which separate men, mainly in place and station, let compassionate love be a continual outward proof that we are one in the inner ground of faith. On the other hand, such fellowship of love in fruitful measure is only possible where there is a consciousness of the fellowship of faith.—F. MÜLLER:—Such love, we rejoice to believe, will again awake in our days; the hearts of Christians have become warm and intent on remembering the need of their brethren, whether it be in showing love to the distant heathen, or to those who, though in the midst of Christendom, yet live no better than heathen, or to oppressed brethren in the faith, who, surrounded by a hostile communion, lack the most necessary means for the maintenance of their church life. But such love is still far from prevailing fully among us.

[LUTHER:—True religion is ever in need. Wherefore a true and faithful pastor must have a care of the poor also.—BURKITT:—The faithful ministers of Christ ought, upon first and fit occasions, to excite and stir up their people to duties of charity, as well as piety; to costly and expensive duties, as well as those that are easy and less burdensome; these being no less profitable to the Church, and much more evidential of a real work of grace upon the heart.—WORDSWORTH:—Paul here shows 1. His fraternal coöperation with the other Apostles; 2. His love for the Jewish Christians; 3. That his non-compliance with the requirements of the false brethren was from no lack of charity to them. He became a suitor to the Gentiles for alms to the Jews, and at length a victim to the rancor of the Jews, when he was engaged at Jerusalem in the act of promoting this very thing.—R.]

[Unity in beneficence: 1. a fruit of the Spirit in the early Church; 2. a hopeful sign in the Church of the present day.—Paul forward in this work of beneficence; first in time, first in effort.—He continued to be forward. Just after writing this Epistle, he made a tour, gathering the alms of the Greek churches for the saints at Jerusalem, whence came the impugners of his office and doctrine. Christian beneficence, like God's, overlooks unworthiness and ingratitude. "The false brethren" would be "forward" at the distribution of alms to the "saints," yet Paul's forwardness was not affected by this.—R.]

---

3. On one occasion (in Antioch) he therefore asserted, and, with the independence of an Apostle, dared assert, even in opposition to a Peter, the principles of his Gentile Christian preaching.

(Chap. ii. 11–21.)

11 But when Peter was come [Cephas[1] came] to Antioch, I withstood him to the face,
12 because he was to be blamed [was condemned][2]. For before that [omit that] certain
[certain *persons*] came from James, he did eat [was eating together][3] with the Gen-
tiles: but when they were come [came][4] he withdrew and separated himself, fearing
13 them which were [omit which were][5] of the circumcision. And the other Jews[6] dis-
sembled likewise with him; insomuch that Barnabas also [ὥστε καί, so that even
14 Barnabas] was carried away with [by] their dissimulation. But when I saw that
they walked not uprightly according to the truth of the gospel, I said unto Peter [Ce-
phas] before *them* [omit them] all, If thou, being a Jew, livest after the manner of
Gentiles, and not as do the Jews,[7] why compellest thou [how[8] *is it that* thou art
15 compelling] the Gentiles to live as do the Jews? We *who are* [we *are*][9] Jews by
16 nature, and not sinners of the Gentiles, Knowing [yet[10] knowing] that a man is
not justified by the works of the law, but [ἐὰν μή, except or but only] by the faith of
Jesus Christ,[11] even we [we too] have [omit have][12] believed in Jesus Christ [Christ
Jesus],[13] that we might be justified by the faith of Christ, and not by the works of the
17 law: for[14] by the works of the law shall no flesh be justified. But if, while we seek
to be justified by [in] Christ, we ourselves also are found sinners, *is* therefore Christ
18 the minister of sin? God forbid [or Far from it]. For if I build again the things
19 [very things][15] which I destroyed, I make [prove][16] myself a transgressor. For I
20 through the law am dead [died] to the law, that I might live unto God. I am
[or have been] crucified with Christ: nevertheless I live; [omit;] yet not I, [it is,
however, no longer I that live][17] but Christ liveth in me: and [yea] the life which
I now live in the flesh I live by [in] the faith of the Son of God,[18] who loved me,
21 and gave himself for me. I do not frustrate the grace of God: for if righteousness
*come* by the law, then Christ is dead [died] in vain [without cause][19].

[1] Ver. 11.—Here also the preponderance of authority is in favor of Κηφᾶς. [As also in ver. 14. The simple past "came" is the best rendering of the aorist ἦλθεν.—R.]

[2] Ver. 11.—[Κατεγνωσμένος ἦν; "was condemned." The E. V., follows the Vulgate: *reprehensibilis*, which is incorrect. Some adopting a slightly different exegesis, render "had been condemned," but this is not so literal. See Exeg. Notes. Schmoller renders ἀνέστην: *entgegentrat*, "opposed," but "withstood" does not seem too strong.—R.]

[3] Ver. 12.—[The imperfect συνήσθιεν expresses the idea of "habitual eating in company with." So too the other verbs, ὑπέστελλεν and ἀφώριζεν; "he began to withdraw himself." *etc.*; but to express this fully would require a periphrasis in English. "Himself" is the object of both these verbs.—R.]

[4] Ver. 12.—Ἦλθεν instead of ἦλθον, probably an old mistake, from ver. 11, is found in ℵ. B. [The latter reading is adopted by modern editors on good MSS. authority.—R.]

[5] Ver. 12.—["Which were" should be italicised if retained.—R.]

[6] Ver. 13.—ℵ. adds πάντες. [No other authority; ℵ.[3] disapproves.—R.]

[7] Ver. 14.—"Καὶ οὐκ Ἰουδαϊκῶς is wanting in Clar., Germ. [two very ancient Latin versions.—R.], Ambrosiaster, Sedulius, Agapetes: but the authorities are much too weak to permit us, with Semler and Schott, to take the words as a gloss." Meyer. [There is some doubt respecting the proper order; ℵ. A. B. C. F. G., Lachmann, Meyer, Ellicott, Alford (in later ed.), Lightfoot read: καὶ οὐκ Ἰουδαϊκῶς ζῇς, while D. E. K. L., most cursives, Rec., Tischendorf, Scholz, Wordsworth have ζῇς κ. οὐχ Ἰουδ. The former seems best sustained. The want of two adverbs equivalent to ἐθνικῶς and Ἰουδαϊκῶς makes it impossible to render literally in English, but the E. V. gives the correct sense.—R.]

[8] Ver. 14.—Πῶς, not τί, is the correct reading. So Lachmann, ℵ. [A. B. C. D. F., most cursives, Meyer and the majority of modern editors. Rec. (followed by E. V.) and Tischendorf have τί.—R.]

[9] Ver. 15.—[The insertion of "*who are*" in the E. V. has made this passage very obscure. "We" might be taken as the subject of "believed" (ver. 16), and all between as explanatory, but if "are" be supplied, the meaning is sufficiently clear. Ellicott adds "truly."—R.]

10 Ver. 16.—"Δέ is wanting in Elz., but against the weight of authority. The omission was occasioned by taking εἰδότες as a definition of what precedes [*i. e.*, "sinners of the Gentiles"—R.], with which construction δέ would not agree. The omission was furthered by supposing a new sentence to begin with εἰδότες." Meyer. [Retaining δέ, the pointing of the E. V. is correct: "We are Jews," *etc.*, "yet (δέ slightly adversative) knowing," *etc.*—R.]

11 Ver. 16.—[Tischendorf omits Χριστοῦ, but apparently on insufficient authority. The omission probably arose from an attempt to avoid the frequent repetition of Χριστός, which occurs three times in this verse. Some read Χρ. Ἰησοῦ.—R.]

12 Ver. 16.—[Ἐπιστεύσαμεν, "believed," better than "have believed."—R.]

13 Ver. 16.—[Here the order Χριστὸν Ἰησοῦν is better supported.—R.]

14 Ver. 16.—[Rec., C. E. K. L., Ellicott, Wordsworth read διότι, which was probably imported from Rom. iii. 20; ὅτι is supported by ℵ. A. B. F. G., Lachmann, Tischendorf, Meyer, Alford, Lightfoot.—The order of Rec., οὐ δικ. ἐξ ἔργ. is not well sustained.—R.]

15 Ver. 18.—[Literally: "if what things I destroyed, these I build again."—R.]

16 Ver. 18.—[Συνιστάνω is adopted by modern editors on uncial authority; συνίστημι of Rec. is probably a grammatical gloss.—R.]

17 Ver. 20.—[The pointing of the E. V. alters the meaning, and weakens the force of this passage, by making two clauses where there is really but one. As, however, δέ occurs three times in quick succession, and with a variation in its force, elegance demands this translation: "It is, however (δέ), no longer I that live, but (δέ) Christ liveth in me, yea, (δέ *resumptive*) the life," *etc.*—R.]

18 Ver. 20.—Lachmann has τοῦ θεοῦ καὶ Χριστοῦ, following B. D. F. G. "It is highly probable that this reading originated in the transcriber's passing immediately over from the first to the second τοῦ, so that only τοῦ θεοῦ was written; as what followed was incongruous, καὶ Χριστοῦ was inserted. Meyer.

19 Ver. 21.—[Δωρεάν may be more properly rendered: "Without cause." Tittmann, *sine justa causa*, not *frustra, sine effectu.* So Meyer, Ellicott, Lightfoot.—R.]

## EXEGETICAL AND CRITICAL.

Ver. 11. **I withstood him to the face,** *etc.*—"To the face"=not behind his back, in his absence. [It does not mean "publicly," that is asserted below (ver. 4). Some of the fathers, "to salve the authority of Peter" introduced the gloss κατὰ σχῆμα, "in appearance," because he had been condemned by others. This view is opposed nobly by AUGUSTINE. See ALFORD and WORDSWORTH, *in loco*.—R.]

**Because he was** or **had been condemned:** the reason why Paul opposed him. It was not therefore any attack on the part of Peter himself, that occasioned Paul's taking a stand against him. Ἀνέστην, therefore not=I withstood him, but=I took a stand against him. [Yet Peter's conduct was an attack on gospel liberty; and Paul "opposed" sufficiently to "withstand" him.—R.]—The reason was, the indignant feeling of the Christians of Antioch, the unfavorable judgment passed upon him by them. Moreover, the scandal which he had given, was notorious, and Paul was obliged to do what he did. But he certainly did not do it out of personal irritation or from arrogance or malice; his own words prevent such a charge. For himself he did it unwillingly, would have avoided rebuking Peter "before them all." But a definite reason, viz., regard for the brethren, the Gentile Christian church, impelled him to it. And in this there was also a command, so that even regard for Peter on the other hand, was no ground for holding back. [It must be remarked that the Greek only states indefinitely that Peter "was condemned," by whom is a matter to be inferred. Various answers are given: by God, by his own previous conduct, by Paul himself (ALFORD), by the church at Antioch. The last is most probably meant, else the rebuke would not have been public. It is not necessary to suppose that only the scandal at Antioch drove Paul to this course, for the conduct of Peter was in itself *reprehensible.* "Had been condemned" must be preferred, if it be referred to a definite condemnation on the part of the Gentile Christians at Antioch.—R.]

Ver. 12. **For before certain persons came from James, he was eating together with the Gentiles,** *i. e.*, with the Gentile Christians. He designates them according to their nationality, because it is on this that the matter turns. Peter therefore neglected the limitations of the Levitical law of meats. This is the simple sense of this remark. "A Jew could not without Levitical defilement eat with Gentiles" (even if these adhered to the decrees of the apostolic council). "Peter, however, had through Divine revelation (Acts x.) been taught the untenableness of this isolation within the sphere of Christianity." This Jewish law of meats he disregarded, that is he lived ἐθνικῶς καὶ οὐκ Ἰουδαϊκῶς, at all events here in Antioch.—"Before certain persons came from James." "From James" is not to be connected with "certain persons" as if="certain adherents of James" (for "James would then be marked out as the head of a party, something which it would be neither necessary nor wise to do here"), but with "came," either generally="from James," that is, from his circle of helpers, or="sent by James." But at all events they were such as held like sentiments with James, *i. e.*, Jewish Christians, who themselves still adhered strictly to the Mosaic law, lived Ἰουδαϊκῶς καὶ οὐκ ἐθνικῶς, and who because, they felt obliged thereto as born Jews, regarded this Ἰουδαϊκῶς ζῆν as necessary for all born Jews, and accordingly for all Jewish Christians, but by no means demanded any such thing as the ἰουδαΐζειν of the Gentile Christians in Antioch, as WIESELER, perverting the state of facts maintains. They stood, therefore, upon the platform of James. "Certain persons" is not therefore= such as without ground, appealed to the authority of James; neither were they of the "false brethren" (ver. 4), who occupied a very different position from James. What views they had respecting the Gentile Christians, is not stated, for these were not at all in question; it is therefore natural to assume, that their views were those of James, and that the latter, when he sent these people, still thought as he did not long before, at the council (ver. 9; Acts xv.). [SCHAFF:—"It would seem from this passage that, soon after the council, James sent some esteemed brethren of his congregation to Antioch not for the purpose of imposing the yoke of ceremonialism upon Gentile Christians—for this would have been inconsistent with his speech—but for the purpose of reminding the Jewish Christians of their duty and recommending them to continue the observance of the divinely appointed and time-honored customs of their fathers, which were by no means overthrown by the compromise measure adopted at the council. It is unnecessary therefore to charge him with inconsistency. All we can say is that he stopped half-way and never ventured so far as Paul, or even as Peter, who broke through the ceremonial restrictions of their native religion. Confining his labors to Jerusalem and the Jews, James regarded it as his mission to adhere as closely as possible to the old dispensation, in the hope of bringing over the nation as a whole to the Christian faith."*—R.] But with Peter, as a Jewish Christian and an Apostle to the Jewish Christians, they found fault, undoubtedly on account of his eating with the Gentiles, that is, with his neglect of the Mosaic law of meats, his ἐθνικῶς ζῆν. Yet it is by no means expressly said that they reproached him with it, for "fearing them of the circumcision," may merely mean, that he feared possible reproaches, such as those, Acts xi. 3. But as he then justified himself in this, and the justification was accepted (Acts xi. 18), there is the more reason to doubt whether the Jewish Christians, who came from James, really made reproaches against Peter, or even whether they would have done it, and whether it was not an empty fear on Peter's part, which was blamed the more on this account, as a causeless denying of the convictions which he then successfully vindicated, a retreat out of weakness, from the position he had then joyfully assumed and justified, supported as he was by the experience through which God had led him. Peter must of course have feared possible reproaches to this effect: that although his conduct at that time respecting Cornelius had afterwards been approved, it would be a different thing for him now, in the presence of Jewish Christians, to live ἐθνικῶς, and moreover that, in the absence of so definite an occasion as then, he would now be regarded as one also standing outside [*i. e.* with the Gentile Christians.—R.], his authority with the Jewish Christians might be diminished, *etc.* But even if such reproaches were really made to him, these persons nevertheless are not to be regarded as agreeing with the "false brethren" and standing upon an entirely different platform from James himself, for neither Acts xi. 18, nor Acts xv. is to be regarded as unhistorical. Out of fear, therefore, **he withdrew and separated himself.**—The imperfects are adumbrative, cause the events to go on, as it were, before the eyes of the reader.—MEYER.—He ate no more with the Gentile Christians, and as appears to be intimated, discontinued this without giving any explanation: he again attached himself to the Jewish Christians, that is, he behaved himself all at once as if the Jewish law of meats were still sacred in his view, inasmuch as he began again to observe it. He did not therefore give up his freer convictions, his practice alone lost its freedom, and stood therefore in contradiction with his convictions. In the act itself there was nothing different from that indulgent regard to the prejudices of those still weak, which Paul himself so often urges as a duty. But the *motive* of Peter's conduct in this case was not anxiety to avoid a possible scandal to the faith—this was not to be feared here—but the fear of men, fear of reproaches, and most likely also of losing consequence and authority. [It must be noted that such a withdrawal was a withdrawal from the very frequent *agapae* and the frequent Lord's Supper. Though the decree of the Apostolic council did not command or forbid the common participation of Jewish and Gentile Christians in these services, yet Peter had thus communed with the Gentile Christians; he ceased to do so, and of course made great scandal. While not violating the letter of the decree, he yet treated these brethren as unclean.—R.]

Ver. 13. Paul therefore fastens on the conduct of Peter (and of the other Jewish Christians who did likewise) the sharp censure of the term ὑπόκρισις, **dissimulation**, and he is the more severe, because along with the consideration for the Jewish Christians, begotten of fear, there was a non-consideration for the Gentile Christians; and thus they were both scandalized and perplexed, since by the change of conduct in Peter they were tempted to the thought that the Mosaic law must after all be binding. It is of course entirely incorrect to find the "dissimulation" in the former association with the Gentile Christians, as if this had been a momentary unfaithfulness towards actual Judaistic convictions.

[**Even Barnabas.**—"My co-laborer in the work of heathen missions and fellow-champion of the liberty of the Gentile brethren." SCHAFF.—LIGHTFOOT: "It is not impossible that this incident, by producing a temporary feeling of distrust, may have prepared the way for the dissension between Paul and Barnabas, which shortly afterwards led to their separation (Acts xv. 39). From this time forward they never again appear associated together. Yet whenever St. Paul mentions Barnabas, his words imply sympathy and respect. This feeling underlies the language of his complaint here, '*even* Barnabas.'" Comp. 1 Cor. ix. 6, and also the mention of Mark, Col. iv. 10.—R.]

[The conduct of Peter must be judged by the facts here stated, not by a desire to advocate or deny the primacy claimed for him. The occurrence is indeed characteristic of that Peter whom the Gospels describe; "first to confess Christ, first to deny Him; first to recognize and defend the rights of the Gentiles, first to disown them practically. His strength and weakness, boldness and timidity are the two opposite manifestations of the same warm, impulsive and impressible temper" (SCHAFF). The fault was one of practice, not of doctrine. The receiving of the rebuke is a sign of Peter's genuine piety. Whether he went out again and wept bitterly we know not. But there was no "sharp contention," and Peter's love for Paul remained. On the early discussions respecting this occurrence see LIGHTFOOT, p. 127, sq., showing how much the church is indebted to AUGUSTINE for a correct view of it. Comp. DOCTRINAL NOTES.—R.]

* [When we consider this position of James, and look at the Epistle which bears his name, we are led, not to doubt its inspiration and place in the canon, but rather to believe that it must be inspired, else it would have differed more from the writings of Paul, and that its place in the canon is a proof of the wisdom of God, who made His Word complete, by making it many-sided, and yet never contradictory.—R.]

Ver. 14. **But when I saw that they walked not uprightly,** *etc.*—We are to supply from ver. 11: "And at the same time heard the Gentile Christians expressing themselves in condemnation of it." [The necessity of supplying this makes it the more doubtful, whether the reference there is to the "condemnation" on the part of the Gentile Christians.—R.] Πρὸς τὴν ἀλήθειαν τοῦ εὐαγγελίου hardly = "according to," which would be κατά, but "in the direction of," = in order to preserve uprightly and further the truth of the gospel.

The sense, therefore, is the same as in ver. 5. This agrees with the context, for Paul, in the conduct of Peter and the other Jewish Christians, beheld an infringement of the "truth of the gospel," especially of the principle of Christian freedom founded in the gospel, on account of its effect on the Gentile Christians: "How is it that thou art compelling the Gentiles to live as do the Jews?" (MEYER).—[The force of πρός is open to discussion, especially as the word ὀρθοποδεῖν is not only ἅπαξ λεγόμενον, but very rare. LIGHTFOOT says it denotes here "not the goal to be attained, but the line of direction to be observed. See WINER, p. 424." And ELLICOTT in reply to MEYER, who claims that κατά would have been used to express the idea of rule or measure, observes that the instances he quotes are all after περιπατεῖν. If the line of direction be the meaning, the E. V. is correct, and the implication is that Peter did not deviate from the "truth of the gospel," but from the line of conduct which the truth of the gospel marked out, hence the verb retains a semi-local meaning, "walk straight."—R.]

**Before all,** "very probably = in an assembly of the Church, although not convened immediately for this purpose" (MEYER)—before Jewish and Gentile Christians.—**If thou, being a Jew, livest after the manner of Gentiles:** means the accustomed practice of Peter, from which he only then receded.—**How is it that thou art compelling the Gentiles to live as do the Jews?**—Paul shows him the self-contradictoriness of his behavior, by a kind of ironical address. "Thou thyself a Jew, livest as a Gentile—and how comes it, then, that thou constrainest Gentiles to live Jewishly? Is not that an utter contradiction?" It is true Peter does not *constrain* the Gentiles directly; it is a turn which sharpens the censure; in reality, it was only an indirect constraining through the authority of the example of Peter. The opinion is, therefore, quite unfounded, which supposes that the messengers of James had preached the principle of the *necessity* of the observance of the law—even for Gentile Christians—and that Peter had at least tacitly supported this principle. Thereby they would have directly oppugned the view of James himself (Acts xv.), and Peter would have oppugned his own. His "dissimulation" at this time by no means authorizes the assumption that he had changed his view as to the indispensableness or dispensableness of the law itself.—But at all events the Gentile Christians in Antioch looked upon Peter as one who, previously not observing the Jewish law, all at once began to observe it. That it was mere "dissimulation," and not an actual change of view respecting the law, they did not at first know; and, therefore, they might easily, even if no one attempted directly to impose the law upon them, feel constrained to regard it as something necessary, and also to guide themselves in practice according to it—at least, in this one point respecting meats. There was at all events the danger that such a *moral compulsion* might be exercised; and when once a single point was regarded as necessary, matters might go farther. —Against WIESELER'S explanation: "You so act that the Gentiles also must live as Jews, if they wish any longer to eat with you" (which is connected with his erroneous view respecting the journey of the Apostle narrated ii. 1 sq.), let it be here remarked only: Had Peter, by his conduct, only imposed on the Gentile Christians of Antioch the necessity of again observing the decrees of the apostolic council, in order to be able to eat with the Jewish Christians, and had Paul himself so regarded it, Peter would certainly not have received this public rebuke from Paul. Peter's conduct, his yielding from fear, would indeed have been censurable, yet the consequences of this for others could only have given occasion for a public rebuke, provided they endangered the *life of faith*; but on Wieseler's supposition this could not have resulted.—Ἰουδαΐζειν is, without doubt, different from Ἰουδαϊκῶς ζῆν, and is not merely another expression for this, but it is with design that Ἰουδ. ζῆν is not repeated. With Peter, at that time, a relapse into Ἰουδ. ζῆν took place—at least in practice, and through it a misleading of the Gentile Christians into ἰουδαΐζειν was to be feared. Ἰουδαϊκῶς ζῆν was in the Jewish Christian something in itself quite irreprehensible, was only a maintenance of national usage; in the Gentile Christian a Ἰουδ. ζῆν became a ἰουδαΐζειν, that is, a Judaizing, being a Judaizer. [Hence, when Peter, who had been living ἐθνικῶς, occupying the position of the Gentile Christians, began again to live Ἰουδαϊκῶς his action was constructively ἰουδαΐζειν, and a moral compulsion put upon his late associates, the Gentile Christians, to do the same.—R.] The distinction is difficult to render in a translation; it is something like, "to live Jewishly,"—"to be Jewish."

Vers. 15-21. That this is a continuation of the address to Peter, is self-evident to every unprejudiced reader, and the assumption that an address to the Galatians suddenly comes in here is so utterly at variance with the context that it is unnecessary to refute it. To mention no other reasons against it, let any one read the historical narrative, extending from as far back as chap. i. 13, up to this point, and imagine now, all at once, without any transition, an address to the Galatians, beginning, "We are, by nature, '*Jews*.'" This view, it is true, has found again decided advocates in WIESELER, VON HOFMANN. True, on our view also, the exposition is somewhat difficult, but it commends itself too distinctly to allow us to hesitate on account of the difficulties of the interpretation. And has not this difficulty, in part, its ground in this, that Paul only cites words, spoken on *another* occasion, and perhaps somewhat condensed also.—At all events the words are not to be regarded as merely addressed to Peter personally. Paul passes over into a more general exposition, for the instruction of the Gentile and Jewish Christians that were then present. "He makes out of the transaction, which then arose respecting the eating or not eating with the Gentiles, a *locum communem* (an article of doctrine), which extends much further than the transaction itself. He speaks of the works of the law generally."—Roos. Paul cites with such detail his words then uttered for this very reason, that the substance of what he then said corresponds so well with the purpose of his letter, suits the case of the Galatians so precisely. Of course it cannot be affirmed that Paul cites the words that he then used, with literal exactness; his expressions may have been modified to a nearer correspondence with the particular purpose for which he here adduces them, although there is nowhere in the expressions themselves any necessity for such an opinion.

Ver. 15. **We are by nature Jews,** *etc.*—Vers. 15–17 give the ground of the censure in ver. 14: We, as Jews, have the law, which, of itself, exalts us above the Gentiles, who, as "without law," are to be regarded as "sinners;" yet we have surrendered the preëminence which we had, and emancipated ourselves from the law in the knowledge that a man is not justified by it, but by faith in Christ,—how then can one of us wish to bring the Gentiles under the law, over whom it was never in force?—would be the very obvious conclusion, which Paul, at all events, compels the hearer to draw, but he himself makes the more general, but more pointed one: How then can any one of us press the observance of the law again, as though otherwise we fell into the category of Gentiles of sinners? One who does this makes Christ thereby a minister of sin—that is, he declares, by this reëstablishment of the law, that faith in Christ itself, as it involves the giving up of the law, brings men into the category of sinners (ver. 17).—**Not sinners of the Gentiles.**—Spoken from the national and theocratic point of view, on which Paul expressly places himself by the emphasizing of their Jewish descent. From that point of view, the Gentiles, as ἄνομοι, in contrast with the Jews, who are ἔννομοι, are, in themselves, ἁμαρτωλοί κατ' ἐξοχήν, although it is, of course, certain that Paul, in another sense, enforces the truth that there is also an ἐν νόμῳ ἁμαρτ., Rom. ii. 12; and that, in a deeper sense, they also, as Jews (with the law), were ἁμαρτωλοί, is an essential thought of the following context, inasmuch as they found justification only through faith in Christ.

Ver. 16. **Yet knowing that.**—It is simplest to take εἰδότες δέ, "knowing that," *etc.*, as the protasis, so that the apodosis begins with καὶ ἡμεῖς, "we also," and to supply ἐσμέν in ver. 15. The objection of Meyer, that the statement of how Paul and Peter had come to the faith, would not be historically accurate, inasmuch as the conversion of neither had come to pass in the discursive way implied in εἰδότες . . . ἐπιστ., is whimsical. The foundation of their faith in Christ was the knowledge, or at least the feeling, that in this faith alone "justification" was found. Only in the measure in which they acquired this conviction, did their faith in Christ become a full, ripe faith.—**A man is not justified,** *etc.*—As Paul here is merely citing words spoken on another occasion, the doctrine of the justification of man not by works of the law, but by faith in Jesus Christ appears here only as a doctrinal principle of the general Pauline theology. It is uttered in a very definite manner, is almost dogmatically formulated, yet strictly speaking it is not demonstrated, but presupposed as familiar. (Chap. iii. contains not so much an elucidation of the nature of justification as a demonstration that it results from "faith," not from "the law," instructive as this demonstration doubtless is for the apprehension of its nature.) Hence the philological investigation of the word δικαιοῦν belongs rather to the exposition of the Epistle to the Romans. On the doctrinal conception of justification, see Doctrinal Notes below.

Looking at the present context alone, we should be disposed to refer the expression, **works of the law** to merely ceremonial requirements of the law; but by thus doing we should miss entirely the Apostle's meaning. The meaning of the phrase "not justified by the works of the law" is not to be gathered from the immediate context merely; it is, as intimated above, a proposition, elsewhere set forth in detail, and only cited here with the presupposition that it is familiar.—The idea ἔργα νόμου is to be taken in the universality implied in the expression. It denotes simply works prescribed by the law, whether of a more ritual character, or, in the stricter sense, moral injunctions. For a more particular consideration, see Doctrinal Notes below.

[The E. V. renders ἐὰν μή rather weakly, "but," since the meaning is "except," "but only," *sola fide* (Luther, Meyer). The justification is not at all by works of the law; which is also the meaning of the formal, final clause of the verse.—Διὰ πίστεως, *per fidem.* Faith is the means by which justification is received. Hooker: "The only hand which putteth on Christ to justification." The Apostle also uses ἐκ with πίστεως; that preposition may imply *origin*, but as it is used with πίστεως in this connection, that idea is forbidden; perhaps the reason of the change was merely to make the correspondence, ἐξ ἔργων—ἐκ πίστεως. It is here used in each case with ἔργων, where the thought of origin may be implied.—**We believed in Christ Jesus.**—Not "became believers in" (Lightfoot), but "have put our faith in." The preposition (εἰς) retaining its proper force, and marking not the mere direction of the belief, but the ideas of union and incorporation with (Ellicott).—There seems to be some ground for the change from "Jesus Christ" to "Christ Jesus" here; it is more elevated than the usual form (Meyer), brings the Messiahship into prominence, as "we also" refers to Paul and Peter, who were Jews (Alford). Still this must not be insisted on.—The genitives Χριστοῦ and νόμου throughout are objective genitives (Meyer, Ellicott, Alford).—R.]

**For by the works of the law shall no flesh be justified.**—[Schaff: "Literally, 'shall all flesh not be justified,' 'find no justification.' For the negation attaches to the verb, and not to the noun." This justifies the force of ἐὰν μή above. No justification at all from works, even in connection with faith.—R.] This is founded on Ps. cxliii. In the parallel passage, Rom. iii. 20, ἐνώπιον αὐτοῦ, "in his sight," is further added. WIESELER: "The words ἐξ ἔργων νόμου Paul has added entirely in the sense of the original passage; for when the Psalmist said, that before God no flesh shall be justified, he of course had in mind the works prescribed by the O. T. law. Since then this law prescribes not only outward works, but also holy dispositions, we must understand the latter also as included both by the Psalmist and Paul among the works of the law."—"Shall be justified."—"It remains undetermined whether the Apostle writes δικαιωθήσεται [future] in view of a final issue in the case of the individual or of mankind, but a final judgment is indicated by the future both here and in the original passage. Only thus, too, is there a progress of thought; otherwise the discourse would be intolerably indefinite. The entrance upon the way of faith (ἐπιστεύσαμεν) is explained from the knowledge that in the present it is the only means of becoming righteous, and the exclusion of the way of legal doing (καὶ οὐκ ἐξ ἔργων) has its ground in the unprofitableness of it, for appearing before God hereafter as righteous." VON HOFMANN.

Ver. 17. **But if, while we seek to be justified in Christ.**—"In Christ" not=through communion with Christ, as ἐν Χρ. εἶναι, although of course faith brings us into inward union with Christ, but it "denotes Christ as the ground of our justification, as the *causa meritoria* in which it rests" (WIESELER). [The phrase ἐν Χριστῷ is a formula of such deep significance in Paul's Epistles, that it is perhaps better always to find in it the idea of union, fellowship with Christ. Why not understand it thus: justified because in Christ by faith? See ELLICOTT, and compare MEYER *in loco*.—R.]

**We ourselves also.**—On our side also, so that we too came into the class of "sinners of the Gentiles." If we came into this class in and through the effort to be justified in Christ, Christ would thus be a **minister of sin**, would make sinners and not "righteous," and would therefore render a service to sin. On this interpretation of the protasis, the apodosis cannot be an interrogation (against MEYER); for from this apodosis it is now justly concluded that Christ would be the minister of sin.—**God forbid** negatives therefore the protasis on account of the consequence resulting therefrom—a consequence in fact utterly inadmissible. It is true, everywhere else in Paul's writings, μὴ γένοιτο negatives a question. If it be thought on this account necessary to assume a question here, the protasis must be taken differently, somewhat thus: "But if we, while we were seeking to be justified in Christ, were ourselves found sinners—because we would thereby declare, that the law has not availed us for justification, but that we were notwithstanding the law sinners, still needing justification—is Christ therefore a minister of sin?" Only we should then expect, as in Rom. iii. 3, 5, μὴ Χριστὸς ἁμ. διάκονος; as VON HOFMANN remarks. He therefore supplies εὑρέθημεν in the protasis, making it a complete sentence, and translates: "But if as those, who seek to be justified in Christ, *sc.*, we are found, then are we also found sinners." But this explanation is evidently forced. It must also be noted that, while Paul elsewhere only uses μὴ γένοιτο after an interrogation, he as constantly introduces that interrogation with οὖν. As a deviation from his usual practice must be admitted in any case, the further deviation, that μὴ γέν. is not preceded by an interrogation may well be conceded. But in any case the explanation is difficult. [LIGHTFOOT fairly discusses the various explanations. 1. As an attack on the premises through a monstrous conclusion (as above). 2. An illogical conclusion deduced from premises in themselves correct. This view, which makes an interrogation in the last clause, is preferred by him, and by most English commentators. "'Seeing that in order to be justified in Christ it was necessary to abandon our old ground of legal righteousness and to become sinners (*i. e.*, to put ourselves in the position of the heathen) may it not be argued that Christ is thus made a minister of sin?' This interpretation best develops the subtle irony of ἁμαρτωλοί: 'We Jews look down upon the Gentiles as sinners; yet we have no help for it but to become sinners like them.' It agrees with the indicative εὑρέθημεν and with Paul's use of μὴ γένοιτο." It paves the way for the words which follow: "I, through the law, am dead to the law." Ἆρα is to be preferred to ἄρα in this case. The former hesitates, the latter concludes.—R.]

Μὴ γένοιτο,* in no way whatever is Christ a "minister of sin," for it is not the seeking justification in Him, that makes me a sinner, but I am found a sinner in an entirely opposite case. [LIGHTFOOT: "Nay verily, *for*, so far from Christ being a minister of sin, there is no sin at all in abandoning the law; it is only converted into a sin by returning to the law again."—R.]

Ver. 18. **For if I build again the very things I destroyed.**—In this opposite case, I represent myself as a sinner, but the blame does not rest on Christ. "Build up again," *etc.* Thus Paul describes the conduct of Peter, "who previously, and even in Antioch had at first declared the Mosaic law not binding, as Christians had therefore, as it were, torn it down as a now useless building; but afterwards through his Judaizing conduct (even though it did not arise from conviction), represented it again as binding, and hence, as it were, built up the demolished edifice anew."—"The first person veils what had taken place *in concreto*, under the

*[WORDSWORTH: "On this formula, derived from the LXX. it is to be observed that the Septuagint render—(1) אָמֵן (Amen) by γένοιτο. See the remarkable instance in Deut. xxvii. 15-18, *etc.*; and (2) they render חָלִילָה, *i. e.*, *absit*, literally *profanum sit*, by μὴ γένοιτο (Gen. xliv. 7. 17; Josh. xxii. 29). Μὴ γένοιτο is something much more than a direct negation, such as '*No verily.*' It is a vehement expression of indignant aversion, reprobating and abominating such a notion as that by which it is looked. And therefore the English, *God forbid!* properly understood, *i. e.*, God forbid that any one should so *speak*, is a fit rendering of it. It is used fourteen times by St. Paul (ten times in the Epistle to the Romans, thrice to the Galatians, and once in 1 Corinthians), and is generally employed by him to rebut an objection supposed by him to be made by an opponent, as here."—R.]

milder form of a general statement" (MEYER).—WIESELER, according to his view of the whole section, gives the sense thus: "But if we also, who seek to be justified in Christ, are convicted as sinners, that is, should sin; Christ is not therefore a promoter of sin. For then I am myself to blame for the transgression, since what I have destroyed (namely, the dominion of sin!) this I build up again." According to this, Paul is here laying stress upon the indissoluble connection between justification and sanctification. Certainly a striking example of dogmatizing exegesis!—**I prove myself a transgressor**:—*i. e.*, of the law. In what way? we must ask, for it might be the "destroying" itself in which the sin consisted, not the "building again." The latter certainly; in ver. 19 Paul tells us why.

Vers. 19-21. [BENGEL: "*Summa ac medulla Christianismi.*"—R.]

Ver. 19. **For I through the law died to the law.**—"'I' for my own part, letting my own experience speak, to say nothing of the experience of others." MEYER. "For" introduces a proof, found in "through the law." "Whoever has been freed from the law through the law itself, in order to stand in a higher relation, acts in opposition to the law, proves himself a transgressor if notwithstanding this he returns again into the legal relation." MEYER. Νόμος is of course in both cases the Mosaic law, since otherwise the passage would have no demonstrative force; not the law of Christ in the first case as Rom. viii. 2. [The distinction made by LIGHTFOOT in his notes on this passage, must be regarded. The law is here spoken of, not as to its *economical purpose* (as WORDSWORTH who limits the meaning here to the law as a covenant), but rather in its *moral effects*.—R.] "I through the law died to the law" that is, the law itself caused me to die to it. But what now is the meaning of 1. "*I died to the law*"? That thereby a becoming free from the law is affirmed is clear. But in the first place this "dying to the law" is not (with many expositors) to be construed as an activity bearing upon the law=it has come to this, that I have acquitted myself of dependence on the law, *etc.* The Apostle means to affirm something as having happened *to* him, not something as having been done *by* him, although of course this event has had a basis in his ethical nature. In the next place, however, the conception of dying, which is involved in the expression, is not to be at once transmuted into that of becoming free; or else justice is not done to the Apostle's turn of thought, which here, as the sequel shows, revolves about the ideas of life and death. Compare the analogous expressions: ἀποθανεῖν ἁμαρτίᾳ, νεκρ. ἁμαρτίᾳ, Rom. vi. 2, 10, 11, where also the Apostle, as the connection in each passage shows, means an event coming to pass through dying, ver. 10 in the physical, vers. 2, 11, in the ethical sense. Still more closely analogous is Rom. vii. 1 sq. In ver. 4 of that passage we have the analogous expression—only there it is passive, while here it is expressed by the neuter verb θανατωθῆναι τῷ νόμῳ and in ver. 1 he gives us the key to the figure in the sentence; "the law hath dominion over a man as long as he liveth." The becoming free from the law is therefore, of course, the *result* of the dying to the law, but not immediately this itself. "Died to the law" is=I have died with this effect, that the law has lost me, who had hitherto belonged to it, that is, that its dominion over me, its claims upon me ceased, so that it could no longer urge its requirements upon me, as heretofore. While "died" of itself already intimates the legitimacy of this acquittal from the law, the complete demonstration of this is contained in the fact that this dying "to the law" has come to pass "*through* the law" not by a power residing outside of it has this death to the law been effected, not in any antinomistic way, not in conflict with the law, so that this would have any ground of complaint. But now the question is 2. how has he "*through the law*" died to the law? how has the "law" itself brought about in him a state of death as regards the law, and therewith a release from its dominion? Thus much, that the law leads to death, Paul plainly declares, *e. g.* Rom. vii. 5, 10, 11, 13. The middle term there is, that it is the νόμος itself which excites sin into ἀναζῆν. This thought is of obvious application here, The explanation would then be; by the fact that the "law" brought me death, its dominion over me reached, it is true, its culmination, but thereby also was broken and done away. For with him who has died, the dominion of the law ceases—according to the principle cited above. And deducing the reason from the passage itself, we might thus state it; for the law can no more come forward with the claims that I should keep it, in order to justification, when its effect is rather death. The objection that the Apostle could not well affirm this "dying" of himself, as something actual since by his conversion he had been preserved from this effect of the law, will not hold; for Paul, Rom. vii. 10 affirms this very thing himself. This explanation is, however, at variance with the fact that according to iii. 24, the νόμος is, indeed παιδαγωγὸς εἰς Χριστόν, but of itself, without Christ, does not yet lead to man's becoming free from it. Now it is true, that this passage reads as if Paul here refers the dying to the law directly to the law itself, but he then proceeds to give the elucidation of this, by giving the immediate cause of the dying, namely, "I have been crucified with Christ." This statement therefore explains the former one. In the same way the dying unto sin, mentioned Rom. vi. is by means of the "dying with Christ," and in Rom. vii. the death of Christ is made the cause of the becoming dead to the law. Thus much then is already clear, that the "law" in both cases is of course the same (Mosaic) law, but in each case it comes into view in a different relation; in νόμῳ in its requirements, in διὰ νόμου in its effect. This explains in a simple way the paradoxical expression, according to which the law appears as making free from itself. But since it is still the same law, Paul is entitled to say, that he who will nevertheless again live unto the law although "through the law he died unto the law" exhibits himself as a "transgressor" *sc.*, of the law.

Let us now consider the first statement of the purpose of this dying namely: **that I might live unto God**, with the dying to the law the living to the law, has, as the very terms imply, come to an end. As long as this existed, no living unto God was possible, but with the dying to the law every hinderance to this living unto God is removed. "Live unto God:" just as Rom. viii. 11. As the dying to the law may not be treated as immediately convertible into a being released from the law, obliterating the conception of dying; so on the other hand the realism of the Pauline expressions requires the like in the case of the antithetical expression: "live to God." Paul wishes first to oppose to the being dead a being alive, therefore this means: that I might be living as regards God=with this effect, that God should have me, after the law has lost me. As from the being dead there resulted the dissolution of a connection—with the law—which had hitherto existed, so from the life there results the formation of a new connection, namely, with God. (Why precisely this results, appears first from what follows, for from the dying "to the law through the law" of itself, there would certainly not as yet result any new life at all, and especially a life for God.) Hence by "living unto God" as well as by "dying to the law" Paul wishes to express, chiefly, an event, not an activity, something which should be accomplished in him, not something which should be done by him in consequence of the dying to the law. Comp. the way in which Paul, Rom. vi. 11 sets forth the "living unto God" of Christians as something that actually comes to pass in their case, not as something which is as yet their task. According to this it would be about=εἰς τὸ γενέσθαι ὑμᾶς ἑτέρῳ, Rom. vii. 4; to belong to God, which involves both a being under God's authority and a communion with God. So far it rather affirms the possession of a good, the attainment of a position, the gaining of a profit, than the proposal of a work. The next verse especially leads us to refer it to the full filial status in relation to God, as it appertains primarily to Christ. This filial status would then be opposed to the condition under the law. Comp. iii. 23 sq. The fact that Paul here contrasts "God" and "law," "living unto God" and "living to the law" would then be explained by the essential difference existing between the full filial position of God's children and the state of bondage under the law. And the antithesis would be essentially the same which Paul sets forth, Rom. vi. 14, as an antithesis between being "under the law" and "under grace." Life, however, is not merely a state, but essentially an activity also, actualizing itself and having permanence only as such. Hence "living to God" indicates, though not primarily, yet as immediately resulting, an activity and course of conduct with reference to God, and the more so indeed for the very reason, that by this "living to God" especially a good is gained; on which account also Paul, *e. g.*, Rom. vi. 12, 13, affirms as an obligation contained therein, the obligation "to yield one's self to God." Since he there derives this obligation from the "being alive unto God," we should doubtless assume it here also, as a secondary idea implied in "that I might live unto God." In the first place the expression ἵνα—statement of design—points to something, which even if it is on the one hand already given, yet on the other is also still to be looked for. And in the second place the connection points to this ethical interpretation, for Paul means to repel the allegation that by faith in Christ, by abandoning the position of the law, one becomes a sinner: and he cannot do this more emphatically than by describing the release from the law as the operation of the law itself, and as having for its purpose the living unto God. "Living unto God" then passes over into the meaning: to dedicate one's life to God, the dative thus acquiring of course a yet fuller meaning, denoting not merely possession, but devotion, surrender to. The antithesis between "living unto God" and "living unto the law" is also to be explained as Rom. vii. For the law leads "to sin" (and to death). The living to the law then in truth sunders from God. The "dying to the law" thus acquires the sense of dying unto sin (Rom. vi.), though of course it is not to be identified with it.

[Ellicott thus sums up the results; while his views do not differ materially from those given above, the statement is so succinct that the substance of it may well be inserted here: 1. Law in each case has the same meaning. 2. The Mosaic law is meant. 3. The law is regarded under the same aspect as in Rom. viii. 7, 13, a passage in strictest analogy with the present. 4. It was not διὰ νόμον or κατὰ νόμον but διὰ νόμου, through the instrumentality of the law, that the sinful principle worked within and brought death upon all. 5. "Died" is not merely "*legi valedixi*," but expresses generally what is afterwards more specifically expressed by "I have been crucified with." 6. The dative "to the law" is not merely "with reference to," but a species of dative "*commodi*:" "I died not only as concerns the law, but as the law required." He paraphrases thus "I *through the law*, owing to sin, was brought under its curse; but having undergone this, with, and in the person of Christ, I *died to the law* in the fullest and deepest sense—being both free from its claims and having satisfied its curse." So Lightfoot: "The law is the strength of sin. At the same time it provides no remedy for the sinner. On the contrary it condemns him hopelessly, for no one can fulfil the requirements of the law. The law then exercises a double power over those subject to it; it makes them sinners and punishes them for being so. What can they do to escape? They have no choice but to throw off the bondage of the law, for the law itself has driven them to this. They find the deliverance, which they seek, in Christ. Thus then they pass through three stages 1. Prior to the law—sinful, but ignorant of sin; 2. under the law—sinful, and conscious of sin, yearning after better things; 3. free from the law—free and justified in Christ. The second stage ('through the law') is a necessary preparation for the third ('died to the law')." So Meyer and many others, following Chrysostom in the main.—R.]

Ver. 20. **I have been crucified with Christ.**—Χριστῷ συνεσταύρωμαι. "I have come into fellowship with Christ's death on the cross, through faith, so that what happened to Christ has also happened to me." The Apostle declares thereby in what way the dying to the law through the law has been effected. Christ died "through the law," for in the crucifixion the curse of the law was fulfilled upon Him. Whoever therefore is "crucified with Christ," has also died "through the law"=the curse of the law is fulfilled on him too. But Christ, dying *through* the law, died also *to* the law, *i. e.*, His life of subjection to the law came to an end (comp. iv. 4) even according to the principle, Rom. vii. 1, and the more so in His case, because it brought the curse undeservedly upon Him, and therefore forfeited its claim. As now the one "crucified with Christ" has died "*through* the law," he has at the same time thereby also died "to the law"=he has, for the law, become a dead man, such an one as is no longer subject to the law, is free from it and its claims. The law over against him has no right of possession, having lost it. Comp. Rom. vii. 2: "dead to the law through the body of Christ." An equivalent sense is contained in chap. iii. 25: "faith having come, we are no longer under a schoolmaster." For "crucified with Christ" rests essentially upon "faith." As "I have been crucified with Christ" was the proof of the precious declaration (ver. 19), so ver. 20 first makes clear, why in consequence of the "dying to the law through the law," he has attained to a "living unto God." For as it is especially true of Christ that through the law, He died to the law, so it is also especially true of Him, that this came to pass that He might live unto God. Comp. Rom. vi. 10. For His death on the cross was for Him the departure from that life in which He also had been subject to the law (iv. 4), and through His resurrection it led in His case to the entrance into a life of another kind, into a life, in which He without any medium stood in immediate relation to God, in a pure filial relation, something which is most simply expressed by "living unto God." Whoever now believes in Christ, participates, as in Christ's death, so in Christ's new life; as he is crucified with Christ, so he lives with Christ (Rom. vi. 8). But Paul does not stop with this thought; he is not satisfied with a "crucified Christ" that he might live with Christ.—**It is, however, no longer I that live.**—In his case the being "crucified with" has indeed led to a life; but what now lives in him is no more his Ego; this his Ego did live, when he was still under the law, without knowledge of Christ; it is therefore an Ego essentially linked with the law, disappearing with the legal life, so that he after the revolution which has come to pass within him through faith in Christ and the release from the law, must regard it as altogether vanished out of existence. This whole Ego has died with Christ.—**But Christ liveth in me.**—Another life is it, on the contrary (δέ adversative), that is now in him, the life of another personality; and this personality is Christ, *viz.*, as one who has Himself passed through death to life. And as such He is living unto God. Therefore although living with Christ has as its result, living unto God, this must needs become far more complete by a living of Christ Himself in the man.

**Yea the life which now I live in the flesh.**—But while Paul has declared of himself, that Christ Himself lives in him, Christ as the risen and glorified One, he, on the other hand, knows well that even yet there appertains to him as before, a life "in the flesh," *i. e.* a life of terrestrial corporeality, and so far, therefore, a yet imperfect life, which of itself stands in conflict with the life of Christ in him (δέ in ὁ δέ adversative). [It is perhaps better to regard δέ as introducing an explanatory and partially concessive clause (ELLICOTT). "So far as I now live in the flesh; it is still a life in faith." LIGHTFOOT. To avoid the repetition of "but"—the word "yea" will convey the force of the connection—"Even though I do live a life in the flesh, Christ so lives in me, that yea this very life I live by the faith," *etc.*—R.] "Flesh" here does not of course affirm an ethical defect, for he affirms this life at this very moment of himself, but only so to speak, a physical life; the opposite idea is not: in the Spirit, but: in vision, in heaven. Paul does not, however, on this account, recall what he said before, but reconciles the life "in the flesh" with the life of Christ in him by **I live in the faith.**—"Now" is in opposition to the past time before the "dying to the law." Now, after he has died to the law, he lives, it is true, even yet "in the flesh," but he lives "in the faith." "In the faith" is of course opposed, first of all in a restricted way, to "in the flesh," on which account also the two phrases are conjoined; but in fact it constitutes the antithesis to the previous "living to the law." [Not "by faith," but "in faith," "the atmosphere as it were which he breathed in this his new spiritual life" (LIGHTFOOT).—R.] **Of the Son of God,**—Christ, we may believe, is designedly distinguished by this exalted predicate, in order to characterize faith as something great, in that it lays hold on the Son of God Himself. As if to say: what matters it that I still live in the flesh? Even in the flesh I possess through faith the Son of God! At the same time also the preposterousness of the thought, that one can become a sinner, "seeking to be justified in Christ," [or that "Christ is a minister of sin."—R.] is intimated. **Who loved me and gave himself for me.**—"It is indeed natural that I should believe on Him, since He," *etc.* — and on the other hand this is a more definite statement of what faith believes.

Ver. 21 is a simple conclusion from what immediately precedes. Men cannot now say, that **I frustrate the grace of God,** for this manifested itself in the atoning death of the Son of God. But precisely in this do I believe, yea, my whole life is a life in faith thereon. Exactly the reverse: **if righteousness come through the law, then Christ died without cause,** needlessly, and if I through the law sought justification, I should then declare the death of Christ to have taken place in vain, and should thus reject the grace of God: but now this latter is precisely what I did not do, and therefore not the former; I cannot be reproached with this. It is to be supposed, that some accused Paul, on account of his independence of the law in his course of conduct, of a contempt of the grace of God, not recognizing, in their confusion of thought, the truth that just this self-elevation of Christ was the chief manifestation of this grace, that therefore every disparagement of that self-devotion to death, by emphasizing the law, implied a contemning of this grace. This δωρεάν is, in conclusion, a sharply trenchant word. [MEYER: "This death took place unnecessarily, if what it should effect, could be attained through the law. ERASMUS is excellent: *est autem ratiocinatio ab impossibili.*"—R.]

## DOCTRINAL AND ETHICAL.

1. "*Controversy of Paul with Peter*" is a frequent, but incorrect title of this section. It should rather be entitled: *Peter's weak yielding and Paul's open rebuke of it.* For there is not the slightest mention made of a controversy between the two, and especially none of any opposing reply provoked by Paul.

As regards the fault of Peter, the question, in what it consisted, has been answered in the main above. To express it generally, it was a practical denying of the freer, genuinely evangelical conviction, to which he had attained, and that too from an unworthy motive, namely the fear of man, a fear of the censure of legally-minded Christians (and thus at all events an ὑπόκρισις). This of itself gives an important hint as to how we are to show regard for "the weak," and when we may, out of consideration for them, renounce some particulars of Christian freedom. It is right only when it proceeds not from the fear of men or their censure or in any other way from self-interest, but from indulgent care that scandal be not given, and conscience be not perplexed.—Peter's conduct, however, was particularly indefensible on account of the special circumstances under which it took place; at a time when it was of moment to secure the principal of Christian liberty, "the truth of the gospel," which through Peter's behavior was put in jeopardy: for the Gentile Christians, who were witnesses of it, were thereby induced to suppose that the observing of the Mosaic *law* was something necessary for a Christian, were shaken in their previous Christian conviction. A further important hint as to this regard for the weak! it may be duty, it may also be forbidden, when the fundamental principle of evangelical freedom would thereby be rendered doubtful to any one (or when, on the other hand, it might be perverted so as to establish the legal position, and to support an attack upon evangelical liberty).

The nature of the fault determines also our judgment respecting it. It was a fault: and on this account Paul's correction of it, and that in the way in which it took place, *i. e.*, publicly, before all, was warranted, nay, necessary: necessary, not so much on account of the fear of man betrayed in it, as on account of the perplexity of conscience among the Gentile Christians, which was to be apprehended. This was the reason why Paul took occasion to set forth with such distinctness the evangelical doctrine of justification by faith. That a Peter should be set right by Paul, ill accords with the Romish view of the primacy of Peter. The transaction in Antioch will therefore also be urged with propriety against the assumption of such a primacy. The narrative is also instructive for the just apprehension of the general personal characters of the Apostles, and constitutes a corrective against exaggerated notions of these, as though a shortcoming, and unwarranted step, or even a sin, were never possible in their case. —But on the other side, more must not be made of Peter's fault than it really was. It must not be regarded as anything else than a sin of weakness. If even Peter's denial of his Master, rightly judged, can only be regarded as such, much more, and with entire certainty must this case in Antioch be so regarded, and this case, although in some measures analogous to his denial, is much less scandalous as indeed, considering that meanwhile he had been endued with the Holy Ghost, might be expected. That he strove with the Spirit, is not even to be imagined, *nam quo rectore apostoli utebantur, spiritus sanctus neque sublata illos omni virium humanarum efficientia neque ita moderatus est, ut labe quavis eximerentur vel castigationi fraternæ locus non esset* (ELWERT, p. 16), as little as that sins of weakness generally are impossible in those who have received the Holy Ghost. Moreover, as this lapse of Peter was a lapse in practical conduct, and not in teaching, it cannot be pretended that it overturns faith in the inspiration of the Scriptures. The apostolic dignity of Peter and of his teaching, Paul does not in the least assail, and does not speak of them as impaired; as indeed it is precisely in his teaching on this particular point that Peter here comes into view as occupying the right position, failing of faithfulness to it in his practical behavior only. But in any case, the uncertainty of the senior Apostles respecting the obligation of the law, the existence of which is plainly enough attested by the Acts, does not warrant us in drawing a conclusion as to the truth of apostolic teaching generally. There was in this matter a learning, a growth and advancement to clear knowledge of the evangelical truth: and just in this point the corrective is given and the genuine truth of the gospel shown to us by means of Paul, in whose calling we are not to see a chance, but the significant dispensation of the Head of the Church, who knew her needs. We need not therefore isolate one from the other, but as and because both are given together, they should also be taken together, and out of both together we should gain the full light of evangelical knowledge of the truth. — Least warranted of all is the misuse of this passage to maintain the existence of a standing difference and permanent ill-feeling between Paul and Peter. Their agreement of view appears in a way hardly to be expected in Peter, inasmuch as he too set forth the principle of evangelical freedom (from the law) by his eating in common with the Gentile Christians; and if in consequence of Peter's weakness there arose a difference, nothing whatever points to anything permanent, to any deep division, but what took place in a single case was rebuked by Paul, and the unjustifiableness of this conduct openly demonstrated. The publicity of the rebuke, moreover, is by no means to be regarded merely as making it keener, but as showing no less the *brotherly* way in which the matter was handled, inasmuch as a reproach addressed to Peter in private would have been far more apt to make the impression of a personal strife, and had there been a deeply seated difference, it were inconceivable that Peter would have suffered himself to be thus publicly rebuked.—As it is important rightly to understand Peter's fault, on the other hand Paul's correction of it must not be misinterpreted; it was not an exaltation of himself, but flowed only from zeal for the "truth of the gospel," for the confirmation of Christian consciences; and the decision with which Paul stood forth in behalf of this without fear of man, is instructive. Although, indeed, not every one is competent to such a procedure, but ordinarily only one who has a public standing, like Paul, yet the principle expressed in his procedure is important, namely, that in matters of faith, no human authorities, however high they stand, can give law, but that their acts remain always subject to the test, according to the norm of "the truth of the gospel."—As the facts here testify against a primacy of Peter, so the ground and warrant of the act of rebuke witness most strongly against the idea of the Papacy in general, and against everything that borders on it under the protection of the principle of authority.

[SCHAFF, *Apost. Church*, p. 258, gives the following *resumé:* "This event is full of instruction. We cannot, indeed, justly infer from it anything unfavorable to the inspiration and doctrine of Peter; for his fault was rather a practical denial of his real and true conviction. But it shows that the Apostles, even after the outpouring of the Holy Ghost, are not to be looked upon as perfect saints in such sense as to be liable to no sinful weakness whatever. We here discern still the workings of the old sanguine, impulsive nature of Peter, who could, one hour, with enthusiastic devotion, swear fidelity to his Master; and the next, deny him thrice. Paul, too, on his part, may have been too excited and sharp against the senior Apostle, without making due allowance for the delicacy of his position, and his regard for the scrupulosity of the Jewish converts; which certainly go far to excuse, though not to justify Peter. Then again from the conduct of Paul we learn not only the right and duty of combatting the errors even of the most distinguished servants of Christ, but also the equality of the Apostles, in opposition to an undue exaltation of Peter above his colleagues." On the bearing of this passage against the Papal claim to infallibility, see WORDSWORTH, who makes the error of Peter to have been "imposing unjustifiable terms of communion."—R.]

2. *The Pauline doctrine of Justification.*—We have in this section, in a short dogmatic form, the Pauline doctrine of Justification in the sentence: *οὐ δικαιοῦται ἄνθρωπος ἐξ ἔργων νόμου, ἐὰν μὴ διὰ πίστεως Ἰησοῦ Χρ.*, "a man is not justified by the works of the law, but [only] by the faith of Jesus Christ."

*a*) *The idea of "works of the law"* is first to be determined. It does not, for instance, signify merely the observance of ritual prescriptions, and the reason why "a man is not justified by the works of the law," is not that such ceremonial works are not sufficient. For then Paul would simply have directed attention from these works to others (better, or more difficult ones), and not, as he does, have diverted attention from works, altogether to something totally different, namely, "faith." No, as the law itself contains not merely ritual prescriptions, but also precepts peculiarly ethical, undoubtedly the entirely general expression "works of the law," also denotes works of either kind. More accurately—Paul does not divide the law, but takes the law as an integral whole, as a divine institute, which, with all its precepts, the ritual as well as the specially ethical, morally obliges man, and, as an expression of the Divine will, requires and expects obedience from him. (Therefore, even if only ritual observances were meant, yet in reality the ground of non-justification could not be found simply in the externality of these precepts; in them also God has expressed His will; their observance also is to be regarded as a moral service.) "Works of the law," therefore, are generally all works that are done (and are) in conformity with the requisitions of the Divine law.—Yet this is only a preliminary and entirely general definition. For then the question immediately arises: But why then no justification by them? or (since the idea of "being justified" itself still awaits elucidation), why does Paul then point entirely away from them to something entirely different? for thus much at least is implied in it. The common answer is: If man only performed such "works of the law," all would be well, he would then be justified thereby: but this he does not, and cannot do; therefore of course in this way there is no justification possible. But this answer of itself cannot satisfy; it reminds us too strongly of a *lucus a non lucendo;* the "works of the law" would then, strictly speaking, have their name from the fact that they are not performed, from their non-existence. On the other hand a man certainly can (even of himself) do "works of the law," can fulfil moral demands of the law (nay, he can do that much easier than have faith). But what he thereby accomplishes, is only *ἔργα*, "works" (on which account Paul in the Romans instead of *ἔργα νόμου* uses also the abridged expression *ἔργα*), *i. e.*, 1. They are only single, isolated acts of obedience, here an *ἔργον*, there an *ἔργον*, and therefore even if the particular act corresponds to the particular requirement, yet this never completely satisfies the idea of the law, as an integral whole, and all trust in these, therefore, as if one could by these isolated "works" really fulfil the will of God, is perverted trust. The *whole* law=God's will, demands fulfilment. This presents the unsatisfactoriness of the "works of the law more particularly as extensive. But 2. it presents it also intensively: the works, even because they are works, are only *external* acts of obedience. But the law demands fulfilment by the *whole* man. "Works of the law" can never satisfy it; and confidence in them, therefore, as if one could endure God's judgment on the ground of these, is always unfounded. The fulfilment of the law requires first and last a *temper of mind* answerable thereto. In the law God requires obedience to His will: to fulfil it, therefore, man must himself be filled with the spirit of this obedience, and that not a merely external, seeming obedience, but a genuine one, whose source is in love to God. But now the fulfilment, both of the former requirement and of this letter, is shipwrecked on the sinfulness of man, in consequence of which he cannot of himself rise above that want of unity and this externality of his moral acts, in consequence of which he accomplishes only "works of the law," and for that very reason does not attain to δικαίωσις. First of all then there would be held up before the man the duty of perfectly fulfilling the law extensively and intensively, in contrast with the mere "works of the law." But this would really accomplish nothing, because the defect is grounded in the sinfulness of man. There is therefore either no δικαίωσις, or it must come in an entirely different way, and this way is "the faith of Jesus Christ."

These "works of the law" Paul nowhere calls "good works:" he uses the term "good works" only in the full sense of the word, to denote works which are really good, as being works of faith; which is just what the "works of law" are not, else δικαίωσις would come from them, and Faith would be superfluous.—Far less than by these even is the name of "good works" deserved by those "works" which have come up within the Christian period and been imposed as conditions of salvation. These have been only a new form of the "works of the law," and therefore LUTHER, as is well known, found in the Pauline declarations respecting these his most effective weapons against the Romish "works of the law" and the false confidence reposed in them. On the other hand, it is true, he urges most distinctly and forcibly that, as being mere human ordinances, the ecclesiastical "works of the law" do not even stand on an equality with the "works of the law" of the Jews, which at least were commanded by God, and that therefore it is so much the more perverse to trust in them. This is the Roman Catholic form of the "works of the law." But they are perpetually undergoing new transformations, and coming up again with the old pretensions (less and less justified as these continually are), agreeably to the natural leaning of man to a righteousness of works. Especially does he find it easy (to say nothing of observances essentially and from the beginning serving this perverse end) to turn even well intended usages and institutions, in themselves salutary, into a "law," and then to set his trust upon the observance of these. Nay, even the exercises which are meant to further the life of faith as opposed to the legal life, are themselves too often turned again into "works of the law."

*b) Signification of* δικαίωσις. Passing now to δικαίωσις, the term of chief import, we ask what is the signification of this?

This question is most easily answered, if we start from Paul's denial: "not by the works of the law." The Jew believes that he ἐξ ἔργ. ν. δικαιοῦται. What does this mean, what is expected by the man who believes this? Evidently this belief does not imply his making to himself the *ethical* statement: if I do the "works of the law," I shall be — made righteous (*justus reddor*), that is, by God. For certainly he who does the works of the law, does not expect a subsequent *justum reddi* by God; his doing the works of the law in itself constitutes him and proves him (according to the supposition) a *justus*. He is not therefore expecting, as necessary to this, that God shall first translate him into the moral conditions of a *justus*. No: the thought "justified by the works of the law" conveyed to the Jew the idea of a *judgment* of God pronounced upon him, as being one who accomplished the "works of the law:" and nothing can therefore be better established than the *forensic, declaratory* signification of δικαιοῦν: taken, in the first instance, in its most general sense. As to the precise nature of the judgment, it was primarily, simply the sentence: Thou art a δίκαιος [righteous, just man.—R.]. This was what the man needed to render complete his living "after the law," and thus δικαίως, what he needed to make his claim before the law perfect: namely, the Divine judgment that he was thereby δίκαιος; even had he wished to derive from it nothing else than the *certainty* that he was δίκαιος. With this he would then have had the lofty, ennobling, and blessed consciousness of God's *taking pleasure* in him, of God's *gracious dispositions* towards him. But the judgment of God, we know, is never, so to speak, a mere judgment in words, but is also a judgment in *deeds*, that is, the favor of God to any one shows itself in actual blessing. To this, to the obtaining of the blessing of God, and averting of His curse, the expectation of him, who occupied himself with the works of the law, was directed, agreeably to the Divine promises. This blessing was, as is known, primarily a temporal one, temporal good fortune and prosperity, the dwelling in the promised land.

If we apply this to the position which the gospel, denying δικαίωσις ἐξ ἔργ. ν. assumes: "a man is justified by the faith of Christ," the sense naturally is: the judgment is uttered respecting him who believes on Jesus Christ, that he is δίκαιος. (How this is brought about, so that the sentence: Thou art δίκαιος, is itself δίκαιον, righteous, by reason of the sacrificial death of Christ, is in this passage only intimated, vers. 19, 20, 21, and is elsewhere more explicitly established by Paul.) The main point is first the fact [*das "dass"*] of this judgment, namely that the Divine complacency and satisfaction is attested thereby: but then, as intimated above all, the whole weight falls upon the manifestation of this in act, upon the effect of this judgment, and hence, upon the certainty of Divine *Blessing* (instead of curse). This blessing then, it is understood, comprehends a sum of manifestations, partly internal, and enjoyed even in the earthly life, but in part such as are only realized in eternity, and make up the fruition of the heavenly "inheritance." This elucidation makes it clear that δικαίωσις is not to be taken as immediately identical with the forgiveness of sins; for the theory of a δικαιοῦσθαι ἐξ ἔργ. ν. implies the expectation of a δικαίωσις not connected with forgiveness of sins; since the claim is here to a justification founded on a *doing* of the works of the law, and not on a transgression of the law. In this justifying "by the faith of Christ" then, which becomes necessary for the very reason that, on account of our sinfulness being justified, is not possible "by the works of the law" — the forgiveness of sin, of the transgression of the law, is no doubt an integral, nay, more, the fundamental element of the δικαίωσις, it is in the full sense an Act of Pardon. — The elements into which the δικαίωσις resolves itself, or, if the phrase is preferred, the consequences which grow out of the δικαίωσις, are then found in detail (partially at least), in chap. iii., (and also in chap. iv.), where the reference to the "Blessing," in opposition to the "curse" (agreeably to our exposition), as well as to the "inheritance," is instructive. And if at the beginning of chap. iii. the receiving of the Holy Ghost is described as an effect of "faith" (as opposed to the works of the law), it is unwarrantable to urge this against the forensic, declaratory sense of justification, as if it signified an internal transformation, a translation from the flesh into the Spirit, *etc.* For the immediate reference here is to the receiving of the Spirit as a Divine *blessing*, the communication of a gracious benefit, as a sign and evidence of the Divine good will, an evidence of pardon. This gift of the Spirit, it is indisputably true, creates a new life, and it is given to this end, but this view is second in order.—Nay, this new life itself is also to be regarded as a Divine grace. Δικαιοῦν therefore is an effective act only in the above named sense, that God's approving judgment is shown also in act, or that God's judgment consists in real blessings. It is not an effective act in the sense that δικαιοῦν of itself *signifies* an *infusio justitiæ* of any sort, new life, or the like.—Unquestionably the "faith of Jesus Christ" leads not merely to δικαίωσις, but also to a new "living with Christ," which is grounded upon a "dying with Christ" (of which there is a brief mention of this section vers. 19, 20). But this is not comprehended in δικαίωσις as Paul uses it; for this idea he has the entirely different turn of thought and expression quoted above. Therefore no one should confound what Paul expressly keeps apart (*e. g.*, as he plainly does in the relation of Rom. vi. to the preceding chapters). Δικαιωθῆναι is not identical with the origination of a new life. In this passage especially (ver. 19 sq.) Paul's allusion to the new life that had arisen in him through faith in Jesus Christ, serves, strictly speaking, only as a reason why he no longer seeks δικαίωσις through the "works of the law," but through faith in Christ. Through the crucifixion with Christ the man of the law has been slain in him, and a new man has arisen who lives in "faith in Christ." The new man therefore is he who knows his δικαίωσις to be grounded on faith in Christ. It is a sign of the new man, it belongs to his nature to live "in the faith of Jesus Christ," and to seek and find in that, instead of in the law, his δικαίωσις. But it does not follow from this that δικαιωθῆναι means the same as to become a new man.

But, allowing that δικαίωσις is not to be identified with the origination of a new life, does not the latter precede the δικαίωσις, and is it not. not unfrequently, the material ground of it? This brings us

*c*) *To the idea of "faith," and its relation to justification.* "The faith of Jesus Christ" leads to justification, and this alone does not the works of the law, is what Paul declares with such distinctness. But in what way? Has Faith this effect inasmuch as, according to what has been touched upon above, the believer appropriates to himself the death and the life of Christ = the old man is slain and a new one planted in him, so that God, with reference to this, even though the new life is only in its beginning, yet recognizing in the beginning the guarantee of the rest, acquits him of sin, and bestows upon him blessing and grace, that is justifies him in the forensic sense, and then implants in him still further such life, with the effective method of the justification? This must be denied decidedly: for this simple reason, that otherwise the ground of justification. in the mind of God, would consist in something else than that which the faith of the believer apprehends as its ground, and so his faith would really be an illusion. For 1. "The believer believes on Christ," is equivalent to saying that he recognizes in Christ, and particularly in Christ's sacrificial death, the ground of his justification. 2. The believer, through his faith in Christ, undoubtedly comes to a new life, but this life is and abides, as our passage itself shows, essentially and above all a life in faith, and in faith on Christ's death (ver. 20); in the conviction of being justified before God by this death, from which then follows a life according to God's will in the special ethical sense, and transformation of the whole direction of the will. The real ground of justification, therefore, cannot consist in the believer's new life itself, but in that in which he himself, renouncing the works of the law, seeks and continually finds it, namely, in Christ's atoning death. Else were he entangled in a delusion. And faith justifies simply because it is, as it were, our unreserved assent to the reconciliation already effected in Christ. It needs only that, for through the atoning death of Christ, provided any one will not deny its value, the grace of God is already won for us all; therefore, there remains nothing on our part but to say Yes to it (*manus apprehendens*). Without this, that grace cannot become our own; through it, it does become our own, since an earning of it, or a making ourselves worthy of it, is no longer needful; but, on the contrary, every such thought derogates somewhat from the merit of Christ. Nothing further then is needed than just this "believing;" we need not fancy this too little when taken in its simple sense = "to trust," "to place confidence in," and we need not suppose we must first make its idea as it were more complete by taking in its effects, in order to be able to acknowledge faith as the condition* of justification. Were faith to be made more than the condition of justification, were it to be made its ground, we might intensify its idea as much as we would, it would still be too little. But now, as on the one hand, Faith utters its Amen to the reconciliation accomplished in Christ, and thus makes the man partaker of it,—that is, justifies him, so does it also lay hold of this death itself, which has wrought for it so great a benefit = the man who has heretofore lived, dies with Christ and through Christ, but there comes instead (not out of faith, but out of Christ, yet not without faith), a new man, who lives to God, but ever henceforth seeks the ground of God's favor in nothing else than in Christ. This trust comes more and more completely into exercise with the new life that springs up, instead of being now superfluous. (This is the double hand of faith.)

* [There need be no mistake about the meaning of "condition" here: *conditio sine qua non*.—R.]

By what is said above, the idea of faith is not in any way unduly weakened. Even though man can do nothing more than *apprehendere* what is in God and Christ, yet this very *apprehendere* is the greatest and especially the hardest thing that (sinful) man can do. For it implies nothing less than a giving of all honor to God, and not to one's self, a willingness to renounce one's own reason, one's own merits, one's own will. Hence, even this man cannot have of himself, but God must bring him thereto. And he does it by the pedagogy of the "law" "unto Christ." On this, see the next chapter, although it is already intimated in ver. 19 of this.

### HOMILETICAL AND PRACTICAL.

Vers. 11-13.—STARKE:—The Apostles also had their faults, and sometimes committed great errors of conduct (1 John i. 8). What? Are ministers then, whose authority is so much less than that of the Apostles, to be expected not to err and sin? Therefore, follow them no further than they follow Christ.—Even though a thing be done with good intention, yet, so far as it is wrong in itself, or as any scandal arises thereby, it cannot be excused or defended by its good intention. When of two evils one must be chosen, it is better to let a scandal arise than to do anything that may prejudice evangelical truth.—Even children of God and great saints are capable of being very easily and suddenly surprised and overcome by the fear of man, when they do not sufficiently watch over themselves.—HEDINGER:—When faults, scandals in doctrine and life are prevalent, it is not for us to be silent, to strike sail and run before the wind, but to stand fast in our place.—QUESNEL:—The higher one stands, the more measured and guarded his conduct should be.

[CALVIN:—How cautiously we ought to guard against giving way to the opinions of men, lest we turn aside from the right path! If this happened to Peter, how much more easily to us.—LUTHER:—Such examples are written for our consolation. If Peter fell, I may likewise fall. If he rose again, I may also rise again. This comfort they take away, who say, the saints do not sin.—This is a wonderful matter! God preserved the church, being yet young, and the gospel, by one person. Paul alone standeth to the truth, for he had lost Barnabas, his companion, and Peter was against him. So sometimes one man is able to do more in a council than the whole council besides.—R.]

[BURKITT:—Such as sin openly, must be reproved openly.—No bands of friendship must keep the ministers of God from reproving sin. A notorious fault must be reproved with much boldness and resolution. If such as are eminent in the church fall, they fall not alone; many do fall with them.—What a constraining power there is in the example of eminent persons. He is said to compel, in Scripture, not only who doth violently force, but who, being of authority, doth provoke by his example.—The errors of those that do rule, become rulers of error. Men sin through a kind of authority, through the sins of those who are in authority.—R.]

[How many rejoice at Paul's defence of the liberty of the gospel against Peter's weakness, who themselves will not receive rebuke as Peter did—nay, are very popes at heart. For there are popes in pews as well as in pulpits, besides the pope who openly claims to be such; Christian liberty suffers from them all.—The fear of man, of popular opinion often becomes to us as authoritative as decrees and Papal bulls to others.—Peter will not commune with Gentile Christians longer; so he might act if he would, as Peter, but as an Apostle, he thus made terms of communion against the truth of the gospel. He was condemned; do we never seek to bind the conscience not only "in meats and drinks," but as respects communion with other Christians?—When such conduct ceases to be a private choice, and becomes public scandal, it should be rebuked by one set for the defence of the truth of the gospel.—The yet remaining power of narrow national and social and religious prejudices in those who profess Christ as "all and in all." How strong in Peter; once so strong in Paul, but now crucified with Christ.—R.]

Ver. 14. SPENER:—The whole life of Christians has, besides God's glory, the end and aim that the truth of the gospel and pure doctrine may be established; those sins, therefore, are great above others, whereby any may be misled as to the truth of the gospel.—STARKE:—So soon as it is taught by words or deeds that anything more is necessary to salvation than the grace of God and faith, so soon is the truth of the gospel wounded.—In the matter of scandals, one who either maliciously or heedlessly causes them, has justly reckoned against him and imputed by God, what thereafter arises out of them, and thus the sin may become more grievous through its consequences.—RIEGER:—O God! if I ever err, give me a frankspoken Paul to warn me and make me on the spot or afterwards as mild in yielding, as Peter!—HEUBNER:—Things that trouble peace may arise even among children and messengers of God. In Acts xiii. 13. xv. 31, similar things are mentioned. Behold the imperfection of the earthly life! only above is harmony forever undisturbed. The kingdom of Christ, nevertheless, advances even through weak instruments.

Public rebuke: 1. admissible, yes, necessary, when anything has been done that perplexes consciences; 2. how shall it be conducted? Undoubtedly by free exposition of its evil consequences, but then chiefly by renewed and more thorough assertion of the truth of the Gospel: not with personal reproaches; and above all, in brotherly love; 3. difficult; therefore examine thyself well, whether thou be called or at all events fitted therefor, that thou destroy not more good than thou restorest; and if thou perceivest thyself not skilled, leave it: for after all it is not thou that rebukest and God knows well enough how to choose His own instruments. In all cases do it not without earnest looking up to God, that in the discharge of it He will keep thee as from the fear of man, so none the less from vanity, haughtiness and a loveless temper.

Ver. 15. STARKE:—The preëminence which we who are born of Christian ancestry have above others, must not be misused to the prejudice of divine grace; we must be none the less certain that the grace of Christ alone, not our descent from Christian parents, can save us.

Ver. 16. LUTHER:—Understand we this article rightly and purely? Then have we the true heavenly sun. But if we lose it, we have nothing else than a hellish darkness.—A troubled, wretched conscience should keep no thought or remembrance of the law, nor should oppose to the anger and judgment of God anything else than the sweet comforting word of Christ, which is a word of grace, of forgiveness of sins, of everlasting life and blessedness. But to do this is especially hard. For the fearfulness of the conscience keeps us from well apprehending Christ, and temps us often to let Him go, and to fall back upon the thought of law and sin.—As a Jew, through the works which he does after God's law, cannot be justified, how then should a monk be justified, by his order, a priest by his authority, a philosopher by his skill and wisdom, a sophistical theologian by his sophistry? Wise, pious, and righteous as men may become on earth through their reason and God's law, yet they are by all their works, merits, masses, and by the best of all their righteousness and acts of worship, not righteous before God.—RIEGER:—What thou art by nature and canst boast concerning thy good bringing up, thy refined education, thy works of the law, distinguish thee doubtless above many others. Thou art not bidden to throw that entirely away. What of quiet days, and advantage to thy health, and the like this secures to thee, enjoy. But into the secret chamber of judgment, where God and the conscience have to do with one another concerning the forgiveness of sins, this is not to intrude. Through no work of the law shall we ever bring it to pass that God will justify us, forgive our sins, bestow on us access to His grace, and the hope of future glory; that we learn alone from God's word and promise in Christ.

Ver. 17. RIEGER:—If I would suffer this thing again to become uncertain to me, namely, that I, leaving all works behind, should be justified through Christ alone; if I would be mistrustful about that, as if I had brought myself into sin by such a disparagement of works; if I fell back again upon works, as chanced to Peter, I should make Christ a minister of sin.—LUTHER:—Every one who teaches that faith in Christ doth not justify, unless a man also keep the law, such a one makes Christ a minister of sin, *i. e.* he makes out of him a law-teacher, who teaches just that, and nothing else that Moses teaches. So can Christ then be no Saviour and grace-giver, but would be only a cruel tyrant, who required of us merely impossible things, not one of which any man can fulfil. [For the other view of this passage see EXEG. NOTES.—BURKITT:—The Apostle rejects the inference of the adversaries of the doctrine of justification by faith with the greatest abhorrence and detestation. It is no new prejudice, though a very unjust one, against this doctrine of justification by faith alone, that it opens a door to licentiousness and makes Christ the minister of sin.—R.]

Ver. 18. STARKE:—Teachers should take good care, that what they tear down with one hand, that they may not build up again with the other.

Ver. 19. RIEGER.—I have not run away from the law like an escaped rogue. It has cost a death, I have made trial of the law before, and learnt well, how far the law carries us, and what is impossible to it. But now, as in the case of a marriage dissolved by death, I am lawfully divorced from the law. I have no desire to knit this bond again.—LUTHER:—St. Paul could have said nothing of mightier force against the righteousness that is supposed to come through the law, than just what he here saith: I have died to the law, I have nothing at all more to do with it, it concerns me nothing, nor can it justify me.—These words are most full of comfort, and let them come in mind to any one in time of temptations and afflictions, and be in his heart rightly and thoroughly understood. Such a one would without doubt be well able to stand against all danger and dread of death, against all manner of terrors of conscience and of sin, though they fell as vehemently upon him as ever they could.—Happy he who, when his conscience falls into distress and temptation, that is, when sin assails and the law accuses him, then can say: What matters that to me; for I have died to thee. But if thou wilt ever dispute with me concerning sins, go, bury thyself with the flesh and its members, my servants pass then in review, plague and crucify them as thou wilt; but me, the conscience, it is for thee to leave, in peace as queen. For thou hast no concern with me since I have died to thee and live now to Christ.—It is a strange, curious, and unheard of speech, that to live to the law is as much as to die to God, and to die to the law as much as to live to God. These two sentences are completely and entirely athwart the reason, therefore also no sophist as law teacher can understand them. But do thou give diligence that thou learn well to understand them, namely thus, that who now will live to the law, that is, practise himself in its works, and keep the same, in order that he may thereby be justified, such a one is a sinner and abides a sinner, and therefore condemned to everlasting death and damnation. For the law can make him neither righteous nor blessed, but if it begins to accuse him in right earnest, it only kills him. Therefore to live to the law is, in truth, nothing else than to die to God, and to die to the law is nothing else than to live to God; now to live to God, this is to become righteous through grace and faith on Christ, without any works or law.—STARKE:—The end of our freedom from the law is not, that we may live to ourselves, but that we may live to God and Christ.

Ver. 20. In STARKE:—Christ on His cross was to be regarded as the surety and head of the whole human race; therefore, in His person the whole human race was also crucified. Especially have believers part in the death of Christ, because faith brings with it a perfect union and fellowship between Christ and the faithful.—BERLENB. BIBLE:—Faith binds us to the cross of Christ, and there nothing of the old man will remain and be spared. Faith and the cross are to one another very near. Therefore, worldly wisdom turns its back on faith. Many with their faith will even separate the cross from itself; they make of faith a cross before the cross, and say of the other, away, away with it!—This is the method of stepping over from the law to the gospel, only through the death of the old

Adam, and his peculiar life. It makes a huge corpse. "I live."—No more after my own willing and working, but in another spirit. We must lose ourselves. A man lives then most blessedly, when he lives not to himself. There must be in the heart another I. The old I must lose itself. But what says the self-love and selfishness that would gladly keep its life, and seek in everything what pleases it, that will not hate its own soul, affections, desires, dispositions, and sensual cravings? Its word is: That am I! that is from me! that is in me! therefore, that is mine! that befits me! that pleases me! that is so with me! It demands, therefore, from God and man rest, life, love, honor, obedience, trust, help, assistance, comfort, and enjoyment. O what a heavy stone of stumbling is self-love in Christ's way!—[BUNYAN:—They only have benefit by Christ to eternal life, who die by His example as well as live by His blood; for in His death was both merit and example; and they are like to miss in the first, that are not concerned in the second.—R.]

LUTHER:—The very life that I live is Christ Himself, and therefore Christ and I are in this matter altogether one thing. None the less, it is true, there remains outwardly cleaving to me the old man that is under the law, but so far as concerns this matter, namely, that I be justified before God, Christ and I cannot but be bound in the closest wise together, so that He lives in me and I again in Him.—Christ and my conscience should become one body, so that I should keep nothing else before my eyes than Jesus Christ. But if I turn my countenance away from Christ, and look alone upon myself, it is at once all over with me. For then straightway flashes into my mind: Christ is above in heaven, and thou here below on earth, how wilt thou now find the way up to Him? Then the reason quickly answers: I will lead a holy life, and do what the law bids me, and so enter into life. But when I thus look upon myself, and consider only what I am, or what I ought to be, and what I am bound to do, I lose Christ forthwith out of my sight, who yet alone is my righteousness and life; but when I have lost Him, there is no longer either help or counsel, but at the last desperation and eternal damnation must needs follow.—BERLENB. BIBLE:—Christ is life not for Himself alone, but a benefit that willingly and freely communicates itself. Where now it finds a man who hates and forsakes his own life, and lives no longer in his own self-love, in him Christ lives.—RIEGER:—If a man should hear of the fellowship of the cross of Christ alone, a man might form to himself too joyless an image of my religion; but it is also a fellowship with His life. And my life in the flesh, my tarrying upon this battlefield of sin and grace, is given me for a proof how the Son of God once made a journey through the world, and remained constant to His Heavenly Father.

[JOHN BROWN:—Paul here declares his experience. The law has no more to do with me, and I have no more to do with it in the matter of justification.—Christ died and in Him I died; Christ revived and in Him I revived. The law has killed me, and by doing so, it has set me free from itself. The life I now have, is not the life of a man under the law, but the life of a man delivered from the law.—*Christ's* relations to God are *my* relations. His views are my views; His feelings my feelings. He is the soul of my soul, the life of my life. My state, my sentiments, my conduct are all Christian.—"It is but right that I should be entirely devoted to Him who devoted Himself entirely for me."—R.]

LUTHER:—It is very true that I still live in the flesh, but be it now what life it may, that is still in me, I count it yet for no life at all; for it is, if one will view it aright, indeed no life, but rather a mask, under which another lives, namely Christ, who is truly my life, that thou canst not see, but hearest it alone. I live, to be sure, in the flesh; but I live not from the flesh or after the flesh, but in faith, from faith, and according to faith.—"Who loved me and gave Himself for me." With these words Paul describes in most comforting wise Christ's office and priesthood. This now is His office, that He should reconcile us with God, give Himself up for our sins, &c. Therefore, thou must not make of Him a new law-giver that does away the old law and establishes a new in its place. Christ is no Moses, no taskmaster and lawgiver, but a grace-giver and compassionate Saviour. He is nothing else than a purely measureless and overflowing compassion, that suffers itself to be bestowed upon us, and also bestows itself. Setting forth Christ after such a way, thou rightly depictest Him. But if thou suffer Him to be portrayed to thee in other guise, thou mayest, in the time of temptation, be easily and quickly overthrown.—These words of Paul are an excellent example of a genuine and assured faith.—Accustom thyself to this, that thou apprehend this brief word, "me," with certain faith, and doubtest not thereof, that thou also art in the number of those who are named with this little word "me." For, as we cannot deny that we are one and all sinners, so can we also not deny that Christ died for our sins, that He might justify us through His death. For surely He has not died for this, that He should justify those that were righteous before, but that He should help poor sinners. Because then I feel and confess that I am a sinner, why should I not, on the other hand, also say that I am righteous because of Christ's righteousness, especially because I hear that He has loved ME and given Himself for ME. St. Paul believed it steadfastly and assuredly, and, therefore, also does he speak of it so freely and confidently. But may He who hath loved us and given Himself for us, bestow on us grace, that we may be able, if only in part, to do the like and speak thus concerning ourselves.—[LIGHTFOOT:—Paul appropriates to himself, as CHRYSOSTOM observes, the love which belongs equally to the whole world. For Christ is, indeed, the personal friend of each man individually; and is as much to him as if He had died for him alone.—R.]

Ver. 21. STARKE:—The rejection of the grace of God, may take place: 1. by a denial of the perfect satisfaction of Christ; 2. by setting along side of it our own merits, worthiness and righteousness, as Popery does in doctrine, and many even in our churches do in fact; 3. by abusing this grace to favor presumption, and to supersede sanctification; 4. when even sincere souls, in the feeling of their unworthiness, are much too timorous to appropriate grace to themselves, and think they must first have arrived at this or that degree of holiness, before grace can avail them any thing; 5. when tempted ones from a lack of feeling conclude that they have fallen out of grace again.

LUTHER:—The righteousness that comes from the law is nothing else than mere contempt and rejection of God's grace, whereby the death of Christ becomes unworthy and unavailing. Who is, indeed, so eloquent that he can sufficiently portray and bring to light, what it is to reject the grace of God? or to make out that Christ has died in vain? It is hard to have to talk of any useless dying; but to say that Christ has died in vain, that is too much, that is quite too villanous a word, for it is nothing less than to say that Christ is wholly unprofitable, is nothing worth.—If any one will make out Christ's death an unprofitable thing, he must also make His resurrection, His glorious triumph over sin, death, *etc.*, His kingdom, heaven, earth, God Himself, God's majesty and glory, and in brief all things together contemptible and useless.—These great, mighty, and terrible thunderclaps, which St. Paul in his writings brings down from heaven against our own righteousness, that comes from the law, ought, by good right, to terrify us from it.—When the world hears such a charge, it will not at all believe that it is true; for it does not allow that a man's heart could be so wicked that he should reject the grace of God, and count Christ's death a despicable thing, and yet for all that, this sin is of all in the world the most common. Whoever will be righteous outside of faith in Christ, such a one casts away God's grace, and despises the death of Christ, though in words he speak as highly and honorably thereof, as ever he knows how to speak.

Vers. 19-21. To live to God, our end; 1. What is thereby required? 2. Condition of accomplishing it; the way thereto is dying—to the law: this again is possible only through being crucified with Christ.—To be crucified with Christ: 1. something difficult, requires nothing less than that we place ourselves under God's sentence of condemnation; 2. indispensably necessary: else there can be no life to God.—To die with Christ—to live to God; this is the pregnant definition of true Christianity.—I live, yet no longer I, but Christ liveth in me: a bold expression; but so must it be in the case of a Christian; one's own Ego must vanish, and in place of it Christ must rule in us.—Christ lives in me: 1. can we say so, when even yet there is much sin in us? 2. When can we say so? when at least it is He, in whom alone we seek our righteousness? The Christian's life a double life: *a.* Proof: 1. the joyful attestation: Christ lives in me; 2. he must humbly acknowledge and in manifold ways experience; I yet live in the flesh. *b.* What is to be done, that he, so long as he lives and whatever his life in the flesh, may not live to the flesh, but to Him who, *etc.*—Living in faith on the Son of God, who loved us, and gave Himself for us: 1. the blessed prerogative, 2. the sacred duty of the Christian.—In LISCO:—The life in the faith of the Son of God: 1. what it presupposes in us. Ver. 19: the death of the old natural life—the being crucified with Christ; 2. wherein it essentially consists? Ver. 20: in entire self-surrender to the Son of God, in being filled and permeated with His love, which to the true Christian is the one moving spring of all his actions; 3. what value has it? Ver. 21, it serves to the glory of the grace of God, and the praise of the death of Christ.

To say Christ has also loved *me*, and given Himself for *me*, is the height of faith's achievements, simple as it appears.—Reject not the grace of God! an admonition as earnest as needful.—To reject God's grace the greatest of all sins. When is this done? (see above.)—Christ died in vain! 1. that cannot be; such a deed of love *must* have a high end; 2. and yet, for how many has He died in vain!—Christ would have died in vain! the severest condemnation possible of every kind of righteousness of works.—To seek righteousness from works; as foolish (for Christ *cannot* have died in vain), as simple (it rejects that which was God's own most glorious work of Love). ["Then Christ died without cause." Did such a person *die*. Then while we may account for His life by other theories, there is no sufficient reason for His death, save that which Paul preached: Full pardon, entire salvation, to every one who by faith lays hold of Christ as dying for him. Any other view is inconsistent with God's wisdom, frustrates God's grace as well.—Self-salvation must ever deny a sufficient purpose in that death.—R.]

# II.

## Paul opposes the LEGAL VIEW itself, which through the false teachers had found entrance among the Galatians.

### Chapter III. 1—VI. 10.

### A. Remonstrance and expression of astonishment, at the contradiction into which this brings them with their own experience respecting the receiving of the Spirit.

(Chapter iii. 1–5.)

1 O foolish Galatians, who hath bewitched [did bewitch][1] you, that ye should not
obey the truth [omit this clause][2] before whose eyes Jesus Christ hath been [was][3] evi-
2 dently set forth, crucified among you [set forth among you, crucified]?[4] This only
would I learn of you, Received ye the Spirit by the works of the law [was it by
the works of the law that ye received the Spirit],[5] or by the hearing of faith?
3 Are ye so foolish? having begun in [with][6] the Spirit, are ye now made perfect by
4 [being made[7] perfect with] the flesh? Have ye suffered [or experienced][8] so many
5 things in vain? if *it be* yet [really] in vain. He therefore that ministereth to you
the Spirit, and worketh miracles among [or miraculous powers in][9] you *doeth he it* by
the works of the law, or by the hearing of faith?

[1] Ver. 1.—[As a rule the English simple past tense is the better rendering of the Greek aorist.—R.]

[2] Ver. 1.—Τῇ ἀληθ. μὴ πείθεσθαι is to be omitted with Lachmann and Tischendorf. A gloss from Gal. v. 7. [Omitted in ℵ. A. B. and others; by Meyer, Alford, Ellicott, Wordsworth, Lightfoot.—R.]

[3] Ver. 1.—Ἐν ὑμῖν is probably to be retained, on account of its difficulty, with D. E. F. L. K., although it is wanting in ℵ. A. B. C. and omitted by Lachmann. [The uncial authority for it is not much stronger than for the clause above, but its omission is so much more readily accounted for than its insertion, that it is retained by Meyer, Ellicott, Wordsworth. Alford rejects it, Lightfoot is doubtful.—R.]

[4] Ver. 1.—[The E. V. by putting "among you" after "crucified," destroys not only the emphasis which belongs to the latter, but also the proper connection of the former phrase.—R.]

[5] Ver. 2.—[The order of the Greek, given above, is to be preserved, as rendering the contrast more striking.—R.]

[6] Ver. 3.—[The E. V. renders the datives in this clause differently. Πνεύματι . . . σαρκί, not "in the Spirit" and "by the flesh," but "with the Spirit," "with the flesh."—R.]

[7] Ver. 3.—[Ἐπιτελεῖσθε, passive, not middle, "being made complete," not "completing yourselves."—R.]

[8] Ver. 4—[The meaning of ἐπάθετε is open to discussion. Schmoller renders "*erfahren.*" See Exeg. Notes.—R.]

[9] Ver. 5.—[Δυνάμεις ἐν ὑμῖν; the two interpretations of this phrase are indicated above. See Exeg. Notes.—R.]

#### EXEGETICAL AND CRITICAL.

Ver. 1. **O foolish Galatians.**—Direct address, because Paul now, for the first time after his historical account, turns to the readers. It is, therefore, a trustworthy intimation that a new section begins here, and that all which precedes belonged together. "Foolish:" that they had given up the better, genuine knowledge, is what Paul wishes to prove to them in the whole Epistle; this is, in fact, implied in the very opening words, chap. i. 6. His particular motive for expressing himself precisely thus here, and in general for expressing himself with especial emphasis, is that, although a new section begins here, yet, for the writer, this beginning presupposes what precedes—that is, in the first instance the proof of the full apostolicity of his preaching generally, and then particularly the just cited rebuking of Peter for conduct similar to theirs, concluding with the powerful words: "For, if righteousness come by the law, then Christ died without cause." This very thought, so painful, that the Galatians, by their conduct, are declaring the greatest act of God's grace, the death of Christ, to have been in vain, may have been what impelled him to the vehement exclamation: ὦ ἀνόητοι Γαλάται. For here also his astonishment and his censure have primary reference to this death of Christ: "set before you, crucified." [Jerome and others have imagined a national peculiarity to be referred to here, which is altogether inadmissible. The Galatians were sprightly, not stupid, and ἀνόητος, marks not so much "dullness" as "foolishness," want of νοῦς, improper use of it. They were not μωροί, but ἀνόητοι.—R.] **Who did bewitch you?**—So senseless and therefore incomprehensible is the apostasy of the Galatians, that Paul explains their being led astray as an effect of magic. For what he immediately subjoins had actually taken place among them; naturally, therefore, this apostasy—to Judaism—was least to be expected of them. For Christ's atoning death and Judaistic legalism are at opposite poles to each other; the stronger the emphasis laid on the former, the most distant must be any thought of the latter. Comp. ii. 21. [LIGHTFOOT:—"The word βασκάνειν originally referred to witchery by spells and incantations, but in actual use it denotes the blighting influence of the evil eye. It here involves two ideas: 1) The baleful effect on the recipient, and 2) the envious spirit of the agent. The false teachers envy the Galatians this liberty in Christ, have an interest in subjecting them again to bondage. This idea, however, is subordinate to the other." See WORDSWORTH, who quotes authorities for both ideas. There may be allusion to the notion that the power of the sorcerer was felt whenever the eye of the recipient rested on him,* in the expression "before whose eyes," as if keeping their eyes on that object would have preserved them from this bewitching; but this must not be pressed.—R.]

**Before whose eyes Jesus Christ was evidently set forth.**—Portrayed before the eyes, of course, by means of preaching, but the expression hints at the pains which Paul took to make known to them the **crucified** One, and to bring Him as near as possible to them. This is done designedly, in order to contrast the more strongly with this the apostasy that had taken place, and to justify the astonishment which he expresses.—**Among you** strengthens the statement still further: in the midst of you, by oral communication, not merely from a distance by letters. The following is the simplest explanation: "Before your eyes," so distinctly points out the meaning; "to paint," as that of προεγράφη, that we cannot hesitate to accept it, although the compound verb does not occur elsewhere in this sense. WIESELER: "But as γράφειν is very frequently used of painting, there is little occasion for hesitation in extending the signification to the regularly formed compound, even though there were no further warrant for it. In the New Testament there are other ἅπαξ λεγόμενα, both in form and meaning, and as to the latter in this case we have also the voice of the Greek Fathers." To give προ a temporal reference [MEYER, ALFORD, and others. —R.] is less suited to the context, while the local signification corresponds with "before whose eyes." [The safest rendering is that of the E. V. LIGHTFOOT says of the verb: "This is the common word to describe all public notices and proclamations; hence: *programme;*" and this is, on the whole, preferable. WORDSWORTH finds here an allusion to the heathen practice of carrying amulets to guard against witchcraft, and to the Jewish custom of binding phylacteries between the eyes. "Who bewitched you, before whose eyes was written and bound up by me, as your frontlet of Faith, your spiritual Phylactery, *Christ crucified;* and who had, as I thought, been thus guarded by me against all the envious fascination of your spiritual enemies." This is ingenious, but it presses unduly the allusion in the word "bewitched."—R.]

Ver. 2. **This only would I learn of you.** —The unreasonableness of the apostasy is still further, and now, indeed, for the first time, expressly exposed. Not merely has the proclamation of Christ's death on the cross been made among them, but, through faith thereon, they have already attained to the receiving of the Holy Ghost,—and yet are you disposed to turn away from that which has already so attested itself? "*Vide, quam efficaciter tractat locum ab experientia.*" LUTHER. ["Learn" = obtain information, not used ironically in the stricter sense of "learning as a disciple," as LUTHER, BENGEL, and others.—R.] He refers them to the receiving of the Spirit through faith, as a proof that it is *Faith* which works justification. For the Spirit can only be given by God to the man whom He justifies (not whom He reprobates); the gift of the Spirit is a token of grace, not of wrath.—"Only," for this is the main question; by this—so far as the proof is to be sustained by facts—the thing is proved.—**The Spirit**, generally, not merely as the principle of miraculous gifts; "for Paul reminds the collective body of his readers of their receiving of the Spirit; not till ver. 5 are the δυνάμεις, as a species of the Spirit's workings, particularly cited." MEYER. —**By the hearing of faith.**—"Through the preaching concerning faith," is the right translation, although not quite congruous with the first member, which has a subjective reference. ['Ακοή, "hearing," has a passive sense always in the New Testament, *i. e.*, it refers to what is heard (see MEYER, ELLICOTT), "the preaching." —Πίστεως, "of faith," evidently an objective genitive. See LIGHTFOOT, WORDSWORTH, against both the above positions. Most modern expositors agree with Schmoller's next remark on the meaning of πίστις.—R.] Not = "through listening to the faith," since πίστις is never = *doctrina fidei*, but is only the subjective believing. "That in the first member of the double question their own strength, and, in the second, the power of the gospel (= of preaching) is made prominent, is quite natural, as it was through human strength that the Judaizing teachers would fain achieve that which was in truth only to be bestowed by the might of the gospel." WIESELER. That the "hearing" was *accepted* is understood, of course, since, from the "hearing," the gift of the Spirit proceeded (comp. Rom. x. 17); from preaching (*sc.* from believing) comes faith, and with it the Holy Ghost.

Ver. 3. **Having begun with the Spirit.** —You have made a beginning in the Christian life through the receiving of the Holy Ghost (ver. 2). Where a beginning is made, the next question is about the completion. Now—remarks Paul with cutting irony, bringing home the sense of this ἀνόητον of their conduct—such a completion there is also with you; but **with the flesh!** *i. e.*, according to your and your false teachers' fancy, this now is the true completion; yet, in truth, it is no completion, but the direct opposite of it, an annihilation of the work begun, because it is a completion with the flesh. "Flesh" is the opposite of "Spirit," and where the "flesh" reigns, the "Spirit" must

[* Coleridge paints this in his wierd lines:
"So deeply had she drunken in
That look, those shrunken, serpent eyes,
That all her features were resigned
To this sole image in her mind." *Lady Christabel.*—R.]

give way. "The flesh," of course, rises again to dominion, where there is a retrogression to the legal position; for therewith the Holy Ghost, which has been obtained only through faith, is necessarily lost; and where the "Spirit" is wanting, there is the "flesh." [MEYER:—"*Spirit* and *flesh* do not describe Christianity and Judaism themselves, but the specific vital agencies in each, the Holy Spirit, and the unspiritual, corporeally-physical human nature, leading contrary to God and to sin." The datives are both modal, indicating the manner in which the two actions took place.—R.] Ἐπιτελεῖν signifies not merely "to end," but "to complete," *consummare*. Ἐπιτελεῖσθε may be middle; if so, then it is simplest to take it as = do ye now bring to completion (*s. c.* the work begun) in the flesh. But ἐπιτελεῖσθαι does not occur in the New Testament in a middle sense, though it is thus used by profane writers. Hence, others take it as passive, *e. g.* MEYER = you are brought to completion, *sc.*, by the false teachers, inasmuch as they make of you people who lie under the dominion of the "flesh." This renders the reproach still sharper. So also LUTHER: instead of saying, *carne consummastis*, he suddenly turns the address, and says: *carne consummamini*, which strictly signifies: Will you then let the matter be carried through with you in the flesh, and thereby be made completely righteous?—The present tense denotes that the Galatians are now engaged in this ἐπιτελεῖσθαι. Comp. i. 6.—Νῦν = *cum magis magisque deberetis spirituales fieri relicta carne*. BENGEL.

Ver. 4. [**Are ye so foolish?**—"So very foolish are ye then?" οὕτως being emphatic.—R.] **Have you experienced** [or **suffered**] **so many things in vain?**—MEYER, in connection with his explanation of "being made perfect," interprets it as referring to the many burdensome performances connected with observing the law, which they had been obliged, by their new teachers, to undergo, in order, according to their notion, to become complete Christians. Having (according to MEYER) reminded them of these by ἐπιτελ, he then lays before them the uselessness of such things by the exclamation (not question): "So many things," *etc.*—This is evidently a strained interpretation, and it is, by no means, probable that this would have been described as a παθεῖν, or even that any such παθεῖν is to be presumed to have taken place. It is, therefore, to be understood, either of sufferings and persecutions, that they underwent, on account of their faith, or, since nothing is otherwise known of such, παθεῖν is to be taken as *vox media*, with the general signification, "to experience," here "to experience manifestations of Divine grace." [While the use of the aorist seems conclusive against the view of MEYER, it is more difficult to decide which of the other two interpretations is to be taken. Though nothing be known of such "sufferings," yet what more likely to occur? And if these arose from Judaizing influences, as was generally the case in Apostolic times, additional point is given to the Apostle's language. The other view, however, seems to give a greater logical unity to the passage, since vers. 3 and 5 both refer to "benefits." But was not Paul, who gloried in tribulation, likely to cite "sufferings" also as evidences of spiritual benefits? These considerations, in connection with the fact that there is no other instance in the New Testament of such a neutral meaning of πάσχειν, render it more prudent to follow the ancient versions and expositors, and adopt "suffered," instead of "experienced."—R.]

**If it be only** [or **really**] **in vain.**—That is, if rather you are not in much worse case, as notorious backsliding is apt to make the man worse than he was before. This addition has special force against the interpretation of ἐπάθετε as denoting persecutions, as with this it gives a scarcely intelligible sense: for the mitigating thought, that perhaps the Galatians will yet bethink themselves, so that the παθεῖν will not have been in vain, can hardly be in Paul's mind here, where he meditates only severe rebuke [?], while the explanation: "if only in vain!"="if it do not rather turn to your loss and greater condemnation," in its turn is not in keeping with the reference of παθεῖν to sufferings endured. For although, when sufferings have been endured for the faith, assistance rendered by God in bearing them may make the guilt of a subsequent apostasy greater, the sufferings themselves cannot well be said to increase it. [Notwithstanding the high authorities for this interpretation, which intensifies instead of softening "in vain," it does seem more probable that Paul here leaves "a loophole of doubt." If suffered is the thought implied, then as he recalled their sufferings, would be the very moment for a flash of doubt, or rather of hope, to enter. In this view it is better to render: "If it be really in vain," "I would fain doubt whether it can be, that all this was in vain."—R.]

VER. 5. **He therefore that ministereth to you the Spirit.**—With this Paul returns to the decisive question of ver. 2, but with some variation of the thought. He no longer sets the matter back into the past, but represents (no doubt designedly) the communication of the Spirit as something still going on, on the ground of faith. They were to recognize themselves as still experiencing this gracious operation of God. Besides this, he singles out and notes particularly the miraculous powers which God communicates through the same medium. [The word "ministereth" means "to supply bountifully." The ἐπί in the compound indicates the direction of the supply, not an enlargement of it. Δυνάμεις ἐν ὑμῖν may be rendered either, as E. V., "miracles among you," or better, "miraculous powers in you," *i. e.*, the peculiar powers there brought by the Spirit, which Paul everywhere alludes to, as observable in the Christians to whom he writes (1 Cor. xii. 28). MEYER decides for the latter from the analogy of 1 Cor. xii. 6, and it suits better the line of argument, which refers throughout to their personal experience.—R.] Moreover he now designates God expressly as the Bestower of the Spirit, doubtless, in order to bring home with special emphasis the truth that God Himself declared for the preaching of faith. For the Scripture proof which follows supports this idea. God declares for this among the Galatians because He has declared for it in His word, and He must ever agree with Himself, His acts with His testimony.

### DOCTRINAL AND ETHICAL.

1. *A Christian church without a "receiving the Spirit"* is not conceivable. It may lose the Spirit again (comp. σαρκὶ ἐπιτελεῖσθε), but it must once have received it. Paul, therefore, because he knows that the Galatians have been converted to Christ, assumes of course that they have received the Spirit. The primary reference is undoubtedly to the Holy Ghost only as a charism from God. The immediate reference is not to definite ethical effects on the hearts of recipients, though it is true that these cannot be wanting, if the Spirit received is *retained.* But as the Holy Ghost here is to be apprehended primarily as a charism (comp. ver. 5: ἐπιχορηγῶν), it is quite intelligible that what is given elsewhere as the condition of justification appears here as the condition of "receiving the Spirit," namely: Faith. "Receiving the Spirit" is, it is true, not immediately identical with "being justified," but is nevertheless an inseparable consequence. At all events no receiving of the Spirit" can take place without the "being justified," because the receiving of the Spirit is a token of Divine grace. Hence from the "receiving of the Spirit" "by the hearing of faith" it is concluded that the "being justified" comes by the same method. See also on this point the remarks on the previous section.

2. *The personal experience* of the operation of the preaching of the gospel is rightly (according to the example of Paul) regarded as a principal proof of the truth of the same. The proof lies more particularly in the receiving of the Holy Ghost: if I receive this through the preaching of the gospel, then this must doubtless be true, be the Divinely ordained way to salvation. Thereby does God declare Himself for this preaching; for the Holy Ghost is certainly a gift of God. A special application of the "witness of the Holy Ghost" which it might not be amiss to call the strict and original meaning of this doctrine.

3. *All evangelical preaching* should in its essence be nothing else than a portraying of Christ, the Crucified, before the eyes of men. It is by this that it leads them to the receiving of the Spirit.

### HOMILETICAL AND PRACTICAL.

Ver. 1. "O foolish Galatians."—In Starke:—It must not be supposed that this is such a phrase of contumely as "Fool," Matt. v. 22, but it is a sorrowful and earnest representation of their spiritual blindness. Christ also addresses His disciples with a similar term of rebuke. Luke xxiv. 25.—Severe reproofs, when they flow from a zeal for the wounded honor of God, and from love to our neighbor, and a desire to save him, are not wrong. The sharp tongue of good men is many times more wholesome than the friendly tongue and flattering words of the ungodly.—As to know Christ aright is the true wisdom, so on the other hand it is the greatest folly not to know Christ aright and not to cleave fast to Him.—[Luther:—A carnal man would interpret this to be a reviling, rather than a godly reprehension. Not so. So parents, of a fatherly and motherly affection, do sharply reprove and rebuke their children, which they would not bear if another should do it. Therefore one and the self-same word in the mouth of Paul is a benefit; but in the mouth of another it is a reproach.—R.]

Würt. Summ.:—False doctrine is, as it were, an enchantment, wherewith the devil bewitches men's hearts. For as through sorcery men's minds are blinded, so that they think they see something, when yet they see nothing, and nevertheless it is hard to fetch them off from the notion; even so, when the devil through false doctrine engages the hearts of men, he bewitches them so that they fancy they have the truth before them, when yet it is mere error and lies. Let us therefore the more diligently take heed to ourselves, that we be not taken in and infected with doctrine; let us the more diligently cleave to God's word, and moreover pray heartily with David, Ps. cxix. 18, 37.—[What spell is this that holds so many eyes, before which Jesus Christ has been set forth so plainly as the crucified One, who dies not "without cause!"—R.]

"Jesus Christ evidently set forth before your eyes, crucified."—Starke:—By this way of speaking is indicated the clearness of the evangelical doctrine of the cross of Christ. In the Old Testament Christ was portrayed to the Jews under many images and types, as in the type of the high priest, of the paschal lamb, *etc.;* but in the New Testament, He was, through the preaching of the gospel, without any shadows such as these, clearly placed before men's eyes, inasmuch as His suffering, shame, satisfaction on the cross, were most clearly published and proclaimed. That was, as it were, the programme which the Apostles *placarded* in all places whither they came.—Spener:—The best church-paintings are plain instructions concerning Divine truth; thereby can a matter be brought as plainly, and more plainly into the hearts of the hearers, than by the skilfullest painter of them all, yea, those things also which no painter can set forth. Actual paintings in the church are to be by no means utterly rejected, they have their use as memorials; but the other painting of doctrine must be joined therewith, and Christ must be portrayed in the heart, else outward paintings, if men are to learn only by gazing upon them, are a lifeless affair.—[Calvin:—Paul intimates that the actual sight of Christ's death could not have affected them more powerfully than his preaching. Such a representation could not have been made by any eloquence, or by enticing words of man's wisdom. When the Church has painters such as this, she no longer needs the dead images of wood and stone, she no longer requires pictures. Such things come, when pastors become dumb.—R.]

Ver. 2. "Was it by the works of the law that ye received the Spirit?"—Hedinger:—A definite, keenly importunate question, with an "either—or," from which there is no escape, appealing to actual experiences, in which no debate is possible,—well fitted to dispel the sorcery (ver. 1) of the false teaching.—A hint as to the right way of convincing and freeing misguided souls out of such enchantment.—Law quickens not, but enjoins, commands, threatens and terrifies, it is true, yet without life. Bondage, constraint; good appearances enough, hypocrisy enough; carefully contrived clockwork, but mute wheels, without soul. Of such are many, that are praised as Christians. Hourglasses are they, that punctually show the time, but where is there Spirit, Heaven, marks of grace? On that hangs all.—SPENER:—The only means of receiving the Holy Ghost, is the preaching of the gospel, as being a word of the Spirit. Where this is heard, and its energy not resisted, the Holy Ghost comes into the soul, not only to work, but also to dwell therein.—STARKE:—Whatever doctrine the Holy Ghost brings to man, assuring him of Divine grace, and impelling him to all good, that is the true saving doctrine.

Ver. 3. It is not enough to have begun well, the matter must also be carried through. The beginning and the continuing of our salvation must be after one way, and we must not desire to be perfected otherwise than we have begun, else is it folly to us.—SPENER:—That is a doctrine to be abhorred, which to be sure ascribes the beginning of salvation to faith and so to the Spirit, but afterwards feigns that the rest must be accomplished and completed with works.

Ver. 5. STARKE:—It is God alone who gives the Holy Ghost. The Apostles also imparted it through their preaching and imposition of hands, but they were only instruments of God. Now-a-days teachers and preachers impart the Holy Ghost, so far as they preach the Word, which in itself has power, and has the Holy Ghost with it.—It is a truly Divine property of the gospel that God aforetime accompanied it with the most excellent miracles. No one who passed over to Judaism, received from God the power of working miracles, but those did who turned from Judaism to Christianity.—Hast thou, O man, the Holy Ghost and His energy in too small measure? Seek the cause in thyself, in that thou usest not the stated means aright.—SPENER:—Where the Holy Ghost is, there He works, although not always outward miracles, yet in the conversion and renewal of men themselves, which is a greater miracle than to make the sick well.

On vers. 1–5. To portray Jesus Christ before men's eyes as the Crucified is the soul of all preaching of the gospel: 1. This it *must* do, because in the cross of Christ alone salvation is found, and it must do it unweariedly and explicitly, with all earnestness, all fidelity, and all zeal. 2. But more it *cannot* do; the inscribing on the heart it must leave to God; although indeed it must ever admonish of the necessity of this, and exhort men to prove whether this has taken place (must warn against dead faith).—Jesus Christ has been portrayed before your eyes as the Crucified; is He also portrayed in your hearts?—Whoever seeks his salvation elsewhere than in Christ, the Crucified, 1) lacks understanding, for he leaves the living spring, which God Himself has opened for us, and hews out for himself broken cisterns; 2) is entangled in an enchantment, bewitched by the deceiving spirit of self-righteousness.—Who hath bewitched you? A question which must be sounded forth in many a congregation; for 1) Christ, the Crucified, is portrayed before their eyes, and yet 2) there is such an utter neglect to seek salvation in Him.—How is the Holy Ghost obtained? 1. Not from works of the law, this follows from the nature of the law, but 2. through faith in the gospel—simply because it is the good news of Christ, the Crucified.

Faith in Jesus Christ the true way to salvation; for through it alone is the Holy Spirit received, not through the works of the law.—How have you received the Spirit? A question to strengthen and warn those who are in danger of embracing the righteousness of works.—Faith in Christ Jesus, 1) it is true in itself, not yet a proof that a man has received the Spirit, for there is also a dead faith; 2) but yet the only way to receive Him.—The preaching of faith the way to the receiving of the Spirit. Therewith is condemned all fanaticism with which, indeed, a righteousness of works of some kind or other is commonly joined.—It is God who bestows the Spirit, but only through the preaching of faith.—The Holy Ghost is the true heavenly gift.—Where God gives the Spirit, He also gives power (Spirit and power always conjoined).—To begin in the Spirit, to end in the flesh, is the most preposterous folly, and yet how frequent.—Hast thou begun in the Spirit? Continue in like manner, and end in the Spirit!

[Christ only, Christ plainly, Christ crucified! the Gospel we preach.—That which is "so foolish" is yet so natural.—Take heed that what God blessed to your spiritual profit, be not despised by you. What means He has honored with His Spirit, do not dishonor by your treatment of them.—Is it indeed in vain? All past sufferings for the Gospel's sake? Aye, and worse than in vain. These have no power to save. Christ's sufferings alone can save.—Our works do not earn God's works.—The Gospel, "the hearing of faith," still has the "witness of the Spirit," is still the δύναμις of God, by which He works δυνάμεις.—R.]

## B. Doctrinal Exposition

CHAPTER III. 6—IV. 7.

### 1. Salvation is not to be attained by works of the law, but through faith alone.

(CHAP. iii. 6–18).

#### a. Demonstration from Scripture.

(VERS. 6–14.)

6 Even as Abraham believed God, and it was accounted to him for righteousness.
7 Know ye therefore that they which are of faith, the same are the children [sons] of
8 Abraham. And [Moreover] the Scripture, foreseeing that God would justify [or justifieth][1] the heathen [Gentiles] through faith, preached before the gospel [proclaimed beforehand the glad tidings][2] unto Abraham, *saying,* In thee shall all nations be
9 blessed.[3] So then they which be [who are] of faith are blessed with [together with
10 the][4] faithful Abraham. For as many as are of the works of the law are under the [or a] curse: for it is written,[5] Cursed *is* every one that continueth not in all things
11 which are written in the book of the law to do them. But that no man is justified by the law [in the law no man is justified][6] in the sight of God, *it is* evident: for,
12 The just shall live by faith. And [Now][7] the law is not of faith: but, The man
13 [He][8] that doeth [or has done] them shall live in them. Christ hath [omit hath][9] redeemed us from the curse of the law, being made [having become][10] a curse for
14 us; for [as][11] it is written, Cursed *is* every one that hangeth on a tree: That the blessing of Abraham might come on [unto][12] the Gentiles through [ἐν, in] Jesus Christ [Christ Jesus];[13] that we might receive the promise of the Spirit through faith.

1 Ver. 8.—[Δικαιοῖ, present—Ellicott calls it the "ethical present." "God justifieth," this is His one way (Alford).—R.]

2 Ver. 8.—[Since "gospel" has a distinct meaning now, it is perhaps better to take the more etymological phrase in rendering προευηγγελίσατο. Schmoller: "*Gab die Verheissung.*"—R.]

3 Ver. 8.—Elz. has εὐλογηθήσονται instead of ἐνευλογηθήσονται against decisive authorities.

4 Ver. 9.—["Together with" is more distinct than "with." The article of the Greek is retained to emphasize "faithful."—R.]

5 Ver. 10.—According to the best MSS. ὅτι should be inserted before ἐπικατάρατος. [The generally received reading does not affect the English form, since ὅτι is here a mere quotation mark.—R.]

6 Ver. 11.—[Since ἐν νόμῳ must be rendered "in the law;" to avoid the too close proximity with "in the sight of," it is better to retain the Greek order, which is emphatic also.—R.]

7 Ver. 12.—[Δέ "logical, introducing the minor proposition" (Alford). "Now" is perhaps better than "but."—R.]

8 Ver. 12.—After αὐτά, Elz. reads ἄνθρωπος against decisive authorities.

9 Ver. 13.—[The aorist ἐξηγόρασεν is historical, hence the simple past is better.—In ver. 12, ποιήσας, aorist participle, should be rendered "hath done" to bring out its proper force.—R.]

10 Ver. 13.—[Γενόμενος, "becoming," but as it explains the manner of the past act "redeemed," "having become" is more accurate. "By becoming" would be still more forcible.—R.]

11 Ver. 13.—Lachmann and Tischendorf, following weighty authorities, read: ὅτι γέγραπται instead of γέγραπται γάρ. [So Meyer and modern English editors. ℵ. has γέγ. γάρ.—R.]

12 Ver. 14.—[Εἰς, "unto." The clause were perhaps better read in this order: "That unto the Gentiles the blessing of Abraham might come in Christ Jesus" (so Ellicott).—R.]

13 Ver. 14.—[Χριστῷ Ἰησοῦ is the reading of most MSS. (ℵ. B. Ἰησοῦ Χριστῷ), and is adopted by most modern editors.—R.]

### EXEGETICAL AND CRITICAL.

Ver. 6. **Even as Abraham believed God.**—This stands in immediate connection with the preceding, and gives the answer to the question in ver. 5, by an affirmation of the second part of it (for Paul views the gift of the Spirit previously mentioned as a proof of justification, and can therefore answer the question in ver. 5 with the statement in ver. 6). Through the preaching of faith God bestows the Spirit of faith, and thereby justifies, even as Abraham attained to justification in the same way. But inasmuch as Paul in going on still keeps Abraham in view, we may, and ought to begin here a new section. This verse does not contain a citation proper, but Paul gives what is contained in Gen. xv. 6 respecting Abraham, as his own immediate declaration. (Comp. Rom. iv. 3.) That **accounted to him**

**for righteousness** is understood by Paul entirely in the sense of "being justified" needs no demonstration.*

Ver. 7. Here, in the first place, he only draws from it the conclusion, that a man by faith becomes a son of Abraham. (Οἱ ἐκ πίστεως, "the spiritual character represented under the form of the causal relation," those that are born of faith, have as it were their nature from it. EWALD explains it somewhat differently: those whose efforts and achievements proceed from faith, as the deepest, and at the same time highest power.) This conclusion of course rests on the presupposition that faith was an essential trait in Abraham's character, and is directed against the Judaizers, who believe that they can prove themselves genuine children of Abraham by works of the law. [The older commentators took γινώσκετε as indicative; "ye know then;" modern ones generally consider it an imperative: **Know ye therefore**.—So MEYER, DE WETTE, ELLICOTT, WORDSWORTH, also Syriac, Vulgate. ELLICOTT: "The imperative is not only more animated, but more logically correct, for the declaration in the verse is really one of the points which the Apostle is laboring to prove." He contends that ἄρα is most properly joined with the imperative. ALFORD and LIGHTFOOT adopt the other view, the latter suggesting that the verb means "to perceive" rather than "to know," which makes the indicative more suitable. There is not necessarily any "argumentative irony" (ALFORD) here. On the whole the imperative seems preferable.—R.]

Paul has made reference to Abraham as the type of justifying faith; he does not, however, content himself with that, but, going deeper, he finds still more striking proof in the significance of Abraham as the bringer of blessing for all the heathen. He dwells the longer on the Old Testament because it was to this that the false teachers naturally appealed against Paul, and by their appeals to it imposed on the Galatians. So he on the other hand seeks to establish his doctrine from the Old Testament, simply by going more deeply into it. [LIGHTFOOT: "The passage vers. 6-9 was omitted in Marcion's recension of the Epistle, as repugnant to his leading principle of the antagonism between the Old and New Testaments."—R.]

Ver. 8. **Moreover the Scripture foreseeing.**—Δέ is simply continuative. [Neither "and" nor "but" gives the precise force.—R.] What God has promised is ascribed to the Scripture itself, not simply because it is related in the Scripture, but because the Scripture, as inspired by God, is conceived as the organ of the Spirit of God. The same then is true of God's foreknowledge, from which the promise proceeded. Yet Paul has not gained from some other source a knowledge of the fact that the Scripture foresaw, and in this foresight gave the promise (WIESELER), but he draws the conclusion as to the "foreseeing" simply from the promise itself: because it is promised, that "all nations shall be blessed in Abraham," the "justifying of the Gentiles through faith" must also have been predetermined. Why, he then explains in what follows.—[ELLICOTT calls δικαιοῖ an *ethical present*, with significant reference to the eternal and immutable counsels of God. ALFORD: "Present, not merely because the time foreseen was regarded as present, not present as respected the time of writing, but because it was God's *one* way of justification—He never justified in any other way—so that it is the normal present: 'He is a God that justifieth' through faith."—R.] Paul cites as proof Gen. xii. 1-3; xviii. 18. The chief emphasis lies upon "shall be blessed," which is therefore placed first in the Greek; yet only so far as it is a "being blessed in Abraham." The sense is: The blessing bestowed upon thee includes a blessing hereafter to come upon all the Gentiles (ἔθνη here of course in the pregnant sense=Gentiles). From this the conclusion is drawn in

Ver. 9. **So then they which be of faith.**—"So then"= agreeably to the promise in ver. 8. Ver. 9 is nothing else than an exposition of the promise cited in ver. 8. In Abraham, it was promised, all the heathen are to be blessed, a promise which has the sense indicated above. Now, he was the *believing one*, and it was (as follows from ver. 6) on account of his faith that he received the promise of blessing. *Therefore* it is, of course, *believers* that are partakers of the blessing promised to him, it is they who are his children, and it is to them therefore that the promise of blessing holds good.—**Are blessed with [together with the] faithful Abraham.**—In this sentence the ἐν is dropped, for the sense is: because the "being blessed in him," is promised to all the heathen, therefore "they which be of faith" (the heathen, if they are "of faith") are blessed *with* him, that is, primarily, in like manner as he; but still further: it expresses the sameness of the lot into which they entered with him, and through this one lot they entered into inner communion with him.—[The preposition shows their community with him in the blessing; the adjective "faithful" renders prominent that point of ethical character in which they must resemble each other, in order to partake of the same blessing. (So MEYER, ALFORD.)—R.] "Are blessed."—As to the meaning of this, there is little occasion for dispute. If we look at the original passage, this is, of course, to be understood quite generally, as is implied in the idea of Blessing=Manifestation of Divine Favor. This again is more specially defined in different ways, and so here; so far as concerns the blessing received by Abraham himself: "together with the faithful Abraham," the primary meaning is that he should obtain a posterity, and as concerns the blessing of the Gentiles in Abraham, the passage is justly regarded as a

* [CALVIN thus refers to "the idle cavillings of certain persons who evade Paul's reasoning. Moses, they tell us, gives the name of righteousness to goodness; and so means nothing more than that Abraham was reckoned a good man because he believed God. Giddy minds of this description, raised up in our time by Satan, endeavor, by indirect slanders, to undermine the certainty of Scripture. Paul knew that Moses was not there giving lessons to boys in grammar, but was speaking of a decision which God had pronounced; and very properly viewed the word *righteousness* in a theological sense. For it is not in that sense in which goodness is mentioned with approbation among men, that we are accounted righteous in the sight of God, but only where we render perfect obedience to the law. Righteousness is contrasted with the transgression of the law, even in its smallest point; and because we have it not of ourselves, it is freely given to us by God."—R.]

Messianic promise in the wider sense=the Gentiles shall have part in the salvation brought by the Messiah, in the salvation that proceeds from one who is Abraham's offspring. The latter is the sense here. *Which* side of this Messianic salvation, however, Paul has in mind, is to be made out solely from the connection, most simply from what is put in opposition to it, namely, to be "under the curse," and, to that again, the simple antithesis is "justified" (ver. 11). Paul of course views "blessed" and "justified" as essentially correlative, coincident ideas: and hence in ver. 8 the one, namely, "justified," is inferred from the other, "blessed." Only, as is easily understood, "blessed" still remains the more general idea; what kind of blessing is meant must be shown by the context. Somewhat more restricted, again, than "justification," is "receiving the Spirit," which, however, is not only connected with the "justification," but is really the true "blessing," on which account Paul, starting from "receiving the Spirit" in the beginning of this chapter, returns to it again in ver. 14.—The ground of the promise in ver. 8, and also of the statement expository of it in ver. 9, is given in ver. 10. A blessing to be bestowed upon the Gentiles in Abraham, and therefore one resting upon faith, is promised; such a one is, and only such a one *can* be, contemplated.

Ver. 10. **For as many as are of the works of the law, are under a curse.**—The force of this is: it must be those "of faith" who are blessed; for those who busy themselves with "works of the law" (the only alternative possible, if not "of faith") cannot be blessed; since these are under the curse, and therefore a bestowal of blessing cannot avail for them. [This negative argument (vers. 10, 12,) strengthens the position taken in the preceding verses, and has an immediate application to the Galatian errors, to which however no allusion is made in this strictly argumentative passage.—R.] "Of the works of the law;" the form is the same as in the antithetical expression, "of faith," but more fully stated.—**Cursed is every one,** *etc.*—Deut. xvii. 26, freely quoted from the LXX. The passage proves what it is cited to prove, viz., that "as many as are of the law are under the curse," provided a non-continuance can be established. This shows that the reference here is to ethical requirements, and not merely to ritualistic ones; thus confirming the view of "works of the law," given in chap. ii. At the same time the passage shows that the ground of "a man is not justified by the works of the law," is that those who "are of the works of the law are under the curse;" the non-justification has then of course its ground, not in the externality of the law, for that would not of necessity involve a curse, but in our not keeping it.

Ver. 11. **But that in the law no man is justified,** *etc.*—Those who are of the works of the law are under the curse. This includes not being justified, but only *implicite*. Paul now states it expressly, in order to support it by declarations of Scripture, as he previously did the positive side. The course of thought might, perhaps, be still more accurately defined as follows: Cursed, it has been declared, is every one that continueth not in all things; but, on the other hand, it might be said, such as entirely fulfil the law will be blest. But, remarks Paul, that is excluded by the tenor of the two Scripture passages about to be cited, for according to them man ζήσεται ἐκ πίστεως, but the law is in no wise ἐκ πίστεως, therefore no one is justified ἐν νόμῳ; the thought that "in the law" justification is possible, is to be entirely put aside.—**In the sight of God.**—Παρὰ θεῷ defines more particularly the idea of "justified," and sets it in antithesis to any (justifying) human judgment. The proof that "in the law no man is justified," Paul derives from two Scripture passages. According to the one (Hab. ii. 4) "to live," results from "faith," according to the other (Lev. xviii. 5) the law does not take note of faith, but of doing; through doing, fulfilling the law, a man has life.—This, of course, has demonstrative force, for "no man is justified" only on the presupposition that this doing (in the second passage) remains only a requirement, and does not actually take place, and that it is with the knowledge of this state of things that the prophet represents faith as the condition of life.—**The just shall live by faith.**—אֱמוּנָה in the original has, rightly explained, not the signification "faithfulness," but as Paul translates it, "Trust, Faith." [The first is undoubtedly the primary meaning of the Hebrew word, but the other is implied in it. It is noteworthy that this passage is one of the two in the Old Testament, where the word "faith" is used in the E. V. See a very suggestive note in LIGHTFOOT, p. 152.—R.]—יִחְיֶה he then naturally understands, agreeably to the New Testament knowledge of salvation, in the higher sense of the Messianic life, that which renders its consummation in eternal life. Ἐκ πίστεως must be joined as in the original with ζήσεται, and not with ὁ δίκαιος. WIESELER justly remarks: In proof of the connection ὁ δίκαιος ἐκ πίστεως, it is alleged that the origin of justification was to be shown, not that of salvation or life. It must not be forgotten, however, that according to the connection the emphasis does not rest upon δικαιοῦσθαι in itself, but upon the fact that this results ἐκ πίστεως; moreover that Paul is not here using his own words, in which case instead of ἐκ πίστεως ζήσεται he would undoubtedly have chosen another term of expression, such as ἐκ πίστεως δικαιοῦσθαι, but that he had to choose from the actually existing passages which treated of the central significance of faith. Whoever examines these more particularly will not be able to deny that the choice made is a happy one. For what does ἐκ πίστεως ζήσεται signify, but that Faith is the fundamental condition through which a man becomes well-pleasing to God, and partaker of the gracious gift of life? In this formula, therefore, the δικαιοῦσθαι ἐκ πίστεως, or the statement that one is declared righteous or well-pleasing to God, in consequence of faith, is in truth included. Δίκαιος, on the other hand, signifies the righteous or devout man, and has here nothing more than an etymological connection with δικαιοῦσθαι. That ἐκ πίστεως is joined by Paul in the Galatians with ζήσεται, appears, moreover, from its antithesis, ζήσεται ἐν αὐτοῖς: "he will live through the commandments." [It is difficult to decide this question of connection; either would be grammatical, both are sustained by high authorities. WINER, DE WETTE, EWALD, ELLICOTT agree with WIESELER; while BENGEL, PAREUS, MEYER, ALFORD, and very many others connect "by faith" with "the just." The former conforms better with the Hebrew; the latter with the general course of Paul's thoughts here and elsewhere. The former is safer, the latter more pointed, but from either the same truth would be deduced.—R.]

Ver. 12. **Now the law is not of faith.**—[Δέ, logical, introducing the minor proposition: "The just shall live by faith." "Now the law is not of faith" (so MEYER).—R.] "The law is not an institution whose nature is determined by faith." WIESELER. [LIGHTFOOT: 'Faith is not the starting-point of the law. The law does not take faith as its fundamental principle. On the other hand, it rigidly enforces the performance of all its enactments.'—**Has done them.**—Actual and entire performance of all requirements. Doing, not believing.—R.]

Ver. 13. **Christ redeemed us from the curse of the law.**—"The asyndeton makes the contrast more energetic."—MEYER. ["Redeemed." WORDSWORTH: "The aorist is important to be observed, as intimating that the Redemption was effected by *one act, i. e.*, by the shedding of His blood, paid as the price of our ransom, when He became a curse for us by dying on the *cross*."—R.] That Paul here proceeds to speak of the redemption from the curse, and therefore presupposes the latter as existing, is of easy explanation. In ver. 10 it had been declared that "as many as of the works of the law are under a curse;" and, on the other hand, it needed no demonstration that all those who had the "law," and as yet nothing else, that is, the Jews, are "of the works of the law" and therefore "are under a curse." "Us," therefore, naturally refers primarily to the Jews, for these, who alone had the "law," alone stood under the "curse of the law." Comp. also, particularly, chap. iv. 5: "to redeem them that were under the law." WIESELER also justly remarks, that particularly in the doctrinal exposition in the Galatians, Paul loves, from easily intelligible reasons, to include himself with the Jewish people, in the first person. Yet I would not be disposed wholly to reject the more general sense of ἡμᾶς. It is true, it was primarily only the Jews who stood under the curse of the law; but Paul here may be thinking not only of the actual, but also of the ideal or possible being under it; that is, through Christ the true way to justification by faith in Him is opened to all, it could not therefore be any longer demanded of the Gentiles (and they could not be tempted) to concern themselves with "the works of the law," through which they also would have come under the curse of the law. Ἔθνη, ver. 14, need not be taken as the direct antithesis of this; doubtless it has the emphasis, and on this account stands first, but the ἔθνη may have been made particularly prominent, only because the fulfilment of the promise given in relation to *them* has become possible through the atoning death of Christ, and in the blessing of the *Gentiles* the reality and effect of the death of Christ is chiefly manifest. But that the effect of this extends of course to the Jews, also is added in the clause introduced by ἵνα. In this clause at least MEYER, WIESELER, and others, understand the first person plural generally, of Jews and Gentiles. MEYER, limiting ἡμᾶς, ver. 13, to the Jews, understands the somewhat difficult connection of vers. 13 and 14 peculiarly, almost too artificially: as long as the curse of the law stood in force, and the Jews therefore were unredeemed, the Gentiles could not become partakers of that blessing; for it was involved in the preëminence which, according to the Divine plan of redemption was bestowed on the Jews, that salvation should proceed from them to the Gentiles. When therefore Christ through His atoning death freed *the Jews* from the curse of their law, God must necessarily have had the design therewith, of imparting to *the Gentiles* the promised justification, and that not in any such way as through the law, but in Christ Jesus, through whom already redemption from the curse of the law had been effected for the Jews. More simple, and more congruous also with the interpretation of ἡμᾶς in the general sense, is USTERI'S explanation: Christ has, by His vicarious death, redeemed us from the curse of the law, in order that (if now henceforth justification is attained through faith) the Gentiles may become partakers of the blessing of Abraham, as from now henceforth there is required for justification a condition possible for all, namely, Faith. The simplest and best exposition of "redeemed from the curse of the law" is MEYER'S: "The law is personified as a potentate, who had subjected those dependent upon him to his curse; but from this constraint of the curse, out of which they would not else have come, has Christ redeemed them, and that by His having procured for them, through His *mors satisfactoria*, the forgiveness of sins (Eph. i. 7; Col. i. 14; Rom. iii. 24 *et al.*), so that now the curse of the law had no more relation to them (objectively—to which must then be added—and nothing else can be added—'faith,' in order that this redemption may also be subjectively realized.)

**Having become a curse for us.**—The *mode* of the redemption is here expressed, namely, by His crucifixion, in which he was set forth as burdened with the Divine ὀργή. The *emphasis* therefore rests on the word κατάρα, which on this account is attracted to the end, and the use of which is immediately to be justified by a declaration of Scripture. The abstract instead of the concrete is chosen, in order to represent with more of vigorous precision the adequacy of the satisfaction which Christ has rendered (comp. the previous ἐκ κατάρας), and it stands *without the article*, because the thought is not, that Christ suffered the *definite*, just named curse of the *law*, to which the subjects of the law are exposed, but in a general sense, that He became an accursed one; it is meant to express not *what* curse he became, but *that* He became a curse (the *that* moreover appears from the following Scripture passage).—Ὑπὲρ ἡμῶν: "ὑπέρ in all places where the discourse is of the atoning death not=instead of, but=in behalf of. The satisfaction, which Christ rendered, was rendered in our behalf; that it was vicarious is implied in the nature of the act itself, not in the preposition. The curse of the law would have had to be realized in that all who did not completely satisfy the law (and this no one could), would have been compelled to endure the execution of the Divine ὀργή against them; but for their deliverance from this sentence Christ with His death has intervened, inasmuch as He died as *Accursed*, whereby, as through a ransom, that damnatory relation of the law was dissolved." See the DOCTRINAL NOTES below.

**As it is written, Cursed is every one,** *etc.* —Scriptural justification of the declaration just made respecting Christ, "having become a curse:" from Deut. xxi. 23, cited freely from the LXX. "The original passage has reference to persons stoned, and then far greater ignominy, publicly hung up on a (probably cruciform) stake, who, however, must not be left to hang over night, because such accursed ones would else have defiled the holy land. Deut. xxi. 23; Num. xxv. 4; Joshua x. 26, 27; 2 Sam. iv. 12. And in that Christ also when executed hung upon a stake, the epithet ἐπικατάρατος applies also to Him." MEYER. [WORDSWORTH notes a remarkable conformity of the prophetical reference to Christ in the passage here cited. The body must be taken down, but "if He had been crucified on some ordinary day, not on the day before that High Day, the Jews would have been as eager that He should remain on the cross as they were then earnest that He should be taken down. Thus, in crucifying Him, and taking Him down from the cross, they proved unconsciously that He whom they crucified is the Messiah, and that it was He who, bearing the curse of the law, has taken away that curse from all who believe."—R.] "Therefore, even if in the original passage crucifixion proper is not meant (which was not an ancient Israelitish punishment), yet that which particularly made both kinds of punishment a curse, the hanging and exposure on the wood was common to them. Ξύλον, used of the wood of the cross, undoubtedly on account of the עֵץ of the Old Testament passage, is found also Acts v. 30; x. 39; xiii. 29; 1 Pet. ii. 24." WIESELER. [ELLICOTT: "It is interesting to notice that the dead body was not hanged by the neck, but *by the hands*, and not on a tree, but on a piece of wood."—R.]

Ver. 14. **That unto the Gentiles might come.**—Respecting the connection see above on ver. 13.—**The blessing of Abraham** = the blessing before announced to Abraham.—**In Christ Jesus.**—"In Christ (in His expiatory death) the bestowal of the blessing has its ground. The following διὰ τῆς πίστεως expresses the matter from the point of view of the subjective medium, while ἐν Χριστῷ sets forth the objective fact." MEYER.—**That we might receive the promise of the Spirit.**—"Climatically parallel to the first clause of intention." MEYER. The first person, "that we might receive," applies undoubtedly to Christians generally, Jews or Gentiles.—"Receive the promise of the Spirit"=to receive the promised Spirit. [ELLICOTT: "Not merely the promised Spirit, but the realization of the promise of the Spirit." This is to be preferred.—R.] Is this to be taken as a nearer definition of the "blessing of Abraham?" It is not immediately identical with this as (see on ver. 9) the "blessing" (in itself quite general) in the connection means primarily the "justification." However not only does the receiving of the Spirit stand in immediate connection, both of thought and fact, with the justification, but although in "the promise of the Spirit," the primary reference is to such a promise as that in Joel iii. [E. V.], yet this again stands, at least in the history of salvation, in connection with the promise given to Abraham in reference to the heathen, so that the two promises are combined on satisfactory grounds in this relation also. In any case Paul is looking back to the beginning of ver. 2. [LIGHTFOOT: 'The law, the greater barrier which excluded the Gentiles, is done away in Christ. By its removal the Gentiles are put on a level with the Jews; and thus united, they both gain access through the Spirit to the Father.' Comp. Eph. ii. 14–18. ELLICOTT: "After a wondrous chain of arguments, expressed with equal force, brevity and profundity, the Apostle comes back to the subject of ver. 2; the gift of the Holy Ghost came through faith in Jesus Christ."—R.]

### DOCTRINAL AND ETHICAL.

1. *Abraham's justification on the ground of his faith* (or rather the direct declaration of the Scripture respecting it), is adduced by Paul as an argument for Justification on the ground of Faith here, and particularly, as is known, in Romans iv. also. The faith in Christ must therefore be regarded by Paul as one in kind with that of Abraham. But it by no means follows from this, as WIESELER justly remarks, that Abraham himself already believed on the Messiah. "For in the Old Testament history of Abraham the idea of the Messiah is nowhere mentioned, often as there was occasion for it, but only the idea of a salvation and blessing coming from Abraham to all nations, the first traces of a universal kingdom of God, to which however the Divine Head is yet lacking. In the New Testament also the idea of the Messiah is nowhere attributed to Abraham. The passage John viii. 5, 6, hardly signifies any thing else than that Abraham, in the theophanies, *etc.*, experienced by him, already beheld the preëxisting Christ." Yet Paul, with entire justice, places the Christian faith in parallelism with that of Abraham; for the one, as well as the other, was essentially a trustful laying hold of a promise coming from Divine grace, as to which, moreover, WIESELER points out that with Abraham, the promised heir of his body came into view at the same time as the future bearer of the collective blessing promised to Abraham, and faith on the promise respecting Him was therefore faith also on the kingdom of God originating in his posterity. It by no means follows from this, that then the *matter* [*Inhalt*] of the Christian and of the Abrahamic faith would be a different one, and that faith would justify on account of its subjective character, while yet it justifies only on account of its matter and object. In the promise given by Divine grace, the faith of the Christian, as of Abraham, has its common matter. For such a promise the Christian lays hold of in faith on Christ, as much as Abraham did in his faith. The real ground of justification in both cases is therefore the grace of God, which gives man something that he could not of himself attain to, and on natural conditions could not even expect, and faith is, as that which nevertheless confi-

dently lays hold of this grace, only the *conditio sine qua non.*—It is very true, this grace of God itself has a different matter with Christians and with Abraham; with Christians its matter is essentially the reconciliation accomplished in Christ, and the forgiveness of sin implied therein, with Abraham it is what has just been mentioned—a distinction which is conditioned simply by the course of the economy of salvation, and which does not prejudice Paul's parallelizing of the two; for Paul speaks here—comp. v. 7, 8, 9—quite generally of πίστις, has in view, therefore what constitutes its generic nature.—Agreeably to this the definite matter of the δικαιοῦσθαι in the two cases is different, *i. e.*, the generic unity is the becoming acceptable to God and accordingly being blessed by Him, and this community of character fully justifies this parallelizing also. But with Christians this general idea is still further defined as follows: to be delivered from the divine wrath incurred by their sins, and to become partakers of the forgiveness of sins. A distinction, to this extent at least, between the δικαιοῦσθαι of Abraham and that of Christians, must be conceded even by those who assume the Messiah to have been the object of faith in the case of Abraham also. For even on this assumption, it will not be alleged that "accounted to him for righteousness" in the case of Abraham has exactly the sense: his sins were forgiven him. This is not treated of in any way in this passage.—That this appeal to Abraham's faith is in no respect an arbitrary laying hold of a single chance passage, that accords with the line of argument, is clear. For, allowing that this judgment respecting the faith of Abraham is found only here, yet confessedly faith in God's gracious promise was that which specifically characterized Abraham, was precisely that which made him the child of God, nay, the Friend of God, and so of course acceptable to God. This would be irrefragably established by the history of his life, even if we had not this direct declaration, Gen. xv. 6.—With perfect justice therefore Paul can designate those who are "of faith" as Abraham's sons. A strong, crushing expression against the Jewish national pride, corresponding to the words of John the Baptist, Matt. iii. 9, and of Jesus Himself, John viii. 39—and yet not in conflict with the truth that according to the Divine purpose the Jewish nation as such, agreeably to its natural descent from Abraham, was the chosen nation. For this people itself, as a whole, was meant to be of the faith of its ancestor, in order to be a true people of God; and the Divine judgment made, we know, a perpetual distinction among the mass of the people between such as were "of faithful Abraham" = were his legitimate [*i. e.*, spiritually legitimate.—R.] children, and such as were not.*

2. *The Scripture is the exposition of a Divine plan of salvation*, connected and of uniform tenor throughout, which has had its definite historical unfolding. In it therefore the earlier has respect to the later, the first to the last; a word of God, belonging to the beginning, is already shaped in view of the consummation; to this is added, that the God who beholds at once the beginning and the end, ideally anticipates with direct words of promise the future development of His counsel of salvation.—To recognize even in the germ the development, requires, doubtless, an apprehension intimately conversant with Scriptural truth, an eye illumined by the Spirit.

3. *The curse of the law.* As the blessing comes from God, as a revelation of His favor and grace (in gifts), so also the curse, as a revelation of His wrath (in judgments, which concentrate themselves in the κατάκριμα of death). In that this revelation of wrath is a consequence of the non-fulfilment of the *law*, the curse is called "the curse of the law," ver. 13 (under which therefore, in the first place, only the Jews stood, as being alone those who hold to the law, but under which of course all would come, who are "of the works of the law"). More precisely: a man comes under this "curse," is under bonds to it, and held prisoner by it, if he is "of the works of the law" (ver. 10), that is, performs indeed *single* works, but nothing more, and yet believes himself thereby to have satisfied the law, which is in no wise the case (see above on "works of the law" in the preceding section).

4. *Christ a curse for us.* To avert this curse of God and to bring His blessing upon all men, Christ has become "a curse for us." Here we stand in presence of the deepest mystery of atonement; we may not, in order to make it more comprehensible, weaken the fact, but must take the words even here, as they say and sound, without artifices of interpretation. Since Christ has freed us from our curse, by having become a curse for us, then, if our redemption from the curse is not to be an illusion, but something real, He became also really *the bearer of the Divine curse*, He has borne the Divine ὀργή passively, has felt it, and also actively has sustained it. And this has come to pass by His death on the cross. Only we must of course not suffer the monstrous thought to arise that God was angry with Him, something that *could not* be; nay more, it was in His death on the cross that He was above all an ὀσμὴ εὐωδίας, "odor of sweetness," unto God. Nevertheless He has, in the first place, *undergone* the Divine wrath by suffering death, whereby there was accomplished on Him the κατάκριμα, "condemnation," of death, and so the curse upon sin; the mode of death, moreover, exhibiting this death, even in form, as a death under curse. Yet that is not all, He has, in the second place, also felt the wrath of God, in that the enjoyment, the sense of the blessed communion of love with God vanished from Him without the reality of this communion itself thereby ceasing. He was, it is true, an ὀσμὴ εὐωδίας to God, but the sense of it vanished from Him, although perhaps only momentarily in those instants of anguish when He uttered the complaint upon the cross that God had forsaken Him. But what was lacking in duration, so to speak, was most completely, as it were, compensated by the fearful intensity of such a sense of abandonment by God, in the soul of the beloved Son of God. To this extent He has fully become a curse, has

* [STANLEY (*History of the Jewish Church.* Vol. I., Sect. 1,) gives a more poetic view of Abraham's faith. Fascinating as these lectures are, it is easier to see whither they tend as one studies this argument of Paul. The stress which this brilliant author puts upon "obeyed" in this very connection, may sound like the voice of a broader Christianity, but tested by Paul's argument here, it proves to be the echo of a narrowing Judaism: "of the law." LIGHTFOOT'S note, p. 156, is much more satisfactory.—R.]

felt the wrath of God, even as condemning wrath. But if it is objected, "but not as eternally condemning," we must again refer to that intensity of the sense of wrath as an adequate expiation.—He has thus become a curse for us = in our behalf; but in our behalf only inasmuch as He thereby came *in our place*. The vicariousness does not lie in the expression ὑπέρ, but in the fact; if we, by the very fact that He became "a curse," have been made free from the "curse," in that there is of course involved that He came in our place; an exchange of positions occurred.—For it is stated that the effect of Christ's "becoming a curse" is to "redeem us from the curse of the law," and so at all events an entire acquittal therefrom, and averting of it. Christ is here represented as showing Himself (immediately, yes alone) *active* in the work of redemption; He offered Himself, is the sense. in becoming a curse, and therewith He presented a ransom—to whom? to "the curse of the law" which had dominion over us. The ransom consisted in Himself; He devoted Himself in this very "becoming a curse" to the power of this potentate, and thus in return let us go free. Analyzing the conception thus, we see that it is a figurative one; in order to reduce it to its exact expression, we must take in the idea (which Paul does not here introduce in so many words) of the sin-offering. In becoming a curse Christ became a sin-offering, and this, because it was an unblemished one, and for this reason an ὀσμὴ εὐωδίας, was accepted by God; and in return Christ, as it were, discharged us from the curse of the law which He represented, took it from us. (Inasmuch as Christ Himself brought this sin-offering in free obedience, He is with justice described as the one active in it, as here; the action of God Himself being of course understood.)—This is only the negative side, the positive is then added ver. 14, where the positive (and moreover subjective) effects of the redemption "from the curse of the law" are named; generically, the being blessed, specially, the receiving of the Spirit. Upon this, especially upon the relation of it to justification, see above in the EXEG. NOTES. We add only the observation: in the Apostle's apprehension of the history of salvation, the operation of the death of Christ is taken out of its isolation; we recognize in it only the fulfilment of the promise given in the beginning of the redemptive revelation; in Christ it is nothing else than the blessing of Abraham that comes to fulfilment; Beginning and End are united. (See upon this the next Sections.)

5. [*The two curses.* WORDSWORTH thus sums up the doctrinal points implied: "Two curses pronounced in the law are here referred to by St. Paul. All mankind was liable to the former one. How was it to be removed?

(1) He who was to *remove* it must not himself be *liable* to it. He who was to be a substitute for the *guilty* must himself be *innocent* He who was to suffer in the stead of the *disobedient* must himself be *obedient* in all things.

(2) He who was to be the substitute for *all* must have the *common nature* of *all*. He must not take the person of one individual man (such as Abraham, Moses, Elias), but He must take the *nature* of all, and sum *up all mankind* in himself.

(3) He who was to do more than counterbalance the weight of the *sins* of *all* must have infinite merits of *His own*, in order that the scale of Divine Justice may preponderate in their favor. And nothing that is not divine is infinite. In order, therefore, that He may be able to suffer for sin, he must be *human;* and in order that He may be able to take away the sins, and to *satisfy* God's Justice for them, He must be *Divine*.

(4) In order that He may remove the *curse* pronounced in the law of God for disobedience, He must undergo that *punishment* which is specially declared in the Law to *be* the *curse* of God.

(5) That punishment is hanging on a tree. That is specially called in the Law the curse of God. Deut. xxi. 23.

By undergoing this curse for us, Christ, He who is God from everlasting, and who became *Emmanuel*, God with us, God in our flesh, uniting together the two natures—the Divine and the Human—in His One Person—Christ Jesus, redeemed us from the curse of the Law. Thus, having accepted the curse, He liberated us from it."—R.]

## HOMILETICAL AND PRACTICAL.

Ver. 6. RIEGER:—This reckoning somewhat, for righteousness rests most of all on God's taking pleasure in faith, and on the fulfilling of His promises, those to which faith trusts. True, even faith gives God the honor, and is in this respect greater than any work. But even faith cannot always give to God the honor so willingly, so fully, with such victory over all doubts arising from the reason, as it should. Therefore God's *imputation* is still the best, according to which good pleasure of His will He counts even a weak spark of faith for righteousness, and therefore I may be assured that, though I now and then be somewhat doubtful of His gracious will, which He has towards me, mistrust Him, become in spirit sad and heavy, I am yet surrounded and overspread with the broad heaven of His promises, and especially of His forgiving grace, and even then His gracious imputation remains valid.

Ver. 7. HEUBNER:—Abraham's spiritual children are only those like-minded with him, *i. e.*, believing souls. By faith thou becomest like the old patriarchs; they acknowledge thee for worthy offspring, whether thou be derived from the same nation, according to the flesh, as they, or not. Spiritual genealogy and probate is of another sort from civil.

[CALVIN:—Paul has omitted one remark, which will be readily supplied, that there is no place in the Church for any man who is not a son of Abraham.—HOOKER:—The invisible Church consisteth only of true Israelites, true sons of Abraham, true servants and saints of God.—R.]

RIEGER:—The footsteps of faith and the walk therein prove this descent (Rom. iv. 12).—Ver. 8.—O man be assured, all thy temptations also, and needs, He hath seen beforehand! Only go with confidence to the Scripture, therein to seek God's consolations.—Who reads the Old Testament enough with the view of finding Christ every where therein?

Ver. 9. BERLENB. BIBLE:—Already with Abraham began the stream of blessing that proceeds from God to believers. This now is the blessing of the one God, flowing from the like grace of God, even though in the most manifold manifestations.—Companionship in blessing a blessed companionship.—Wilt thou have blessing? Believe! Other way there is none.—We see then, where the trouble is, if one finds in his soul no such well-being or blessing, but rather the curse, and disquietness in his conscience. It is in this matter of faith, which a man will not frankly receive from God, and let old matters go, and deny them for Christ's sake. But a man must himself be *of faith*, as Paul here expresses it, that is, thou must have so committed thy heart to the Spirit of Christ, that He has been able to gain possession of thee, and through faith bear thee as a child of God. Then is a man "of faith," that is, he has, as to the spirit, a Divine origin.

Ver. 10. "As many:" let there be as many of them as there will; and were there of them as many again who declare for this party and make their boast and glory of it, and will have their salvation from it.—"Of the works of the law:" this expresses the inner ground of the man, what fashions his soul, and whose child he is. It is not people who teach the law, but such as are born of the same. It means not: who give diligence to live after the measure of the law, but who live legally, take here a work and there a work, approach therewith before God, and so place themselves under the curse. "Under" signifies imprisonment, for these people bar themselves in.—LUTHER:—Our Lord God has two manner of blessings, a bodily, that appertains to this life, and a spiritual, that appertains to the life everlasting. Such bodily blessing have the ungodly in fulness and abundance. To banish the eternal curse, that is, the eternal wrath of God, death and damnation, there avails neither the world's nor the law's righteousness. Therefore those that have not more than the corporeal blessing alone, are for this reason not God's children, and blessed before God, but under the curse they are and abide.—If now God's law puts men under a curse, how much more other laws, which are of much less worth?

HEUBNER:—If we will be saved by the law, we must do all, and must be able to say, that we have never neglected any thing commanded, nor done any thing forbidden. In brief, the matter stands thus: if we will merit salvation, amazingly little will come of it, for our virtue is piece-work; against one or two legal performances God can oppose ten transgressions. Whoever does not view the requirements of the law with the diminishing glass of light-mindedness, and his own works with the magnifying glass of self-love, must acknowledge this.—[JOHN BROWN:—It is absurdity thus to seek for justification from that which is and must be the source of condemnation. To expect to be warmed by the keen northern blast, or to have our thirst quenched by a draught of liquid fire, were not more, were not so incongruous.—R.]

Ver. 11. CRAMER:—The religion that teaches us to believe that we are saved by grace without works, is the true, original, Catholic religion, to which also Habakkuk and the old prophets bear witness; therefore the Romish religion, which contradicts this, can be neither the original, nor the true Catholic church, but must be a new church.—STARKE:—The regenerate, who are already righteous through faith, continue in their righteousness and blessedness, and become at the last perfectly blessed, but still only through faith.

Ver. 12. The law will have doers, that deserve Heaven by works. The gospel will have only sinners, who have done working, but who, repenting them of their sins (or broken into contriteness by the law), seek medicine, help and grace in Christ and His Father's compassion. They now see aright their guiltiness, together with the loathsomeness of sin; they now first understand and love Moses aright, and walk after his law; not out of constraint or hope of reward, but as being already righteous in Christ, and minded to show forth the profit, purpose, joy and might of such righteousness in all manner of works possible.

Ver. 13. LUTHER:—God hath cast all sin of all men upon His Son. Then forthwith comes the law, accusing Him and saying: Here find I this one among sinners, yea who hath taken all men's sins upon Himself, and bears them, and I see in the whole world besides not another sin, except upon Him alone; therefore shall He suffer for it and die the death upon the cross.—Insomuch then as through this only Mediator, Jesus Christ, Sin and Death are taken away, without doubt the whole world were so pure that our Lord God therein could see nothing except mere righteousness and holiness, if we only could believe it.—On that side there is no lack. But the lack is with us, who believe it so faintly. If we believed it fully, doubtless we should already have been blessed and in Paradise, but the old sack, that still hangs around our neck, holds us back from arriving at such certain faith.—We should not look at Christ after the flesh, as if He were a man, righteous and holy for Himself alone, and having nothing to do with us. True it is that Christ is the holiest person of all, but thou must not stop with that knowledge, that does not yet give thee Christ. But thou knowest Him aright, and obtainest Him for thy own, when thou believest that this holiest Person of all has been bestowed upon thee by the Father, that He should be thy High-priest and Saviour, yea, thy minister and servant, who should lay from Him His own innocence and holiness, and take upon Him thy sinful person, and therein bear thy sin, death and curse, and thus become a sacrifice and a curse for thee, that He might so redeem thee from the curse of the law.—All virtue lies in the little words: for us.

[Two curses are here mentioned by Paul. The one: "Cursed is every one that continueth not," *etc.* That curse lay on all mankind. The other: "Cursed is every one that hangeth on a tree." This curse Christ took, that He might redeem us from the first. Both were curses in and of the law. The one specifies the guilt, the other the punishment. Christ bore the accursed punishment, thus He takes away the accursed guilt. He stood for the "every one" who continueth not, by becoming the *very one* who hung upon the tree.—R.]

[WORDSWORTH:—How much reason have we

to abominate *our sins*, which were the principal causes of the crucifixion of Christ! They were indeed the traitors which, by the hands of Judas, delivered Him up. The Jewish priests were but our advocates; we by them did adjudge and sentence Him. Pilate was but our spokesman, the Roman executioners were but our agents therein. The Jewish people were but proxies acting our parts; our sins were they which cried out: "Crucify Him," with clamors more loud and more effectual, than did all the Jewish rabble.—The second Adam hung on the tree in Calvary, in order that by hanging on the tree He might abolish the sin committed by us in the first Adam, when he ate of the fruit of the tree of good and evil in Paradise.—There on the cross He extends His hands to all and calls all—Gentiles as well as Jews.—R.]

Ver. 14. LANGE:—The blessing comes not alone *from* Christ, but also *in* Christ. For whoever does not receive it in Christ, receives it not from Christ; as indeed many wish to have it from Christ, but not to take it in Christ, that is, receive it so that they thereby suffer themselves to be brought into His fellowship and in it enjoy the blessing with large addition.

*On the whole Section:*—The Christian's walk, a walk in the footsteps of the faith of Abraham.—Those who occupy themselves with works of the law, are under the curse: (1) a fearful word, (2) yet only too true.—Blessing or Curse? Other alternative there is none.—Christ has turned the curse into blessing.—The redemption from the curse of the law through Christ.—He became a curse for us. (1) How is that possible? and yet (2) it was necessary, for (3) thereupon rests our salvation.—Our righteousness before God is grounded alone upon faith: (1) this is taught by Abraham's example; (2) proved by the promise given by God to Abraham; (3) attested by the innermost essence of the law; (4) made sure by the redemption established by Christ.—Only through faith in the Crucified One have we part in the redemption accomplished by Him. I. That faith generally is the condition, vers. 6–12. (1) Proof from the example of Abraham's faith, vers. 6–9; (*a*) on account of his faith was Abraham accounted righteous before God, ver. 6; (*b*) the promise given to him of the blessing of the Gentiles, presupposes in these also faith. (2) Demonstration from the impossibility of any one being redeemed from the curse of the law through any manner of works, vers. 10–12. II. That the redemption accomplished by Christ is the essential matter [*Inhalt*] of faith on Him. (1) That Christ has redeemed us from the curse of the law; (2) that He has effected this by Himself becoming a curse for us.—The death of Christ deserves an imperishable remembrance, because in it He became a curse for us. (1) He became a curse for us: (2) Therein lies the power of His death for blessing.

[COWPER:—

Oh, how unlike the complex works of man,
Heaven's easy, artless, unincumbered plan!
No meretricious graces to beguile;
No clustering ornaments to clog the pile.
From ostentation as from weakness free,
It stands, like the cerulean arch we see,
Majestic in its own simplicity.
Inscribed above the portal, from afar
Conspicuous as the brightness of a star,
Legible only by the light they give,
Stand the soul-quickening words—BELIEVE AND LIVE.]

---

b. Demonstration from the chronological relation of the Lord to the Covenant of Promise.

(VERS. 15–18.)

(Vers. 16–22. *The Epistle for* 13*th Sunday after Trinity*.)

15 Brethren, I speak after the manner of men; Though *it be* but a man's covenant,
yet *if it be* [*when it has been*][1] confirmed, no man disannulleth [annulleth][2] or addeth
16 thereto. Now to Abraham and his seed were the promises made. [Now to Abra-
ham were the promises made and to his seed.][3] He saith not, And to seeds, as of
17 many; but as of one, And to thy seed, which is Christ. And [Now] this I say,
*that* the covenant, [A covenant][4] that was confirmed before of God in Christ [that
has been before confirmed by God to Christ][5], the law, which was four hundred and
thirty years after, cannot disannul [does not invalidate][6] that it should make the
18 promise of none effect [make void the promise]. For if the inheritance *be* of the
law, *it is* no more of promise: but God gave [hath freely granted][7] *it* to Abra-
ham by [through] promise.

[1] Ver. 15.—[Κεκυρωμένην, simply "confirmed." If anything be supplied, it need not be in the conditional form of the E. V.—R.]

[2] Ver. 15.—["Disannulleth" is now obsolete, the simple form being of precisely the same signification. "Addeth thereto" *i. e.* new conditions.—R.]

[3] Ver. 16.—[The change in order is necessary to emphasize "and to his seed." Ἐῤῥέθησαν, ℵ. A. *et al.* Lachmann, Tischendorf, Meyer, *et al.*, instead of Ἐῤῥήθησαν, Rec.—R.]

[4] Ver. 17.—[The structure of this verse is cumbrous, but the insertion of "that" renders it still more so.—R.]
[5] Ver. 17.—Εἰς Χριστόν is lacking in several MSS. including א. The connection however favors the belief in its genuineness, since otherwise the argument in ver. 16 would hardly be turned to practical account. [Omitted in א. A. B. C. many versions, by Lachmann, Tischendorf, Meyer, Alford, Lightfoot. Retained by Griesbach, Wordsworth, bracketted by Ellicott. If retained, may be rendered "to Christ," or "for Christ." See EXEG. NOTES.—R.]
[6] Ver. 17.—[Οὐκ ἀκυροῖ—"cannot" may be implied, but is not expressed. "Invalidate" is preferable to "annul," as the Greek word differs from that rendered "annul" (ver. 15).—R.]
[7] Ver. 18.—[Κεχάρισται, "has given freely," "given of grace." We have no single word to express it.—R.]

## EXEGETICAL AND CRITICAL.

Ver. 15.—[**Brethren.**—An affectionately pathetic address. How different from ver. 1! The tone is greatly softened.—MEYER. "Here is a pause, at which the indignant feeling of the Apostle softens, and he begins the new train of thought which follows with words of milder character, and proceeds more quietly with his argument" (WINDISCHMANN).—R.]

**I speak after the manner of men.**—Κατὰ ἄνθρωπον. Paul thus excuses himself for comparing a man's διαθήκη with a διαθήκη of God, he will not (he says) regard the matter from a higher point of view, but simply according to the analogy of human relations. [CALVIN: "By this expression he intended to put them to the blush. It is highly disgraceful and base that the testimony of God should have less weight with us than that of a mortal man."—R.]

Διαθήκη is not to be taken here in the sense of covenant (although approved by MEYER and WIESELER). [See below.—R.] The sense is that of Testament. It is true God made with Abraham a covenant, hence God's covenant of promise with Abraham is here spoken of. But in these verses, Paul takes up this covenant in the aspect of a Testament, in order to emphasize the fact that in it God has made a free promise (of an inheritance) in contrast with the law, which imposes injunctions, making everything depend on merit. This character of the covenant of promise reminds him of a human Testament, and the principles of jurisprudence which are valid with respect to such an instrument, furnish the basis of his argument. [The majority of modern commentators take the other view. The reason here advanced is based upon the idea of "inheritance," which belongs to a covenant as well as to a Testament. The usage of the LXX. is decidedly in favor of the rendering "covenant." So the New Testament usage (the exceptional case, Heb. ix. 15–17, beginning with this idea also). So that while doctrinally considered it is not of much moment (CALVIN, who however prefers the meaning "covenant"), the order of the words and the comparison require this meaning (ELLICOTT). Comp. BAGGE, MEYER, LIGHTFOOT. The influence of the Vulgate in substituting "Testament" for "covenant" in the name of the two parts of the Bible is perhaps to be deplored.—R.]

**No man annulleth**—*i. e.*, of course, legitimately. [Ὅμως belongs here logically. But the sense is well preserved in the E. V.—R.]—**Addeth thereto**=adds specifications to it, of any kind whatever.—From what is true of a human Testament [or covenant], Paul now argues as to the Testament [or covenant] of God; this also "no one annulleth or addeth thereto"—"no one" and hence not "the law" either. But before he draws this conclusion (ver. 17), he furnishes (ver. 16) the necessary premises for it (WIESELER). He does this, by showing that the διαθήκη referred to the time after as well as before the giving of the law, and *in substance* remains still in force, without which necessary link the demonstration, that the law made no change in the character of the διαθήκη, would be without value or meaning. For if the διαθήκη had been of limited duration, confined to Abraham for instance, if the promise had been made only to him, it would, when the law came, have been long before fulfilled and thereby done away; the two would not have come in contact. But this is not the case.

Ver. 16.—**Now to Abraham were the promises made** [lit. **were spoken**], **and to his seed.**—This, as shown by "were spoken," and still more by what follows, refers to particular passages, and such moreover as contain the clause "and to thy seed" as also the promise of an "inheritance;" not, therefore, such as Gen. xxii. 18[?], but xiii. 15; xvii. 8 (and according to the LXX. also xxiv. 17). The sense is therefore: not merely to Abraham was there in the διαθήκη a promise, *sc.*, of an inheritance, made by God, but also to his seed; the διαθήκη was not exhausted in him, but was valid also for his seed. But especially must it be shown that it has validity *even now*. Therefore, says Paul, inasmuch as these promises were given "also to the seed of Abraham," they were given also to Christ. This seed of Abraham (he says), is indeed no other than Christ. This, he says, follows from the very fact of the singular form "his seed" being used. "In order to explain this emphasizing of the singular form in the exegesis of Paul, appeal has been made to the fact that the Rabbins of his time also now and then strain the singular or plural to serve an exegetical turn, and in the passages Gen. iv. 25; xix. 32, themselves explain זֶרַע of the Messiah. This comparison is admissible, if only we do not overlook the extraordinary contrast which exists between ordinary Rabbinical caprice, and Paul's exposition in this passage. That in the Abrahamic promise the idea of the Messiah is concealed, and that the 'seed of Abraham' may be actually understood of the Messiah, is unquestionably the true view, on which the whole exposition of Paul rests, and which he has a little before demonstrated from the connection of Scripture and the deepest reality of the fulfilled truth. But the form in which he, in this passage, rather casually than otherwise, expresses this view, correct in itself, namely, that it is already indicated by the use of the singular in the text which gives the Abrahamic promise, appears to demand the explanation given by most interpreters, as derived from the Rabbinical training of his youth." WIESELER.

[The ground of this assumption of Rabbinical method in his argumentation is this: that the stress of the argument rests on a grammatical, error; the Hebrew word, which he renders σπέρμα, having no plural answering to σπέρματα or "seeds." Granting this, it must yet be remembered that the consequences involved in an admission of such "playing" with Divine truth, in a writer, who claims to speak for God, are too grave, to permit us to make such an admission hastily. Is there no other reasonably satisfactory explanation, which denies any Rabbinical influence, implying the slightest quibbling? If there be, justice to such a writer as Paul, aside from any reverence for this Epistle as inspired, should lead us to adopt it. JEROME's application of κατὰ ἄνθρωπον to this verse is hardly allowable. He would not intentionally weaken his own cause thus. LIGHTFOOT well says: "It is quite as unnatural to use the Greek plural with this meaning as the Hebrew. This fact points to St. Paul's meaning. He is not laying stress on the particular word used, but on the fact that a singular noun of some kind, a collective term, is employed, where τὰ τέκνα or οἱ ἀπόγονοι, for instance, might have been substituted. Avoiding the technical terms of grammar, he could not express his meaning more simply than by the opposition 'not to thy seeds, but to thy *seed*.' The singular collective noun, if it admits of plurality, at the same time involves the idea of unity." ELLICOTT: "We hold that there is as certainly a mystical meaning in the use of זֶרַע in Gen. xiii. 15; xvii. 8, as there is an argument for the resurrection in Exod. iii. 6, though in neither case was the writer necessarily aware of it. As the word in its simple meaning generally denotes not the mere progeny of a man, but his posterity viewed as one organically-connected whole; so here in its mystical meaning it denotes not merely the spiritual posterity of Abraham, but Him in whom that posterity is all organically united, the πλήρωμα, the κεφαλή, even Christ. This St. Paul endeavors faintly to convey to his Greek readers by the use of σπέομα and σπέρματα." Comp. WORDSWORTH, OLSHAUSEN *in loco*. How Pauline this conception is, will appear to every student of the Epistles to the Romans and Ephesians. Paul's Rabbinical training undoubtedly made him quick and close in discrimination respecting the Old Testament; that it ever made him quibble, and institute false distinctions is against his character as well as against his inspiration.—R.]

That any explanation of the passage which maintains that Paul does not mean to interpret "seed" of the person of Christ is incorrect, needs no proof. [Against this, see ALFORD *in loco*. —R.] Doubtless, secondarily, those who are "of Christ" are also "the seed of Abraham" (ver. 29), but it is only because, primarily, Christ is this seed. This reference of "seed" to the person of Christ is not disproved by alleging that thereby the διαθήκη, the inheritance would be promised to Christ as well as to Abraham. But, it may be asked, is then the inheritance promised to Christ; is He designated as the Heir, and not rather as the Mediator and Bringer of the inheritance? Doubtless the latter, but primarily He is Himself the universal Heir; therefore in ver. 19 he is called distinctly the universal Heir: "the seed to whom the promise was made." Let us only vividly apprehend the course of prophecy that sketches the history of redemption. The Messiah Himself, according to it, is He who occupies the promised inheritance, that is, who takes full and abiding possession of it, and by this very fact, brings in the time of salvation and of God's kingdom. The conception is therefore one somewhat different from that in ver. 14, but both are equally according to truth, and the two modes of conception are most intimately connected. For Christ is certainly the Heir, only, He is the Heir in order to procure for His people the participation of the inheritance and therewith the blessing of God. And, as is self-evident, it is this truth, namely, that He in turn *brings* the inheritance into the possession of His *people*, which is here mainly in mind. Inasmuch as the διαθήκη had reference to Him, it had and has reference also to those that are "Christ's"; the question as to them therefore still remains to be answered; nay, it is as to them that it occurs, *how* they become partakers of the inheritance promised in the covenant. For that the covenant with the promise of the inheritance is valid also for the Christian dispensation, that it is "confirmed by God to Christ," is only one side of the truth. On the other side it was maintained with reference to the law that had come between, that the attainment of the inheritance had now become encumbered with the condition of the fulfilment of the law, that it came now *of the law* and no more *simply* "*of promise*." This assertion Paul now opposes, by applying what was said in ver. 5 about a covenant in general, to the covenant of God.

Ver. 17. **A covenant that has been before confirmed by God to Christ.**—This passage, as WIESELER says, is rightly understood only by considering that the assertion which Paul undertakes to refute is not the assertion of an entire abrogation of the Abrahamic covenant by the law, but only that of a modification in the Judaistic sense by the law of an invalidating, so that it should make void *the promise* (which would be an "invalidating," because thereby the character of the covenant as a promise given by grace, and thus its specific peculiarity would be taken away). This alone gives the sense of ver. 18: I have a right to say: it "does not invalidate that it should make void the promise;" *for* if the inheritance is obtained by law, it no longer comes "of promise;" but "of promise" it *is* to come, for it was assured by God to Abraham through promise, and of grace. We cannot therefore concede an invalidating, so that the promise is made void through the law, for this would take away something essential to the covenant; but, according to ver. 15, this cannot be.—[Various interpretations of εἰς Χριστόν have been suggested. The simplest and most obvious one is: "unto Christ," *i. e.*, as the second party to whom the covenant was ratified. ELLICOTT suggests "to be fulfilled in Christ," and renders "for Christ." Perhaps that of WORDSWORTH is implied: "*unto Christ:* so as to tend toward, and be consummated in Christ as its end, who, as man, sums up all Abraham's seed in Himself." But on the whole it is best to reject the words as a gloss.—R.]

**The law which was four hundred and thirty years after.**—Paul has taken the number from Exod. xii. 40, but apparently from the text of the LXX. which adds καὶ ἐν γῇ Χαναάν thus including the sojourn of the patriarchs in Canaan (as do also the Samaritan text and Josephus *Ant.*, 2, 15, 3), while according to the Hebrew text this number covers only the duration of the sojourn in Egypt. Therefore "it is hardly to be said, that Paul has here made a mistake of memory, but only that, on account of his Greek-speaking readers, who used the Septuagint, he has here, as commonly in his Old Testament citations, adhered to the tradition of the LXX., which he could the more easily do, because the precise numbers of the years was a matter of no moment." WIESELER. [Though the precise number is of no moment as respects Paul's argument, the chronological difficulty is a grave one. The period from the call of Abraham to the departure of Jacob into Egypt is fixed at two hundred and fifteen years. The question is: must we compute the sojourn there as extending over four hundred and thirty years, or only two hundred and fifteen years. The Hebrew text, Exod. xii. 40, seems to demand the former term (and also Stephen, Acts vii. 6, "four hundred years," as in the prophecy Gen. xv. 13, both of which passages give round numbers). The latter term is that of the commonly received chronology. If it be adopted, the difficulty is thrown mainly upon the passage, Exod. xii. 40, to which the LXX. add as above. ALFORD and ELLICOTT suggest this strong point in favor of the shorter term, viz., that from the data respecting ages and births, the longer term would make the age of Jochebed, the mother of Moses, at least two hundred and fifty-six years when Moses was born. So that the longer term makes the accurate statement of numbers overthrow the accurate statement of genealogies and events, which was far less likely to be tampered with. The gloss, if it be a gloss, of the LXX. affords the easiest solution of the difficulty, and Gen. xv. 40, Acts vii. 6, are then to be explained in the same way. Comp. USHER, WINDISCHMANN, HALES.—R.]

Ver. 18 **But God hath freely granted it to Abraham through promise.**—Prominence is to be given to the fact that God has not limited His promise, which He gave to Abraham, by conditioning it on a fulfilment of the law, but that it was a promise of pure grace; therefore, says Paul, God has, out of grace, by means of promise, bestowed, *s. c.*, the inheritance on Abraham, *i. e.*, not put him in actual possession, but assured it to him. The two expressions, "freely granted," and "through promise," are conjoined to exclude most definitely the idea "of the law."

## DOCTRINAL AND ETHICAL.

1. *Epochs of Revelation.* In the preceding section, as well as this, Paul has not cared to conduct a Scripture demonstration merely by the citation of isolated passages, but has used a freer and nobler method with the Scriptures. He showed in the revelation of God to Abraham a prophetic setting forth of the perfect revelation of God exhibited in Christ (especially at the close of ver. 14 had this become evident), and thus placed the Scripture in the light of a history of the revelation of redemption. This view of it has become, in the present section (as far as to chap. iv. 2), the controlling one. The law also here constitutes for him an epoch of the revelation of God, so that there are three of these epochs represented by Abraham, Moses, and Christ. They are not, however, simple stages of development, but the first and the third belong essentially together in one order, as germ and fruit; for the middle epoch, so diverse in character, a false claim is made, which it is his endeavor to refute, and to assign and establish its just position.—The suggestions which Paul here gives are important starting points for a just historical apprehension of Revelation, and at the same time an example of a proper adjustment of relations and reconciliation of apparent contradictions in it.

2. *The Law is not a complement of the Covenant of Promise.* It is not till in the next section that the purpose and meaning of the law, and its relation to the covenant of promise, are expounded positively. The negative proof, however, here adduced, is of itself important; viz.: That the law is not, and is not to be regarded or treated as a complement and rectification of the Covenant of Promise, so that whatever at first was freely promised as a boon "should be now encumbered with a burdensome condition." Or rather, this was so, indeed, but only for a time, for a definite season (as is shown afterwards). In this way, however, the inheritance was not *actually* attained, but as it was originally assured purely by promise, so is it now attained only through faith, the subjective correlative of the promise; and only this is required.

[3. *The sum of the Apostle's argument.* "This, then, is the sum of the Apostle's argument: A ratified, unrepealed constitution, cannot be set aside by a subsequent constitution. The plan of justification by believing was a ratified and unrepealed constitution. The law was a constitution posterior to this by a long term of years. If the observance of the law were constituted the procuring cause or necessary means of justification, such a constitution would necessarily annul the covenant before ratified, and render the promise of more effect. It follows, of course, that the law was appointed for no such purpose. Whatever end it might serve, it could not serve this end; it could never be appointed to serve this end."—BROWN. What end it serves, the Apostle states in the section immediately following.—R.]

4. *Christ the Seed of Abraham.* "'Seed,' comprehends posterity generally, and therefore of course a plurality. But among this posterity one nevertheless was found upon whom the whole expectation of faith was directed, and through whom also all promise first received its fulfilment. As Christ at His actual coming into the world humiliated Himself to live as a man among men, and had to be discovered and sought out by means of the words and works that were His alone, in like manner was He in the promise also concealed, as it were, among the seed, or among the collective posterity of Abraham, so that only when the time was fulfilled could any plainly distinguish Him and say: This is Christ, this is He who sanctifies and blesses, who yet is of the same descent with those that are sanctified and blessed; therefore also He is not ashamed to call them brethren, and it was not unbefitting Him, that all should be comprehended in the one Seed."—RIEGER.

### HOMILETICAL AND PRACTICAL.

Ver. 15.—"Brethren."—RIEGER: By this address the Apostle noticeably softens the sharpness used in the first verse. Nothing calls for so much consideration, for so thorough a mingling of sharpness and gentleness, as when men fall back under the law and the blindness as to the gospel conjoined therewith. For the bewitching arts of the prince of this world, which are implied therein, and the mischief to be feared therefrom, demand sharpness; the hunger and thirst after righteousness yet alive in the conscience, and the love to the truth, demand to be appealed to with the utmost possible tenderness.—In the word of God throughout there is much condescension to our weakness, or much that is presented in human style, suitable to our power of comprehension. God has also actually so arranged it, that between the visible and the invisible, between the ordinances in the realm of nature and in the realm of grace there is much that is similar, and we therefore through the images furnished us by our experience in human life, obtain a true conception of the ordinances of grace. The Incarnation of the Son of God has such an influence on the whole economy of God forward and backwards, that God everywhere deals with us after the manner of a man.—LANGE:—Human ordinances and institutions, which in themselves serve for the outward well-being of human and civil society, are in themselves not to be contemned. Since God counts them worthy that His apostles should therewith make clearer the economy of His kingdom.—In STARKE:—If a great lord gives us his hand and seal, we are satisfied and believe, that the heavens will fall before such a promise will be broken. Why do we not rather trust the sealed handwriting of our God who cannot lie.—"Addeth thereto."—In divine things the human addition is often discernible, but very improperly, often causing that nothing pure is left.—[So the annulling by the addition of the law would make void the promise.—R.]

Ver. 16.—SPENER: In the Holy Scripture all is written with Divine wisdom, therefore no word, no letter, no arrangement of the words is settled at random.—Divine truth must be found in the Holy Scripture itself and the letter of it, and may not be expected by separate communication from the Holy Ghost. Else Paul could not insist upon a little word and thereupon rest his argument.—[Paul, who takes such a broad view of the Scriptures as the one great history of Redemption, is the one who notices the truth in the least details of the word. One need not be a loose expositor, in order to have broad views; the accurate reader is not contracted by his accuracy.—R.]

Ver. 17. STARKE: Sacred chronology gives a great light, for a more accurate insight into the ways of God.—[How many read their Bibles, as if the whole were written at one time. They acknowledge a history there, but it sheds no light for them upon the great truth of God as a whole.—Abraham and Moses. How prominent, how related.—How often the followers of Christ stop at Moses, when they ought to go back to Abraham!—The covenant was confirmed of God to Christ. Through Abraham, indeed, yet it is essentially a covenant between God and our Redeemer. So the Old Covenant is the new and everlasting Covenant.—R.]

Ver. 18. STARKE: It is impossible to have righteousness and salvation partly from the works of the law, and partly from grace. For these are opposing things, that destroy one another. It must either be of works alone or of grace alone; now it is not of works, therefore it is of grace alone.—RIEGER:—So long, indeed, as the human heart in falsehood still parts its love between light and darkness, nothing were more pleasing, than if it could thus turn from side to side between the promise and its own merit, that is, if, so far as might be, it could boast itself of merit and the law, and where these were too scant, could put forward, under cover of the promise, the grace and merit of Christ. Then, moreover, there would be in this way no great need of going deep in either quarter; it would only be to bend a little to the law, and as to the appropriation of grace, it need not call for any very special humility. But with such a divided heart, one has neither access to grace, nor entrance into the everlasting inheritance.

All that we have from the Gospel or from the promise, is a gift, a free gift of grace, and nothing is attained by obedience as a condition. We are not, therefore, to regard a godly life as a condition of obtaining the blessings of grace, but as a part of the grace itself which the Lord shows us.—[How old this method of grace by covenant of promise! Older than Moses. Yet how new! for we never apprehend it until God reveals it to us by His spirit, and then it seems as though it were a revelation of something entirely new.—The benefits of the gospel are all through promise. Hence all of grace, all to faith, all for the glory of the Promiser!—R.]

2. The law had undoubtedly its value, and that for the attainment of salvation itself, but only a preparatory, and therefore also a transitory value. Believers are free from it.

(CHAP. iii. 19—iv. 7.)

a. The law had its own sufficient end, having respect to transgressions, and so far from opposing an obstacle to the promises, it had the office of preparing the way for their fulfilment, as a schoolmaster unto Christ.

(VERS. 19–24.)

19 Wherefore then *serveth* the law [lit. what then *is* the law][1]? It was added[2] be-
cause of [the] transgressions, till the seed should come to whom[3] the promise was
[has been] made; *and it was* ordained [being ordained][4] by [by means of] angels
20 in the hand of a mediator. Now a mediator is not a *mediator* of one, but God is
21 one. *Is* the law then against the promises of God?[5] God forbid: for if there had
been a law given which could have given life, verily righteousness should [would]
22 have been[6] by the law. But [ἀλλά, But, on the contrary][7] the Scripture hath con-
cluded [shut up][8] all under sin, that [in order that] the promise by faith of [or in]
23 Jesus Christ might be given to them that believe. But before faith came we were
kept under the law, shut up [kept in ward, shut up[9] under the law] unto the faith
24 which should afterwards be revealed. Wherefore the law was [So that the law
hath been or become][10] our schoolmaster *to bring us* [omit *to bring us*] unto Christ,
that we might be justified by faith.

b. But for this very reason it has fulfilled its purpose, when it has brought us to faith, and believers, as children (sons) of God and heirs, are no longer under the law.

(VERS. 25–29.)

25 But after [now][11] that faith is come, we are no longer under a schoolmaster.
26, 27 For ye are all the children [all sons] of God by faith in Christ Jesus. For as
many of you as have been [were][12] baptized into Christ have [omit have] put on
28 Christ. There is neither Jew nor Greek, there is neither bond nor free, there is
neither male nor female [no male and female][13]; for ye are all [all are][14] one in
29 Christ Jesus. And [But, δέ] if ye *be* Christ's, then are ye Abraham's seed, and [or
omit and][15] heirs according to the promise.

(Vers. 23–29.—*The Epistle for New Year's festival.*)

[1] Ver. 19.—[The E. V. is sufficiently accurate. Ellicott renders "what then *is the object of* the law?" Schmoller: *Wie verhält es sich mit dem Gesetz?*—R.]

[2] Ver. 19.—Griesbach and Scholz have ἐτέθη, which is not sufficiently supported. [So Rec., but προσετέθη is adopted by most modern editors.—The article should be retained with "transgressions" in the E. V. So Ellicott, Alford.—R.]

[3] Ver. 19.—Instead of ᾧ ἐπήγγελται, J. and many cursives, some Fathers also, have ὅ ἐπήγγελται; but this is poorly supported, probably arising from the fact that ᾧ was not understood.

[4] Ver. 19.—[The italics in the E. V. separate διαταγείς too much from the first clause, with which it is closely connected.—"By means of" brings out the purely instrumental force of διά.—R.]

[5] Ver. 21.—Τοῦ θεοῦ, bracketted by Lachmann. The omission is not well sustained. ℵ. retains it. [B. is the main authority for rejecting it. Meyer rejects it mainly on exegetical grounds.—R.]

[6] Ver. 21.—Ἂν ἐκ νόμου ἦν. [Rec.] There are different variations: ℵ. has ἐκ νόμου ἦν ἄν, the best attested order is ἐκ νόμου ἂν ἦν. [So A. B. C., Lachmann, Tischendorf, Meyer, critical editors generally.—R.]

[7] Ver. 22.—[The strongly adversative αλλά requires the insertion of "on the contrary" (Alford, Ellicott).—R.]

[8] Ver. 22.—[As the E. V. renders the same verb (συγκλείειν) ver. 23, "shut up," it is substituted here as less ambiguous than "hath concluded."—R.]

[9] Ver. 23.—Συγκεκλεισμένοι is in all probability the correct reading—not συγκλειόμενοι. Yet ℵ. has it [συνκλειόμενοι (*sic.*) The perfect of the Rec. is adopted by Tischendorf, De Wette, Meyer, Wordsworth, Ellicott (on critical and exegetical grounds). Lachmann, Scholz, Alford, Lightfoot, adopt the other. The order is changed; "under the law" seems to be best joined with "shut up."—R.]

[10] Ver. 24.—["So that the law hath become" is more literal. "Schoolmaster" is retained, since we have no better word with which to translate παιδαγωγός. "Tutor" (Alford) is no more exact.—"*To bring us*" is better omitted, since it presents but one side of the meaning.—R.]

[11] Ver. 25.—["Now" brings out the idea that *it is so*.—R.]

[12] Ver. 27.—[The aorist verbs in this verse are better translated by the simple past tense of the English.—R.]

[13] Ver. 28.—[The change of particles in Greek with this last pair is thus noted. On its peculiar force see EXEG. NOTES.—R.]

[14] Ver. 28.—Εἷς ἐστε ἐν Χριστῷ Ἰησοῦ. A. has ἐστε Χριστοῦ Ἰ. "But εἷς would easily be overlooked after the preceding ὑμεῖς, and then ἐν Χρ. Ἰ. was first followed by Χριστοῦ as a gloss, from the beginning of ver. 29, and afterwards supplanted by it. The reading ἕν instead of εἷς is an explanation." Meyer. ℵ. has ὑμεῖς ἐστε ἐν Χριστοῦ, but ἐν is marked doubtful [marked for erasure; the marks afterwards removed, ℵ.[3] reading as Rec.—It is doubtful whether we should read πάντες or ἅπαντες. ℵ. has the latter.—R.]

[15] Ver. 29.—Καί is omitted in good MSS., including ℵ., by some versions and Fathers, but may very easily have been overlooked, as it follows κατ' (Meyer). It is rejected by Lachmann, Tischendorf, Scholz, [also by Meyer in 4th. ed., Alford, Ellicott, Lightfoot, on the authority of ℵ. A. B. C. D. As Schmoller follows Meyer in retaining it, it may be rejected here on the same authority.—R.]

## EXEGETICAL AND CRITICAL.

Ver. 19. **Wherefore then serveth the law?**—["What then is the object of the law?" —R.] If the inheritance is not to come by the law, but still "of promise," the objection is obvious: why then did not God suffer the promise to stand alone? Why then did the law come afterwards? Certainly this was in that case superfluous!—To this Paul answers, in effect, thus: was the law then purposeless, if it had not precisely *this* purpose, of mediating the obtaining of the inheritance? Could it not have another purpose? Yes, this was the case, it had a purpose, but one very different from that of being the means of securing the inheritance. What then?

The direct answer is not given immediately, but is introduced with: "**It was added because of the transgressions.**—This means, simply, on account of transgressions was the law added. "Transgressions," multiplying and becoming aggravated, gave, in the first place, occasion for adding the law, necessarily brought it to pass that God came with respect to His people into an *entirely* different, more distant relation than existed, in the covenant of promise, between Him and the patriarchs. Instead of the more fatherly relation existing hitherto, God was constrained to place Himself in a relation involving the exercise of severe discipline, involving rigorous requirements and commands, nay, sharp threatenings, as it is afterwards expressed: "We were kept in ward, shut up under the law." And as this relation so different from the former had been occasioned by "transgressions," it was of course precisely in its right place where the "transgressions" of men prevailed, and it was designed, with reference to this, not so much in order to prevent them, as rather, by its commandments and prohibitions, and the threatenings annexed, to bring them under a more stringent accountability (which now first became possible), and a plainly expressed curse. Comp. EWALD: In order, because offences had come into the world, to punish them the more severely. (At first the judgment of death had kept the sense of sin alive. As men now were too accustomed to this, the law then came, and therewith the stricter imputation of sin, the curse more severely denounced, the obedience more rigorously required. RIEGER.) At the most this is as far as we are to go in the explanation of παραβάσεων χάριν. A more precise declaration as to the positive purpose of the law in relation to "transgressions" is not yet given here; and cannot therefore be deduced from the general expression; for then the second objection (ver. 21) would no longer be possible; it is in the refutation of this that Paul first expresses himself more particularly. The common explanation therefore: "For the sake of transgressions" = to induce them (agreeably to what Paul elsewhere says of the effect of the law to promote sin), is at least in no way indicated. The question whether Paul had it in mind would not arise before vers. 22, 23, 24. That the word χάριν does not necessitate this explanation, is shown by such passages as Luke vii. 47; iii. 12. [The view here suggested seems to be in the main that of ELLICOTT and WORDSWORTH (*Milton. Paradise Lost*, vii. 285). The purpose of the law as here set forth was, not (1) to prevent transgression, nor (2) to create, multiply transgressions, though elsewhere this is mentioned as its effect, but (3) to bring to light "the transgressions" of it already occurring and to occur, to make them "palpable, to awaken a conviction of sin in the heart, and make man feel his need of a Saviour" (ELLICOTT). Thus "the law had a supplementary, parenthetical, provisional and manductory character, and came in, as it were, *incidentally*" (WORDSWORTH).—R.] To this purpose of the law there then agree also:

1. The limited duration of its binding force, continuing only **till the seed should come,** for with that its purpose in reference to "transgressions" was fulfilled. (Why? is answered ver. 23, sq.) "The seed" **to whom the promise has been made** (see on ver. 16) is Christ, for He is the universal Heir; those who are Christ's are then, it is true, included also in this seed, and become therefore joint-heirs with Him (ver. 29). 2. The manner of its origin: **ordained by means of angels in the hand of a mediator.** As agents in giving the law (not as its authors), Paul designates the angels, agreeably to the ancient tradition, which appears first LXX. Deut. xxxiii. 2 (not in the original); and also Heb. ii. 2; Acts vii. 53; Josephus, *Antiq.* 15, 5, 3, and in the Rabbins. "In the hand of a mediator" = Moses. Moses received the tables of the law from God, and brought them down to the people. "In the hand" is therefore to be taken strictly. The explanation of most of the Fathers [so BARNES.—R.] referring it to Christ is incorrect. [LIGHTFOOT remarks: "It will be seen that St. Paul's argument here rests in effect on our Lord's Divinity as its foundation, otherwise He would have been a mediator in the same sense in which Moses was a mediator. In another and a higher sense St. Paul himself so speaks of our Lord (1 Tim. ii. 5)."—R.] SCHNEIDER refers it to the angel of the law, who, according to Jewish theology, had the special com-

mission to teach Moses the law. Unquestionably the Rabbins speak of an angel of the law, but it is no more possible to prove this Theologumenon to have existed in Paul's time, than it is to establish it from the Bible (MEYER). The purpose of this reference to the origin of the law is not to demonstrate its inferior dignity, and still less, indeed, is it, as even MEYER and WIESELER strangely assume, to bring the glory of the law, in the magnificence and solemnity of its institution, before the reader. The dignity of the law itself is not under consideration, but its design, as compared with the covenant of promise. We are not, in reading this verse, to pause without reason at *προσετέθη*, as though this were a complete idea, but should read the whole verse together. It is true, we first read: on account of transgressions it was added, but the complete statement is: on account of transgressions it was added in the definite way which is described, 1. by "till the seed," etc., 2. by "ordained by," etc. In this way did it originate, that is, 1. in an entirely different way from the covenant of promise; it was not an immediate giving of a promise, not a fatherly provision and agreement on the part of God, but was introduced by a mediation, and a double one, first of angels, and then, and not before, of a human mediator expressly chosen; the former mediation being on the side of God, the latter being given at the desire of the people themselves. ("How strangely does this appear in contrast with the former manifestations of God, in which the promises were given." REIGER.) This is meant to point out how much more of strangeness God used towards the people in the law, how much more distant a relation it established than the covenant of promise; how could it then have had the same purpose as the covenant?*—But this manner of origin 2. corresponded entirely with the purpose of the law as it has been stated: "because of the transgressions." As these made the law in general necessary, so, moreover, they were the reasons why God came, only through angels, into relation to His people, and that the people on their side had need of a mediator, to hold intercourse with God. The difference indicated in the latter circumstance between the law and the covenant of promise, is then moreover expressly dwelt upon in the following verse.

Ver. 20. **Now a mediator is not a mediator of one.**—The first words are simple and plain: A mediator (*ὁ μεσίτης*, the Art. generic) can never be mediator of a single party, the very idea presupposes more than one, two at least, between whom he is *μέσος*. The question can then only be, whether the design of the remark is, primarily, to express something respecting the mediator himself, personally, or something respecting his function. In the first case the sense would be: He belongs not merely to one, but to the two, the two parties between whom he mediates. So now here *in concreto:* the mediator of the law belonged to the two parties whose mediator he was, viz.: God and men; and the sense more particularly would be: therefore not merely to God, but also to men. The remark would then be intended as an affirmation respecting the nature of the law, that is, has not only a Divine, but also a human character.—Yet this explanation by no means commends itself. If we join *ἑνός* with *οὐκ ἔστιν*, the interpretation: He belongs not merely to one, is much less obvious than the other: He has to do not merely with one, but with two, mediates between two. Still simpler is the construction of EWALD, who joins *ἑνός* immediately with *μεσίτης*=the mediator of one is not, does not exist, is an impossibility. [So WORDSWORTH.—R.]

**But God is one.**—The words can mean nothing else: *εἷς* has a numerical signification, *i. e.*, it can have no other meaning than that of the preceding *εἷς*, hence not=the same, One with Himself, etc. It is these words especially that have given rise to such an enormous number of attempts at explanation. As regards these the reader is referred to the monographs of C. F. BONITZ, C. F. ANTON REIL, KOPPE, or the ordinary commentaries, such as those of MEYER and WIESELER, where the more important modern explanations are arranged in order. A detailed examination may be spared here, especially as the passage of itself is not doctrinally important. [MEYER thus remarks on the course of exegesis: "The many different explanations of the passage, and there must be more than 250 of them, have been thus multiplied especially in more modern times; for the Fathers pass lightly over the words, which are plain in themselves, without regarding their pragmatic difficulties, for the most part applying the first clause, which is generally taken correctly, to Christ, who is the Mediator between God and men, some however casting a side glance at the opponents of the Divinity of Christ. Although there was no special dogmatic interest connected with the passage, the variety of interpretations in the 16th and 17th centuries (see POOLE'S *Synopsis*) was such, that every expositor of importance took his own separate course, yet without polemical spirit, since no dogmatical question was at issue. The variety has become still greater since the middle of the 18th century, especially since the rise of grammatico-historical exegesis (the philogical errors of which exegesis it has however fully experienced), and is still increasing. How often too the absurdest fancies and crudest attempts have availed themselves of our text, the explanation of which seems to be regarded as an exegetical work of art!" He then answers fifteen, of the later opinions, besides alluding to others. JOWETT reckons 430 interpretations! What a testimony to the amount of exegetical labor bestowed on the Scriptures! That too on a passage which is at best but a general statement in support of a single point in a long argument, which seeks not so much to set forth the gospel, as to remove mistaken views respecting the law! How thankful we should be that the gospel texts are so pellucid; had they been less so, we should doubtless have 250 interpretations of them also. As the exegesis now stands, it is perhaps better to admit that the verse is *δυσνόητον*

*[JOHN BROWN: "The existence of a mediator is certainly no proof that a dispensation is not a dispensation of mercy, for the new covenant has a mediator. But the facts connected with the law being given by the hand of Moses as a mediator, plainly show that the law was not, in its literal meaning and direct object, a revelation of the way of obtaining the Divine favor."—R.]

τι (2 Pet. iii. 16). The passage is undoubtedly genuine, and does not refer to Christ. Thus much seems clear. Schmoller gives below an exposition, to which he has added in the second edition another (on which comment is made in the proper place). To this the reader will find added the views of ELLICOTT and LIGHTFOOT, which have been chosen on account of their clearness, a quality especially desirable, when the explanation has so often been *lucus a non lucendo*.—R.]

The question is mainly this: Is δέ (of the second clause) simply metabatic, or adversative? A decision in favor of the one view, gives an entirely different sense from that arrived at by adopting the other.—In the first case we have simply the minor premise of a syllogism, ὁ θεός is with εἰς subsumed under the εἰς denied with μεσίτης. The mediator is not a mediator of one, *now* God is one, therefore, &c. The conclusion now may be various. WIESELER gives it: Therefore the mediator has reference not *merely* to God, but also to men. But the thought that there is found in ὁ δὲ θεὸς εἱς ἐστίν, namely, God is only one party, appears to have too little force. EWALD gives it: Therefore the Mediator has not reference to God, for God is only one, consists not, for instance, of two internally distinct Gods, or of an earlier and later God; it is clear therefore that Moses as mediator, did not mediate, say between the God of the promise and the God of the law, and thereby confound the law with the promise, and so annul the former by what was latter and later, but that he only mediated between God and the people of that time. Ingenious, but far-fetched. The chief objection, however, to this whole view of δέ as metabatic is, that the following sentence in ver. 21 points too evidently in νόμος and θεός to a previous antithesis, from which then οὖν deduces an inference. The above-mentioned explanations are wanting in the recognition of the inner connection of the two verses (MEYER); the thought breaks off, and an entirely new one begins. Besides, according to EWALD's explanation the question as to a κατά would not have been in place here, as this κατά is precisely what the foregoing thought would have denied. Δέ is therefore doubtless to be taken adversatively, and the δέ of the first member is the metabatic δέ of a minor premise. Paul had said: The law was given through a mediator. Now with one there is no mediator, while on the other hand God is One, therefore it might be inferred that the law is against the promises. MEYER: ver. 20 contains two *loci communes*, from which a possible inference (ver. 21) with respect to the two concretes which are under consideration, is drawn. Sense: A mediator presupposes two, therefore also the law does; in the case of that, there were two parties, between which the mediator intervened;—on the other hand God is One, not a plurality; if the promise therefore, of which God is author (comp. vers. 18 and 21), had its origin through Him alone, there was only a single personage active thereby, it was a purely Divine act, not resting upon a contract of two parties. How entirely different in origin, therefore, was God's covenant of promise, from the law? (Was it not thereby clearly indicated, that the purpose of the law was not to be the same and therefore is not the same, as that of the covenant of promise, that therefore its purpose *in specie* cannot have been, to secure—directly—the κληρονομία for men?) But can it not be inferred from this, that the law is *against* the promises of God? that it stands in conflict with them? so that, because the law has come, the promises are no longer to be regarded as valid, and a fulfilment of them is not to be looked for; as at the giving of a constitution by compact between prince and people the qestion may arise whether previous promises given on one side are still to be fulfilled? The main point is to understand κατά (ver. 21) rightly (even MEYER does not explain this correctly). *One* objection, that the law is then purposeless, if "the inheritance is not of the law," Paul has refuted in vers. 19 and 20, by pointing to the fact that it was given for an entirely different purpose, as appears from the very manner of its origin. But out of this refutation of the first objection arises a second, whether by this superadding of the law (προσετέθη) the purpose of the covenant of promise be not hindered; first a free promise on the part of God (without regard to παραβάσεις), and then a *law*, coming through a mediator, who intervened between God and the people, originating therefore by a compact of God and the people (with definite reference to παραβάσεις); does not this then hinder the first, and so far do it away?—This abrogation however is not to be taken in the sense of ver. 17, that the law came in *the place of* the promise, so that the inheritance would now come "of the law," for this is already refuted, first by the very course of the argument ver. 15 sq. from the idea of a διαθήκη, then also by the refutation of the objection that then the law is purposeless, vers. 19, 20. The question in ver. 21 is to be understood as implying an apprehension that by the law the attainment of the inheritance (which, it is presupposed, according to the proof already given, can only be attained "by promise") may be hindered, may be made, comparatively speaking, impossible. It is not, therefore, the *form* of the "promise" which is here meant, but the *substance*; on which account we have here again the plural ἐπαγγελιῶν; the question being, whether the law does not render the fulfilment of the promises of God impossible. This alone gives a progress of thought, and this alone is entirely congruous with what follows. Paul now refutes this second objection also. The law in no wise interposes an obstacle to the promises of God, but rather, in itself, agrees fully therewith, nay, although it had not itself the ability or function of bringing the promises immediately into fulfilment, it was meant nevertheless to serve the purpose of rendering men partakers of this fulfilment by faith in Christ (vers. 23, 24), and with this the law itself then attained its end (ver. 25 sq.).

I allow this explanation, given in the first edition, to remain. It was grounded on that of MEYER, and has at all events this in its favor, in distinction from other explanations, that it puts ver. 21 in immediate connection with ver. 20, and understands the question in ver. 21 as seemingly resulting from ver. 20, while the other explanations, though otherwise having much in their favor, assume that the thought breaks off with ver. 20, and that in ver. 21 Paul merely turns back to ver. 17 or 19.—However a new explanation of ver. 20 has been given by Dr. VOGEL in the *Studien und Kritiken*, 1865, Heft 3, which, it is true, also fails to give a connection between ver. 20 and ver. 21, but which, on the other hand, points out the connection between vers. 19 and 20 with better success than usual, and which, in particular, gives due weight to the statement, the law was "ordained by means of angels." In the other explanations full justice has not been done to this statement, which though otherwise so abrupt, could not have been made without a purpose. VOGEL starts from the usually neglected point of the signification of *μεσίτης*, and shows that *μεσίτης* by no means signifies merely, and not even predominantly—as is commonly assumed in advance—one who stands in the midst between two, but that it means most commonly one who acts instead of some one, and cares for his affairs.—A genitive joined with it signifies either the matter, which is accomplished by the mediation, or the person whom the *μεσίτης* represents, or (which however cannot be shown of Paul's use of it) the several parties between whom he discharges his function (as in 1 Tim. ii. 5). When now it is said of the *μεσίτης*: *ἑνὸς οὐκ ἔστιν*; this of course involves the positive affirmation: a mediator can only be the mediator of more than one. And here VOGEL admits that it would be most obvious to understand this plurality of a plurality of parties, between whom the mediator stands in the midst, but decides nevertheless in favor of the other interpretation of *μεσίτης*: representative—of several persons, for the discharge of their affairs. It is true a representative may very well represent one person only; but then we must understand a representation for the purpose of mediation. In that case it is most natural, only one having to conclude a compact, that he should do it in his own person. But if several have it to do, and that in such a way that the transaction cannot be completed by all, a mediation by one person acting instead of many becomes necessary, and such a person is a *μεσίτης*. The sense would then be: where a mediator appears, we are obliged to understand him as representing a number of persons. VOGEL is led to this interpretation, in the first place by the sentence immediately following: *ὁ δὲ θεὸς εἷς ἐστίν*=but (adversative) God is one. He therefore is not that plurality, which the mediator as such implies. Therefore—the strict logical inference—the mediator is not God's mediator, does not appertain as mediator to God. But whose mediator is this mediator? who is this plurality?

The answer, given ver. 19 is: *ἄγγελοι*—in these we have the plurality we were looking for. The law is, according to Paul, *διαταγεὶς δι' ἀγγέλων*. (Comp. ver. 15, *ἐπιδιατ.*: the law is not an *ἐπιδιαταγή* in the sense that the covenant of promise was thereby prejudiced, or destroyed; it is, however, a *προσδιαταγή*—comp. *προσετέθη*—which, however, was not intended to annul the covenant of promise, for it was only meant to be in force "till the seed should come," etc., that is, only for a time, only till the fulfilment of the covenant of promise should take place. The covenant, therefore, neither could nor should be in any way infringed upon.) The author of the law is not mentioned here, as He had not been at *προσετέθη*. Of course God is to be understood. But Paul is not specially engaged, in making this authorship prominent. He stops with declaring that the law was ordained—promulgated—through angels, having in mind thereby to place it on a lower level than the covenant of promise. With "in the hand of a mediator" (by which of course no one else than Moses is to be understood) Paul now proceeds to name the signs by which the inferior dignity of the law may be known. The disposition of it committed to the angels, took effect through a *μεσίτης*, who, it is manifest, is to be regarded then as their delegate. The angels, the sense might be, did not even themselves promulgate the law in their own person, but this was done through a (human) mediator. The sense therefore would be: ordained for men, that is, the people of Israel, through angels, who, moreover, availed themselves of a mediator.—Yet Paul, by "in the hand of a mediator," is not so much giving a fresh sign of the inferior rank of the law, as strengthening the previous affirmation, "ordained by angels." The circumstance that a mediator was engaged in the work, was not meant so much to explain the manner of the angelic ministration, as to establish the fact of it. The presence of a mediator was in Paul's mind closely connected with this, but by no means so closely connected in the current doctrine. How far this circumstance, that a mediator (namely, Moses) had a joint agency in the giving of the law, is a proof of this ministry of angels, is explained in ver. 20. "In the hand of a mediator" Paul has said and had to say: but where a *μεσίτης* is present, a plurality of parties represented by him is to be assumed; God however is not a plurality, but One: The law, therefore, at whose promulgation a plurality intervened, did not proceed from God, but from the angels (these being the only two parties conceivable)—and therefore form a plurality. The clause would not then be properly a proof (as indeed it is not introduced by *γάρ*), but the fact of the "being ordained in the hand of a mediator" would be simply alluded to for confirmation of the "by means of angels." It would then in fact be best to include the clause in a parenthesis. This interpretation is not disproved by the fact that in many other passages Moses is explicitly named as dealing with the people by commission from God Himself. Paul could still have the right to say that if in a single passage, as here, the giving of the law is represented as the work of angels, Moses must necessarily be regarded as their delegate; comp. Acts vii. 38.—It might also deserve attention, that in ver. 21 the *ἐπαγγελίαι* are expressly distinguished by the epithet *τοῦ θεοῦ*. Is not this connected with the fact that previously at the mention of the law, its Divine origin was entirely passed over and the giving of the law represented as the work of angels?

The question in ver. 21 would not then express a conclusion apparently resulting from the immediately preceding statement. It would rather express amazement, as to how any one could even imagine that the law, which is proximately, to be referred to the angels, could invalidate the promises of God. It is too weak for that. And what would thus be improbable on account of the mode of the law's origin, would then be further refuted by the truth, that the law is incapable of giving life.

Even on this interpretation of ver. 20, however,—independently of the explanation of *οὐν*—the sense given by us to the *κατὰ τῶν ἐπαγγελιῶν* (see above) and to *εἰ γὰρ ἐδόθη* (see below) might be preserved.

[The above view to which such prominence is given on account of its novelty and originality, is in all essential features the same as that of GFRÖRER (*Geschichte des Urchristenthums, das Jahrhundert des Heils; Erste Abtheilung*, pp. 228, 229, Stuttgart, 1838). So that, although thirty years old, it has met with less consideration from commentators than is here given to it in its revived form. As GFRÖRER himself intimates that this interpretation is "easy to be perceived by the eye which has been sharpened by accurate acquaintance with the Jewish mode of thought," it may be allowable to suggest that were this Paul's meaning, his Rabbinical training would be more apparent than in ver. 16. Besides this view would make Paul apparently disingenuous in his attempt to lower the claims of the law, which is God's law,—"through angels, by the hand of a mediator." And yet the chief peculiarity of this novel interpretation is its ignoring that fact. This vitiates the whole, in our view. As Schmoller remarks ver. 19, "the purpose of this reference to the origin of the law is not to demonstrate its inferior dignity."*

Subjoined is the view of ELLICOTT (2d ed.): "The context states briefly the four distinctive features of the law with tacit reference to the promise, 1) restricted and conditioned; 2) temporary and provisional; 3) mediately, not immediately, given by God; 4) mediately, but not immediately, received from God. Three of these are passed over; the *last* as the most important, is noticed; 'the law was *with*, the promise was without a mediator.' Ver. 20 thus appears a syllogism of which the conclusion is omitted: '*Now a mediator does not appertain to one* (standing or acting alone); *but* (in the promise) *God is one* (does stand and act alone); THEREFORE (in the promise) A MEDIATOR DOES NOT APPERTAIN TO GOD. *Is then the law* (a dispensation which, besides other distinctions, involved a mediator) *opposed to the promises which rested on God* (and involved no mediator)? *God forbid.*' According to this view the only real difficulty is narrowed to the minor proposition. *How* was God one? And the answer seems,—not because He is essentially unity, nor because He is one by Himself, and Abraham is one by himself, nor yet because He is both the Giver, the Father, and the Receiver, the Son, united (as held in ed. 1), but, with the aspect that the last clause of ver. 18 puts on the whole reasoning,—because He dealt with Abraham singly and directly, stood alone, and used no mediator." This has the merit of simplicity and is a safe view. LIGHTFOOT is perhaps not so close in his explanation, but it may well be added: "The very idea of mediation supposes two persons at least, between whom the mediation is carried on. The law then is of the nature of a contract between two parties, God on the one hand, and the Jewish people on the other. It is only valid so long as both parties fulfil the terms of the contract. It is therefore contingent and not absolute. *But God* (the Giver of the promise) is one. Unlike the law, the promise is absolute and unconditional. It depends on the sole decree of God. There are not two contracting parties, there is nothing of the nature of a *stipulation*. The Giver is every thing, the recipient nothing. Thus the primary sense of 'one' here is numerical. The further idea of unchangeableness may perhaps be suggested; but if so, it is rather accidental than inherent. On the other hand this proposition is quite unconnected with the fundamental statement of the Mosaic law, 'the Lord thy God is one God,' though resembling it in form."—R.]

Ver. 21. **God forbid. For if there had been a law**, *etc.*—That the law is not in the sense indicated "against the promises of God," Paul proves first by the consideration, that if a law had been given which could make alive, *δικαιοσύνη* would have proceeded from it, *i. e.*, not as it is commonly and altogether erroneously explained, in connection with the erroneous view as to the force of the objection: if a law that could do this had been given, and *δικαιοσύνη* came from it, then were the law actually "against the promises of God (a sense to which *γάρ*, rightly taken, is unsuitable); but Paul really wishes to show that the law accords with the promises, and cannot be intended to annul these; for if the law were able to make alive, *δικαιοσύνη* would actually proceed from it, that is the same effect which is to be wrought through the promises. The law cannot, therefore, in itself, have any tendency hostile to "the promises." But, he continues, "the Scripture has shut up all," *etc.*=the power to "give life" (*ζωοποιεῖν*) was, as it were, denied the law, in order that "the promise might be given by faith in Jesus Christ." It *could not* "give life," and thereby bring "righteousness," if only on account of the sins of men; but, in truth, it *was not* to do this, this was in no wise its design, for the promise was to come *ἐκ πίστεως Ἰησ. Χρ.*—**Given life.**—*Ζωοποιεῖν*=to make inwardly living, not=to give eternal life, for the sense is: if the law could awaken man from his death in sins, and give him spiritual life, "righteousness" (=*δεδικαιωμένον εἶναι*), would actually proceed from the law, for with the *ζωοποιηθῆναι*, the condition of justification would be of course perfectly realized. The conclusion is therefore from cause to effect. MEYER incorrectly takes it "from effect to cause," in connection with his explanation of *ζωοποιεῖν* as the bestowment of eternal life. The "making alive" is not indeed actually the cause of "justification," but this is only because a making alive through the law is not possible. It is however precisely this unrealized case, viz., a making alive through the law, that is here spoken of. [The being dead in sins is here taken for granted; what is meant by "life?" WIESELER's view is given above. MEYER as usual restricts it to future eternal life; but LIGHTFOOT well says, it includes "alike the spiritual life in the present and the glorified life in the future,

*[See TURNER *in loco.* to whose valuable remarks I am indebted for the discovery that this view is not a new one.—R.]

for in the Apostle's conception the two are blended together and inseparable." This seems to accord better with New Testament usage. The reasoning then is not from the whole to its part (ALFORD), for the "justification" is not strictly a part, but a condition of "life," nor from cause to effect, but from effect to cause. "Life" does not comefrom the law, it does not, was not designed to justify, it is not against the promise, but has another purpose afterwards set forth.—R.]—**Verily.**—Ὄντως = in fact, and not merely according to the fancy of the Judaizers, as is now the case, the hypothesis being denied.—**Righteousness.**—Δικαιοσύνη is of course not immediately identical with "the inheritance," but it is an essential element of it, and the one treated of throughout the Epistle, which to be attained by faith.

Ver. 22. **But on the contrary, the Scripture shut up all under sin.**—Συγκλείειν is the strengthened κλείειν, to shut up, (not to shut together): then more tropically with εἰς to deliver up as a prisoner to some one; and generally, to give up into the power of any one, to deliver over. Ὑπό in this verse and the next one expresses this state of subjection still more strongly. Ἡ γραφή: the Scripture, generally, the written word of God: not the law. Τὰ πάντα: the collective whole=all men;* as a fact, doubtless including Gentiles as well as Jews; although, as the context shows, the immediate reference is only to those who have the law, and of whom the Scripture speaks, that is, the Jews.—The sense of this somewhat peculiar expression is easily deduced from ver. 21. It is meant to explain, why the law (and generally, any law) *could not* make alive=impart spiritual life. "If the law had been able ζωοποιεῖν, then δικαιοσύνη would have proceeded from it; an impossible thing, for the Scripture has placed all under the power of sin," it was therefore not possible to fulfil the law and in this way to come to spiritual life; for the law certainly has not the power to destroy the dominion of sin, such a dominion as exists; it has not the power to break as it were the yoke of sin. But how far now can such a "shutting up under sin" be ascribed to the *Scripture?* Of course only in so far as it bears witness to this "being shut up." The sense therefore is: according to the testimony of the Scripture all are subjected under the power of sin=sin exercises a *dominion*, and that over all. This was the fault of men, but the active expression: the Scripture has done it, points nevertheless to an activity, which, it is true, could not have been exercised by the Scripture (for this, in itself, could only be a witness), but which yet was exercised by the Author of the Scripture, God. He has placed all under the *dominion* of sin (and that, as appears afterwards, with the design that the promise might be given by faith, *etc.*). But this, of course, He could only do for the punishment of men, on account of their "trangressions;" it is a punishment ordained of God, that sin should exercise a formal dominion over men.—The connection stated with the previous verse excludes an explanation which otherwise would have a good deal for it, especially because then a function would be ascribed immediately to the Scripture. The explanation is this: the Scripture has, by its declaration, its portrayal, as it were, shut up=subjected all men without leaving any escape or exception, to the *sentence:* Thou art a sinner! and therewith has also shut them up under the curse which sin brings.—Still less is it meant to be said that the Scripture constrains all to *acknowledge* that they are sinners. Nor is there any allusion here to the truth, that the law, instead of restraining sin, has promoted it. Unquestionably, however, we are warranted by what Paul elsewhere says of the law, to bring in this thought, not in order to explain the words, but in order to gain a clearer conception of the fact.

The purpose of this "shutting up all under sin" was, that "the promise" should not be given "by the law" but "by faith of Jesus Christ" and therefore that matters should proceed according to the "covenant" of God, that is, that the promised good should be given, in a certain sense attained, not by merit of works, but of free grace. (This was the purpose of God of course with the foreknowledge that this end, on account of the sinfulness of men, cannot be reached through the law.) But more specially this "shutting up under sin" had as its aim, **that the promise might be given** ἐκ πίστεως Ἰησοῦ Χριστοῦ. For the law was given until the seed should come to whom it had been promised: this shutting up all under sin in consequence of which the law could not make alive, had therefore as its aim, that the promise should be given "by faith" on this Seed, that is, this Seed is Himself first made partaker of the promised good, since, according to ver. 16, the promises were given also to Him, and to others only through Him. Therefore also the duplicate expression **by faith of Jesus Christ—to them that believe.**—It no longer concerns the writer merely to show that the promise is given "by faith" or "to them that believe," agreeably to its original nature, and therefore really "of promise," or of grace. This has already been established in vers. 17, 18, but now, after the new epoch of the history of redemption, the epoch of law, is expressly called an adventitious [*hinzugekommene*] period, and the *sinful condition* of men having been made prominent, the discourse is directed more definitely to the point that the promise is given by faith on Jesus Christ, as the Redeemer, of grace therefore, but of grace ministered in this way. [It is perhaps best, with ELLICOTT and ALFORD, to take the genitive "of Jesus Christ" as both objective and subjective; the Object and the Giver of faith. St. Paul's opponents, as nominal Christians, might hold that the promise came to believers only, but he insists that it came not "by the law, but by faith of Jesus Christ." Hence there is no tautology (LIGHTFOOT)—R.]—"The promise:" here of course, in the objective sense, the object of promise. Taken generally this is=the inheritance; in a more special application that which is attainable for sinful men "by faith of Jesus Christ," is the "being justified," as is simply stated in ver. 24.—The pro-

*[CALVIN, BENGEL, ALFORD. JOWETT are disposed to give this a wider meaning: *omnia humana*, everything which men are, possess or can accomplish. But of this there is no indication in the context, the neuter being chosen because men are here regarded as a collective whole (MEYER).—R.]

mise, therefore, was to be given "by faith;" it was not possible "by the law" on account of sin: but before faith came, the law—and that on account of being shut up under sin—or more precisely, the peculiar position of men in respect to the law, was in its proper place, in order to open the way for the revelation of faith. This Paul says in ver. 23.

Ver. 23. **But before faith came.**—Neither here nor anywhere else [in N. T.] does πίστις mean the *doctrina fidem postulans*, the gospel, but subjective faith, which however is made objective. When men at the preaching of the gospel, believe on Christ, faith, which before was wanting, was now come, that is, it had entered, so to speak, the hearts of those who had become believers in Christ (MEYER).—**We were kept in ward, shut up under the law.**—"We"=the Christians from among the Jews. "Under the law" (ὑπὸ νόμον) is to be joined with "shut up" (συγκεκλ.), and this is then more closely characterized by "kept in ward" (ἐφρουρ.), which marks the transition to "unto the faith," *etc.* Paul then says first: We were "shut up under the law"=the law was the master to whose power, we were completely subjected, without any freedom of our own. And as such (shut up under the law), we were guarded, kept in ward (ἐφρουρούμεθα)=that we might not become free, in substance: we were held in subjection to the law. What now does this mean? Plainly it characterizes, briefly and strikingly, the nature of the law; it was a pressing yoke, a constraining power, to which men were subject. It was such by its continual holding up of commandments and prohibitions, and especially by what was connected therewith, the continual, terrifying denunciation of the curse in case of transgression in case of the non-fulfilment of the enjoined conditions. According to this, how can the condition of men under the law be more strikingly depicted than as a "being shut up under the law" [the perfect participle, which reading we retain, expressing this continued, permanent state.—R.], and because no manner of dispensation therefrom was bestowed in the whole epoch before faith was revealed as a συγκεκλ. φρουρεῖσθαι? [The meaning of ἐφρουρούμεθα is not "safely kept," but "kept in ward." We were shut up under the law and thus kept prisoners.—R.]

The purpose of this representation of the condition of law is no longer merely "to place in the light" still more clearly the great difference between the law and the covenant of promise in itself (as in vers. 19, 20), but it is now to be shown how the design of the law, in its deeper significance, nevertheless coincided with that of the covenant, how the former was preparatory to the perfecting of the latter. For "we were kept in ward, shut up under the law," says Paul, **unto the faith which should afterwards be revealed.** This is to be taken not merely as temporal, but also as telic=for faith=to the end that it might be possible for faith to be revealed, the same faith therefore, in reference to which it had just been said, that the Scripture shut up all under sin, in order that the promise might be given *through it.* The direct aim of the law, therefore, was the revelation of this faith, and through this we are made partakers of the promise; so absolutely untrue is it, that it stood in the way of the promise.—"Revealed:" for "so long as men had not yet believed on Christ, faith had not yet come into manifestation, it was still an element of life hidden in the counsel of God, which, as a historical manifestation, was unveiled, when the congregation of believers came into being." MEYER. How far now was this being "kept in ward, shut up under the law" preparatory for faith, and pointing to it? This Paul does not state; we must fill out the statement for ourselves, which however is not difficult after the preceding remarks. The Scripture has shut up all under *sin.* But on the other hand these same were kept shut up under the law. What else was purposed thereby (since ζωοποιεῖν through it is already excluded), than to awaken and keep continually awake in the soul, the fearful consciousness of standing under the curse of the law (the curse comprehended in the law itself, against transgression of it, against sin), and by this very means, on the other hand, to ground more and more deeply in the soul the conviction of the impossibility of attaining to "righteousness" through this law. The first effect, the consciousness of deserving the curse is elsewhere (comp. ii. 19) designated by Paul as a "dying," and this operation of the law as a "killing." Comp. 2 Cor. iii. 6. In this way it led to the revelation of faith in men's hearts, as to the only way of escape yet possible, or, it led to the longing for a redemption from sin, and thus made men willing for faith on the Redeemer given by God in Christ. [This was the result, but the state "under the law" was still objectively real, whether this consciousness were awakened or not. ELLICOTT remarks on the unusual order, that it "seems intended to give prominence to μέλλουσαν, and to present more forcibly the contrast between former captivity and subsequent freedom." Comp. Rom. viii. 18.—R.]

Ver. 24. **So that the law hath been.**—Ὥστε: an inference. The fact of this "being kept in ward," etc., "unto the faith which should afterwards be revealed" made the law **our schoolmaster.**—This name it deserves, and that for a twofold reason: 1. The παιδαγωγός* approaches his charge with commands and prohibitions, nay, sometimes with threats of punishment, and in general, with limitations of his freedom, and lays upon him in this respect a stringent yoke; there takes place a keeping in ward, shut up under him. This limitation of freedom, and in general this whole relation of subjection, is not however an end in itself, but

*[As Schmoller omits any detailed reference to the word παιδαγωγός, ALFORD's note may well be inserted here: "The παιδαγωγός was a faithful slave, entrusted with the care of the boy from his tender years till puberty, to keep him from evil physical and moral, and accompany him to his amusements and studies. The E. V. '*schoolmaster*' does not express the meaning fully; but it disturbs the sense less than those have done, who have selected one portion only of the pedagogue's duty and understood by it, 'the slave who leads the child to the house of the schoolmaster,' thus making Christ the schoolmaster, which is inconsistent with the imagery." So LIGHTFOOT: "This tempting explanation ought probably to be abandoned. Even if this sense did not require πρός Χριστόν or εἰς Χριστοῦ, the context is unfavorable to it. There is no reference here to our Lord as a teacher. 'Christ' represents the freedom of mature age, for which the constraints of childhood are a preparation. Comp. Eph. iv. 13." —R.]

has place only as a means to an end, serves a higher purpose, namely, that the pupil may be *trained* for mature age, and for the assuming of that higher grade, for which he is destined; "kept in ward, shut up" only "unto" that, which is afterwards to be revealed. And, according to ver. 23, the function of the law also had precisely this twofold aspect.—This goal that was set for attainment, the second point, was the main thing with the pedagogy of the law; this, therefore, is expressly stated in the added phrase (hath been our schoolmaster) εἰς Χριστόν, **unto Christ**.—This is unquestionably relic; this again is more precisely explained by **that we might be justified by faith.**—The goal was Christ=justification by faith in Him. Justification, which the law itself could not bring, because "shutting us up under sin," it was yet to open the way for, to conduct to; because it could not itself bring it, was yet to impel to the seeking and attaining of it "by faith."

Ver. 25. **But after that faith is come,** *etc.*—The law was preparatory to faith in Christ (and so far, indeed, in agreement with the covenant of promise), but for the very reason that it was preparatory, it had only a temporary validity, it ceased with the coming of that for the coming of which it was meant to prepare. Freedom from the law had the way prepared for it by the law itself, leading as it did to faith (how, see on ver. 23); but actual freedom came in only with faith. How?

Ver. 26 explains how (in connection with the aspect of the law as schoolmaster). By the fact that man through faith becomes a son of God. In this conception, however, we are not unduly to emphasize "son" as is commonly done, and to attribute to it the sense of free, son, come to majority, who therefore no longer stands, as a παῖς, under the παιδαγωγός. No doubt the "son of God" is also the one of full age, and therefore free; but Paul, instead of the bare notion of majority, substitutes at once a higher, theological idea, that of the Child of God. Whoever now stands to God in the relation of child, can no longer remain under the law, that schoolmaster, whose threats of the wrath of God awaken slavish fear.*—Πάντες=**all** without distinction. This word is meant to emphasize strongly the power of faith. Whoever he be that has it, becomes a son of God and free from the schoolmaster, therefore you also are free. "You" writes Paul of set purpose, having before (ver. 25) spoken only of the Jewish Christians as those who had previously been under the schoolmaster. But now: You all, even the Gentile Christians, all you who are become believers,—that it might come into no one's mind, to place himself, of his own accord, under the schoolmaster, the law.—Paul says designedly **in Christ Jesus** instead of a genitive immediately depending on **faith** because he wishes to predicate of Christians that they are in Christ Jesus. For he proves that they are sons of God, from their putting on Christ, ver 27.

*[In ver. 25, the article is omitted before παιδαγωγόν, as if to imply, under any schoolmaster, *unter Pädagogengewalt* (MEYER). Still as MEYER himself suggests, the emphasis must be laid on θεοῦ, "sons *of God;*" therefore not in the old pedagogic bondage.—R.]

Ver. 27. The demonstrative force here appears to be simply in this, that Christ was God's Son (MEYER). WIESELER'S objection that Son of God is not used in a similar sense to that in which υἱὸς τοῦ θεοῦ would be applied to Christ, because it is not used in the sense of a being begotten of God, is a strange one. Certainly that is not meant, but by this very putting on of Him who as begotten of God is God's Son, believers come into the relation of children to God, of course in the measure in which it is possible with them.—It is peculiar that Paul proves that all are the children of God through *faith* in Christ, immediately from the fact that they all have put on Christ by *baptism*, and so, without any intermediate step, puts Baptism in the place of Faith. Faith and Baptism, accordingly, are to him in a certain sense convertible ideas, that is, he does not conceive faith without baptism, or baptism without faith; he can therefore prove an effect of faith from an effect of baptism, and doubtless he speaks only to and of such as were not only baptized as well as believers, but with whom also the act of baptism was at the same time an act of faith.—The transition, however, from the "faith is Christ Jesus" to the **baptized into Christ** is easily intelligible in another view also. For nothing proves so clearly that any one has become a Son of God, as that he has put on Christ, and this takes place through the "being baptized into Christ" in a way that is also objective, and therefore undeniable.* On the other hand, his reference to baptism is of course only secondary; he does not as yet mention it in ver. 26, because, according to the connection he is there concerned directly with the effect of faith.

The full import of **put on Christ** is not developed, yet one thing at least is said, and that is primarily the most important—it involves the having become a son of God. It is not immediately=the putting on of "the new man." For the discussion here respects not the ethical quality of the act, but the relation to God involved in it; it is by justification and the relation of children to God given therewith and not by the subsequent sanctification, that we become free from the pedagogy of the law; the filial relation to God does not result from the putting on of the new man, but the reverse. On the other hand, in becoming a son of God, a man naturally has come into an inner relation to Christ, into communion with Him. This inner relation to Christ, in which we invest ourselves with Him, must then without fail lead to this result, that Christ becomes in us the principle of a new life, and we become inwardly transformed. This result is the more certain in that the entrance into relation with Him is so entirely real, through the act of baptism. One cannot *enter* into such inward relation with Christ without also experiencing this inward transfor-

*[ALFORD says "Observe here how boldly and broadly St. Paul asserts the effect of Baptism on all the baptized." WORDSWORTH also at some length presses the objective grace of this rite. But surely there is as much and more reason for pressing "by faith in Christ Jesus" (ver. 26). Clearly the primary truth is "ye are all sons of God by faith in Christ Jesus;" the thought of ver. 27 is secondary. Where there is baptism and no sonship by *faith*, the question is an open one, as far as this passage is concerned, whether there has been any such "effect of baptism." See DOCTRINAL NOTES, 3.—R.]

mation, at least in its principle. The admonition Rom. xiii, 14: "Put ye on the Lord Jesus Christ," may therefore be understood in the sense of an admonition to a corresponding ethical work=to a becoming like Him through our work.—All are children of God by faith (πάντες, ver. 26; ὅσοι, ver. 27). This Paul carries out in the concrete in ver. 28.

Ver. 28. **There is neither Jew nor Greek.**—All these natural antitheses do not come into account in this relation,=if one only believes on Christ, he is a son of God, let him be what else he may. This is tersely expressed at the end of the verse by **for ye all are one in Christ Jesus.**—For this, according to the connection, can mean nothing else than: these distinctions, in a certain sense, antagonisms, do not, as respects being in Christ, come into consideration. All who are in Christ Jesus, are in the same degree "sons of God," how different soever they may be in other relations, that is, they are all, (ἕν) one and the same. Paul, however, goes somewhat farther yet, and by using εἷς, says that they are capable of being regarded all together, as one (moral) person.—Here, too, we are not to think, at least directly, of "the new man" as if the "one new man" were meant.—Why now precisely *this* concrete explication of the "all" in ver. 26? The connection shows that the Apostle's first concern is to represent the antagonism of Jews and Gentiles as done away in Christ; for by the law this antagonism especially was maintained, and was therefore removed by the falling away of the law. And, on the other hand, the abrogation of the law could not be maintained in full earnest unless that antagonism were regarded as removed. But in order to make this "all" more vivid, or to place in still stronger light the power and meaning of faith in Christ, he adjoins yet other antitheses, and remarks that they too, in the new relation, are no longer reckoned of account; the slave also is through "being in Christ" a "son of God" as well as the freeman, and it is the same with sex. In this also, he appears to have the law still in mind. For these antitheses were maintained by the law; at least the law spoke sometimes of slaves, sometimes of freemen, sometimes of men, sometimes of women, and gave in respect to one class, ordinances which were not in force for another, while in view of faith in Christ, or of baptism in Christ's name—these antitheses fell entirely away. [There is a slight change of construction in the last antithesis. "The alterable social distinctions are contrasted by οὐδέ, the unalterable natural one is expressed by καί. The latter distinction is specially applicable as against the Jews insisting on their own spiritual privileges, and on the perpetual obligation of *circumcision.*"—WORDSWORTH. Of this there may be a hint in the use of υἱοί, "sons," not "children," as E. V. The other sex have now the same privilege once belonging to "sons" alone. "Ἄρσεν and θῆλυ, generalized by the neuter, as being the only gender which will express both" (ALFORD).—R.]

Ver. 29. **But if ye be Christ's, then are ye Abraham's seed.**—Because Christ Himself is Abraham's seed (vers. 16, 19), and those that are His participate in His status.—**Heirs according to the promise**—for it was to Abraham and his seed that the promise was given, therefore=the promise goes then for you also into fulfilment. On the other hand it needs no proof that those who are Christ's (because they are heirs by virtue of *this fact*, that they are Christ's) are heirs in the way of the promise of grace, not of works.

[ELLICOTT: "The declaration of ver. 7, is now at length substantiated and expanded by twenty-two verses of the deepest, most varied, and most comprehensive reasoning that exists in the whole compass of the great Apostle's writings."—R.]

## DOCTRINAL AND ETHICAL.

1. *The Law and the Covenant.* Three points respecting the law are treated of in this section: *a*) the difference between the law and the covenant of promise; *b*) the inner relation of the law to the covenant as the means of preparation for the faith which receives the promised inheritance; *c*) the liberation from the law on the entrance of faith. Upon the first two points we have little more to say in addition to what has been already said in the EXEG. NOTES.

*a. The difference between the Law and the Covenant of Promise.* The law was not only given much later (ver. 17), but had also an entirely different character from the covenant of promise made with Abraham, and is not therefore to be regarded as a sort of renewal of that first covenant. The revelation of God to the patriarchs was essentially a different one from the subsequent one at the giving of the law on Sinai. In the first God gave pure, free promises of grace for faith; in the second He also, it is true, gave promises, but imposed as a condition of their fulfilment, the observance of a complex system of law. Or, primarily, the whole sinful people were placed under a constitution of law, and to this promises were attached, but only in the case of obedience; in the case of disobedience, there were threatenings, quite as distinct. To this corresponded the entirely different way in which the law was brought in—in the formal way of a compact concluded through a third party, a mediator, where both sides make engagements, and take on themselves obligations. By this was indicated a separation of God and His people, and it was therefore not the *normal* relation of God to His people, the one corresponding to the nature of God, but only a relation induced by the circumstances, especially by the transgressions of the people at the time; from the beginning, therefore, it pointed beyond itself, but was, no doubt, for a certain time the proper one, adapted to prepare for the relation of grace between God and His people that had been introduced by His dealings with the patriarchs.

*b. The inner relation of the Law to the Covenant* as the means of preparation for the faith which receives the promised inheritance. Respecting the second point we give here only the apt remarks of RIEGER (although his interpretation of ver. 22 is in itself incorrect): The attestation of God, written down and publicly promulgated in the law, has so taken hold of us and all our doing and leaving undone, that no denying, palliating, justifying of ourselves can any longer avail anything, but we must give ourselves up guilty and prisoners under the curse denounced against every transgression; and through this captivity under the law, become pliant and ready for faith on the promise, as afterwards for coming humbly to the cross of Christ preached in the gospel, and thus seizing the only way of escape left remaining to us. The law, then, by its confining me under sin, so far from having the will or power to close against me the access to grace, on the contrary drives me into a strait, in which I am most apt to find and lay hold on the only means of escape. Deluding hiding places of the caves of sin, it indeed closes; but the appointed fleeing to the wounds that have atoned for me it furthers, rather than hinders. In brief: the promise ratifies to man everything, the law comes between and denies him all. Thereupon it is thought, God is against Himself, that must be allowed; but at last it turns out, that the law itself has had to help to this end, namely, that faith and the promise should have the victory. Christ is the law's honor, end, and fulfilment.

*c. The liberation from the Law on the entrance of faith.* Christ is the law's honor, that is, what honors the law is precisely this, that it leads to Christ. But at the same time and on this very account is He the law's *end and fulfilment.* The end of the law, for this beyond question is the intention of the whole Epistle, to demonstrate that Christians are no longer under the law, and in ver. 25, this is expressly declared: now that faith is come, we are no longer under the schoolmaster; he has fulfilled his office.—This is, in the first instance, to be understood historically. With the coming of Christ the epoch of the law, when it exercised dominion, is past, and a new epoch has begun, that of faith on Christ. Hence, also, those who in this new epoch are added to the people of God, through faith in Christ, that is, the Gentiles, are no longer to be held subject to the law, as though faith were not sufficient for salvation.—But this is to be understood also more specially, in a subjective sense; the man who has attained to faith in Christ, is thereby no longer under the law, but may and ought to view himself as free therefrom, and to appropriate to himself the full consolation of God's grace, and to oppose it to all accusations of the law.

2. *The Law has still its use, and must be preached among Christians.* But if now from (*c*) it were inferred: The law then no longer concerns us, and ought not to be preached among Christians! this would be a false conclusion. A *usus justificatorius*, unquestionably, cannot be made of the law under any circumstances, and we must, with Paul, warn men against any such use; and to this extent the position of the Christian preacher, as respects the law, is a negative one. But such a *usus*, indeed, did not belong to the law in itself, according to its Divine intention (as Paul teaches us), even though it was actually so employed. What belonged to the law, was the *usus pædagogicus*, and that it has still, and so far it has a function even in this, the New Testament era. For although the epoch of the law as a historical preparation for redemption, ceased with the coming of Christ, and with that the epoch of faith began, yet in the individual the "coming of faith" is always at first inchoate, and in this respect it cannot be said that in the Christian era we simply admonish the soul to have faith in Christ, and lead it at once to the true source of justification. This may indeed take place, nor can it be disputed that there is such a thing as coming to faith in Christ at once. But its depth, its steadfastness, its true, full worth, this faith receives, now as ever, only through the service of the law. This must be held up before each man, and that distinctly and repeatedly, in order to bring him to the knowledge of his incapacity of fulfilling it, of the impossibility of attaining in this way to justification, and of the necessity of faith in Christ. Even the ceremonial part is applicable to this end, in order to make the value of its fulfilment in Christ the more plainly visible. Naturally, however, the specially *ethical* precepts come into the foreground. (That, in the application of the law within the Christian sphere, these latter, of the whole complex system of the "Mosaic law," are most prominently in mind, and that, therefore, when we speak of the law as still having a use at the present time, the word is not to be taken in its full sense, is, of course, easily understood.)—In this holding up of the law, in its *usus pædagogicus*, there is, it is true, only an analogon of what took place in the actual epoch of the law; for the subjection under the law is renewed, so to speak, only in an ideal way. At most, it may be said to him who will not be persuaded of the impossibility of being justified by works of law: then make trial of the law awhile! But on no one may the law be actually imposed, for the sake of having it do its work on him, to prepare him for faith; and no one ought to impose it on himself to this end. And as to the "bondage under law" of the Christian Church before the Reformation, we may, it is true, view in it a permissive Providence of God, and therefore something that was salutary, but we are bound to stigmatize the fact in itself as indicating an entire misconception of the true character of Christianity.—Yet, if the law is to have its *usus pædagogicus*, an actual subjection under the law must take place, namely, through the medium of the conscience. Only where this "law written in their hearts" exercises its function (but not where there is a mere agitation of feeling or conviction of the intellect), is it possible for a vitally active faith to come into existence. Only for *conscientiæ perterrefactæ* do the consolations of the grace of the gospel in reality exist. And these exactions and threatenings of the law in the conscience are in turn essentially enlarged, more clearly defined and intensified by the positive law of God, so that in this sense it amounts to a complete "shutting up under the law." How long then this "keeping in word, shut up," *etc.*, is to last, how soon faith is to be revealed, and justification to be brought in, is reserved to God's secret counsel, who in the history of His people alone knew when the time was fulfilled, and who in the case of each soul also, alone knows it. To wish to continue "shut up under the law" would be perverse, for Christ is come, we must press through to Him, and in Him find consolation. But even when faith has been attained to, the *temptation* may come, to a retrogression "under the law," which must therefore be *overcome* with all appropriate means of strengthening faith. In this case then we are

to take a decidedly negative position with respect to the law, turning from it, suffering it not to terrify us, nor to expel Christ, and set Moses again in His place. Comp. also, on the whole subject, the admirable observations of LUTHER below, in the Homiletical remarks. This no doubt is the *usus*, which the law even since Christ's coming has retained. But this use manifests Christ more than ever as the End of the law; the law is only meant to drive us to Him. But Christ is also the Fulfiller of the law. The question therefore arises, whether the law have not another *usus* also, for the Christian. Upon this see below, in the remarks upon chap. v. 15 sq.*

3. *The significance and the blessing of Baptism.* Upon the idea of the "sons of God" see DOCTRINAL NOTE 7, on the following Section. Those are "sons of God," who believe on Christ, the more certainly so because they have received *Baptism*, and therewith have been baptized "unto Christ." For therewith they have "put on Christ" = have come into Christ = into Christ's relation to God = into the relation of the sons of God. Two things are implied in this passage. (1) Baptism is only a "putting on Christ," because joined with faith, it is therefore to be considered as such only when this connection really exists. That is: whoever positively does not believe on Christ, of him it is true, even if he chance to have received baptism outwardly, that he has not put on Christ. (Indeed, his being baptized could hardly be called "baptized into Christ.") On this ground, however, our practice of infant baptism remains legitimate. In the case of those, who do not yet believe when they are baptized, only because they are not yet capable of believing, but in whom there is just as little unbelief, or perverted faith in any thing else; in the case of children, who are *brought* by their believing parents to baptism, nothing certainly hinders us from assuming that they *in fact* "put on Christ." Let us consider only what this means. Not, to become a new man (see above, in the EXEG. NOTES), but in the first instance only to enter into the relation of children to God. For children certainly are not yet "under the law," and are not placed under the law (and consequently slavish fear of the Divine wrath and curse is out of the question), but are consciously placed by their parents under the promise of God in Jesus Christ. And if any significance at all is to be attributed to the parental care in this behalf, it must be assumed that an actual transfer under the promise takes place, where no positive opposition can exist. They receive from God the adoption of children, although as yet they do not use or comprehend it, that is, God comes into the relation of a Father to them, and accepts them as His children "in Christ Jesus," although as yet, they know it not. From this possession in fact, to the conscious use of it, those baptized then make the transition in the measure in which they themselves apprehend in faith the promise of God in Christ, and the most efficacious means for promoting this conscious apprehension in faith, is precisely the translation in fact into this relation to God, that has already taken place in baptism. What therefore with the adult, come to self-consciousness, is one act, namely, the communication of the blessing and the consciousness of having it, the translation into the adoption of children and the use and enjoyment of the same, is, with the child, divided. The possession is assured to it, in order that from the very beginning of self-consciousness, it may feel itself already in possession of the good, and may so much the more certainly make use of the same.* And yet—more nearly regarded—the distinction is not even so great as this, for with the adult also, the possession in fact of the adoption of children (the "putting on Christ") and the consciousness and enjoyment of it—are two things by no means always coincident, but the latter is lacking only too often, from the weakness, nay, want of faith, that may intervene, and then the first concern always is to apprehend the promises of God afresh in faith, or more exactly, by recalling to mind that we possess them in fact, to quicken anew faith, that is, the consciousness of the possession. (2) But it is to be observed, that on the other hand also, the power of effecting the putting on of Christ, and of making one a child of God is ascribed to faith only because it is joined with the being "baptized into Christ," and therefore also, we may further conclude, can be ascribed only to it, when it is joined therewith. So then the candidate's longing after faith inheres, as it were, in his baptism, and finds first through this its realization, so the converse is true: Faith not without Baptism! *i. e.*, not merely that baptism must be added to faith, to perfect and to seal it, &c., but although a beginning of faith, more, however, in the nature of an *inquiry* of the heart after the salvation in Christ, than any thing more definite must precede baptism,—faith itself comes to the *certainty: I* have salvation in Christ, that is, in fact, comes really to be faith, only upon the ground and in virtue of that acceptance of the individual on the part of God, and that giving of himself up to God, which takes place in the act of baptism. Only on the ground of baptism, therefore, does the actual putting on of Christ take place, and therewith the becoming a child of God. Unquestionably this is the blessing and the significance of baptism, that it would thus help us to faith, to certainty as to our personal state of grace in Christ, even though in special circumstances it is reserved to God to lead a man without baptism to the certainty of faith.

*[This third use of the law, viz.: as a guide to duty, is denied by Schmoller in form, but not in fact. That we must have a guide to our new life is evident enough. The only dispute is, as to whether we shall call it a *law* or not. Paul certainly does so in v. 14, vi. 2. And when this New Testament guide to duty is compared with the ethical precepts of the Mosaic law, it is found to be nothing else than the Decalogue itself, as Christ interpreted it, and as it was from the first designed to be understood. Compare the position of the law in the third part of the HEIDELBERG CATECHISM, *Of Thankfulness*, especially Questions 90, 91, 115.—R.]

*[Although any wider discussion of the subject of infant baptism would be inappropriate in this place, yet it must be added that any consistent pedo-baptist view must admit as much as Schmoller maintains here. The practice, however cherished from "custom or superstition," must inevitably fall into disuse (where there is no law compelling it), unless parents and children are brought to look at it in this light. Undoubtedly to my mind, it were better that it should fall into disuse, than be a mere public naming of a child, without any such delightful reality in it, as is here held. Of its efficacy as a means for promoting "the conscious apprehension of the promise of God in Christ," in after years, instances are still occurring, despite the prominence of "spasmodic" over "educational" Christianity in these days.—R.]

[CALVIN's remarks on ver. 27, present the middle ground of the Reformed Confession: "It is customary with Paul to treat of the Sacraments in two points of view. When he is dealing with hypocrites, in whom the mere symbol awakens pride, he then proclaims loudly the emptiness and worthlessness of the outward symbol, and denounces in strong terms, their foolish confidence. In such cases he contemplates not the ordinance of God, but the corruption of wicked men. When, on the other hand, he addresses believers, who make a proper use of the symbols, he then views them in connection with the truth —which they represent. In this case he makes no boast of any false splendor as belonging to the sacraments, but calls our attention to the actual fact represented by the outward ceremony. Thus, agreeably to the Divine appointment, the truth comes to be associated with the symbols.—The sacraments retain undiminished their nature and force; they present both to good and to bad men, the grace of God. No falsehood attaches to the promises which they hold out of the grace of the Holy Spirit. Believers receive what is offered; and if wicked men, by rejecting it, render the offer unprofitable to themselves, their conduct cannot destroy the faithfulness of God, or the true meaning of the sacrament. With strict propriety, then, does Paul, in addressing believers, say, that when they were baptized, they 'put on Christ.' In this way, the symbol and the Divine operation are kept distinct, and yet the meaning of the sacraments is manifest; so that they cannot be regarded as empty and trivial exhibitions."—R.]

4. "*Ye are all one in Christ Jesus.*" In this sentence there are two truths expressed, complimentary to each other, respecting the faith of Christians: *a. All* are one, that is, the natural differences, relative antitheses, which exist among men, place no limitations in the way of Christian faith. No one is hindered, by nationality or rank or sex, nor even by his religious belief, from becoming a Christian. Christianity is destined for absolutely all; as certainly as it is the specifically Divine, God-revealed religion; so on the other hand, this character of universality shows it to be the genuinely human religion, the religion destined for mankind as such.—Inasmuch as all can thus attain to faith in Christ, they can therewith, and this is the main thing, all attain also to the blessings contained therein, can all become God's children, all become heirs of the heavenly kingdom.—*b.* All, moreover, are also *one* in Christ. Inasmuch as the Christian faith embraces all, it also unites all, comprehends all in one great whole, and so first realizes in the full sense the idea of the unity of the human race, which by it is transformed into a great family of God. This it was meant to be, but is not of itself, not so much in consequence of the naturally established distinctions, as of the continual influence of (falsely uniting as well as) falsely sundering sin, to which so many false distinctions owe their first origin (as that of slaves and freemen), and which has given to those naturally existing a false tension, and turned them into sundering antagonisms.—This implies at the same time, that Christianity, while it unquestionably does away all artificially established distinctions, does not level down natural ones, grounded in the Divine order of creation (such as sex, age, and also nationality), although it will have them divested of all harshness and false exaggeration (comp. also ANACKER).

[The truth here set forth by the Apostle contains also the principle of true evangelical catholicity. As *all* are one, irrespective of the natural differences, relative antitheses, which previously existed; so all, who are "in Christ Jesus" are *one*, irrespective of the differences and antitheses, which remain after they become Christians. That through the influence of yet remaining sin, these antitheses become antagonisms, does not destroy the real unity, since all "in Christ Jesus" are at least tending towards assimilation to Him. This unity (or catholicity, as applied to the church) is something superior to external uniformity, whether of rite, order or mere theoretical creed. But, at the same time, it is something widely different from latitudinarianism. The latter has no positive basis, but this is the actual unity "in Christ Jesus," the real catholicity of those who are "one," not from outward constraint, or ecclesiastical regulations (however excellent), but from their position "in Christ Jesus," which necessarily involves oneness of life from Him, with Him and in Him. Such a catholicity will lead neither to attempts to unite the visible church by means of external uniformity, nor to less earnest holding fast to the truth as it is in Jesus. In the Catholic Church, as thus constituted, "neither circumcision availeth any thing, nor uncircumcision" (rites, polity, philosophic or speculative theology), "but a new creature." Gal. vi. 15.—R.]

## HOMILETICAL AND PRACTICAL

Ver. 19. LUTHER:—Even as it does not make sense for a man to say: Money maketh no one righteous, therefore it is worth nothing, just as little does it profit to say: The law maketh no one righteous, therefore is it a useless thing. But a man should so acquaint himself with the matter, as to attribute to each particular thing its own functions, that suiteth and appertaineth thereto. [BUNYAN:—He that is dark as touching the scope, intents and nature of the law, is also dark as to the scope, nature and glory of the gospel.—R.]

LUTHER:—See here most evidently the evil consequence of transgressions. On account of these God was constrained to change His countenance towards His people, and could no longer simply give promises of grace. A separation had ensued, and a mediator must intervene, who yet could only throw a bridge over, but could not do away the schism; the people were placed under a law, that commanded, and promised also, it is true, and yet the promises could not receive their fulfilment.—Essentially this, even now, is always the result of transgressions. The law comes in, held up by the conscience, but this is only a mediator, which throws a bridge over, so that there is still a connection, but the separation cannot thus be taken away. —Yet as it was true of the people collectively, so is it true of the individual, that the law came indeed because of transgressions, but only *until* the seed should come. It is to find its end when it has done its work; is then to yield again to the Divine grace in Christ. Christ also it is true was called a Mediator, for He also was to unite that which was severed. But He has really united it, and not merely thrown over a bridge. For He received from God and brought to the people not merely the law, but came for the people's sin and transgression "with His offering of Himself, and so removed the separation." Whereas when Moses interceded upon the Mount for his sinful people, his office of mediator approached, indeed, to that of Christ; but after the intercession, although it preserved the people from destruction, he still came back to them with new tables of the law, and with the glory on his countenance which the people feared, and which he must therefore hide. Entirely different is the glory of the new Covenant.

Ver. 21. SPENER:—What God has ordained, is not at variance within itself, and therefore law and gospel are not at variance. Both agree together. But that we sometimes think they are contrary to one another, comes from our want of understanding. If we find therefore any two things in the Holy Scriptures that seem to contradict one another, we must yet believe otherwise concerning them, because both are spoken by God, and the defect is in us alone, that we cannot comprehend it.—[JOHN BROWN: —What a sad aptitude is there in our depraved nature to misapprehend the design of the gifts and works of God, and to pervert that to our destruction which was meant for our salvation, rendering such an exuberance of illustration necessary to prevent fatal mistake as to the purpose of "the law."—R.]

BERLENB. BIBLE:—The law cannot make living. It commands only: This shalt thou do, else thou art accursed. It does not give spiritual energies, but presupposes them. It cannot bring new Divine life into the dead heart of man. Therefore also it cannot justify. If it could do this, "then would be extolled and revealed to man, not God's grace, but rather men with their own power, merit, and work, which would be wholly opposite to the gospel, wherein God alone is recognized as righteous, but all men as false and powerless."

Ver. 22. The Scripture does not acknowledge in man the ability to help himself. It is the revelation of the general ruin, of the dominion of sin, over all men, showing how it began with the fall of the first man, and has extended itself over the whole. There follows from this the necessity of a redemption. This testimony of Scripture, still continued, should persuade *us* also, of the impossibility of attaining through works, that is, through our own strength, to justification, and of the necessity of entering, for that purpose, upon the way of faith. If the *Scripture* has *shut up* all under sin, it is an idle fancy, if thou thinkest thou canst nevertheless, in contradiction thereto, fulfil the law.—"That the promise," *etc.* Blessed purpose of the terrifying judgment: God would thereby only close up the false way, and therewith, as it were, procure Himself space for the redemption through Christ, and thus for the manifestation of His free grace agreeably to the covenant of promise.

Ver. 23. LUTHER:—The law is a prison, both bodily and spiritually. Bodily, it guards the ungodly outwardly, and restrains them so that they may not according to their will and pleasure practice all manner of villainy without fear. Then it shows us also spiritually our sin, terrifies and humbles us, in order that, when it has so terrified us, we may recognize our misery and perdition. And this is its true work or office, which it is appointed to discharge in us; yet so that it endure not forever.—The law with its custody is meant to serve our best good, namely, that when we are terrified thereby, grace and the forgiveness of sins may become to us so much the sweeter and more amiable, such as man can attain to by no works, but only through faith.—Whoever now is so well skilled, that in time of temptation he can bring together these two things, which are yet else of all things most opposite to one another, that is, whoever knows, when the law terrifies him most vehemently, that then the end of the law is at hand, and also the beginning of grace and faith, such a one knows rightly how to use the law. Know thou, that the law slays thee to this end, that thou mayest, through Christ, be made truly alive?—What has happened historically, at a certain point of time, since Christ has come, has done away the law, and brought freedom to light; the same happens day by day, spiritually, in every Christian man. For in such a one the matter is wont to take such a course, that now the time of law and the time of grace, ever one after the other, has room and place.—The law has its time, when it urges him, torments and plagues him, and brings him to feel his sin and acknowledge its greatness, to be afraid of death and God's judgment. And when it does this, it accomplishes its fitting and becoming work, which a Christian, while he yet lives in the flesh, feels more and oftener than he would fain feel it. But the time of grace is, when the heart, through the promise of Divine grace, is again helped up, so that it gains confidence through Christ towards God, and says: "Why then art thou cast down, O my soul, and why art thou disquieted in me?" Seest thou then nothing at all than merely law, sin, terror, mournfulness, despair, death, hell and the devil? Is there not also such a thing as grace, forgiveness of sins, righteousness, consolation, joy, peace, life, the kingdom of Heaven, God and Christ? We should with diligence learn to distinguish both manner of times, not with words only, but also in the heart, wherein they have their working. But this is above all things difficult. For although these two times, of law and grace, are widely different from each other, as concerns their unlike working, yet are they of all things *most closely joined together*, namely, in one heart. Yea, no one thing is to another so near as fear and faith, law and gospel, sin and grace. For so near are they to one another, that one consumes away and devours the other.—The law is *abused*, first, by all such as set their holiness in works, and indulge themselves in such dreams as that men can be made righteous by the law.—The law, secondly, is also abused by those that would set Christians wholly free therefrom, as the enthusiasts essayed to do, and who dream that Christian freedom is such a freedom as that every one, after his own pleasure and presumptuous mind, may do what he will.—The law is abused, thirdly, by those that are terrified thereby, and yet understand not, that such terror should not endure longer than until they reach Christ. These, through such abuse of the law finally fall into despair, even as hypocrites by their abuse of the law, become proud and presumptuous. On the contrary, one can never highly enough estimate and value, what a dear, precious, and excellent thing it is to have the law, when it is rightly used.—[Such wrong use of the law is made by those who, appointed to lead children to Christ, continually din in their ears such false doctrine, such old legalism, as this: "My child, be good, do thus and so, or God will not love you." What wonder when parents and teachers make the first wrong use of the law above referred to, that the little ones, whom a better training would speedily bring to Jesus, waiting to receive them, make the third wrong use of the law, and are terrified by it. "Forbid them not" thus! Parents do not stand in the place of the law as a schoolmaster, but, as it were, in the place of God, the Father.—R.]

Ver. 24. [BURKITT:—Moses and the law is a rigid and severe schoolmaster, who by whips and threats requires an hard lesson of his scholars, whether able to learn it or not; but Christ and the gospel, is a mild and gentle teacher, who by sweet promises and good rewards, invite their scholars to duty, and guide and help them to do what of themselves they cannot do; by which means they love both their Master and their lesson, and rejoice when it is nearest to them to direct them in their studies—R.]

LUTHER:—If the law is done away, we are never henceforth under its tyranny, but are under Christ, and live in all security and joy, through Him who now reigns in us mildly and graciously by His Spirit. Therefore, if we could rightly apprehend Christ, the dear Saviour, this severe and wrathful schoolmaster would not dare to touch a hair of our heads. From this it follows, that believers, as concerns the conscience, are by all means free from the law; on this account the schoolmaster [*Zuchtmeister*] should not rule therein, *i. e.*, he should not affright, threaten, or take the conscience captive, and though he should undertake it, the conscience should not care for it, but should behold Christ on the cross, who through His death had freed us from the law and all its terrors. Nevertheless there is sin still remaining in the saints, whereby their conscience is accused and plagued. Yet Christ helps it up again through His daily, yea, continual drawing near. For like as Christ, when the time was fulfilled, came once upon earth, that He might redeem us from the insupportable burden and power of our schoolmaster, even so does He come every day, yea, every hour, to us spiritually, that we may grow and increase in faith and the knowledge of Him, and that the conscience may from day to day better and more certainly apprehend Him, and on the other hand, that the law of the flesh and of sin, the fear of death, and terror before God's wrath and judgment, and whatever else my unhappiness is, that the law is wont to bring with it, may continually grow weaker and weaker, and diminish more and more.

Ver. 26. [CALVIN:—It would not be enough to say that we are no longer children, unless it were added that we are freemen; for in slaves age makes no alteration. The fact of our being children of God proves our freedom.—R.]—In STARKE:—Even among God's children are many found that still are burdened with many weaknesses, as is witnessed by the example of the Galatians.

Ver. 27. LUTHER:—To put on Christ according to the gospel, means not, to put on the law and its righteousness, but means, by baptism to receive the unspeakable treasure, namely, forgiveness of sins, righteousness, peace, comfort, joy in the Holy Ghost, blessedness, life and Christ Himself with all that He is and has.—STARKE:—The putting on of anything is such a union with that which we put on, that it becomes quite our own, that we therewith cover our nakedness, adorn ourselves, yea, it may even be, are superbly attired. Considering this matter, we may remember how our first parents, before their fall, needed no clothes to cover their nakedness, but after the fall sought them idly in fig-leaves, as an image of their own righteousness, in the place of which God made them other clothes of skins, as an image of the righteousness of Christ; for this is our beautiful garment, because it covers our nakedness, and protects us against the wrath of God, and adorns our soul.—O exceeding benefit, that we were baptized into the name of Jesus, even in our childhood! The remembrance of our baptism should be to us a continual assurance of participation in Christ and the kingdom of God; but not the less also give to us a continual impulse to all the faithfulness which the covenant of grace requires.—Believing Christians have in their daily putting on of apparel, especially when they put on new and clean garments, a beautiful figure, whereby they should bethink themselves, partly for comfort, of their legitimate nobility in Christ, partly of their bounded duty towards Him.

Ver. 28. [BURKITT:—Now since the coming of Christ there is no difference or discrimination between one nation and another, no regard to any national privilege, either of Jew or Gentile, no distinction of conditions either bond or free; or of sexes, either male or female; but circumcised or uncircumcised, we are all, one as good as another, in respect of outward privileges, or external advantages; but being sincere believers, we are all equally accepted of God in Christ. No external privilege or prerogative whatsoever, without faith in Christ, is any whit available to salvation; none are debarred from Christ, nor more nor better accepted with Him for any of these things.—R.]—LUTHER:—"For ye all are one in Christ Jesus." These are great and admirable words. Before the world and according to the order of the law, there is a very great distinction of persons, which should be most diligently maintained. For if the wife in the family would be husband, the son father, the scholar master, the servant lord, the subject ruler, what would come of it all? Truly a wild confusion, so that no one could know which was which.* But because Christ's kingdom is not a kingdom of the

* [*Dass Niemand wüsste wer Koch oder Keller wäre.*]

law, but of grace, there is also no distinction of persons therein. The Christ whom St. Peter and St. Paul, together with all the saints, have had, even the same I, thou, and all believers, also have, the same have all baptized children also. Therefore a Christianly believing conscience knows nothing at all of the law, but looks alone upon Christ, through whom it comes to the unspeakable glory of being God's child.—LANGE: —If all men are one in Christ, as respects the Divine benefits or blessings of salvation, so no less do the rules of life given, and the duties inculcated by Christ, apply to all, so that no one may except himself.

Ver. 29. STARKE:—The seed of Abraham is Christ with all His Christians, who cleave to Him in faith. He the Head, they as His members; He as the One through whom the blessing comes; they as His associates. Intimate and glorious union!

On vers. 15–22. (*The Epistle for the 13th Sunday after Trinity.*) HEUBNER:—The covenant of God with Abraham an everlasting covenant with the good. 1. Establishment, character of the same in itself: *a*) it is truly Divine, inviolable (ver. 15) and *b*) had reference as to its contents to all men and their redemption through Christ. 2. The continuance of the same even under the law (vers. 17-20): *a*) The law cannot abrogate the covenant of grace (vers. 17, 18). *b*) On the other hand the law is meant as a dispensation on account of sin to prepare the way for the perfect dispensation of the covenant (vers. 19, 20). 3. The perfecting of the same by Christianity: *a*) necessity of this covenant even according to the law (ver. 21), *b*) the condition of the same is faith in Christ (ver. 22).—The false and the right use of the law.—The dispensations of God for the salvation of men: Abraham, Moses, Christ. (The three stages of the economy of Salvation in their relation to each other.)—The unity of God with all the external difference of his revealed dispensations. —The one purpose of all the institutions of salvation.—Christ the consummation of all revelations.—GENZKEN: Promise and law: (1) Both given by God, (2) have both one divine purpose. —WESTERMEIER: The testament of our God: (1) its excellence, (2) its irrepealableness.— JOH. CHR. STARR: The use of the gospel for our salvation: whoever uses the same aright, regards it as a Testament, *a*) to which he adds nothing, because it is God's Testament (vers. 15 sq.), *b*) as a testament confirmed by the death of Christ (ver. 17), *c*) as a free irrevocable gift of grace (vers. 18–20), *d*) in which alone righteousness and life are to be sought.—In LISCO: The purpose of the law: (1) what it is not, (2) what it is.—God's covenant of promise an unchangeable one=not abrogated by the law: (1) the law might not abrogate it, because it had long before been established (vers. 15-18); (2) could not abrogate it, because it could not replace it= could not help to justification (vers. 21, 22).

Vers. 23–29. (*Epistle for New Year's Day.*)* HEUBNER: The happiest entrance into the new year: (1) When we grow out of sin and the law's constraint and through faith become children of God (ver. 23). (2) When we begin a new life after Christ's example, and become united in love (vers. 27, 28). (3) When we keep in mind the hope of one day celebrating in Heaven the eternal year of jubilee.—The free, courageous mind with which the Christian enters upon the new year.—WESTERMEIER: The precious New-year's gifts out of God's word, which this epistle offers: (1) Golden freedom; (2) A high rank; (3) A beautiful garment; (4) Peace and unity; (5) The best hopes for the future.—In LISCO: At the entrance upon a new year how important for all believers is the certainty that we are God's children.—SCHAZZER:— How happy our life in the new year will be, when it is a life in the new covenant! (1) What means it: to live in the new covenant? *a*) not to live without God; *b*) nor as in the old covenant =under the law; *c*) it means: life in the faith of the Son of God—in the adoption of God's children—in communion also with all the children of God. (2) Such a life is happy; for (*a*) it takes from us what makes us wretched: love of the world and the servile mind; (*b*) it gives us what makes us truly happy: the joyfulness of faith, the filial feeling, the blessing of Christian communion; (*c*) it promises us eternal life.—The blessing of being children of God consists (1) in the inward fear; (2) in the brotherly union; (3) in the promised inheritance.

CONARD: We are God's children: (1) this ought to give us repose; (2) impel us to holiness; (3) fill us with blessed hope.—HARLESS: Freedom in Christ: (1) freedom out of Christ; (2) actual slavery out of Christ; (3) the law and freedom in Christ.

Vers. 19–29. How is the law related to the covenant of promise? (1) It is essentially distinct therefrom, vers. 19, 20; (2) yet it is not in conflict with it, for it does not aim to justify (vers. 21, 22); (3) it is on the other hand advantageous for it, vers. 23, 24; (4) it must however recede before it (vers. 25 sq.)—Christ, (1) the law's honor=this is the law's honor, that it points to Christ; (2) the law's end.—The law points to Christ, but also ends in Christ [1, historically, 2, ethically].—Justification before God (1) comes into effect not without the law, (2) yet not through the law. Or (1) only through faith in Christ, (2) yet not without the law.

[Vers. 27, 29.—CHRYSOSTOM (in Turner):— Thus we say, with regard to friends, such a one has put on such a one, when we mean to describe great love and increasing harmony and union. For he who has clothed himself appears to be that with which he is clothed. Let Christ, therefore, always appear in us.—AUGUSTINE:— We having put on Christ are all Abraham's seed in Him, and we are Christ's members; we are one man in Him.—R.]

[Vers. 26–28. True freedom in Christ, hence true equality and true unity! How often are they sought by the world and even by the Church in some other way!—R.]

Of vers. 21–29 each one is suited to *immediate* homiletical application. Special suggestions are not needed.

*[In the Lutheran Church, etc., not in the Church of England.—R.]

c. In their condition of minority the sons of God were indeed held as servants—were under the law; but with the sending of the Son of God the time of majority, and therefore of the full position of sons and heirs, is come.

(CHAP. iv. 1–7.)

*(The Epistle for the Sunday after Christmas.)*

1 Now I say, *That* the heir, as long as he is a child, differeth nothing [in nothing]
2 from a servant, though he be lord of all; But is under tutors and governors [guar-
3 dians and stewards][1] until the time appointed of the father. Even so we, when we
were children, were [or were kept][2] in bondage under the elements [στοιχεῖα, rudi-
4 ments][3] of the world: But when the fulness of the time was come [came], God sent
5 forth his Son, made [born][4] of a woman, made [born] under the law, To redeem
[That he might redeem][5] them that were under the law, that we might receive the
6 adoption of sons. And because ye are sons,[6] God hath [omit hath] sent forth the
7 Spirit of his Son into your [our][7] hearts, crying, Abba, Father. Wherefore [So
then, ὥστε] thou art no more a servant, but a son; and if a son, then an heir of
God through Christ [heir through God][8].

[1] Ver. 2.—['Επιτρόπους . . καὶ οἰκονόμους: the first referring to controllers of his person, *i. e.* "guardians," the latter, to managers of his property, *i. e.* "stewards." See Lightfoot.—R.]

[2] Ver. 3.—[῏Ημεν δεδουλωμένοι: the force of the perfect participle is more accurately expressed by "were kept in bondage."—R.]

[3] Ver. 3.—["Rudiments" is preferable to "elements," as bringing out more distinctly the *ethical* meaning. See EXEG. NOTES.—R.]

[4] Ver. 4.—[Γενόμενον must be rendered alike in both cases. "Born," *natum*, is the interpretation now generally adopted. So Koppe, Schott, Meyer, and later English commentators.—R.]

[5] Ver. 5.—["It seems more exact to indicate the repeated ἵνα by the same form of translation" (Ellicott).—R.]

[6] Ver. 6.—[On the exact force of ὅτι κ. τ. λ, see EXEG. NOTES. "Sent forth" is the better rendering of the aorist.—R.]

[7] Ver. 6.—Elz. has ὑμῶν against preponderating authority. Altered to conform to the foregoing ἐστέ. ['Ημῶν, ℵ. A. B. C. D. F., adopted by the best editors.—R.]

[8] Ver. 7.—The reading κληρονόμος διὰ θεοῦ is with good reason approved by Lachmann, Tischendorf, [Meyer, Ellicott, Alford, Lightfoot.] ℵ. has it. "It is commended also by its comparative difficulty." The κληρονόμος θεοῦ διὰ Χριστοῦ of the Rec. has arisen from a wish to lighten the difficulty, and is founded on Rom. viii. 17. So also the simple θεοῦ. The reading κληρονόμος alone is without any authority. [Wordsworth alone, among many recent English editors, adopts the longer reading.—R.]

## EXEGETICAL AND CRITICAL.

This section depends on the proposition which Paul announced at the close of the preceding one, that Christians are no longer under the νόμος παιδαγωγός, because they are sons of God, and heirs. It distinguishes, with a reference to Israel, which was God's son, and yet was under the law, a twofold condition of the sons of God, the condition of minority, when they were still kept in bondage, and the condition of majority, when that bondage ceased, and therewith the proper position of sons first began.

Ver. 1. **Now I say, that the heir, as long as he is a child.**—"The heir"=the son, as the one who—by law and descent—is heir, even though he does not until afterwards come into possession of the property. He is **lord of all** =has the right thereto; nay, if the father is dead, he is actual possessor, only he cannot enjoy it, cannot assert his character as master, so long as he is under guardians as νήπιος, a child, [an infant, a minor. LIGHTFOOT: "The minor was legally in much the same position as the slave. He could perform no act, except through his legal representative. This responsible person, the guardian in the case of the minor, the master in case of the slave, who represents him to the state—was termed in Attic law κύριος. Prospectively, however, though not actually, the minor was κύριος πάντων, which the slave was not."—R.] The most natural reference is to a child placed under guardianship, whose father is dead, especially on account of the expression κύριος πάντων; and this is favored by the direct application to the son, of the term κληρονόμος, heir. Some interpreters, it is true, cite the expression: "until the time appointed of the father," as inconsistent with this, on the ground that the age of majority was *legally* determined; but this objection has too pedantic a character. [ALFORD: "The question, whether the *father* of the heir here is to be thought of as dead, or absent, or living and present, is in fact one of no importance; nor does it belong properly to the consideration of this passage. The fact is, the antitype breaks through the type, and disturbs it; as is the case wherever the idea of *inheritance* is spiritualized. The supposition in our text is, that a father has pre-ordained a time for his son and heir to come of age, and till that time, has subjected him to guardians and stewards. In the *type*, the reason might be absence, or decease, or even high office or intense occupation of the father; in the *antitype*, it is the Father's sovereign will; but the *circumstances* equally exist." So ELLICOTT and LIGHTFOOT.—R.]

Ver. 2. **Guardians and stewards.**—Ἐπίτροπος also usually signifies guardian. Here, as =he who counsels the ward, defends him, and directs him. It is distinguished from οἰκονόμος =agent, a steward of the estate. The twofold expression is meant to bring out more strongly the idea of dependence.—**Until the time appointed of the father.**—Προθεσμία: "*tempus præstitutum*, appointed term, only here in N. T., but frequently in the classics, Philo and Josephus." MEYER. [Objection is made to the view that the definite time was appointed by the father (MEYER and others), since the term was fixed by statute in Roman law. Some suppose a reference to some exceptional legislation as respected the Galatians. But this difficulty arises only on the supposition that the father is conceived of as *dead*, which is but a supposition. Besides it is unnecessary, as implied above, to press the illustration.—R.]

Ver. 3. **Even so we.**—To be taken strictly= the Jewish Christians. They must be such as were "under the law" (ver. 5). [MEYER objects strongly to this limitation and with reason, urging 1) the sense of "rudiments of the world," 2) that in ver. 5, where the first clause evidently refers to the Jewish Christians alone, the second, taking up ἡμεῖς again, as evidently refers to Christians generally, since ver. 6 addresses such, and 3) that οὐκέτι (ver. 7) and τότε (ver. 8), applied to the Galatians, refer back to the servile condition. ALFORD, ELLICOTT and others admit only a secondary reference to the Gentile Christians. This is perhaps sufficiently satisfactory, but the whole context seems to refer it to Jews and Gentiles alike (LIGHTFOOT).—R.] **When we were children,** νήπιοι.—The pre-christian state is regarded as a childhood in relation to the Christian state of the same persons, only the Christian state then is regarded as ripe age (the comparison is differently applied 1 Cor. xiii. 11; Eph. iv. 13). In childhood a state of bondage existed [the perfect indicating a continued state.—R.]; the external position was that of a servant, not that of the free son. For we were yet ὑπὸ τὰ στοιχεῖα τοῦ κόσμου, **under the rudiments of the world.**—For the different explanations which this difficult expression has received, see MEYER or WIESELER. According to my view the expression applies in any case only to Judaism, especially to the "law" (an Apostle Paul could not possibly comprehend Heathenism and Judaism under one idea, regarding them thus as virtually equivalent); and moreover στοιχεῖα, especially in view of iv. 9, is to be taken in any case in a spiritual sense=beginnings of religion, elementary wisdom; for only with that do the expressions ἀσθενῆ καὶ πτωχά, "weak and beggarly," agree. [Στοιχεῖα, originally the letters of the alphabet, as being set in rows. The question here is, has it a *physical* or an *ethical* reference. The fathers adopted the former view. The latter: "elementary teaching," is now generally received, and is supported by its simplicity, its accordance with the idea of "minor" running through the context, as well as by Col. ii. 8. See notes on that passage. Against the limitation to Judaism, see below.—R.]

Τοῦ κόσμου is either general = Mankind; "the collective human world is conceived as an individual subject, needing the Divine training, to which God, in its boyish age, lasting till the sending of Christ, gave the elementary instruction of the law" (WIESELER). It is true that the heathen world=this part of the κόσμος, had not these rudiments, but for that very reason does not here, where the object is the exposition of the Divine pedagogy, come into consideration. Or could "the world" be taken in a more specific sense, more fully characterizing the "rudiments" themselves=elements, which primarily belong only to the sphere of "the world," of the visible, the external, and hence themselves having the like character, themselves external (comp. LUTHER), opposed to the higher stage, as pneumatic or heavenly? Comp. τὸ ἅγιον κοσμικόν, Heb. ix. 1 (WIESELER). [The first view seems preferable, but without the limitation to Judaism, which grows out of Schmoller's view of "we." For there was a Divine pedagogy in heathenism also, under which most of these to whom Paul wrote "were kept in bondage." Lexically such a limitation is highly improbable. MEYER refers "world" to non-Christian humanity, and "the rudiments of the world" would then mean, not anti-Christian teachings, but the rudimentary training of non-Christian, ante-Christian humanity, including both Judaism and the strivings of heathenism, which may indeed have generally taken the form of external ceremonies, but which were alike propædeutic, the one containing besides an element absolutely good, absorbed in the gospel, the other, an element absolutely bad, antagonistic to the gospel. The Christian view of Ancient History, now generally received, strongly favors this interpretation. See CALVIN, MEYER, and comp. Col. ii. 8; also a thoughtful note of LIGHTFOOT, p. 170 sq., comparing the component parts of Judaism and heathenism.—R.]

Ver. 4, 5. **But when the fulness of the time came, God sent forth his Son.**= When the measure of time was full: and this was full when the time appointed by God had elapsed. The time is conceived as a measure. [LIGHTFOOT: "It was 'the fulness of time.' *First:* in reference to the *giver*. The moment had arrived which God had ordained from the beginning and foretold by His prophets for Messiah's coming. This is implied in the comparison 'the time appointed of the Father.' *Secondly:* In reference to the *recipient*. The gospel was withheld until the world had arrived at mature age; law had worked out its educational purpose and now was superseded. This educational work had been twofold: 1. *Negative:* It was the purpose of all law, but especially of the Mosaic law, to deepen the conviction of sin and thus to show the inability of all existing systems to bring men near to God This idea which is so prominent in the Epistle to the Romans appears in the context here, vers. 19, 21. 2. *Positive:* The comparison of the child implies more than a negative effect. A moral and spiritual expansion, which rendered the world more capable of apprehending the gospel than it would have been at an earlier age, must be assumed, corresponding to the growth of the individual; since otherwise the metaphor would be robbed of more than half its meaning.—The primary reference in all this is plainly to the Mosaic law; but the whole context shows that the Gentile converts of Galatia are also included, and that they too are regarded as having undergone an elementary discipline, up to a certain point analogous to that of the Jew."—R.]

**Born of a woman.**—Conveying no allusion to His miraculous conception, but simply an emphatic designation of the Incarnation, defining precisely "sent forth." The reality of the Incarnation is emphasized, in order, in the first place, to bring fully into view the humiliation which God imposed on His Son, and to make this contrast felt: He humbled Himself—we were exalted. But this humillation did not consist in the Incarnation alone, it was only the beginning; its full expression is found in **born under the law,** and the contrast becomes thereby still stronger: He was brought under bondage—we, into freedom. Yet of course the object is not merely to make the contrast sensible, but "born of a woman" and "under the law" is mentioned, because it was the means of attaining the end which was to be attained, namely, **that he might redeem,** *etc.*—*i. e.*, primarily and principally the being "born under the law" was this means, but this again was only possible through His really becoming man.—Γενόμενον ὑπὸ νόμον, probably simply=born under the law, not: brought under the law. The primary meaning of this is, in general, that by virtue of His Jewish birth, He, like every Israelite, was subordinated to the requirements of the law, and we are therefore to supplement "redeem them that were under the law" with ἐκ τοῦ νόμου, "from the law=that He might make those subjected to the law free from the law=that He might free them from the state of subjection under it, from their obligation to it, from the "bondage" just mentioned. The sense of "redeem" is given by the simple addition: ἵνα τὴν υἱοθεσ. κ. τ. λ.,= might translate us from the position of servants into the free position of sons. Primarily, only this is implied in the words, and the expression therefore is not immediately convertible with the narrower, more defined one in iii. 13; although, indeed, if we look for the causal nexus between Christ's being born under the law and His redeeming those under the law, we shall be led back to the thought expressed iii. 13, as the connecting one, namely, that the one who stood "under the law" became by this law "a curse" =bore also the curse of this law, and thus freed the men who stood under the curse of this law from this curse of the law, and therewith from the law altogether, from dependence on it, since in the place of that dependence there now naturally came a believing self-surrendering to the Liberator. This filling out the thought by a reference to the death of Christ, gives moreover to "born of woman" also, its full significance; for only through this was death itself possible, as only through the being "born under the law" was it possible as a death under the curse of the law.

**That we might receive the adoption of sons.**—Properly the *position* of sons [υἱοθεσία] as opposed to the position of servants. Even "under the law" they were *in themselves* υἱοί, but as yet differing in nothing from servants; through Christ they first attained also to the *position* of sons, differed from servants. Υἱοθεσία here means then more exactly: the right of the free, major son. This may very well be designated simply as υἱοθεσία, since sonship *de facto* really begins with it, the son thereby first becomes properly a son.—That a sonship relatively to *God* is here treated of, is made apparent by the connection. [Schmoller evidently refers "we," in this clause, to Jewish Christians alone; but the objections of MEYER and others to such a limitation (see on ver. 3), apply with great force here. That it breaks the force of the Apostle's argument, and destroys the connection of the whole passage, to restrict it thus, is evident from the explanation into which Schmoller is forced in his remarks on the succeeding verse. It may be allowed that, in the previous clause, "those under the law" refers to Jewish Christians alone, but a wider reference of "we" to all Christians must be insisted upon.—R.]

Ver. 6. **And because ye are sons.**—Remarkable is the abrupt transition into the address to the Galatians, whereas what preceded applied to the Jewish Christians; for these were "those under the law," while the Galatians were, at all events, predominantly Gentile Christians. But through the sending of the Son the Gentiles also were to obtain the sonship with God, and they did actually obtain it through faith in Him. He can therefore naturally say to Gentile Christians also: Ye are sons,—and can appeal to the witness of the Spirit concerning this, which they have in themselves. And the discussion had properly direct reference to the Gentile Christians, the Galatians, to their freedom from the law; the remarks ver. 1 sq., were only as it were episodically woven in [?!], in order to explain the peculiar position of Israel under the law.—[Accepting the wider reference of "we," (ver. 6), we find here no "abrupt transition," but a change to the second person, in order to apply to the Galatians, what had been affirmed of all Christians. Of course this obviates the necessity of such an explanation of the connection, as Schmoller makes.—R.]—With this sentence Paul wishes to confirm to the Galatians, in a way indisputable to themselves, that they actually have the position of sons and no longer that of servants; they also (he says) have this, as well as the Jewish Christians, as certainly as the Spirit also utters His voice in them. The primary *purpose* of the sending of the Son, stopped with this υἱοθεσία. That the purpose has been *accomplished*, is shown first in this, the Spirit's witness of adoption. Ver. 7 therefore contains the simple conclusion from ver. 6: Accordingly thou art, etc. [It is a question whether ὅτι should be rendered "because," *quoniam*, or "that," *i. e.*, to show that ye are sons (ELLICOTT). Most commentators incline to the former view. ALFORD in his notes opposes MEYER, who adopted the latter view, which in his fourth edition, however, he characterizes as "harsh and unusual." Still the proof of sonship remains. He would not have sent the Spirit, if they had not been "sons."—R.]

**God sent.**—At the regeneration of each of the readers, or what may here be taken as identical, at their baptism. Yet naturally a continuous sending from that time forward, is not excluded but included. [The aorist is used as in ver. 4, referring to a definite act. MEYER notes the similarity of form, as "a solemn expression of the objective (ver. 4) and subjective (ver. 5) certainty of salvation," and also as indicating doctrinally "the same personal relation of the Spirit, which God has sent from Himself as He did Christ."—R.]—**Spirit of His Son.**—A peculiar expression; not immediately convertible with the conception: spirit of sonship, but = the Spirit, which the Son of God has; plainly, moreover, which He has peculiarly as Son; hence, the Spirit, in which, with Him the consciousness of sonship relatively to God rests and expresses itself, and so = the Son of God's Spirit of sonship. God gives the very same Spirit into the hearts of those whom He has accepted as His sons for the sake of His Son Christ; and therewith they also attain to the consciousness of sons relatively to God, so that they cry: Abba, etc.—**Crying.**—This strong word, κράζειν, doubtless expresses, first and chiefly, the assurance and the strength of the persuasion, the full undoubting faith of having in God our Father; also, however, as resulting from this, the fervor with which the soul turns to this Father, yet without direct reference to a condition of trouble, in which a call is made for help.—**Abba, Father!**—"It is simplest to suppose that the juxtaposition of the two equivalent expressions is meant to emphasize more strongly the idea of Father." WIESELER. MEYER with less probability thinks, that Ἀββᾶ had become so settled and sacred a term, as an address to God in Christian prayer, that it had acquired the nature of a proper name, admitting thus the addition of the appellative ὁ πατήρ. The ancients found in it an intimation: *quod idem Spiritus fidei sit Judæorum et gentium.* [It seems best to regard this repetition as taken from a liturgical formula, which may have originated among the Hellenistic Jews, who retained the consecrated word "Abba," or among the Jews of Palestine, after they became acquainted with the Greek language. The latter theory best explains the expression as used Mark xiv. 36 (LIGHTFOOT). There may be a reason for retaining "Abba" in its affectionate character, "My Father" (ALFORD). And the repetition may contain the hint, which the Fathers, LUTHER, CALVIN and BENGEL find, of the union of Jew and Gentile in Christ. Certainly an advance from the "Abba" of childhood to the "Father" of maturity, on the part of the believer, is not implied, nor is there a reference "to the fact that a *freedman* might by addressing any one with the title Abba, prepare the way for adoption by him," since they are enabled thus to cry, "because ye *are* sons."—R.]

Ver. 7. **So then thou art.**—A progress in individualizing for a practical purpose; namely, to bring home fully to each one separately, what he possesses through Christ.—**No more a servant.**—This refers back to the being "in bondage under the rudiments of the world," and applies to the Jewish Christians in its full sense, and then to the Gentile Christians also, in this respect, that in consequence of the sending of the Son, the necessity of giving themselves up to be held in bondage "under the rudiments of the world" was done away for them also; that in Christ these have lost their force. [In the wider view of "we" (ver. 3) this explanation is unnecessary.—R.] In what special, still more wretched sense, they too were actually slaves, and so the state of servitude was abolished for them, appears immediately after in ver. 8.—**But a son.**—The contrast between "servant" and "son," as applied to the Jewish Christians, is limited to their being now in actual enjoyment of the son's privileges; as applied to Gentile Christians it is without restriction.—**And if a son, then an heir through God.**—"Through God" makes prominent that the one character, as well as the other, proceeds from grace, as opposed to all desert of works. Because a son (*sc.* of God), therefore according to the well-known hereditary right, also an heir, *sc.* of God. The controversy, whether Jewish or Roman right of inheritance is meant, may be called pedantic. Heir of God = to whom God's possession appertains, eternal life. [The briefer reading, διὰ θεοῦ, now generally adopted, is thus remarked upon by WINDISCHMANN: "It combines, on behalf of our race, the whole before-mentioned agency of the Blessed Trinity: the Father has sent the Son and the Spirit, the Son has freed us from the law, the Spirit has completed our sonship; and thus the redeemed are heirs through the Triune God Himself, not through the law, nor through fleshly descent."—R.]—This gives another basis for "heirs," iii. 29, and the train of argument thus reaches its conclusion.

## DOCTRINAL AND ETHICAL.

1. *The rudiments of the world.* Respecting the characterizing of the law as "rudiments of the world," comp. the remark of LUTHER: Learn from this, when it concerns the business of justification before God, to speak of the law most contemptuously, following the Apostle. But when we are not treating of how a man may become acceptable and righteous before God, we are to reckon the law most highly and honorably, and with St. Paul, to call it holy, righteous, good, spiritual, and divine, as indeed it truly is.—St. Paul is alone among all the Apostles, in speaking so scornfully as it may appear, of the law. The other Apostles make it not their wont, so to speak. Therefore ought every one, who will study in the Christian theology, to take careful note of this diverse manner in St. Paul's writings. He has been called by our Lord Jesus Christ Himself His chosen vessel, and therefore also He gave him an elect mouth, and a diverse way of speaking above the other Apostles, so that he, as chosen vessel [*Rüstzeug, lit.* weapon], might most firmly and most faithfully found the citadel of the faith, even the article which teaches how a man must become righteous before God, and might teach the same most perspicuously, and most clearly,

2. *Law and Old Testament.* "Law is not synonymous with Old Testament, gospel with New Testament; as if we could say: The law has been abrogated by the gospel, Christ is the end of the law, therefore for us Christians the Old Testament has no more validity. It is not so, but the Old Testament as well as the New, contains gospel promise of grace, and the New as well as the Old contains law Only that in the Old Testament the law, the schoolmaster unto

Christ, prevails, the gospel, on the other hand, appears in the form of promise of the future salvation, and so is more veiled; but in the New Testament the gospel of the accomplished salvation strikes the key-note, and the law, as a threatening might, only opposes itself to the despisers of salvation, and is written in the hearts of believers. And since the gospel extends through the whole Holy Scripture of the Old and New Testament, every Christian must necessarily count the Old Testament also honorable and holy. It is true here also: What God hath joined together, let not man put asunder." ANACKER.

3. *The fulness of the time.* For a full historical demonstration of Christ's having come in the fulness of time, see *e. g.*, ANACKER. [SCHAFF: *History of the Apostolic Church*, and *History of the Christian Church*, vol. I. "It was a great idea of Dionysius 'the little,' to date our era from the birth of the Saviour. Jesus Christ, the God-man, the prophet, priest, and king of mankind, is, in part, the centre and turning point not only of chronology, but of all history, and the key to all its mysteries. All history before His birth must be viewed as a preparation for His coming, and all history after His birth as a gradual diffusion of His spirit and establishment of His kingdom. He is 'the desire of all nations.' He appeared in the 'fulness of time,' when the process of preparation was finished, and the world's need of redemption fully disclosed."

"As Christianity is the reconciliation and union of God and man in and through Jesus Christ, the God-Man and Saviour, it must have been preceded by a two-fold process of preparation, an approach of God to man, and an approach of man to God.—In Judaism the true religion is prepared for man; in heathenism man is prepared for the true religion. There the divine substance is begotten; here the human form is moulded to receive it. Heathenism is the starry night, full of darkness and fear, but of mysterious presage also, and of anxious waiting for the dawn of day; Judaism, the dawn, full of the fresh hope and promise of the rising sun; both lose themselves in the sunlight of Christianity, and attest its claim to be the only true and the perfect religion for mankind."

"The way for Christianity was prepared on every side, positively and negatively, directly and indirectly, in theory and in practice, by truth and by error, by false belief and by unbelief—those hostile brothers, which yet cannot live apart—by Jewish religion, by Grecian culture, and by Roman conquest; by the vainly attempted amalgamation of Jewish and heathen thought, by the exposed impotence of natural civilization, philosophy, art and political power, by the decay of the old religions by the universal distraction and hopeless misery of the age, and by the yearnings of all earnest and noble souls for the unknown God. 'In the fulness of time,' when the fairest flowers of science and art had withered, and the world was on the verge of despair, the Virgin's Son was born to heal the infirmities of mankind. Christ entered a dying world as the author of a new and imperishable life."—R.]

4. *God sent His Son, born of a woman.* In these few words we have the sum of the second article [*i. e.*, of the Augsburg Confession]: "Jesus Christ, true God, born of the Father in eternity, and also true man, born of the Virgin Mary." ANACKER.—If the preëxistence of the Son does not follow of necessity from the expression: God *sent* Him, it follows so much the more necessarily from the added clause: "Born of a woman," *i. e.*, from the fact that this is predicated of the Son as something peculiar. Paul cannot have been thinking of a man, to whom the character of God's Son belonged only in some theocratic sense, who had been elevated to it by God: for why then the particularizing clause: born of a woman? It would be absolutely meaningless. It has a meaning only in the case of One, who in Himself was not one born of woman, who only became so, with whom this was something entirely peculiar. The peculiarity and noteworthiness of the fact, also, that the Son of God was born under the law, depended, in reality, upon this, that in His original state He had not human nature.—The supernatural conception, it is true, is by no means implied in the expression: born of a *woman*, in itself, as if *by this* the concurrence of the *man* were to be excluded. But if we take this expression together with "God sent His Son," we are almost necessarily constrained to assume another than the ordinary origin through the generative activity of the man, an immediate activity, instead, of the God who purposed to send the Son.—The Divine Sonship of Christ is one belonging to Him in Himself, essential to His nature, so essential, that even by being born of a woman, and under the law, it was not nullified. It is on this account entirely different from our Divine sonship: this is an acquired, a mediated one; mediated through God's Son Christ.—On the other hand in this passage the true humanity of Christ is most distinctly declared. He did not bring His body from Heaven, and did not pass with it through Mary *quasi per canalem*, nor did He merely assume a body like an angel. Either is excluded by the expression: born of a woman. And the tenor of the passage shows plainly that it is meant, not to declare His preexistent being (this we can infer only by reasoning back), but precisely His true humanity, that God sent Him in such wise that He caused Him to be born and be manifested as man; it was precisely this which made it an actual *sending*, fulfilling the promise. But on the other hand this Man=God's Son; for if not, the purpose would in this way have failed in accomplishment, since it was no other than His Son that God would send.

5. *Born under the Law.* By this is made prominent not the legal *obedience* which Christ rendered, or anything performed by Him, but something to which He subjected Himself, the *dependence* on the law, in which He was placed —according to the whole connection: a *δουλοῦσθαι* (comp. *τοὺς ὑπὸ νόμον*), primarily dependence in general, and then as the culmination of it, the curse of the law, to which He subjected Himself. This passage therefore is no proof of the "active obedience of Christ," as it is termed. Christ, it is true, was in such a sense under the the law that He observed it; He did not resist it; He was content with this dependence, and fulfilled the requirements of the law. But it is inappropriate to designate the *obedience*, which

Christ indeed rendered in fullest measure towards His Father, as fulfilment of the law, and to designate the (active) fulfilment of the law as that which was great and meritorious in Christ. Christ's obedience was an essentially free obedience of a child towards the Father, and thus far surpassing a bare *law*-obedience.—On the other hand, the statement of doctrinal theology, which in many quarters causes scandal, that Christ was *in Himself* not subject to the law, is *in itself* not incorrect. Only we must then take law in the entirely definite Biblical sense. The γενέσθαι ὑπὸ νόμον which was added because of transgressions, was of course something in itself wholly inadequate to His sinless being, wholly obedient as it was to God; He stood, as concerned Himself, in the Son's relation to God, not in the servant's relation, was no minor, needed no παιδαγωγός. This γεν. ὑπὸ νόμον, therefore, was something in itself foreign to Him, imposed upon Him, and undertaken by Him, *for the definite purpose* of the redemption of those under the law. But He was the first one "under the law" who yet was sinless, obedient to God, and this availed to the good of the men who were under the law

6. *Adoption and the consciousness of it.* From the attainment of the filial relation to God [*Gottes-Kindschaft*] Paul distinguishes again the certainty of the same, so to speak, the conscious exercise of the privilege of children. Agreeably to this he distinguishes a twofold sending: the sending of the Son into the world and the sending of the Spirit of the Son into human hearts. On the first is grounded the *attainment* of the adoption of God's children, inasmuch as the sending of the Son led to the ransoming of those under the law. This is the objective side. Yet this hardly denotes merely the redemptive act of Christ, but includes doubtless, even at this point, faith in this act, as without this faith there is not an actual adoption, a being a son (comp. ὅτι δέ ἐ σ τ ε υἱοί). But to this is yet added the sending of the Spirit of the Son into the hearts of the redeemed, or more specifically: His crying Abba in the heart. Primarily this serves for the sealing and making sure of the now established filial right (comp. Rom. viii. 16). Yet it is not bare assurance that is wanted, but the exercise, the use of the right; and this first becomes possible by receiving the Spirit of Sonship, exclaiming Abba. "Should we wish to do it of our own desire and folly (namely, use such an heartily filial address to God), the word would die upon our lips; for *we* cannot make God our Father, only He Himself can do it." It is this Spirit of adoption Himself, says Paul here, that cries Abba in us, of course, by uniting Himself with the spirit of the suppliant, and forming in it the language of filial address to God. Therefore Rom. viii. 15: *We* cry Abba *by* this Spirit.

Paul distinguishes, as has been said, two stages, but yet plainly not in such a sense as if the first were something complete within itself, and the second added to it, as something distinct, but whoever is "son" receives *eo ipso* this Spirit, and if he did not receive it, the Apostle would not predicate the being a son of him. The receiving of this Spirit is for him, and is meant to be for the readers (on which account he alludes to it), the criterion of having become a "son of God." He cannot conceive the being a son without this Spirit in the heart exclaiming Abba. Therefore he affirms it at once and in reference to all: "Because ye are sons, God sent forth," etc. The same faith which translates us into the position of children, opens also the access to this Spirit. Yet of course this receiving of the Spirit of sons or children, is again somewhat successive, and Paul does not mean to say that this crying Abba takes place always with uniform strength and joyfulness; he will not deny that there come times of spiritual conflict; he only expresses what is normal.

7. *Son, not servant.* The idea of Divine sonship is a twofold idea, for the υἱὸς θεοῦ is first (υἱὸς) θ ε ο ῦ and then υ ἱ ὸ ς (θεοῦ). In Rom. viii. 14 sq., the previous context shows the former to be the main idea, for "being a son of God" is opposed to living "after the flesh," and is defined by "led by the Spirit of God." In this passage the essential idea is the second one: the Son of God is *son* and no longer *servant* (with which we may also supply "of God"), or the filial relation of the Christian to God, as it is brought into effect by Christ, involves the idea of religious maturity. The Christian has through his faith come religiously to majority; he no longer stands to God in the relation of the minor son, still kept in bondage. This latter relation of man to God is also one in itself possible and relatively admissible. God Himself placed man in it by the law (ver. 3); Israel itself stood by God's appointment in the relation to God of religious minority, was as yet "kept in bondage under the rudiments of the world." This was at that time what was fitting and wholesome for the people of God. (And in a certain sense the man who as yet knows nothing of Christ, is, even now, in this relation to God, is the unfreed minor, kept in by legal restraints, at least by the inward law of the conscience. It is true this law is a far more imperfect one than the positive law of God. Therefore the natural man without Christ is far more a δοῦλος than Israel was—a δοῦλος rather to the σάρξ or the φύσει μὴ ὄντες θεοί than to God; and there is needed at first a special activity directed to the awakening of the conscience. See below.) It is otherwise with the Christian; he has gained through faith in Christ, or rather through the Spirit of Christ, the position towards God of the free major son: this position, because established through Christ, has its direct analogy in the relation of Christ to His Father. It is true there is in this no independent dignity [*Selbstherrlichkeit*]; but it is not so much that this is forbidden him, as that he himself is the farthest possible from wishing it, recognizing in it, as he does, an illusive image, knowing that thereby he would in truth lose his freedom, that true freedom consists in this very obedience of love towards God, in speaking nothing else than what He teaches, in doing nothing else than what He points out. Thus, although not living to himself, he is yet truly free, even towards God, as one of full age; is, *sui juris*, independent. For his conduct is not prescribed to him in legal injunctions, regulating even the outward life, and seeking in

this way to conform the inner life to God's will; he recognizes the "living to God" as his very element, the condition of his happiness. His obedience is not merely an obedience of law towards a ruler, but a life in trustful love to Him who is recognized as Father and sealed through the Spirit.

But especially does the maturity of the Christian consist in this, that he is *heir*, in possession of the paternal *estate*. For thus the minor is distinguished from the major son; for the former the inheritance is as yet administered by others, and he himself is not yet in enjoyment of it, but only, it may be, from time to time, receives out of it what is necessary for him, and on the other hand, may, on occasion, be kept in straits, or even subjected to punishment. So with man under the law; as he first sees in God One who commands and strictly regulates life, so also he sees in Him one who bestows good only according to desert, and who just as certainly, where punishment is deserved (as is more often the case), inflicts punishment, and instead of a blessing communicates a curse. It is otherwise with the son of full age and with the Christian. He is heir, is in possession and enjoyment of the paternal estate. This actual enjoyment of the inheritance he possesses in the first instance in justification and the state of grace connected therewith. As the major son freely disposes of the paternal estate, so also the Christian, in faith freely applies himself, as it were, when he will and as oft as he will, to his Father's treasure, and takes from it whatever he desires. Only this possession and enjoyment of his is, as it were, still embarrassed by the "sufferings of this present time," and the glory of the inheritance is still "to be revealed" (Rom. viii. 17, 18), as indeed the major son also, who has come into possession of the paternal estate, has still to struggle with many inconveniences, and so cannot as yet give himself up to the undisturbed enjoyment of his estate, and yet is none the less the free son, of full age, and by no means any longer in his minority. From this the simple inference is: (1) That as the Christian may not deprive himself of his position as Christian, if he would not incur the reproach in ver. 9, so also he may not be robbed of this rank or denied it, he may not be again placed under guardianship, and thus reduced from one of full age to a minor again, that therefore in particular the law may not be again imposed upon him, and his relation to God represented as conditioned by that; (2) that a Christian church, which does not regard her members as mature children of God, and train them to be such, but which instead retains them under the guardianship of the Divine law, or, more than that, of self-devised human ordinances, and accords to them only such a share in the benefits of Divine grace as suits her own discretion, if indeed, she does not wholly conceal them and set an inheritance invented by herself in their place—that such a Christian church misapprehends her most essential character (for Christ was no new lawgiver), and that therefore the Romish church, which does this, incurs this reproach, and that the evangelical church would incur the like reproach, so far as she imitated her in this, in a supposed pedagogic interest, or for the sake of discipline and order.* She has simply to be God's almoner by offering the means of grace which excite and strengthen faith, as the condition of adoption as God's children, and what she ordains can lawfully have no other end than directly or indirectly to further such beneficence. True, individually as well as historically, the state of maturity, in the child of God, is preceded by that of immaturity; for just so certainly as a Christian is in the former state, just so certainly is he there no otherwise than through actual heart-faith. But the true way, that agreeable to the Divine order in such a case, is (according to remarks on the foregoing section) to hold up the law for this end and this only, that the man's conscience and with it the knowledge of sin may be awakened, that the law may prove itself in him also "a schoolmaster unto Christ." Now this comes to pass only through the preaching of the word of God in its completeness, inasmuch as thereby the law also is set forth, but now, of course, only with the intention of leading to the Gospel and therewith to the condition of spiritual maturity.

8. *Old Testament believers not of full age.*—As respects Christians the believers of the old covenant were accordingly not yet in the full sense "sons of God," *i. e.*, "major sons." "But how were then the holy prophets, the great heroes, the upright men of God, who lived from Moses until Christ, minor children, that must be kept under the figurative rudiments of divine instruction as under tutors and governors? Doubtless in a certain sense they were. It is true that in much they have surpassed us; but what was spiritual, heavenly, eternally permanent in the kingdom of God, what Paul ever calls 'a mystery,' was not revealed to them so plainly as to us" (Roos). In order to judge correctly, we must however, with the Apostle himself, distinguish the period before the law from that under the law. For example, the patriarchs, although in another respect also children, stood in immediate intercourse with God, were not in the position of servants. On the other hand there certainly was also in the believers under the law, in proportion as the promise of the new covenant was living in them, *e. g.*, in the prophets, an anticipation, in a certain sense, of the position of major sons of God, although rather in some single moments of elevation.

### HOMILETICAL AND PRACTICAL.

Ver. 2. STARKE:—Human ordinances, which are directed to the well-being of the commonwealth, are in themselves in no wise contrary to the Divine law.—When the Prince of Wales in his childhood once refused obedience to his governess, appealing to his dignity as heir to the throne, Prince Albert brought the Bible, read him this passage, and chastised him.

Ver. 3. HEUBNER:—The human race has had authorized and unauthorized guardians. Moses was authorized, for God had appointed him, on

* [There is doubtless a polemical reference in these statements of Schmoller, of no special interest to the American reader. It need only be suggested that Lutheran *antinomism* sometimes seems (but only seems, it may be conceded) to verge on *antinomianism*.—R.]

the other hand the Pope and Mohammed without authority have endeavored to bring back the race, now free and of full age, to minority again. The authority of revelation does not retain us in minority; for the faith which it requires is no blind second-hand piety, but first makes us truly free from all that darkens and binds.—SPENER:—God has His wise distribution of the measure of grace at various times, with which we must be content and learn to accommodate ourselves thereto. He has also His holy order, according to which He leads His children in conversion from the law into grace.—BERLENBER. BIBLE:—This guardianship was designed only for minors; hence it is all wrong when Christians allow themselves to be brought into bondage again under ordinances, which are urged upon souls as good and necessary to salvation, and made a burden, beyond and without God's Word and revealed will, which therefore proceed not from nor are approved of Christ and His Spirit. O how many, that otherwise have a good degree of knowledge and personal piety, are in a pitiable bondage under such things! Either they are things which are counted as belonging to outward worship, or which should otherwise serve to make people pious. Now it is not indeed to be denied that some incitements in themselves innocent may help beginners somewhat. But so soon however as a rule and necessity, or it may be even a holiness, is make out of it, it is a yoke. But the main cause why such ordinances of men are a slavery of souls is, because men commonly therein seek and exalt themselves. Our crafty nature seeks with its tricks to maintain itself in its false life, and conceals itself behind outward observances and human usages. Meanwhile it secretly carries on its sins, as before, and will not drown and die in the death of Christ.—It is enough to suffer that other hard yoke, which presses the man at his first conversion. The law of God itself knows how to press him hard enough then, with its righteous judgments and requirements. Matters go laboriously and wretchedly enough with a young believer.

Vers. 4, 5. For this fulness of the time the fathers and all believers in the Old Testament waited with great pangs and earnestness. Not less longingly then, even now, must he wait and look for this Deliverer, who feels his imprisonment. For the fulness of the time, which began with Jesus' birth, continues ever from then on through all times, our own times among them.—As this took place as to the outward work, so does it now come to pass as to the inward, since the revelation of the Son breaks forth at the time which the Lord has decreed, and His government takes the upper hand in order to bring matters to that stage, to which under the drawing of the Father they could not attain. If thou therefore spyest in thyself a mighty drawing towards faith and hungering after Jesus, take heed that thou neglect it not. For this is even the fulness of thy time, when thy Saviour is about to be sent into thy heart by the Father. In the same hour learn thou to watch and pray, and to forget all else, that thou mayst win thy freedom.

LUTHER:—Hear thou, O law, thou hast no right nor might over me; therefore I concern myself nothing, that thou accusest and condemnest me long and much; for I believe on Jesus Christ, God's Son, whom God the Father hath sent into this world, that He might redeem us poor, wretched sinners, who were in bondage under the law's constraint and tyranny.—Christ hath redeemed us, in that He was made under the law. When He came, He found all of us together guarded and shut up under the law. What did He then? Because He is God's Son and Lord over the law, the law hath no right nor power over Him, nor can it accuse Him. Now, although He was not under the law, yea, was its Lord, He nevertheless willingly subjected Himself to the law. Christ incurred no debt to the law, yet did the law nevertheless behave itself towards this innocent, holy One, &c., even so as towards us, yea, it raged much more and more cruelly against Him than it is wont to do against us men. For it accused Him as if He were the very worst blasphemer and mover of sedition, and pronounced that He was guilty of all the sins of the whole world, and finally it condemned Him by its sentence to death, and moreover to the most shameful of all deaths on the cross.—Because now the law has dealt so cruelly against its God, Christ now appears against the law, and speaks on this wise: Good mistress Law, you are indeed a mighty invincible empress and tyrant over the whole race of man, and have moreover a right thereto; but what have I done to you, that you have so cruelly and contumeliously accused and condemned me the Innocent? Then must the law, because it can by no means answer for this, nor excuse itself, suffer for it in turn, and allow itself also to be condemned and strangled, so that it may therefore retain no right, nor power, not alone against Christ, whom it hath so injuriously assailed, but also against all who believe on Him.—So has Christ now through this His victory chased the law away out of our conscience in such manner that it can no more put us to shame before God. This one thing it does yet, it still continues to reveal sin to accuse and terrify us; but the conscience lays hold against it of these words of the apostle: Christ hath redeemed us from the law, maintains itself thereon by faith and comforts itself therewith. Yea, so proud and courageous moreover does it become in the Holy Ghost, that it dares bid defiance to the law, and say: I care little for all thy threatening. For the victory, which Christ hath won of thee, He hath bestowed upon us; therefore we are now become free of the law unto eternity, if so be we abide in Christ. Therefore let there be praise and thanks to our dear God, who hath given us such victory, through our Lord Jesus Christ. Amen.

[Vers. 4, 5. ROBERT HALL:—(1) The mission of Jesus Christ, and the manner in which He manifested Himself. The Son of God, "made of a woman, made under the law." (2) The design of His mission; "to redeem them that were under the law, that we might receive the adoption of sons." (3) The fitness of that season which God in His infinite wisdom appointed for this purpose.—It was a most favorable time to prevent imposture in matter of fact; an age the furthest removed from credulity, an age of skepticism. The Infinite wisdom saw fit to select this time to silence forever the vain babblings of philosophy, to "destroy the wisdom of the wise."—Because the fulness of the time was come, the event here referred to was the most important that had ever distinguished the annals of the world. The epoch will arrive when this world will be thought of as nothing, but as it has furnished a stage for the "manifestation of the Son of God."—R.]

Ver. 6. LUTHER:—When we stand in the midst and deepest in the terrors of the law, when sin as it were thunders over us, death makes us tremble and quake, the devil roars most cruelly, then begins the Holy Ghost to cry: Abba, dear Father! And this, His cry, is much mightier than the law's, sin's, death's, and the devil's cry, let it sound ever so loud and hideously, it breaks and presses with all might through the clouds and the heavens, comes before God's ears, and is heard, &c.—Although I am on all sides in great terrors and distresses, and it seems as if I, Lord, were wholly and utterly forsaken by thee, yet am I nevertheless child, thou, Father, for Christ's sake. I am to thee dear and pleasant for the Beloved's sake. But for man in his heart to be able to utter the little word "Father" in time of temptation in true earnestness, there needs such a deep skill thereto, as truly neither Cicero, nor Demosthenes, nor any other accomplished orator has had; yea, should they even melt together all their skill in one heap it were not yet possible for them perfectly to utter forth what is meant by the Holy Ghost in the single word "Father" in believer's hearts.—We ought to let go the injurious, damned doctrine (wherewith the pope hath defiled all Christendom), that man cannot be certain whether he is in grace before God, or not, and hold for certain that we have a gracious and compassionate God, who has in us a gracious complacency, cares for us as His dear children in earnest and most heartily —for Christ's sake; *item*, that we also have the Holy Ghost, which intercedes for us with crying and groanings unutterable.—In STARKE:—Behold the nature of ejaculatory prayers [*Stossgebetlein*], as they are called, wherein only the heart is lifted to God. In such a way can a believing soul very well pray without ceasing.—[BUNYAN: —O how great a task is it for a poor soul that comes, sensible of sin and the wrath of God, to say in faith but this one word, Father! The Spirit must be sent into the heart for this very thing; it being too great a work for any man to do knowingly and believingly without it.—That one word spoken in faith, is better than a thousand prayers in a formal, lukewarm way.—I myself have often found that when I can say but this word, *Father*, it doth me more good than when I call Him by any other Christian name.—R.]

Ver. 7. LUTHER:—Because Christ has redeemed us, that were under the law, there is no servant any more, nothing but children; therefore can thy power and tyranny, good mistress Law, have no place upon the lordly throne where my Lord Christ is to sit; therefore now I heed thee not, for I am free and a child, that is to be subjected to no servant's place.—The law may well rule and reign over the body and the old man; but the bridal bed, wherein Christ is to have His rest, it should leave unstained; that is, the law should leave the conscience at ease and undisturbed, for this is to reign alone with its bridegroom Christ, in the realm of freedom and of sonship.—"And if a son, then an heir." No one through his works or merit succeeds in becoming heir, but birth alone brings it to him; even so do we also come to the eternal, heavenly possessions, such as forgiveness of sins, righteousness, the glorious resurrection, and eternal life, not through our coöperation, but without any act of ours—we suffer them to be bestowed upon us, and receive them from God through Christ.—Whoever could believe without any doubt, that it were true, and certainly comprehend, how immeasurably great a thing it is, that one should be God's child and heir, such an one would without doubt take little account of the world, with all that therein is esteemed precious and honorable, such as human righteousness, wisdom, dominion, power, money, possessions, honor, pleasure, and the like; yea, all that in the world is honorable and glorious, would be to him loathsome and an abomination.—How great and glorious a bestowment the eternal kingdom and the heavenly inheritance is man's heart in this life can not understand, and still less express. We see in this life only the central point, but in the life to come, we shall see the whole infinite circle.

Vers. 1–7. There are two degrees of the adoption of God's children: the degree of minority, where one is rather servant than child, and the degree of majority, where one has the place of a child.—The bondage of the law the way to the full adoption of God's children.—The relation of the law and of the gospel to adoption with God.—The son, still a minor, must wait till God declares him of age; while the son of full age is not to abdicate the child's place, else he makes a retrogression displeasing to God. Without Christ, under age, through Christ, of full age.—When Christ came, came the time of majority for the people of God; when He comes *to thee*, it comes also for thee, not earlier—but then, really.—GLÖCKLER: The wisdom and love of God in the sending of His Son: Wisdom: He came, when the time was fulfilled: Love: He came to bring redemption, and the adoption of children.—The true intent, virtue, and fruit of the incarnation of the Son of God.—When the time is fulfilled, God will send also to thee His Son, and His Spirit into thy heart; only wait and doubt not!—Every time, even the longest, has its fulfillment, for it is subject to God, in the service of His purpose.—KAPFF: The blessedness of the adoption of God's children: It is (1) a condition of freedom, (2) of joyfulness in faith, (3) of heirship to God.—W. HOFACKER:—On the family or house of God, into which, to us as children, access stands open in Christ Jesus: 1) The house or the family of God: there is there a Father, God, a mother-free, unmerited grace, a first-born Brother; many brothers and sisters besides, and a ministering retinue in the holy angels. 2) The different relations in which we may stand to the household of God: *a.* there are some, and they are greatest in number, who stand in a far distant and alien relation to the family of God; *b.* a smaller, less considerable number stand to the family of God in a nearer, but yet not the nearest relation; *c.* the third class stands to it in the full, conscious relation of children, as Paul says, ver. 6. 3) The laborious [*aufgabenreiche*] and yet glorious condition of those, who walk as children of the house of God: *a.* the first task is, to learn more and more the true temper of children; *b.* the second, to show faithfulness and diligence in the daily work entrusted to them by the Lord; *c.* the third is, to wait in patience and hope for the promised inheritance.—MÜHLHÄUSER: The Abba cry: 1) a sign of being God's child; 2) but only possible through the Spirit of God.—Christ the Redeemer from the bondage of the law, 2) the redemption itself, 3) the consequence of this redemption.—HESSE: In what does sonship with God consist? 1) In the maturity of the spirit; 2) in the joyfulness of prayer; 3) in the certainty of salvation.—AHLFELD: Redemption through Jesus Christ. 1) From what has He redeemed us? From the law, from the constraint and from the curse of the law. 2) What does God offer us through our redemption? Sonship: the spirit of a child and the inheritance of a child.

---

## C. Rebuke, passing over into Sorrowful Complaint.

CHAPTER IV. 8–18.

**1. Interrupting the doctrinal exposition, Paul rebukes the incomprehensible backsliding into which they are falling.**

(VERS. 8–11.)

8 Howbeit then, when ye knew not God, ye did service [were in bondage][1] unto
9 them which by nature are no [not] gods.[2] But now, after that ye have known God,
or rather are known [have been known][3] of God, how turn ye again [how is it that
ye are turning again][4] to the weak and beggarly elements [rudiments], whereunto
10 ye desire again [again anew] to be in bondage? Ye observe [carefully] days, and
11 months, and times [seasons],[5] and years. I am afraid of [respecting] you, lest I
have bestowed upon you labor in vain.

2. In language agitated by sorrow, he complains of the equally ungrounded estrangement, they had suffered to grow up between him and them through the selfish intrigues of the false teachers.

(VERS. 12–18.)

12 Brethren, I beseech you, be [become][5] as I *am;* for I *am* [also *have become*] as
13 ye *are:* [.] ye have not injured me at all [ye injured me in nothing]: [yea] Ye
know how through [that on account of][6] infirmity of the flesh I preached the gos-
14 pel unto you at the first [the first time]. And my [your][7] temptation which was
in my flesh ye despised not, nor rejected; [,] but received me as an angel of God,
15 *even* as Christ Jesus. Where is then [or What then was][8] the blessedness ye spake
of? for I bear you record, that, if *it had been* possible, ye would have plucked out
16 your own [omit own][9] eyes, and have given them to me. Am I therefore [So then,
am I] become your enemy, because I tell you the truth [or by speaking to you the
17 truth]? They zealously affect you, *but* not well [They pay you court in no good
way];[10] yea, they would exclude [desire to exclude] you,[11] that ye might affect
18 them [may pay them court]. But *it is* good to be zealously affected always in *a*
good *thing* [to be courted in a good way at all times], and not only when I am
present with you.

1 Ver. 8.—[The idea of *servitude* rather than *service* is more accordant with the connection of thought.—R.]

2 Ver. 8.—Lachmann, Tischendorf read τοῖς φύσει μὴ οὖσι θεοῖς, instead of τοῖς μὴ φύσει οὖσι θεοῖς. Rec. [The former reading is that of ℵ. A, B, C, and modern editors generally.—R.]

3 Ver. 9.—[The tense here is the same as in the preceding clause, and the translation must conform.—R.]

4 Ver. 9.—[The construction is like ii. 14.—The rendering above given retains the force of the present: ye are in process of turning.—R.]

5 Ver. 12.—[Γίνεσθε—"become." In the next clause the same verb is to be supplied. The better division of verses would join the last clause with ver. 13, as the better pointing transposes the period and colon.—R.]

6 Ver. 13.—[This rendering of δι' ἀσθένειαν may now be considered as established.—R.]

[7] Ver. 14.—The reading τὸν πειρ. ὑμῶν ἐν τῇ σαρκί μου is followed. So ℵ [[1]A. B. D. [1]F., Lachmann, Tischendorf, Meyer, Bagge, Ellicott, Alford, Wordsworth, Lightfoot.—R.] Rec. reads τὸν πειρ. μου τὸν ἐν τῇ σαρκί μου; its sense is: You have not despised my bodily temptation=me on account of my sickness, by which I was tempted of God. But MSS. authority is strongest for ὑμῶν. Evidently this was not understood, and the Recepta is a conjectural emendation, based on a false interpretation. Πειρασμόν was understood as *calamitas*, as an infirmity in the body of Paul himself, because in ver. 13 this is spoken of; and so ὑμῶν had either to be entirely erased, or replaced by μου; and τόν added to connect ἐν σαρκί μου with πειρασμόν. On the sense of the approved reading, see EXEG. NOTES. [Schmoller follows Lachmann's punctuation, which puts a full stop after σαρκί μου, but this is objectionable, and not adopted by later editors. It is better to put a comma only after "rejected."—R.]

[8] Ver. 15.—There are three readings: 1) The Recepta, τίς οὖν ἦν ὁ μακαρισμὸς ὑμῶν. 2) The same, only without ἦν. 3) Ποῦ οὖν ὁ μακαρ. ὑμῶν, without ἦν, which gives no sense with ποῦ. The last reading is well supported, and found in ℵ., but seems to be a very old gloss; for a change of ποῦ into the more difficult τίς cannot readily be explained. Of the two others, 2) seems preferable, though we cannot definitely decide. [Ποῦ is adopted by Tischendorf, Alford, Wordsworth, Lightfoot; τίς, without ἦν by Ellicott. If we adopt 1) or 2), the E. V. must be altered: "What then was"—*i. e.* of what kind was, etc.—R.]

[9] Ver. 15.—["Own" is not warranted by the simple τοὺς ὀφθαλμοὺς ὑμῶν.—R.]

[10] Ver. 17.—[On the alterations, vers. 17, 18, see EXEG. NOTES. Ellicott's translation has been adopted only in part. —R.].

[11] Ver. 17.—Ἡμᾶς [instead of ὑμᾶς.—R.] is an unnecessary conjecture [of Beza's].

[12] Ver. 18.—The reading ζηλοῦσθε is an unnecessary conjecture in all probability, though found in ℵ. B. [Rejected by all editors of importance. Meyer, Ellicott, Wordsworth, read τὸ ζηλοῦσθαι; Lachmann, Alford, Lightfoot omit the article. It probably disappeared with the incorrect reading of the verb in some MSS.—R.]

## EXEGETICAL AND CRITICAL.

Ver. 8. **Howbeit then, when ye knew not God.**—This sounds as if it continued the doctrinal development, but it takes a practical turn in the very next verse. "Now no longer a servant," Paul had said,—but, he now continues, reverting to the former time, then were ye servants—when ye did not know God. Yet this is doubtless not merely a note of time, but a statement of the ground of the then existing bondage=as certainly as ye are now no longer servants, just so certainly was there a valid ground for your being formerly servants, when ye knew not God, namely, servants of idols. But comprehensible on this account as your earlier bondage was, equally incomprehensible is your present surrendering of yourselves into bondage again. For the "not knowing God" has ceased, hence with the cause, the effect also; they are, as already said, no longer δοῦλοι, and therefore a δουλεύειν in their case has no longer any justification whatever; their new bondage to the law is now as much without warrant as was their former bondage to idols.—**Ye were in bondage to them which by nature are not gods.**—This indicates more precisely the kind of bondage, in which the readers, as being Gentiles, formerly found themselves. From the fact that he so distinctly states of what kind their bondage was, it appears to be beyond doubt that he could not place them, as respected their pre-Christian state, in one category with the Jewish Christians as respected the pre-Christian state of these (ver. 3), nor comprehend them together under "those in bondage under the rudiments of the world." Their bondage was, it is true, also bondage, but nevertheless an essentially different, more wretched one: they were not "kept in bondage" *sc.* by God Himself for a while, from pedagogic reasons, under a law, but it was a bondage resulting from their not knowing God, and being servants, moreover, τοῖς φύσει μὴ οὖσι θεοῖς=to those gods, which yet are in their real nature not gods, but are only so called; they are in fact according to Paul's teaching elsewhere, *demons*. [Undoubtedly there is a "bondage" here referred to somewhat different from that of ver. 3, but the distinction seems to be, that in addition to the pedagogic bondage, in which all were held, these Galatians, or heathen, were in even a worse condition. The sense of the two readings must be noticed; that of Rec., τοῖς μὴ φύσει οὖσι θεοῖς joins the negative μὴ with φύσει; not gods in reality, only thought to be so; but the better sustained order, τοῖς φύσει μὴ οὖσι θεοῖς joins the negative with οὖσι, asserting that they were not gods at all, did not exist; whether 1 Cor. x. 20 justifies us in supposing that the implied antithesis is *demons*, is very doubtful. MEYER and ELLICOTT remark that this is a subjective negation.—R.]

Ver. 9. **Rather have been known of God.**—A corrective climax, in order to give the following "how" still more emphasis. "This knowing on the part of God is of course not used of a theoretical knowing—for in that sense every one is an object of Divine knowledge—but of an affectionate, loving, interested knowledge; comp. 1 Cor. viii. 3; xiii. 12, and in the Hebrew יָדַע as frequently used. The aorist points to an act of God in the past, which was the act of adoption." WIESELER.—**How is it that ye are turning again?**—Πάλιν does not belong to "the rudiments" but to "turn" therefore not as if they had already before served the στοιχεῖα, but πάλιν only affirms that a second, new turning [*Umwandlung*] was taking place with them first from idols to God, now from God to "the rudiments of the world"=how turn you again—namely, to the στοιχεῖα?—In ἐπιστρέφετε, moreover, there is not of necessity implied the idea of turning back, but simply that of turning away; although in the expression: "Conversion from idols to God" the thought of an original apostasy from God lies at the foundation, yet it lay being rather in the background; and as ἐπιστρέφετε has in itself an entirely general signification, it could very well be applied, even in a case where there was no reference to a turning back; indeed there was scarcely another word to express this turning away, this striking into a particular course. [Schmoller, having adopted WIESELER's view of ver. 3, is of course, consistent in following out that interpretation here, but it is very evident that this interpretation is difficult to defend. Here, and especially in the final clause of the verse, there must be a departure from the more obvious meanining of the words, to admit the idea that they had not *relapsed* as well as *lapsed* by their apostasy. Πάλιν does not necessarily imply a turning back to the same things but to similar things, not *retro* but *iterum, i. e.*, not again to heathenism indeed, but to Judaism, both of which are included in "the rudiments of the world." So MEYER, ALFORD, ELLICOTT, LIGHTFOOT and others. The present tense (ἐπιστρέφετε) is used, for the change was still going on. Comp. i. 6 (LIGHTFOOT).—R.]—The **rudiments** are called **weak**, because they have not the power to atone for sinful man, and by communication of the Spirit to transform him inwardly, agreeably to what Paul says of the law, *e. g.* Gal. iii. 21; Rom. viii. 3; comp. also Heb. vii. 18. They are called **beggarly** on account of their relatively imperfect matter in comparison with the perfection and the riches of the gospel. WIESELER.—**Whereunto ye desire again anew to be in bondage.**—"Again" belongs to "serve," not as if they had already once served "the rudiments" but they have already served, they have been δοῦλοι; and now they wish to be so again, although servants of another lord, and thus they wish to begin the δουλεύειν again ἄνωθεν, from the beginning, after it has scarcely as yet come to an end. [ELLICOTT's statement is preferable: "They had been slaves to the rudiments in the form of heathenism; now they were desiring to enslave themselves *again* to the rudiments, and to *commence* them *anew* in the form of Judaism."—R.]

Ver. 10. **Ye carefully observe.**—Proof of the declaration first made: "Ye desire to be in bondage." [The punctuation is a matter of dispute. An interrogation mark is placed at the close of the verse by TISCHENDORF, LIGHTFOOT, and others, but ELLICOTT, WIESELER, and more lately MEYER and ALFORD (both of whom formerly made the verse interrogative) adopt a simple period. This suits the transition to ver. 11 much better.—R.] "Παρατηρεῖσθε: to observe carefully, not to celebrate, or else the objects would have been σάββατα, νεομηνίας, ἑορτάς. The Apostle means to say, that they were not only given to the celebration, but, precisely like the Jews, were already scrupulous also as to the correct reckoning of time for their holy days. Days, with reference to the Sabbath; months, probably with reference to the new moons, not, because certain months, the seventh especially, were regarded as peculiarly holy months; seasons, within the year, with reference to the feasts; years with reference to the Sabbatical year, not the year of jubilee, which was no longer celebrated." WIESELER.—This passage shows how far and how far not, the Galatians had as yet been led astray. [Comp. Col. ii. 16. ALFORD is scarcely warranted in saying that this verse is at variance with any and every theory of the Christian Sabbath, since the reference is evidently to Jewish observances, Jewish days, etc. WIESELER supposes that they were then celebrating a Sabbatical year, because the present tense is used, but this is pressing it too far.—R.]

Ver. 11. **I am afraid respecting you.**—Not superfluously has Paul added the ὑμᾶς, but in the consciousness that it is not his own interest (as for instance his having labored fruitlessly, in itself regarded), but the readers' that his anxiety respects. MEYER.—Luther aptly says: *Lacrimas Pauli hæc verba spirant* [These words breathe the tears of Paul].

Ver. 12. **Become as I.**—The Apostle's reprehension of their conduct naturally prepares the way for the admonition to a change of this. Yet he does little more than briefly indicate the exhortation, without continuing it, but goes on rather to make mention, with painful emotion, of his personal relation to the readers, as it had been and as it had now become.—The sense of the briefly expressed admonition is not quite evident: but probably=become like me in freedom from Judaistic observance; the motive to this is then added: **For I also have become as ye are**, like you Gentiles, through my ἐθνικῶς ζῆν, comp. ii. 14, and moreover the Apostle means, doubtless: when I brought you the gospel.—[Schmoller joins **Brethren, I beseech you**, with what follows, but the punctuation of the E. V. is better. The meaning of the first clause seems plain. In regard to the second, "two interpretations deserve to be considered: 1. 'For I was once in bondage as ye now are.' I once *was* a Jew, as ye now Judaize. 2. 'For I abandoned my legal ground of righteousness, I became a Gentile like you.' The latter sense is simpler grammatically, as it understands the same verb which occurs in the former clause, 'because,' not 'was.' It is also more in character with the intense personal feeling which pervades the passage. 'I gave up all those time-honored customs, all those dear associations of race, to become like you. I have lived as a Gentile that I might preach to you Gentiles. Will you then abandon me, when I have abandoned all for you?' This sense is well adapted both to the tender appeal 'Brethren, I beseech you,' and to the eager explanation which follows: 'Ye did me no wrong'" (LIGHTFOOT).—**Ye injured me in nothing.**—The emphasis does not rest on *me*, a mere enclitic in the Greek, as if implying that they had injured God and Christ. As the verb is aorist like those which follow, it seems best to refer this to that time of his first preaching. In that case the meaning "I have no personal grounds of complaint" (adopted by many from CHRYSOSTOM to LIGHTFOOT) is untenable. He begins with this clause to adduce their former treatment of him, as a reason for "becoming as he is." The next clause is not strictly adversative.—R.]

Ver. 13. **Yea ye know that on account of infirmity of the flesh.**—"The only correct, because the only grammatical explanation, is: On account of weakness of the flesh, so it appears from this, that Paul was necessitated, on his first journey through Galatia, to linger there, although properly it had not lain in his plan, and that he had during this compulsory sojourn preached the gospel to the Galatians. How and from what cause he was suffering, whether from natural sickness, or from injuries undergone for the gospel's sake, we do not know. Paul does not, by the mention of a previously unintended activity among the Galatians, work against his purpose, but rather right in the line of his purpose, since the love which received him so heartily and joyfully, must have been so much the greater, the less it was founded on the duty of a thankfulness owing for a benefit previously intended for the receivers, and for efforts made strictly on their account" (MEYER);—or rather, perhaps; "the less he, considering the impediment of his bodily condition, could expect such a reception" (WIESELER). That is, we suppose, because, through his infirmity he was in many ways impeded in his public labors, because his preaching of the gospel was a variously marred, imperfect one. He means to say then, that he preached *in a state of* bodily weakness. But the words themselves are not to be so translated. [WORDSWORTH: "On account of the *infirmity in his flesh* and the consequent temptation to his *hearers*, he was naturally led—perhaps he was guided by the Holy Spirit —to shun in the *first instance* the more civilized population, of Asia and Europe, as to go rather to the despised Galilees of the world, and then when his reputation was established, to proceed through Macedonia to Athens, and thence to Corinth and to Ephesus, and so finally to Rome." But this learned author can scarcely be warranted in making this the implication in πρότερον, as he does, in order *to deny* a second visit to Galatia.—R.] Πρότερον, apparently not=formerly, referring generally to time past viewed from the present; for the addition would then be entirely superfluous; but special=the first of two definite occasions. The second time of "preaching" is, however, not the present writing of the Epistle, for εὐαγγελίζω is invariably used of oral preaching; but there is a twofold presence of the Apostle among the Galatians presupposed, to the first of which the πρότερον refers. In fact, the book of Acts also mentions two visits of Paul in Galatia, Acts xvi. 6; xviii. 23. "Paul therefore adds τὸ πρότερον, in order to designate with full distinctness the first visit, during which he founded the churches. At his second visit, also, the joyful experiences which he had had τὸ πρότερον were not repeated; the churches were already infected with Judaism" (MEYER).

Ver. 14. With the reading πειρασμὸν ὑμῶν it appears best to set a period after ἐν τῇ σαρκί μου, and to connect the words with οἴδατε ver. 13=you know how you, through my bodily infirmity, and the hampering of my evangelical activity in consequence of it, were put on proof=experienced the temptation to think unfavorably of me. Unquestionably the connection is somewhat difficult. But plainly the connection with what follows is wholly inadmissible, although MEYER accepts it=you have not despised your trial in my flesh. But what is meant by despising the trial, &c.? Who could understand it at all? MEYER himself has to alter the expression somewhat, so as to mean: contemptuously repel. And besides what would be signified by the climatic expression with two words: ἐξουθενήσατε and ἐξεπτύσατε? This, however, manifestly constitutes the antithesis to the strong affirmative expression ἀλλ' ὡς ἄγγελον κ. τ. λ. The one as well as the other therefore refers to himself. He praises this in them, that they did not reject and even spit out *him*, as there was room to apprehend, but—the exact opposite—received him as an angel, nay, as Christ. [The reading ὑμῶν must be adopted, but this by no means compels us to follow the punctuation and connection just indicated. MEYER, ALFORD, ELLICOTT, WORDSWORTH, LIGHTFOOT and most editors reject Lachmann's punctuation, which makes the latter part of the verse intolerably harsh and abrupt, and does little to remove the difficulty of the former part. As WORDSWORTH intimates "the teacher's infirmity is the people's trial." Paul's infirmity, whatever it was, put them on trial, was the thing which tried them (πειρασμὸν ὑμῶν), and yet they did not despise and loathe him on account of this infirmity, but received him, etc.—R.]

Ver. 15. **What was then** [or **where then is**] **the blessedness ye spake of?** [The E. V. gives a sufficiently correct paraphrase, if ποῦ be read.—R.] WEISELER:=How highly blessed you pronounced yourselves, *sc.* that you were able to hear me?—Τίς=how great. Οὖν comes in somewhat abruptly, but is explained by the emotional character of the style. Paul transfers himself vividly into the time when they received him with such veneration, and exclaims: How was it then, what a boasting of blessedness then arose?—With that agrees, as a proof, what follows: **For I bear you record.** —MEYER: Of what character then was you boasting of blessedness?=how inconstant? More farfetched is the explanation: On what was your boasting of blessedness founded? Others supply ἐστί: What then is your boasting of blessedness?=it is nothing any longer; it is at an end, therefore somewhat in the sense of ποῦ. But the following γάρ does not agree with this.

**That, if it had been possible,** *etc.*—A proverbial mode of speech, derived from the high value and indispensableness of the eyes. Puerile is the explanation: Paul had an opthalmia, and says here, that the Galatians, if it had been possible would have given him their sound eyes. [The E. V. "your own eyes," giving an emphasis, unwarranted by the Greek, favors this theory of "opthalmia." It is well defended by Dr. BROWN, *Horæ Subscecivæ*, yet scarcely sustained by this passage.—R.]

Ver. 16. **So then, am I become your enemy.**—A sharp antithesis. The simplest sense: Since you were so minded towards me, can I be afterwards regarded as your enemy only **because I tell you the truth** (instead of speaking according to your fancy). The sentence is introduced somewhat abruptly, or the inference implied in ὥστε is not so very obvious. It may be explained, however, from the emotional character of the language. The emphasis lies on "tell the truth;" but in the first instance "enemy" (ἐχθρός), as constituting a contrast, must be made prominent; it therefore stands first, and by placing ἀληθεύων ὑμῖν *at the end*, this also is emphasized. The Apostle had already told the Galatians the truth, rebuking their errors and short-comings, before the writing of his Epistle (for this they had not seen as yet), at a second visit in person among them. [The present form of the E. V. seems against this, but the participle means "by telling the truth," which of course admits of a part reference. WORDSWORTH renders "being true," to avoid the admission of a second visit.—R.]

Ver. 17. **They pay you court in no honest way.**—[So ELLICOTT. LIGHTFOOT: "As ζηλοῦν would seem to have one and the same sense throughout this passage, its more ordinary meanings with the accusative, as 'to admire, emulate,' must be discarded. It signifies rather 'to busy one's self about, take interest in,' a sense which lies close to the original meaning of ζῆλος, if correctly derived from ζέω." So Schmoller *liebeifern.*—R.] "They also, it is true [*sc.* the false teachers; for we usually abstain from naming those whose very names produce in us dislike and aversion (CALVIN)] will fain have an affectionate zeal towards you, and contend for the possession of you: but in view of the truth, that, while they will bring you out of affectionate zeal, is worse than what you already have, we must say; they are zealous for you to no good." EWALD.—**They desire to exclude you,**—first from me, and thus from the pure gospel to them and their teaching.—Ἵνα, (that) with the indicative present is certainly harsh; but MEYER'S interpretation is altogether too forced. He feels himself obliged on account of this harshness to take ἵνα=*ubi, in quo statu;* whereby, by which exclusion, when it has taken place, you, with your zeal are directed to them as objects of your interest. [The final sense of ἵνα, *i. e.*, they do it for this purpose, is preferable; the indicative being regarded by ALFORD and ELLICOTT as a solecism, though Lightfoot remarks that this usage, while quite unclassical, is often found in later writers. MEYER insists very strongly however upon the local sense.—R.]

Ver. 18. **But it is good to be courted in a good way at all times.**—The "courting" of which they are the objects, he has been obliged to censure, and accordingly he adds (turning to the readers themselves): It is indeed good (καλόν) to be an object of the affectionate zeal of others, good to be zealously loved—but only in a good thing. It is only good to be zealously loved in a good laudable cause, and for the sake of it, but not as now, on account of an evil cause, namely, apostacy from the truth. This thought Paul completes by the addition: At all times it is good to be loved for the sake of a good cause. But (he says) more accurately considered, it is only good, when one is zealously loved *at all times*, for the sake of a good cause, and not merely for a while, or at certain times, *i. e.*, when one is always *worthy* of zealous love (for the sake of a good cause). This thought however, Paul does not leave thus general, but suddenly—disturbing the concinuity of the discourse, though quite in congruity with the emotion expressed in the language of this section—gives it a definite application—**not only when I am present with you.**—Then you showed yourselves worthy of love, but, alas, not now, when I am not with you.—MEYER and WIESELER understand the beginning of the sentence thus: good it is, that zeal is shown, etc.; and not so that the Galatians are understood as the objects of the zeal, but so that the zeal ἐν καλῷ is opposed to the zeal of the false teachers, which was ἐν κακῷ. But justice is not thus done to the passive infinitive. [This verse has caused much discussion. The following results seem clear: 1. That the verb ζηλοῦν is to retain the same meaning throughout. 2. That the last infinitive is passive, and the Galatians the object. But 3. the force of ἐν καλῷ is doubtful. It may be (*a*) merely adverbial (ELLICOTT). "It is a good thing to be the object of courting *in an honest way* (as you are by me, though not by them) at all times, and not merely when I happen to be with you." (*b*) It may indicate the sphere, in contrast with that of the false teachers (ALFORD). It is a good thing (for you) to be the objects of this zeal, *in a good cause*, at all times and by every body, not only when I am present with you. I do not grudge the court that is paid you. Only let them do it in an honorable cause. (*c*) Or the phrase may be pressed, as is done by Schmoller, to imply a contrast between their present and their former state. LIGHTFOOT prefers a view similar to this, but, as he admits, *it supplies too much.* As (*b*) is entirely consistent with the requirements of 1, and 2, it seems preferable.—R.]

[Many commentators (including BENGEL, WORDSWORTH, LIGHTFOOT) put a comma at the close of Ver. 18, thus joining the next verse most closely with this section. There is a sufficient change of tone and thought to justify a full stop, but it seems doubtful whether a new section or paragraph should begin with ver. 19. Most commentators, even those who separate vers. 18 and 19, begin the new paragraph with ver. 21; with more propriety apparently. Schmoller, however, joins ver. 19 with ver. 21, and divides the sections accordingly. While the matter is not of sufficient moment to warrant an alteration of his arrangement, the usual division presents the Apostle's thought more satisfactorily. See EXEG. NOTES on vers. 19, 20 in the next section.—R.]

## DOCTRINAL AND ETHICAL.

1. *The characteristic of heathenism is, lack of the knowledge of God.* A heathen was before his conversion an atheist (Eph. ii. 12). True they had a certain religiosity, but "Knowledge of God" is for Paul at least, a very definite positive idea, essentially distinct from that religiosity. What the heathen worship are by nature not gods.—A hint not to overvalue in an unscriptural manner the religious feeling of the heathen world, which manifested itself in idolatrous worship; also not to see in it too readily anything positive, a prophecy of the true knowledge of God, something only different from it in degree. Rather, it is something negative, a having lost the truth, or at most an echo of that truth which in its main substance is lost. For, according to Rom. i., the heathen also had indeed originally a knowledge of God, but this before they became heathen by their being servants to them which are by nature not gods; with the coming in of this servitude they lost the knowledge of God. Very different then was the standing of the Israelite from that of the heathen, *i. e.*, although he was "in bondage under the rudiments of the world," yes, "shut up under sin," he was yet one "knowing God," not "without God" (ἄθεος) in the world.

2. *Confidence between teachers and hearers.*—"There must be more depending on hearty confidence between teachers and hearers, than is commonly thought, because the Apostle so solicitously strives for it, and assures them he has not lost his affection for them, but is still mindful of their first love." RIEGER.—The preacher, it is true, is in the first place only the bearer and bringer of the divine word, and it is primarily this itself, which opens and wins

hearts. The man, compared with the word which he brings, falls entirely into the background, as appears from the very declarations of Paul in this section. Had not the word which he brought, in itself won hearts, had not these conceived confidence in the word as such, for the sake of its contents, Paul himself would have found no access among them; for in his personal appearance, in view of the weakness of the flesh, with which he came, there was at least nothing captivating to the hearts of men.—But on the other hand, simultaneously with the receiving of the word, there is also formed a personal relation to the bringer of it; he is not a mere instrument, but a personality, and in his bringing of the word comes into consideration as such. A bond of confidence and love is knit between the hearer and the teacher; to him who brings what searches the heart in its inmost recesses, who proclaims to us the word of salvation and eternal life, our heart must also necessarily turn in love, if it has suffered the word to gain any hold of it whatever. And on the other hand the personal bond which is formed, will then in its turn have an essential influence in promoting the reception of the word and steadfastness in faith. The preacher may also, as Paul shows, expressly appeal to this personal relation, may and should value highly the love which he experiences, may—not indeed affect an injured tone when it is withdrawn from him, but may well, when the Church has in any way gone astray, use the personal relation that has been formed, as a motive in his admonitions.

[3. *Observance of days, etc.* The scrupulous observance of "days and months and seasons and years," is to the Apostle a token that his labor in the gospel has not resulted in appropriate effects. These things belong to "the weak and beggarly elements," to which the Galatians were returning. That there is no allusion to the observance of the Lord's Day is evident, for this cannot be classed among these "rudiments," to which they desire to be again anew in bondage. It could not be classed among "heathen rudiments," for they knew nothing of it; nor with "the bondage of the law," for God's Sabbatic law ante-dated the Mosaic law (comp. the fourth commandment, "Remember"). And whatever of legal bondage had been linked with the observance of the Jewish Sabbath was eliminated together with the change to the first day of the week. This at once removes the Lord's Day from the category of "days" (ver. 10), and also of "weak and beggarly elements" (ver. 9). The mode of observance is learned from the Lord's words: "The Sabbath was made for man, and not man for the Sabbath," which at the same time imply, when rightly understood, the perpetual necessity for a Sabbath.—R.]

## HOMILETICAL AND PRACTICAL.

Ver. 8. CRAMER:—"To reflect often on our former miserable condition of heathenism, serves to move us to thanksgiving for the benefit received." LUTHER:—There is a twofold knowledge of God, a common and a special. The common all men have by nature, in that they know that there is a God, who has made heaven and earth, &c. But how our Lord God is minded towards us, what He will give us and do for us, that we may be redeemed from sin and be saved, of that men know nothing. They know not what pleases or displeases God, and so adore, instead of the actual God, something that their own heart has dreamed out and feigningly devised, but which, in very truth, is naught.—[BROWN:—In false religion in all its forms, nothing is more remarkable than its enslaving, degrading influence on the minds of its votaries.—R.]

Ver. 9. LUTHER:—We are known of God, rather than we know Him. For what we do towards such knowledge is nothing else than to hold still, and let God occupy Himself with us, namely, by giving us His word, which we lay hold of through the faith which He also works in us, and thus to become God's children.—We shall not fare better than the dear Apostles themselves fared, who in their lifetime had to see the congregations that had been built up through their office with much pains and labor, so sadly torn down, that for very pity their heart was ready to break.—It may easily and quickly happen, that one apostatize from the truth. For even Christians, who are in earnest as to sound doctrine, consider not sufficiently, how precious and most needful a treasure is the right and true knowledge of Christ. Besides there are exceeding few among those that hear the preaching of faith, that are tried by the holy cross and spiritual conflict, and that sometimes have with sin, death and devil a skirmish, but the greater part live on in all security, without all combat and strife. So long as they have sound teachers with them, they speak according to them; but when these their true teachers are away, and the wolves in sheeps' clothing come creeping in, at once that takes place with them, which happened to the Galatians, namely, that they are soon and easily seduced and perverted.—When the foundation is destroyed, it is then all one, whether men turn themselves to the law, or to idols. Whoever falls from grace upon the law, has as hard a fall as he that falls from grace into heathenism, for out of Christ there is nothing else than idolatry and a vain image of God.—"To the weak and beggarly rudiments." When the law accomplishes its right and fitting work or office, it accuses and condemns men; then it is not a weak and beggarly element, but strong and rich, yea, it is an immeasurable, invincible power and wealth, against which the conscience is indeed weak and poor.—It is most admirable that St. Paul speaks so contemptuously of the law. For he does it to this end, that they who will through the law be made righteous, may from day to day become still weaker and more beggarly. For they are of themselves weak and beggarly, *i. e.*, by nature children of wrath and guilty of perdition, and lay hold then on that which also is nothing else than merely infirmity and beggary, whereby they will fain become strong and rich.

Ver. 10. "Ye carefully observe days." Here might some one say: If the good Galatians did so great a sin, in that they observed days, months, seasons, &c., how comes it then, that ye do not also sin, who yet do the like? Answer: in that we keep Sunday, Christmas, Easter, and the like days of solemnity or festivals, we do it with all freedom, we burden with such ceremonies no one's conscience, nor teach, that men must needs keep them, in order to be thereby justified and saved, or to make satisfaction for sin. But on this account we keep them, that matters may go on in the church in good discipline and order, and that outward unity may not be sundered (for inwardly we have another unity). But the principal cause is this, that the ministry may remain in its full exercise, and that the people may have their certain appointed time, when they may come together, hear God's word, and therefrom know God. *Item*, that they may take the sacrament, pray in common for all necessities of all Christendom, and may thank our dear Lord God for all His benefits. BERLENB. BIBLE:—In such things that is even against Christianity which is urged upon men over and above Christianity. He that can comprehend what mischief the evangelical spirit suffers from such patchwork, has made great progress.

Ver. 11. HEUBNER:—The teacher labors upon an uncertainty, knows not what he accomplishes, he sows upon hope.

Vers. 12–20. RIEGER:—As much depends on such earnest remonstrances for opening the hearers' hearts, as on the most convincing arguments.

Ver. 12. SPENER:—A true pastor is sensitive in no particular, save in what is contrary to the honor of God, and the salvation of His flock.—LUTHER:—That he gives the Galatians so good words, is as much as to mix and temper the bitter wormwood drink so with honey and sugar that it may become sweet and pleasant. Even so do parents, when they have well flogged their children, give them good words, give them gingerbread, apples, pears, nuts and the like, that the children may take note and understand that their parents have at heart their good.

Vers. 13, 14. It may well be that human reason stumbles and starts back, when it beholds the slight, contemptible and weak nature of the dear Christians, wherein there is so much of suffering, yea, the world has ever counted all God's servants for great fools, who will fain comfort, help and counsel others, *item*, inasmuch as they boast of so great heavenly possessions and treasures, of righteousness, power, strength, victory over sin, death and all evil, of everlasting joy, &c., and are yet the poorest beggars, and moreover weak, troubled and despised.—STARKE:—True servants of the gospel are angels of God, as having the name of messengers and heralds of the divine will, even as also the invisible and heavenly spirits bear the name of angels from a like office. — LANGE:—If teachers wish to be looked on as angels of God, and in a certain sense as Christ Himself, they must also approve themselves as good angels, and not as Satan's angels and servants, and discharge their office with such purity, as they have Paul for an example.—[BURKITT:—It is an high commendation to a people, when neither poverty nor deformity, nor any deficiency, which may render a minister of the gospel base and contemptible in the estimation of the world, can possibly diminish any thing of that respect which they know to be due and payable unto him.—R.]

Ver. 15. HEUBNER:—Let the apostate reflect, when he was happiest, how blessed he was before he fell. — BERLENB. BIB.:—As indeed we are owing more than the eyes of the body, to those that have opened to us the eyes of the soul.—HEDINGER:—A beautiful proof of faith, to love those from the heart, that plant faith within us! O the horror, that some would gladly tear out tongue and eyes from those that teach us the word of the kingdom of heaven!—CRAMER:—It is everywhere the same, that new preachers are welcome, and soon get followers and a great concourse. While the sign is new, it is hung against the wall; but when it is old, it is thrown under the bench.—[BROWN:—When the gospel is remarkably successful, the danger is not of converts not being sufficiently attached, but of their being inordinately attached, to the minister who has been the instrument of conveying to them so great a benefit. The being greatly applauded, is scarcely any proof that a minister has been successful; the being highly esteemed and cordially loved, is a considerably strong presumption that he has; the being regarded with indifference and dislike, is a clear proof that he has not.—R.]

Ver. 16. HEUBNER:—Him who tells us the truth, we ought to count for our true and best friend.—LUTHER:—In the world matters go altogether strangely and against reason, namely, he that speaks truth becomes an unwelcome guest, yea, is counted for an enemy; but this is not so among good friends, and still less among Christians.—STARKE:—He that hates any one, because he tells him the truth, such an one betrays himself very clearly as no child of God.

Ver. 17. LUTHER:—This is the way of all false spirits, to put on a friendly behavior, and give people the best words, so as to get a hold. When they first come creeping in, they swear most fervently, that they seek nothing else than alone how they may further God's honor and men's salvation; they promise to those that receive their teaching, that they shall certainly be saved. And with such assumed appearance of godliness and sheep's clothing, the ravening wolves do immensely great harm to the Christian church, where pastors are not active and vigilant and earnest to withstand them. — RIEGER:—Great pains given to any thing, great certainty assumed concerning it, is indeed something very taking to men's minds; but zeal alone gives no certain proof of truth. The doctrine is not to be judged according to the zeal, but the zeal according to the doctrine. The zeal does not make the cause good, but the cause must make the zeal good.—[BUNYAN:—Zeal without knowledge is like a mettled horse without eyes or like a sword in a madman's hands.—RICCALTOUN:—In reading the history of the church it is hard to say whether what has gone, and still goes under the name of *zeal*, has done more good or hurt to religion.—BURKITT: — The old practice has ever been amongst seducers, first to alienate the people's minds from their own teachers, and next get themselves looked upon as alone, and only worthy to have room in the people's hearts.—R.]

Ver. 18. STARKE:—Zeal for good must be enduring.—This is a human feeling, which exists in many, even pious souls. They are zealous in good, when faithful teachers are present, but when they are absent, or it may be dead, they slacken in their zeal.

**D. Confirmation of the freedom of Christians, from the narrative of the Scripture concerning the two sons of Abraham, Ishmael and Isaac, by means of an interpretation referring it to the Jewish and the Christian Church.**

## CHAPTER IV. 19—30.

(Vers. 21-31. *The Epistle for the 4th Sunday in Lent.*)

19 My little children[1] of whom I travail in birth again [with whom I am again in
20 travail] until Christ be formed in you, I desire [I could wish indeed] to be
present with you now, and to change my voice [tone];[2] for I stand in doubt of you
21 [am perplexed about you].[3] Tell me ye that desire to be under the law, do ye not
22 hear[4] the law? For it is written, that Abraham had two sons, the one by a bond-
maid, the other by a free woman [one by the bondmaid, and one by the free wo-
23 man]. But he *who was* of the bondwoman was born after the flesh; but he of
24 the free woman *was* by promise [through the[5] promise]. Which things are an
allegory [are allegorical]:[6] for these are the [omit the][7] two covenants; the one
from the [omit the] mount Sinai, which gendereth to [bearing children unto]
25 bondage, which is Agar [Hagar].[8] For this Agar is mount Sinai in Arabia [(For
Sinai is a mountain in Arabia), or For the word Agar means in Arabia mount
Sinai; or For this Hagar represents mount Sinai in Arabia], and answereth to
[she ranks[9] with] Jerusalem which now is [the present Jerusalem], and is [for[10] she
26 is] in bondage with her children. But Jerusalem which is above is free, which is
27 the mother of us all [and she is our[11] mother]. For it is written, Rejoice, thou
barren that bearest not; break forth and cry, thou that travailest not: for the
desolate hath many more children [many are the children of the desolate more]
28 than she which [who] hath a husband. Now we [But ye],[12] brethren, as Isaac was,
29 are the [omit the] children of promise. But [still] as then he that was born after
30 the flesh persecuted him *that was born* after the Spirit, even so *it is* now. Never-
theless what saith the Scripture? Cast out the bondwoman and her son; for the
son of the bondwoman shall not be heir [shall in no wise[13] be heir] with the son[14]
of the free woman.

[1] Ver. 19.—א. τέκνα. [So B. F. G., Lachmann; but א.[3] A. C. K. L. read τεκνία, adopted by Tischendorf and most recent Editors. Occurs nowhere else in Paul's writings.—R.]

[2] Ver. 20.—[Φωνήν, literally "voice," but "tone" is a more intelligible rendering.—R.]

[3] Ver. 20.—["Am perplexed"; so Ellicott, Alford, Lightfoot. Schmoller (with doubtful propriety) throws this verse into a parenthesis.—R.]

[4] Ver. 21.—'Αναγινώσκετε, an ancient gloss, [followed by the Vulgate, but rejected by all modern Editors.—R.]

[5] Ver. 23.—א. omits τῆς. [Undoubtedly to be retained, and preserved in the English translation.—R.]

[6] Ver. 24.—['Αλληγορούμενα, "allegorical" (Alford, Ellicott). Older English versions vary greatly. Against the meaning "allegorized," see EXEG. NOTES.—R.]

[7] Ver. 24.—Elz. reads αἱ δύο, against decisive authorities. א.[1] inserts, א.[3] omits αἱ.

[8] Ver. 25.—The Rec. reads: τὸ γὰρ Ἄγαρ Σινᾶ ὄρος ἐστὶν ἐν τῇ Ἀραβίᾳ. Besides this we find these readings: 1. τὸ γὰρ Σινᾶ ὄρος—2. τὸ γὰρ Ἄγαρ ὄρος—3. τὸ Ἄγαρ Σινᾶ ὄρος—4. τὸ δὲ Ἄγαρ Σινᾶ ὄρος κ. τ. λ. It is difficult to decide which is the correct reading, since the weight of authority is about equal for some of these readings. The Rec. is supported mostly by cursives. 1. is decidedly better sustained; א. has it, but with an addition found in no other MSS. (ὂν before ἐν τῇ Ἀρ). 2. and 3. are very weakly supported; but 4. is well sustained. The choice then seems to be between 1. and 4.: τὸ γὰρ Σινᾶ and τὸ δὲ Ἄγαρ Σινᾶ; and between these it is scarcely possible to make a positive decision. [It may be remarked that the readings Rec. and 4, differ only in the substitution of δέ for γάρ; since this can readily be accounted for (γάρ first omitted because of the closely following Ἄγαρ, then δέ inserted for connection, or to correspond with μέν, ver. 24), it is perhaps better to regard the choice as lying between Rec. and 1. The former is adopted by Tischendorf, Meyer, Ellicott, Alford, Wordsworth; 1. by Lachmann and Lightfoot among others. In favor of each, see the above-named commentators. Lightfoot has two valuable notes, p. 189 *sq.* 1. is certainly *lectio brevior*; Rec. *lectio difficilior*; Ἄγαρ may have been carelessly inserted from ver 24, but it was even more likely to have been carelessly omitted after γάρ.—The exegetical difficulty is as great as the critical. Of the three English renderings given above, I. follows reading I., II. and III., the Rec. See EXEG. NOTES.—R.]

[9] Ver. 25.—The readings συστοιχοῦσα and ἡ συστοιχοῦσα are not weakly supported, but still must be regarded as exegetical glosses; not without value in the exposition of the passage.—[If a comma be put after "Arabia," it is unnecessary to supply "she."—R.]

[10] Ver 25.—[Rec. δέ; followed by Vulgate, E. V., but weakly supported. ℵ. A. B. C. F. read γάρ; so modern Editors. —R.]

[11] Ver. 26.—The better attested reading, μήτηρ ἡμῶν, is to be preferred, on internal grounds also to μήτηρ πάντων ἡμῶν. "Πάντων has come into the text, partly because of such parallel passages as Rom. iv. 16; Gal. iii. 26, 28; partly because of the multitude of τέκνα in the quotation ver. 27 (Wieseler). [Πάντων, Rec. ℵ.[3] A. C.[3] K. L., many fathers, Wordsworth. Bracketted by Lachmann. Omitted in ℵ.[1] B. D. F. many versions and cursives; rejected by Tischendorf. Meyer, Alford, Ellicott, Lightfoot.—The E. V. "which is" is perhaps more literal, but Ellicott's rendering, given above, is more forcible, and allowable with ἥτις.—R.]

[12] Ver. 28.—"The reading ὑμεῖς-ἐστε is, with Lachmann, Tischendorf and others, to be preferred to the common text ἡμεῖς-ἐσμεν, since the latter appears to be a correction from ἡμῶν (ver. 26) and ὑμεῖς is more lively on account of its application to the readers." (Wieseler). ℵ. however has ἡμεῖς. [Both are well supported, but ὑμεῖς is adopted by most Editors on internal grounds.—R.]

[13] Ver. 30.—[Lightfoot follows ℵ. B. D. in reading κληρονομήσει (apparently a correction from LXX).—The double negative οὐ-μή is rendered by Ellicott, "in no wise."—R.]

[14] Ver. 30.—Τοῦ υἱοῦ is omitted in ℵ., but inserted by the corrector. [Instead of τῆς ἐλευθέρας we find also μου Ἰσαάκ (from the LXX).—R.]

## EXEGETICAL AND CRITICAL.

Ver. 19. **My little children.**—[LIGHTFOOT: "A mode of address common in St. John, but not found elsewhere in St. Paul. Here the diminutive expresses both the tenderness of the Apostle and the feebleness of his converts. It is a term at once of affection and rebuke."—R.] It is more natural to make a break here (the very suddenness of the appeal implies this) and to join "my little children" with "tell me" (ver. 21). It cannot at all events be connected with the preceding context, but the connection with ver. 20 is only possible on the assumption of an interruption of the discourse (comp, δέ). [The presence of δέ in ver. 20 is urged as a reason for connecting our verse very closely with ver. 18, as is done by many commentators. The course of the thought would then be: "I have a right to ask for constancy in your affections. I have a greater claim on you than these new teachers. They speak but as strangers to strangers; I as a mother to her children with whom she has travailed" (LIGHTFOOT). But there is something so sudden in the address, that it is better to separate the verses (so MEYER, ALFORD, ELLICOTT).—R.] On the other hand the contents of ver. 20 fit very well into the discourse as a parenthetical remark. In the "am again in travail" the wish presses itself upon him, rather to be present with them—and this he then expresses—before going on, in ver. 21, to attempt to change the minds of his readers, as being his children, and to bring them back. It is true "tell me," after this interruption, does not connect immediately with ver. 19; the "little children" receives a particular definition in "ye that desire to be under the law," but this only indicates how far a travailing again is necessary, in order to prepare for a continuance of this ὠδίνειν through the following exposition, as indeed all that precedes had been nothing else than such a travail.

[This view of the connection of the passage is open to serious objection. Two vocatives are joined together, which are separated both in position and in tone. Ver. 20 which contains the wish to be present is sundered from ver. 18, where the thought of his presence is introduced. The idea of travailing is joined to a passage of argument by illustration, and separated from the more personal part of the discourse. If there be a difficulty about δέ (ver. 20) as introducing an "opposition," and hence a parenthesis be deemed necessary, this "opposition" may be found (MEYER) "in the tacit contrast between the subject of his wish to be present with them, and his actual absence and separation." It seems best then to connect vers. 19 and 20 together—detaching them as a burst of tenderness from both the preceding and subsequent context, though joined in thought more closely with the former.—R.]

**With whom I am again in travail.**—*i. e.*, the second time.—The labor of his spirit on the hearts of the readers he here compares with the travail of a mother (elsewhere with the begetting of the father), in which the point of comparison is the activity directed to the coming of a child into the world; with the mother—of a natural child; here with the Apostle—of a spiritual child. This image is continued with the expression until Christ be formed in you.—It is a ripe, completely developed child that is in contemplation=in which the life has come to perfect manifestation. Such a child, and only such a one, renders a mother's pangs of labor effectual, for only such a child lives, and therefore only in such a one has she a child. So long as the birth is not that of a perfect child, so long must she ever look forward to new pangs of labor, before she can have this, her wish granted. [ELLICOTT: "The idea is not so much of the pain, as of the long and continuous effort of the travail."—R.] —With justice therefore is the complete formation of the child represented as the aim of the labor, and there is here nothing like an inversion of the physiological process, in which the *formatio* takes place *ante partum.* This is not here the point in question. The natural child is completely developed, in that the natural life, as it were the spirit of life, comes in it to perfect manifestion, gains an actual, corresponding form. What this natural spirit of life is in the natural child, Christ is in the spiritual child, as the principle of spiritual life, and hence the expression of the Apostle: Christ is μορφωθῆναι in them =the inward principle is to come with them to manifestation to gain a form in an established, assured, evangelical conviction of faith; only when this takes place, has Paul as spiritual mother actually a spiritual child. But since this is wanting, as is shown by their apostacy, he is therefore now bearing them once again, in the hope that this perfect formation may come to pass. (If it had not, he would have needed to travail in birth still again, but here, as is natural, he only speaks of a second travail.) That in nature a completely developed child is not hoped for from a second bearing of the same child, is a self-evident incongruity between the fact and the image, but it answers the purpose that the activity is the same—in both cases there is a travail of birth.*—WIESELER incorrectly finds in πάλιν ὠδίνειν the doctrinal conception of the new birth, and takes πάλιν therefore as antithetical to the natural birth. In the first place the Apostle's lamentation over the alteration that had taken place in the readers, brings almost necessarily to our thoughts the probability of a renewed activity among them; and secondly he could well designate the labor bestowed by him upon the Galatians as a bearing of spiritual children, but not as a regeneration in the doctrinal sense, for this appertains to God alone. Paul's travailing in birth with them, it is true, had as its end, their becoming regenerate children of God, but the one is not therefore to be identified with the other.

Ver. 20. **I could wish indeed to be present with you.**—[This rendering, though not literal, brings out the force of the passage, and the "tacit contrast" in δέ. See above.—R.]—**And to change my tone.**—This, in its immediate connection with a wish to be present with them, appears to signify: I should be glad to give my language such a form as suits with oral intercourse; from the written style, with its more formal, unpliable character, less suited to make an impression on the heart, I should be glad to pass over into oral discourse. But φωνὴν ἀλλάξαι does not on this account mean: to interchange discourse with any one=to converse together, as WIESELER singularly assumes. Why he should like to be with them, and to vary his discourse, he then expressly declares: **For I am perplexed about you.**—Ἐν, the perplexity has its ground chiefly in them, in their state of mind.† He knows not with what arguments he can find access to them and dispose them to a return. Therefore he thinks now he could more easily accomplish something by oral discourse with them. MEYER understands φωνὴν ἀλλάσσειν of a wish of Paul, instead of the rigorous tone used in his last visit, to essay a milder tone. But this is far from evident.—RIEGER justly remarks that in a certain sense Paul does immediately after in ver. 21 what he wishes in ver. 20, namely, varies the form of his language, and speaks as if he were present with them: λέγετέ μοι κ. τ. λ. [For the various interpretations of the phrase "change my voice" see MEYER *in loco*. The view given above seems tame, but the reference to the tone during his second visit is doubtful. So also the interpretation: "to modify my language from time to time as occasion demands." Certainly it is improper to think of a desire to change his tone to a more severe one (in contrast with the mild τεκνία). On the whole it seems best to conclude 1) that the desired change was from the severe to the milder address; 2) that the severe tone referred to is that of the present Epistle (so ELLICOTT and many others).—R.]

Ver. 21. **Tell me, ye that desire to be under the law, do ye not hear the law?**—"Hear" is hardly to be taken precisely as implying that the law was publicly read by the pseudo-apostles among them, but generally: Do you not give heed to what is written in the Law? The second time νόμος, according to the Jewish use of תּוֹרָה = the Pentateuch. From the law itself, on which you lay so much stress, you might discover that you are not, and are not meant to be under the law. [MEYER:—"At the close of the theoretical part of his Epistle, Paul now appends a very peculiar *allegoric argument from the law itself*, intended to destroy the influence of the false Apostles with their own weapons, and to root it up out of its own proper soil."—R.]

Ver. 22. **For it is written.**—Γάρ = I must inquire: do ye not hear the Law; for if you really heard the law, you would find in it that which might convince you how unsound and dangerous it is to "desire to be under the law." That to which Paul refers the Galatians, as being found in the law, is the narrative in Genesis, of the two sons of Abraham, Ishmael and Isaac, the one by the bondmaid, Hagar, and the other by the free woman, Sarah. As is known, he had Ishmael first, and he is therefore mentioned first. They were therefore indeed both Abraham's sons, but they had not merely different mothers, but mothers also of entirely different conditions; the one was the son of a bondmaid, the other of a free woman.

Ver. 23. Yet even with that they might have been begotten in like manner, **but** (ἀλλά) this was far from being the case, the son of the bondmaid was begotten **after the flesh**, and the son of the free woman **through the promise.**—Κατὰ σάρκα = entirely in the ordinary way of natural generation, of carnal intercourse; διὰ τῆς ἐπαγγελίας = formally also, it is true, in this way, but materially (by the side of which the other is a vanishing factor), by virtue of the divine promise, which Abraham had received, inasmuch as God in a miraculous manner, restored the long-lost capacity of Sarah to conceive, so that in truth the efficient factor was God. [The preposition διά denoting the *causa medians* (ELLICOTT).—R.]

Ver. 24. **Which things are allegorical,** ἅτινά ἐστιν ἀλληγορούμενα.—Paul thus introduces his interpretation of the narrative which he quotes. He states what the Galatians might learn from it. [ELLICOTT has a valuable note on the distinction between ὅς and ὅστις. His view of ἅτινα is thus expressed: "*all which things* viewed in their most general light." This wider meaning will guard against the assumption that the narrative itself was a mere allegory and not historical.—R.]—Ἀλληγορεῖν = ἄλλο ἀγορεύειν: to say something else than is expressed by the letter, to say something in figures; passively: to have a tropical sense, ἀλληγορούμενον εἶναι = to be something that has such a sense. That Paul understands what is related in Genesis of Abraham, Hagar, Sarah, etc., as history also, needs no proof: but undoubtedly at the same time he

* [WORDSWORTH mentions a curious exposition and extension of this metaphor in the Epistle of the primitive churches of Gaul "who say that by means of the martyrs much joy accrued to the holy Virgin Mother, the Church of Christ, receiving back *alive* those whom she has lost as abortions, and also because through means of the martyrs, very many of her children who had fallen away by apostasy, were again conceived in her womb, and were being brought forth again to life."—R.]

† [Hence ἀποροῦμαι is to be taken, not as passive, with deponent sense (ELLICOTT), nor middle (LIGHTFOOT), but middle with passive signification (MEYER, ALFORD); "the condition of perplexity is conceived of as wrought upon, suffered by the subject."—R.]

sees in the history an intimation of something else, something higher, than the simple history relates. In what sense, see below, in the DOCTRINAL NOTES. [The precise meaning of ἀλληγορεῖν must be noted. It *may* be made to cover the thought: to be treated as having an allegorical sense, but here we must insist on the more definite and strict meaning: to have an allegorical sense. "Which things viewed in their most general light *have* an allegorical meaning;" this interpretation will guard against the assumptions and errors which are based upon a looser view. See DOCTRINAL NOTES.—R.]

To what the history points is then stated: **for these are two covenants.**—Αὗται seems not to refer immediately, *i. e.*, grammatically, to the women, but, according to ordinary Greek usage, to stand for ταῦτα; it would be somewhat different if in ver. 23 the women were the subjects. Substantially no doubt it refers to the two women, in whom he sees types of the two covenants—not however in the twofold marriage covenant of Abraham with Hagar and Sarah (as JATHO assumes, who, in order to sustain this view, is obliged to give an exceedingly forced interpretation of "which is Agar"). It is peculiar, and renders the understanding of this passage somewhat difficult, that Paul, in the first place, designates the women and not the sons themselves as symbols, more particularly as prophetic symbols of the two covenants; and in the second place, it even more perplexes the matter, that he finds in them the two *covenants* = of God with men, which were typified or prophesied (that is, in general, the Old and the New Covenant), and takes these themselves as mothers, and then from these first passes over to the two diverse *churches*, whose motherhood appears more clearly when viewed in connection with their members. Of course, however, the covenants stand in intimate relation to the churches; it is not only they that confer on them their peculiar character, but also that properly constitute them; without the covenants the churches would not exist.—**The one from Mount Sinai**, *etc.*—A pregnant expression = the first covenant is that which originates from mount Sinai and bears unto bondage. Γεννῶσα, feminine, because it corresponds to the mother Hagar. The expression εἰς δουλείαν γεννῶσα is itself to be supplemented so that it = bearing, *sc.* children, as it were into bondage = and translating them into bondage, of course by subjection to the law, for the covenant from Sinai is the covenant of law.—**Which is Hagar.**—This is = this covenant is typified by Hagar, for she too as "bondmaid" bore children "unto bondage." This is of course primarily the ground why he compares the Sinaitic covenant with Hagar; of both alike the "bearing children unto bondage" was an attribute. But this abrupt assertion: the Sinaitic covenant is Hagar, or, Hagar signifies the Sinaitic covenant, because it as well as she "bore unto bondage," is of itself too bold and startling, and Paul therefore in a parenthesis intimates that Sinai and Hagar, far apart as they might seem to be, yet even independently of this "bearing," stand *of themselves* related to one another.

VER. 25. The words setting forth this relation are, according to one reading: τὸ γὰρ Σινᾶ ὄρος ἐστὶν ἐν τῇ Ἀραβίᾳ: according to the other: τὸ δὲ [or γάρ] Ἄγαρ Σινᾶ ὄρος, &c. Accepting the first reading, Paul points to the fact that Mount Sinai is situated in Arabia—that therefore the Sinaitic covenant has one home with Hagar, and so far a relation to her. Both originate from Arabia—are not at home in the Holy Land; while yet they both came in near relation to the people of God; Hagar to Abraham, bearing him a son; the Sinaitic covenant to Abraham's posterity, raising up children to this; for Israel by the Sinaitic covenant first became an organized theocratic people, possessing the principle of self-preservation and hereditary continuance.—Accepting the reading: τὸ δὲ Ἄγαρ, κ. τ. λ. in which δέ is exceedingly well suited to introduce an elucidation, which indeed it properly is, rather than a demonstration [γάρ being however the more probable reading, on critical grounds, see critical note.—R.], the Apostle points out that even as to name there exists a relation between Hagar and the Sinaitic covenant,—that it is not therefore so arbitrary as might seem on his part, to interpret the former as a type of the latter; for that among the Arabians, Mount Sinai has just this name of Hagar, and that—as Paul undoubtedly assumes—after Hagar. It is true we have no other proof of Sinai's having this appellation, and it would have to be assumed that Paul had learned, perhaps from his sojourn in Arabia, that Sinai bore this name also among the Arabs, which he referred back to Hagar. It is certainly probable, that the Arabs named Sinai Ἄγαρ; for this is = Rock, and so corresponds precisely to the character of this mountain chain, and probably also to the signification of the ancient name "Sinai" itself, which etymology renders by "Rock."—Paul would then, only err in the reference of this name Ἄγαρ to the Hagar of the Old Testament, but at all events the name would be the same, and this, in the first instance would be the main thing. Yet this circumstance will always make this reading suspicious.

[In addition to these interpretations, which may be distinguished as I., II., another (III.) must be considered, *viz.*, that of CALVIN, BEZA, ESTIUS, WORDSWORTH (and LIGHTFOOT, if the correctness of the Recepta be established): "For this Hagar (is) represents Mount Sinai in Arabia."—I. is comparatively free from grammatical difficulty, forming a parenthesis, which introduces a *geographical* remark, the point of which is obvious, though on the whole it seems much tamer than the other views. Besides the *critical* grounds for preferring the longer reading (not the least strong being this absence of grammatical difficulties), it may be objected 1. That since a *mere* geographical remark would be unnecessary, the emphasis must lie on ἐν τῇ Ἀραβ.; but to convey such an emphasis, the Greek order should be ἐν τῇ Ἀρ. ἐστίν (ALFORD). 2. MEYER intimates that this view must press as the essential point, the fact that the mountain was "outside of the land of Canaan," and yet this essential point is only implied. Still there is not much force in this objection, since the positive statement "is in Arabia," the land of bondsmen, is after all the main thought, the other being a negative antitheses, that may well be omitted.—II. is adopted by MEYER, ELLICOTT, ALFORD, and many older commentators (CHRYSOSTOM, LUTHER, *et al*). This may be called the *etymological* view. Here the grammatical difficulties are not great, for it may readily be conceded, that τὸ Ἄγαρ means "the word Agar," ἐστίν, "means"—and ἐν τῇ Ἀρ. either "among the Arabians" or "in the Arabian (supply διαλέκτῳ) dialect," and the objection that "the word Agar" cannot properly be the subject of συστοιχεῖ is met by putting a semicolon at the end of this clause, or throwing it into a parenthesis. The real difficulties are far graver. 1. It is extremely doubtful whether "Agar" did mean "in Arabia, Mount Sinai." The testimony of travellers is not strong, that of philology even less so. Granting that the Arabic word for "rock" is similar in sound, we are far from settling the question of identity of name. 2. "If in writing to a half-Greek, half-Celtic people, he ventured to argue from an Arabic word at all, he would at all events be careful to make his drift intelligible" (LIGHTFOOT). Was it likely to be intelligible to them, when in these days of philological and geographical research, this interpretation is still doubtful? 3. The argument or illustration seems fanciful when resting on this identity of name, especially as Hagar had a meaning in Hebrew, and Sarah also, which meanings could well have been used here, were it a question of names.—III. "For this Hagar *represents*," *etc.* This may be called the *typical or allegorical* interpretation, and for that very reason more likely to be correct in this connection. It avoids the objections against I. on the score of emphasis, and tameness; with II. follows the reading which seems more correct, but avoids the fanciful and doubtful features of that view. MEYER considers the neuter article an insuperable objection. But this may be met 1) as is done by WORDSWORTH, by joining the article with Σινᾶ ὄρος not with Ἄγαρ. He contends that this is allowable and that no other order was admissible. Still this seems unnatural. Or 2) by understanding τὸ Ἄγαρ, "the thing Hagar," not the woman, for ver. 24 passes over into allegory, but the allegorical Hagar,—her position as set forth in ver. 24. This is less objectionable. As this is the only real difficulty (ἐστίν, "represents," is of course admissible), we may adopt III. as perhaps the safest view, seemingly that of E. V. As regards punctuation, a comma then suffices after this clause, and Ἄγαρ is the grammatical subject of συστοιχεῖ.—R.]

**Ranks with.**—Συστοιχεῖ δέ might be connected with ἥτις (ver. 24) or back of that with μία, *sc.* διαθήκη. [So DE WETTE, LIGHTFOOT.—R.] "For she is in bondage" is given as the proof of "ranks with," and this evidently refers to "bearing children unto bondage" (ver. 24). The covenant "bearing children unto bondage" "ranks with the present Jerusalem, for she is in bondage with her children." Συστοιχεῖν, to stand in one row with something else, to belong to the same species, to belong together with anything. The Sinaitic covenant, says Paul, and the present Jerusalem, although separated in time and place, yet belong essentially together; the former brought into "bondage," the latter is in that very bondage. The object is to show that an internal relation exists between the Sinaitic covenant and the present Jerusalem. [This is certainly preferable to the view of CHRYSOSTOM and most of the Fathers, LUTHER *et al.*, which takes Σινᾶ as the subject, and renders the verb either "is contiguous to" or "joined in a continuous (mountain) range" with Jerusalem. The thought is irrelevant, and we should then have Mt. Zion, rather than Jerusalem, following the verb. LIGHTFOOT thus shows the exact meaning of the verb: "In military language συστοιχία denotes a *file*, as συζυγία does a rank of soldiers; comp. Polyb. x. 21, 7. The allegory of the text may be represented by συστοιχίαι thus:

| | |
|---|---|
| Hagar, the bond woman. | Sarah, the free woman. |
| Ishmael, the child after the flesh. | Isaac, the child of promise. |
| The Old Covenant. | The New Covenant. |
| The earthly Jerusalem, etc. | The heavenly Jerusalem, etc." |

Accepting this meaning, it is necessary to take exception to embracing the idea of type in the word. Those in each list are σύστοιχοι with each other, but ἀντίστοιχοι to those in the opposite list.—R.]—It seems however more accordant with the context to make Ἄγαρ (ver. 25) the subject. For Hagar is a type of the present Jerusalem, "ranks with"—stands in the same row with it, or better, fits as a type to the antitype [?] Moreover Hagar *was* "in bondage with her children, just as the present Jerusalem." Besides in this connection there is significant reference to the fact that "the present Jerusalem" corresponds to Hagar alone—and not to Sarah; the special proof of which is, what is affirmed of "the present Jerusalem," viz.: "for she is in bondage with her children." [So that not only the proximity of the word Ἄγαρ, but the closer correspondence also, supports the view that "Hagar" is the logical subject of the verb. See MEYER.—R.]

**The present Jerusalem.**—Jerusalem represents here as it always did in the Old Testament, the Jewish people; but this as a collective personality, and moreover a maternal one, the individual members of the people being viewed as children of this mother. Ἡ νῦν Ἱερουσ. is the present Jerusalem in contrast with the μελλ. Ἱερουσ. as it shall become through the Messiah, *i. e.*, through faith in Him, the Jerusalem, which has not, and so long as it has not, received the Messiah. "The present Jerusalem" meaning thus the historical Israel, the Jewish people, its children are of course "born after the flesh" and Paul presupposes this as self-evident.—**Is in bondage.**—This cannot apply to the yoke of the Romans, for this has nothing at all to do with the Sinaitic covenant, but applies to the being in bondage under the Mosaic law. A state of bondage in this sense Paul predicates of the existing Jewish church without further proof, as something which the readers after the preceding exposition of the nature of the law (comp. iii. 23; iv. 3–7), must concede, and indeed that the Jews were strenuous observers of the law was a matter beyond doubt.

Ver. 26. **But Jerusalem which is above is free.**—Paul does not continue the course of thought begun in ver. 24 with "for these are two covenants." He names the first covenant only, not the second one also, but to make the contrast more palpable, opposes at once to the present Jerusalem, which is in bondage, another Jerusalem which is free. Now the present Jerusalem is in a condition of bondage because the first covenant, which is a covenant of bondage, came in her to manifestation. So the freedom of the other Jerusalem would have its ground also in the character of the second covenant, which comes into manifestation in her, and we have a right to find implied a second covenant bearing children unto freedom, which is typified prophetically by Sarah, just as the covenant of bondage by Hagar. If we inquire what this second covenant is, according to the previous context, the answer cannot be doubtful; over against the covenant of law stands a covenant of grace or promise. WIESELER's parallelism goes too far, where he wishes to supply: *δευτέρα δὲ (διαθήκη) ἀπὸ ὄρους Σιὼν, εἰς ἐλευθερίαν γεννῶσα, ἥτις ἐστὶ Σάῤῥα. τὸ γὰρ Σιὼν ὄρος ἐστὶν ἐν τῇ γῇ τῆς ἐπαγγελίας, συστοιχεῖ δὲ τῇ ἄνω Ἱερουσαλήμ. ἐλευθέρη γάρ ἐστι μετὰ τῶν τέκνων αὐτῆς.* ["The second covenant from Mount Zion, bearing children unto freedom, which is Sarah. For Zion is a mountain in the land of promise, and ranks with Jerusalem above, for she is free with her children." This follows from his view of ver. 25, and is objectionable besides for the reason that it forces an allegory beyond the point to which it has been carried by the Apostle himself.—R.] Somewhat too definite also is MEYER's view: The other covenant is the one established in Christ (see afterwards on *ἡ ἄνω Ἱερουσαλήμ*). Paul has not waited till now to give the proof that the covenant of grace is a covenant of promise, and that on this account Jerusalem above is also free. This is in part clear from what precedes and in part results from the nature of the case, since a covenant of promise given of grace, because it has nothing to do with any law, can have no connection with "bondage" either. In addition he now demonstrates to the Galatians this only, that *they* are children of *that* Jerusalem which is free, and that therefore it would be preposterous for them to wish to be under the law. "Free" of course =not being under the law.

The main question is, what *ἡ ἄνω Ἱερουσ.* signifies. "Jerusalem" here also means a church taken as a collective personality, her individual members being conceived as her children. But *ἡ ἄνω Ἱερουσ.* is of course not the "ancient" Jerusalem, the Salem of Melchisedek, nor yet the mountain of Zion, which in Josephus is called *ἡ ἄνω πόλις*. [LIGHTFOOT: "The Apostle instinctively prefers the Hebrew form Ἱερουσαλήμ here for the typical city, as elsewhere in this Epistle (i. 17, 18; ii. 1) he employs the Græcised form Ἱερόσόλυμα for the actual city. 'Ἱερουσαλήμ *est appellatio Hebraica, originaria et sanctior:* Ἱεροσόλυμα, *deinceps obvia, Græca, magis politica,*' says Bengel on Rev. xxi. 2, accounting for the usage of St. John (in the Gospel the latter; in the Apocalypse the former), and referring to this passage in illustration."—R.] On the other hand LUTHER is right in his decided protest against the reference to the *ecclesia triumphans*, for the Christians of this world are here designated by Paul as children of this *ἄνω Ἱερουσαλήμ*. (Only so much is correct, that with the *παρουσία* it is no other than this very *ἄνω Ἱερουσ.* that comes to perfection, so that the Church after the *παρουσία* is essentially identical with that before it. But the eye is not at all directed here to the *παρουσία*; and the very reason why the expression *ἡ μέλλουσα Ἱερουσ.* is not chosen is, that after Christ had appeared upon earth this must be referred to the *παρουσία*. WIESELER is therefore also incorrect in asserting not only that the church of the perfected is meant, but in insisting as he does that these are *expressly* comprehended.)—But yet *ἡ ἄνω Ἱερουσ.* must at all events signify a Jerusalem that is above, an *upper* Jerusalem, and this "above" can only refer to Heaven. Here again LUTHER has a right understanding of it, in the main point at all events, when he remarks that this "above" is to be understood not of place but of character: "when St. Paul speaks of a Jerusalem above and the other here below upon earth, he means that the one Jerusalem is spiritual, but the other earthly. For there is a great distinction between spiritual and corporeal or earthly things. What is spiritual, that is above, but what is earthly, that is here below. Therefore says he then, that the spiritual Jerusalem is above, not that in respect to space or place it is higher than the earthly here below, but in that it is spiritual." The upper Jerusalem would therefore=the spiritual Jerusalem. This explanation, it is true, does not appear to do full justice to the material idea "above," but it leads in the right direction for this, and needs only to be completed by including also the conception of space which is contained in *ἄνω*. That is, *ἡ ἄνω Ἱερουσ.* is not= the Jerusalem that is *localiter*, externally situated above (this is refuted by LUTHER), but the Jerusalem, that as to its *essential character* is an upper, heavenly one, and therefore neither originates from earth nor belongs to earth, but originates from Heaven and belongs to Heaven, let it be situated where it may, of which nothing is expressly said. (In reality Luther also means this and nothing else by his spiritual Jerusalem, and his explanation, therefore, only apparently incurs the reproach of spiritualizing.) Whether the expression is immediately founded upon the rabbinical doctrine of the ירושלים של מעלה "which according to Jewish teaching is the archetype existing in Heaven of the earthly Jerusalem, and at the establishment of the Messianic kingdom will be let down from Heaven to earth, in order, as the earthly Jerusalem is the central point and the capital of the old theocracy, to be the same for the Messianic theocracy" (MEYER), cannot be affirmed with certainty; that Paul did not share the crude and sensuous rabbinical conceptions of this heavenly Jerusalem, but had a scripturally purified idea of it, is in any case clear; so that from the Jewish schools he only derives the expression rather than the substance of the idea. At the most he had only the fundamental conception, which was then essentially modified. [LIGHTFOOT: "With them," *i. e.*, the rabbinical teachers, "it is an actual city, the exact counterpart of the earthly Jerusalem in its topography and furniture: with him it is a symbol or image, representing that spiritual city of which the Christian is even now a denizen (Phil. iii. 20). The contrast between the two scenes, as they appeared to the eye, would enhance, if it did not suggest the imagery of St. Paul here. On the one hand, Mount Zion, of old the joy of the whole earth, now more beautiful than ever in the fresh glories of the Herodian renaissance, glittering in gold and marble; on the other, Sinai with its rugged peaks and barren sides, bleak and desolate, the oppressive power of which the Apostle himself had felt during his sojourn there—these scenes fitly represented the contrast between the glorious hopes of the new covenant and the blank despair of the old. Comp. Heb. xii. 18–22."—R.]

**And she is our mother.**—If we seek to define still more distinctly the idea of the ἄνω Ἱερουσ., we shall find that here also LUTHER had the right sense of it, when he peremptorily declares, and in opposition to the transcendental fantasies, which overlooked the actually operative heavenly forces in the word and sacraments, so strongly insists that: "the heavenly Jerusalem, which is above, is nothing else than the dear church or Christendom, that are in the whole world here and there dispersed, who all together have one gospel, one manner of faith in Christ, one Holy Ghost, and one manner of sacrament." Only here again he makes the idea too special. The upper Jerusalem, which essentially springs from Heaven and not from earth, and belongs to Heaven and not to earth, is in the first instance nothing else than the true Church and people of God in its entire generality; for this has its constitution not in the covenant of law, but in the covenant of grace or promise, and its essential character may therefore with full right, nay must be denominated by Paul a heavenly one.—As certainly now as Paul dated back the covenant of grace as far back beyond the covenant of law as Abraham's time, so certainly did this "upper Jerusalem" properly begin with Abraham himself, although at first indeed rather in the way of promise, in idea, as it were, but yet *realiter*, as certainly as God's covenant of grace was one really concluded. This "upper Jerusalem" then, it is true, first came to full manifestation with the advent of the Messiah, as with this God's covenant of grace first found its true actualization; and so far is the upper Jerusalem=Christendom, but yet even now it must not be identified with it. It is a higher, more general idea, precisely =God's congregation [*Gottesgemeinde*] which the idea of the church does not altogether exhaust, but which continues to rise above it, lying at the foundation of the church, which is its concrete manifestation, but yet to be distinguished from it; and indeed this idea of the congregation of God will never attain its completely adequate expression in the church of this dispensation, but only with the παρουσία will such a complete coincidence of ideas and phenomenon be realized (as indeed on the other hand the present Jerusalem which is in bondage was also not absolutely coincident with the Jewish community, but many members of it raised themselves above this bondage, although no doubt in this case the coincidence was far more nearly complete). [MEYER's interpretation: "the *Messianic theocracy*, which before the παρουσία is the *church*, and after it Christ's kingdom of glory" is substantially correct, provided we sufficiently extend the meaning of the word "Church." Our conceptions of her, "who is our mother," must here be large enough to include all her children, in the Old and the New Dispensations, as militant and triumphant. See DOCTRINAL NOTES.—R.] What Paul now wishes to show is, that Christians are children of this true congregation of God, that is grounded upon the covenant of grace, and therefore of course is free, and not merely that they are children of the Christian community, which certainly would have needed no proof.—From the foregoing we see still more evidently (what has already been touched upon above), that the expression ἡ μέλλουσα Ἱερουσ., although it would have corresponded with ἡ νῦν Ἱερουσ., would not have been suitable here. On the other hand nothing stood in the way of designating the natural Israel as ἡ νῦν Ἱερουσ., inasmuch as every one would refer this expression to the right object; in this sense a κάτω Ἱερουσ. would have sounded strange, and would have been less intelligible, so that the want of correspondence in the expressions is not at all surprising.

Vers. 27 and 28 contain the proof of the proposition that "Jerusalem which is above" is the mother of Christians,—in syllogistic form, only not quite exact, since ὑμεῖς is the more probable reading in ver. 28. Ver. 27, major premise: To the "Jerusalem which is above," although she does not bear, there are many children promised, who therefore, as Isaac, must have been born purely in virtue of Divine promise.—Ver. 28, minor premise: But now are we, or rather, says the Apostle, with definite application to the readers, for whom particularly the proof is intended, ye are the children of promise, after the analogy of Isaac;—therefore (conclusion) ye are children of the Jerusalem above.

**For it is written, Rejoice, thou barren that bearest not,** *etc.*—For the major premise Paul appeals to Isaiah liv. 1. The theocratic nation is addressed during the Babylonian exile, and told that though aforetime in the bloom of Israel's prosperity she was like a woman "who hath a husband," who had by her husband numerous children, she now resembled a woman that is "desolate" = without a husband (for it had been repudiated by God), and in consequence —for στεῖρα is here to be taken in this sense—is "barren," "not bearing," "not travailing," bears no children. (God is to be conceived as the husband, if this part of the figure is also to be interpreted, according to the familiar Biblical image of God's marriage covenant with Israel.) But yet is she to rejoice, and loudly to express her joy (ῥῆξον sc. φωνήν, *rumpe vocem*, let loose the voice), for she shall become richer in children than before! This therefore not in the way of natural generation, but through the immediate extraordinary operation of God: they are therefore children not "after the flesh," but born "through the promise." (Only, so to speak, the natural, carnal relation of God to the people as begetting natural posterity, was dissolved; God yet remained, in the exercise of a higher energy, devoted to the people as His people, for the very end of bringing in something higher than before.) Evidently in this the image of Sarah hovers before the prophet, of that barren one who was "desolate," that is, at least as "barren" could have no conjugal intercourse with her husband, and therefore was so far without husband, and who yet became a mother of a numerous progeny in virtue of the Divine energy. Thus even the prophet sees in Sarah a type of the theocratic nation—not, it is true, in her condition of freedom, but at least in her becoming a mother by promise, and therefore is she a type of the theocratic people, inasmuch as this increases not in the natural way=through natural descent, but through the addition of spiritual children.—Herein also is found Paul's justification for referring this passage immediately to "Jerusalem which is above." Primarily, indeed, it applies to the theocratic people as a whole. But even here, to the natural children, =to such as become members of the theocratic people by natural descent, are opposed spiritual children=such as become such in virtue of Divine operation, without natural consanguinity. The sense therefore cannot be merely: The now depopulated Israel shall again become populous, yea, even more than before, by renewal of the now interrupted conjugal intimacy; but from *that* people of God which increased by natural descent, there is distinguished the people of God in the higher, completely true sense, whose existence does not depend on natural descent, but on Divine operation, that is of course, the operation of the Spirit, inasmuch as God through His Spirit produces faith, and *so* raises up children to His people, regarded as mother, or to Abraham their first ancestor. There is thus contrasted with the natural, empirical people of God, the one ἔχουσα τὸν ἄνδρα, which is now continued in the present Jerusalem, a higher spiritual one, the one which is "barren, bearing not,"=not naturally maintaining and increasing itself, *i. e.*, in short the "Jerusalem which is above."—The fulfilment of the promise then, took place, *i. e.*, numerous children, without being naturally begotten by the theocratic people, were born to it, in particular, through the appearance of the Messiah, for all, who came to believe on Him, became thereby, and not by natural descent, members of God's people (comp. ver. 28).—But it must here be remarked in addition, that Paul's design is not strictly to declare positively of the Jerusalem above (as even MEYER assumes), that it had first been barren, therefore first unpopulated, childless, and had then become the mother of children (with the origin of the Christian people of God); but he means thereby only to distinguish it from the theocratic people that is maintained and continued by natural means. In distinction from this the Jerusalem above is in its *nature*—and *remains* therefore barren, not bearing, not travailing, desolate, for she obtains children indeed, but by no means through becoming fertile, τίκτειν, ὠδίνειν = not by such natural processes, as if these had only failed for awhile, and had then again become operative; on the other hand the children are given to her in a way not to be naturally explained, not as bodily offspring, but spiritually by Divine operation; for she is and remains not "having a husband" (=who does not stand to God in this natural and carnal relation). [ALFORD:—The "husband" of the E. V. may mislead "by pointing at the one husband (Abraham) who was common to Sara and Agar, which might do in this passage, but not in Isaiah: whereas ἔχ. τὸν ἄνδρα means, 'her (of the two) who has (the) husband,' the other having none: a fineness of meaning which we cannot give in English." This goes to sustain the view of Schmoller.—R.] We need not be perplexed because this would create a divergence from the type of Sarah, with whom certainly, after her barrenness, a bearing and travailing took place. But although Paul undoubtedly knew this well, he yet (vers. 23, 29) denies explicitly and roundly that Isaac was born after the flesh and vindicates to him only a being born through the promise, after the Spirit; and he can very well apprehend the contrast thus absolutely, because he looks only at the essential thing, the determining, generative principle, and this was purely "the promise," "the spirit," even though the act did not proceed without the medium of the "flesh." Sarah, is his meaning, did not obtain her son Isaac, because from a naturally unfruitful woman she had become a naturally fruitful one; her obtaining the son was therefore only, as it were, formally, not essentially, a τίκτειν, &c. (see on ver. 23). But if Paul expresses himself thus even respecting Sarah, with whom nevertheless in a certain sense a τίκτειν, and the like, did take place, the same of course holds good in its full sense of the antitype, the true people of God, as Jerusalem above. This is precisely its specific quality, that it obtains children without "bearing" as "barren," and in this very way approves itself as the true people of God, for which God begets children; therefore we have only: "many are the children of the desolate," not: she will *bear* many children. Of course "barren" varies a little; at first it is one who *cannot* bear, because she is deprived of the husband; but from that it becomes one, who does not bear and *is* to bear, *i. e.*, does not in this way obtain children, and is to obtain them, but in another way. But this variation is already implied in the original sense of the passage, which as it were says: "Barren hast thou become, that cannot bear; well, so shalt thou be and remain, but not to thy hurt, but to thy good," &c.—**Many are the children of the desolate more**, *etc.*—MEYER rightly explains: not=πλείονα ἤ, which would leave the numerousness of the children wholly undetermined, but it expresses, that both have many children, but the solitary one, more=numerous are the children of the solitary, far more, than of her who hath her husband.

Ver. 28 places the Galatians, as Christians, among the children of the Jerusalem above, promised her in ver. 27. **As Isaac was.**—Κατὰ Ἰσαάκ, in conformity with, according to the type of, even as Isaac. The antitype of the mother, Sarah, was named ver. 26; even so are Christians antitypes of *her* son, Isaac.—**Children of Promise**,—opposed to σαρκὸς τέκνα, therefore properly children whom the promise has born=who are born in virtue of the promise of God, not through carnal generation. —So was it with Isaac; he was born to Abraham as son in this way. Even so is it with you: you have in this way been born, *i. e.*, become *members of God's people*. This needs no proof, for on one side, it was certain that they as Christians were members of God's people, and on the other side also, that they were not so by nature, by carnal descent, but in a spiritual manner, namely, through their knowledge of Christ, to which God had led them by His Spirit, thereby fulfilling His promise. It therefore follows from this, that they belong, because members of the theocratic people, and yet not such by natural descent, to "the children of the desolate" (ver. 27)=have her (to whom, although desolate, children are promised by God) as their mother, as was affirmed in ver. 26.

Ver. 29. **Still as then he that was born after the flesh.**—Why will you nevertheless be under the law, and so in the condition of bondage? Paul had brought home to his hearers, You are like Isaac, not like Ishmael. This he had deduced from the manner of the birth of each. But now he adds—looking at the subsequent lot of each—a warning, that it is dangerous to place themselves in a position like Ishmael's, for he had been shut out of the inheritance. Even so will it fare—Paul gives them to understand, with those that are like Ishmael=those that are under the law. Ἀλλά: for the thought which Paul first expresses, is in opposition to that in the foregoing verse, where he had described Christians as having a possession, as children of the free woman, because children of the promise. Yet Paul does not affirm this in order to frighten them back from the condition of freedom, as one of persecution, but on the contrary (*ἀλλά*, ver. 30) in order to set forth immediately after the evil lot of the children of the bondwoman, as persecutors, and thus to hinder the Christians from placing themselves, through bondage to the law, in a like position with them.

**Persecuted.**—In Gen. xxi. 9, Ishmael is mentioned only as a scoffer: Paul here then either uses *διώκειν* in a more general sense, or he follows a more developed tradition, traces of which are found in the Rabbins. [*Διώκειν* is a strong word, and we are not justified in altering or extending its meaning to meet a difficulty, arising from the interpretation of another passage. The question then is: Is this statement of the Apostle based only upon the Scriptural narrative (Gen. xxi. 9), or also upon some other reliable source of information, supplementing the Old Testament narrative. The chief objection urged by most modern commentators against the former of these views is, that there is no thought of "persecution" either expressed or implied in the passage referred to. It tells us of Ishmael's "laughing" (מְצַחֵק: which the LXX. expands into *παίζοντα μετὰ Ἰσαὰκ τοῦ υἱοῦ αὐτῆς*"); this has been interpreted as *in play* awakening Sarah's jealousy, and as *in mockery*, arousing her anger. Obviously the latter is more in accordance with the context and is a legitimate rendering of the Hebrew (see LANGE'S *Com.* Gen. *in loco*). But is it said that even this view of the narrative will not justify the assertion "persecuted." WORDSWORTH, accepting the meaning "playing," remarks: "The temper in which Ishmael played with Isaac, may best be inferred from the comment which Isaac's mother made upon it. Sarah's words interpret Ishmael's act. If his play had been loving play, she would not have been displeased by it. It must have been the spirit of spiteful malice, made more offensive by its pretence to sportiveness and love,* which extorted from Sarah the words which the Holy Spirit, speaking by St. Paul, here calls a verdict of Scripture. And Almighty God Himself vouchsafed to confirm Sarah's interpretation of Ishmael's play, by commanding Abraham, although reluctant, to hearken to Sarah's voice in that matter." It would seem that an inspired Apostle, reading the Old Testament narrative in the full gospel light, could interpret the spirit of that occurrence, without relying on *tradition.* If however the objection urged by MEYER, DE WETTE, JOWETT, and others, be deemed valid, as even ELLICOTT admits them to be, the following remarks of LIGHTFOOT may well be taken into account. "1) This incident which is so lightly sketched in the original narrative had been drawn out in detail in later traditions, and thus a prominence was given to it, which would add force to the Apostle's allusion, without his endorsing these traditions himself. 2) The relations between the two brothers were reproduced in their descendants. The aggressions of the Arab tribes on the Israelites were the antitype to Ishmael's mockery of Isaac. Thus in Ishmael the Apostle may have indirectly contemplated Ishmael's progeny; and he would therefore be appealing to the national history of the Jews in saying 'he that was born after the flesh persecuted him that was born after the Spirit.' "—R.]

**After the Spirit.**—The one born according to the Spirit. The Spirit of God was the power by which the generation of Isaac took place. The Spirit however is here conceived not as the power, but as the norm, according to which the generation took place=he was begotten in the way and manner in which the Spirit begets. "After the flesh" is to be interpreted in the same way.

**Even so now.**—Those born after the Spirit =" the children of promise" are persecuted by those born after the flesh=the natural members of the theocratic people, the Jews. But the main point is not the suffering of persecution by the one, although the thought of it occasions the *ἀλλά*, but the persecution of the others. See ver. 30.—To what this specially refers, is hard to say: that there was no lack of persecutions on the part of the Jews, is indeed well known. That the plotting of the Judaizers against the Christians are also meant, is probable; for these Judaizers believed themselves to have a preëminence, precisely as those born after the flesh, and, as our whole Epistle shows, took a position, which though professedly in the interest of others' salvation, was nevertheless really hostile towards those who were only "born after the Spirit," or only set a value on this, and denied to them a title to membership among the people of God. A similar self-exaltation over others and a disposition to suppress them, took place also, he says, in the case of Ishmael with respect to Isaac. But it turned out the other way.

[WORDSWORTH: "St. Paul's comparison here is peculiarly apposite and relevant to the subject before him. The Judaizers, with whom he is dealing in this Epistle, were like Ishmael, the

* [AUGUSTINE: *Sed lusum Paulus persecutionem vocat, quia lusio illa illusio erat.*—R.]

son of the bondwoman Agar, the representative of the Old Covenant not spiritually understood. They professed friendship for the Galatian Christians, who were the spiritual Isaac. In semblance they were *playing* with the offspring of the free woman, but in reality they were *persecuting* him. The Judaizers were endeavoring to rob the Galatian Christians of their Evangelical inheritance derived from Abraham. Thus Ishmael pretended to be playing with Isaac, but was in fact persecuting him. The Apostle, therefore, who had just been comparing himself to an affectionate mother, comes forward as a vigilant *Sarah*, and interferes to part the Jewish Ishmael from the Christian Isaac; and to rescue the children of the promise and of freedom from the treacherous flattery and tyrannical sport of the children of the flesh and of bondage." This beautiful comparison is of course marred by any reference to tradition in our verse.—R.]

Ver. 30. **Cast out the bondwoman and her son,** *etc*—Paul here cites the words of Sarah Gen. xxi. 10 according to the LXX., only instead of μετὰ τοῦ υἱοῦ μου Ἰσαάκ, he substitutes, because the expression is severed from the context, μετὰ τοῦ υἱοῦ τῆς ἐλευθέρας; therewith stating expressly the meaning of Sarah; for it is from this very point of view, namely, that her son is the son of the free woman, that she comes forward so decidedly against Ishmael, as the son of, the bondmaid, declares that he is not entitled to be co-heir with her son, and demands his expulsion. It is not the personal behavior of Ishmael therefore which she urges against him, but his position, although, it is true, she is moved to do it by his behavior. As he is in himself not entitled to be co-heir, this right possessed against him is now urged—and as the narrative shows, made good. The application with an "even so now," Paul leaves to the readers as being obvious, because through the whole argument he desires that they themselves may see the perverseness of the position which they are on the point of assuming. It would be thus supplied: Even so now—will it fare with the children of the bondmaid; they have as little right of inheritance as the son of the bondmaid had then, and this want of title will be brought into force against them on account of their persecution (so that in this particular also they will prove themselves antitypes of Hagar and Ishmael). The reference to the expulsion of these does not as yet apply immediately to the readers, but if they suffer themselves to be made children of the bondmaid—and what that signifies is clear—by going over to the legal Jewish position, they lose at all events their *right* of inheritance, and are on the way to lose also the inheritance itself. Paul specifies the persecution primarily because the Divine exclusion from the inheritance was historically occasioned by that. A searching admonition, "to hear the law better" (ver. 21)=to take better note of the intimations which are contained therein—and therefore not to place themselves under the law.

[Lightfoot: "Shall in nowise inherit! The Law and the Gospel cannot coexist; the Law must disappear before the Gospel. It is scarcely possible to estimate the strength of conviction and depth of prophetic insight which this declaration implies. The Apostle thus confidently sounds the death-knell of Judaism at a time when one-half of Christendom clung to the Mosaic law with a jealous affection little short of frenzy, and while the Judaic party seemed to be growing in influence and was strong enough, even in the Gentile churches of his own founding, to undermine his influence and endanger his life. The truth which to us appears a truism must then have been regarded as a paradox."—R.]

The course of thought begun in ver. 21, concludes therefore with our verse in a complete and satisfactory way: Take heed then to the law, and learn from it: (1) that ye *are* free as Christians and (2) that ye, if ye do not persevere in this freedom, forfeit the inheritance—so that necessarily the conclusion must be drawn with ver. 30, and ver. 31 cannot be viewed as an immediate deduction from what precedes, nor as a conclusion, but only as a sentence summing up once more the foregoing result and introducing a transition to what follows, on which account it is to be joined with it.

### DOCTRINAL AND ETHICAL.

1. *The personal relation between teacher and congregation.* The significance which attaches to the personal relation between teacher and congregation (see on the former section, the first remark), comes most evidently to view in this, that the teacher must regard it as his commission, to beget spiritual children (and that truly living ones)—as father, nay, yet more: to bear them also—as mother. There is thus of necessity constituted an inner bond of personal fellowship between him and the souls on which he labors; but it is true, the existence of such a bond is not to be presupposed as a matter of course, or demanded even where the condition of such a loving labor of spiritual begetting and bearing is wanting.

2. "*Christ is formed* (1) in the understanding of man, when he receives a truly living and spiritual knowledge of Christ's person, offices, and benefits; (2) in the will of man, when (*a*) in regeneration faith in Christ is not only kindled, but also attains to its fit form, so that he hangs simply and solely on Christ, which faith then in justification apprehends and puts on Christ, and unites itself inwardly with Him; (*b*) in renewal, when Christ's Divine mind is daily more and more formed in men, so that the lineaments of Christ's image become ever more discernible.—It reads moreover: Till Christ be formed in you, not, Till you or I form Him in you, because regeneration is no human work."—Starke.

3. *The allegory.* What view are we to hold of the interpretation of the two wives and sons of Abraham in this section? Is Paul a representative of that allegorical interpretation which presupposing a double, yes, multiplex sense of the Biblical text, long prevailed in the church, to the prejudice of the sound historical understanding of the contents of Scripture? The appearance is strongly for it, but in truth it is not so. Paul to be sure allegorizes here, for he says so himself. But with the very fact of his saying this himself, the gravity of the hermeneutical difficulty disappears. He *means* therefore to give an allegory, not an exposition; he does not pro-

ceed as an exegete, and does not mean to say—after the manner of the allegorizing exegetes—that only what he now says is the true sense of the narrative, conceded in the letter, the only sense really worthy of God's word. The question then is only (1) whether this allegorical interpretation is merely a subjective fancy of the Apostle, or whether it is grounded in the actual facts; (2) what use he makes of this allegory. Commonly these two questions are not kept distinct from each other. Respecting the first, no one can speak of a mere arbitrary fancy (of a play of allegorical sharp-wittedness, rabbinism, and the like), who pays the least attention to the typical significance which according to Paul appertains to Abraham and his history,—and who allows any justice whatever in this, the Apostle's view of Abraham. We well know that for Paul Abraham himself is typical by his faith, and in immediate connection with that, Isaac is typical by his birth through the power of the Divine promise, and not of the flesh; he is the type of the true children of Abraham, *i. e.*, of the true theocratic people, whose origin is not that of natural birth alone (comp. Rom. ix. 16 *sq.*). This of itself then gives on the other hand the converse, namely, the typical character of the carnal son, Ishmael. But now, in this section, Paul goes yet a step further. To him not only the manner of birth of the two sons of Abraham is typical, but also the condition in which they were born: the bondage of the one and the freedom of the other. Isaac is thus the type of a theocratic people, that (1) does not become such by natural birth, but by Divine operation; (2) and is also in possession of freedom, is the spiritual and free Israel; on the contrary Ishmael is the type of a merely natural and enslaved theocratic people: that is, the natural people of God is enslaved by its being under the law, something which is not true of the spiritual, genuine Israel. Respecting the warrant for a typological apprehension of the Old Testament generally, WIESELER justly remarks: "Since the whole of the Old Covenant is a σκιά of the New Testament dispensation, the single facts, persons and truths have therefore a prefigurative character, according to the measure in which each has within this whole and in relation to the New Covenant, a conspicuous and central significance." That this applies to the person of Abraham is clear, and equally to the manner in which children were born to him, for through Abraham's children the progress of the history of redemption is determined. But if even with an Isaac it is primarily only the manner of his birth to which this signification attached, yet the *condition* in which he was born, was an inseparable element of that; for from the legitimate, and therefore free, wife of Abraham, came naturally also the legitimate son, the son of promise; the freedom of Isaac was therefore not an accidental but an essential quality of him who was born in virtue of a Divine promise, and so Paul has a right to attribute to the fact of his freedom also, a typical importance, and to attribute the same to the opposite condition of Ishmael. If this prefigurative character of Abraham and his sons is acknowledged, it is clear, that the Apostle's allegory is not arbitrary or accidental, but that it has a point of attachment in the actual history. But—and this is commonly overlooked—the allegory is not on this account eliminated from the passage; the allegory has its ground in the typical relation of Abraham's two children to the two congregations of God, but yet for all this it is in form allegory. For *αὗται γάρ εἰσι δύο διαθῆκαι* is allegory, not typology; the two women were certainly not *prophetic types* of the two covenants. Something like this might be said, that the two women are, as mothers of the two diverse children of Abraham, types of the two churches of God, the external and the spiritual, conceived as collective personalities, as mothers of their members, although even this would be strained; but to say outright that the two mothers are *prophetic types* of two covenants, yields no rational sense. Only by allegorizing can Paul see in the two mothers two covenants, but the allegory is taken from the facts themselves, inasmuch as it is the covenants by which the character of the antitypes of the sons of those mothers is determined. It is necessary to acknowledge this mingling of Type and Allegory, or the passage will not be rightly apprehended. We feel that it is not merely allegory, and look for the type, and again we feel that it is not purely type; the two, in truth, are interwoven with each other.

If we could venture to draw from our section a general conclusion, it would be this: (1) that allegorizing portions of Scripture is not forbidden, provided only that it is acknowledged as such, and not given forth as exegesis proper; (2) that it is warranted in proportion as it has a typological basis which itself is authorized. What this is may be judged by the remarks above.—While we should acknowledge, therefore, that our allegory has an objective foundation, that Paul does not interpolate something into the narrative of Genesis at his own fancy, it is not on the other hand (to come to the second inquiry, as to the use he makes of it), correct to say that "he ascribes to it an objective value as proof." For that he is too sober-minded, for he undoubtedly is, as was remarked, far removed from that allegorizing exegesis which *bona fide* declares: This and this is *meant* in the passage besides the letter [? See below.—R.]. and which therefore upon this assumption proves the "higher truth" by means of allegorical explanation from a Scripture passage. If we look more closely, we find moreover, that he does not at all *argue* his proposition of the freedom of Christians *from* the narrative of Genesis; he does not infer any thing like this: Sarah signifies the upper Jerusalem, Isaac the Christians, therefore Christians are the children of the upper Jerusalem; moreover Sarah is free, therefore the upper Jerusalem is free, and Christians are children of the free congregation, and therefore likewise free. On the other hand he asserts the freedom of the Jerusalem above as self-evident, and resulting from the previously assumed ground of the covenant of grace, on which it rests, as opposed to the covenant of works, and then first expressly demonstrates from a prophetical passage that Christians are children of the Jerusalem above, and so comes to the conclusion that they are free (see the exegesis above). If it is inquired: Why then is the narrative of Genesis adduced, a narrative of type interwoven with allegory? the answer is simple: in order, by reference to the simple relations of things in the beginning of the theocratic people, to illustrate the higher relations of the present, or better: in order to furnish a confirmation of the latter by pointing out the relation between type and antitype = see, at the very beginning it was the same! For that typology may serve, with or without the application of allegory, which of course makes no difference, but not for strict proof; and still less bare allegory, when and where it is acknowledged as such.—We cannot draw a different conclusion from the remark, ver. 21: Do ye not hear the law? The sense is simply: Do ye not then see that matters stood just the same with the ancient typical personages? The spiritually begotten Son was born in the condition of freedom and that should dispose you to give credit to my previous argument! Here the expression sounds, it is true, as if every reader of the law would be constrained to deduce this from the narrative in Genesis, as if this therefore simply signified the higher truth which is now under discussion, and merely expressed it under the veil of history; still whoever gives even cursory attention will not be tempted to press these words, but will recognize in them a rhetorical drapery.

4. [*Paul's treatment of the Old Testament narrative.* A reference to the exegesis of ver. 24 will justify the following conclusions: 1) Paul does not regard the Old Testament narrative as in itself an allegory. He is careful to use a subject (ἅτινα) which is general enough to prevent our making such an unwarranted assumption. 2) His interpretation is not "subjective, fanciful or rabbinical."* The predicate ἀλληγορούμενα means "to have an allegorical meaning." Hence the meaning inheres in the nature of the "things," and does not depend on his acute speculation respecting them. On exegetical grounds, Schmoller is not warranted in affirming that Paul does not imply: "This and this is *meant* in the passage besides the letter." In his proper anxiety to guard against "allegorizing exegesis" he gives some room for assumptions respecting the "subjective" character of this allegory of the Apostle. Against such attempts to represent the interpretation of St. Paul as subjective, *i. e.*, to speak plainly *erroneous*, ELLICOTT properly remarks: "It would be well for such writers to remember that St. Paul is here declaring, under the influence of the Holy Spirit, that the passage he has cited has a second and a deeper meaning than it appears to have; that it has that meaning, then, is a positive, objective and indisputable truth."—3) This passage gives no countenance to "allegorizing exegesis" of the Scriptures. This error, once so common, may have a different origin from attempts to make the Bible narrative a mere allegory, but it tends in the same direction, destroys the true knowledge and perverts the true use of the Scriptures. He may properly allegorize, who has the inspiration Paul had, but only when that inspiration shows him that "these things *have* an allegorical meaning." On this point CALVIN says: "As the Apostle declares that these things are allegorized, Origen and many others along with him, have seized the occasion of torturing Scripture, in every possible manner, away from the true sense. They concluded that the literal sense is too mean and poor, and that, under the outward bark of the letter, there lurk deeper mysteries, which cannot be extracted but by beating out allegories. And this they had no difficulty in accomplishing; for speculations which appear to be ingenious have always been preferred, and always will be preferred by the world to sound doctrine. For many centuries no man was considered to be ingenious, who had not the skill and daring necessary for changing into a variety of curious shapes the sacred word of God. This was undoubtedly a contrivance of Satan to undermine the authority of Scripture, and to take away from the reading of it the true advantage. God visited this profanation by a just judgment, when He suffered the pure meaning of the Scripture to be buried under false interpretations. I acknowledge that Scripture is a most rich and inexhaustible fountain of all wisdom; but I deny that its fertility consists in the various meanings which any man, at his pleasure, may assign. Let us know, then, that the true meaning of Scripture is the natural and obvious meaning; and let us embrace and abide by it resolutely."*—R.]

---

*[Every proper theory of inspiration must admit that Paul's early education had its influence on his character as teacher. But the word "rabbinical" contains a moral or rather immoral implication, which cannot be allowed.—R.]

*[LIGHTFOOT gives Philo's allegory of this same passage, and compares it with Paul's: "Philo's allegory is as follows. Abraham—the human soul progressing towards the knowledge of God—unites himself first with Sarah and then wi[th] Hagar. These two alliances stand in direct opposition t[he] one to the other. Sarah, the princess—for such is the interpretation of the word—is divine wisdom. To her therefore Abraham is bidden to listen in all that she says. On the other hand Hagar, whose name signifies 'sojourning,' and points therefore to something transient and unsatisfying, is a preparatory or intermediate training—the instruction of the schools—secular learning, as it might be termed in modern phrase. Hence she is fitly described as an Egyptian, as Sarah's handmaid. Abraham's alliance with Sarah is at first premature. He is not sufficiently advanced in his moral and spiritual development to profit thereby. As yet he begets no son by her. She therefore directs him to go in to her handmaid, to apply himself to the learning of the schools. This inferior alliance proves fruitful at once. At a later date and after this preliminary training he again unites himself to Sarah; and this time his union with divine wisdom is fertile. Not only does Sarah bear him a son, but she is pointed out as the mother of a countless offspring. Thus is realized the strange paradox that the barren woman is most fruitful. Thus in the progress of the human soul are verified the words of the prophet, spoken in an allegory, that 'the desolate hath many children.'

But the allegory does not end here. The contrast between the mothers is reproduced in the contrast between the sons. Isaac represents the wisdom of the wise man; Ishmael the sophistry of the sophist. Sophistry must in the end give place to wisdom. The son of the bondwoman must be cast out and flee before the son of the princess.

Such is the ingenious application of Philo—most like and yet most unlike that of St. Paul. They both allegorize, and in so doing they touch upon the same points in the narrative, they use the same text by way of illustration. Yet in their whole tone and method they stand in direct contrast, and their results have nothing in common. Philo is, as usual, wholly unhistorical. With St. Paul, on the other hand, Hagar's career is an allegory, because it is a history. The symbol and the thing symbolized are the same in kind. This simple passage of patriarchal life represents in miniature the workings of God's Providence hereafter to be exhibited in grander proportions in the history of the Christian church. The Christian Apostle and the philosophic Jew move in parallel lines, or as it were, keeping side by side, and yet never once crossing each other's path.

And there is still another point in which the contrast between the two is great. With Philo the allegory is the

5. *The two covenants and their children.* The fact that the Apostle recognizes a significance in the Scripture narrative of the twofold character of the wives and sons of Abraham, is a sign of his clear-minded way of viewing the Scripture; by the less reminded of the greater, in the germ already seeing the fruit. It is at the same time a sign of his pedagogic wisdom, that to those who boasted themselves of their descent from Abraham, he so simply discovers the insufficiency, and particularly the perversity of this boast, by referring to the twofold relation of sonship to Abraham, of which the one is so entirely destitute of ground for boasting. On the other hand, he shows here also again, as in chap. iii., his deep and clear view into the economy of salvation, and its guiding principles, in the first place by definitely distinguishing the two covenants in the history of redemption, and then by the way in which he characterizes them. There is a covenant of law and a covenant of grace; and both are mothers, that bear children, only in different wise and with different consequences. The first covenant bears children in the way of natural generation, for it finds its concrete manifestation in the carnal Israel and its members. All the natural children of Israel have part in this covenant; but it is simply a covenant which brings to the participants in it bondage and only that, for it imposes on them the law. It is widely different with the covenant of grace. This also has children, yea a great number of them, but these children God Himself brings to it through the operation of the Spirit (it does not obtain them, as it were, of itself), for this covenant finds its concrete manifestation in the spiritual Israel, which obtains its children in a spiritual way, and not by outward descent. This is the first covenant which brings to its members freedom, and does not transfer them into bondage under a law; for it does not make the attainment of God's blessing dependent on the keeping of legal commandments and prohibitions, but secures it to its members as a pure bestowment of Divine grace. Intimately related therefore as Paul knows these two covenants and communities to stand to each other (for they are still like children of the one father), yet again he keeps them sharply and clearly apart.—Especially noticeable is the conception of the upper Jerusalem, the signification of which has been explained above. In the first place, therefore, Paul distinguishes the spiritual from the carnal Israel, the ideal from the empirical. With the external Israel the idea of the theocratic people was as yet by no means realized as to its true substance; on the contrary this was a conception of much higher range. Therefore all vaunting by the Jews of their nationality, as alone entitled to be reckoned God's people, is ungrounded. Above the theocratic people in its national manifestation within the Jewish community stood yet again the true people of God, that even in this community already found individual members, for under the Old Testament all were not children of Ishmael's, and under the New Testament all are not children of Israel's sort. And indeed from Abraham down, the true people of God was never quite extinct, but yet, so long as the covenant of law, and therewith the carnal Israel were in the ascendant, it could not yet come to developed existence. This it attained only through Christ. It is noticeable, secondly, that Paul in this conception of the Jerusalem above, has a conception, which stands still higher than that of the Christian body; the Jerusalem above is the mother, Christians are only the children. Unquestionably, however, they are actually the children, and so far even in this expression their rank is declared=they are children of no lesser one, and should therefore not forget what they owe to themselves and their rank, should not unworthily lower themselves. But on the other hand, they are only children, and are what they are, only through their mother. The Christian community is not of itself in its empirical manifestation already=the spiritual Israel, but has continually in this its *spiritualis nutrix.* We see how that which Paul expresses with his "Jerusalem above" is what dogmatic theology has endeavored to embody in its conception of an *ecclesia invisibilis*, by which it strives to guard the church against a false emphasizing of her empirical manifestation, and as it were to preserve to her her ideality. Only that the conception of the *ecclesia invisibilis* is in the first place a narrower one, limited more to the church since Christ, and still more, it is a secondary and negative one, first formed by abstraction from the mixed condition of the church on earth, while the idea of the Jerusalem above is a positive, primary one, grounded in the biblical economy of salvation itself.

whole substance of his teaching; with Paul it is but an accessory. He uses it rather as an illustration than an argument, as a means of representing in a lively form the lessons before enforced on other grounds. It is, to use Luther's comparison, the painting which decorates the house already built." The very pleasing character of Philo's allegory is a warning against such interpretations. They always aim to be as captivating as his, and often succeed, only to be most unlike Paul's "in tone and method."—R.]

### HOMILETICAL AND PRACTICAL.

Ver. 19. LUTHER:—The Apostles, all devout preachers and also schoolmasters, are (in their peculiar way) also our parents. For like as we from our natural birth have from our parents the form of our bodies, so do these men help thereto, that our heart and conscience attain within us to a perfect form. Now the perfect form which a Christian heart should have, is faith, whereby we lay hold on Christ, cleave to Him alone and to no other thing besides.—BERLENB. BIBLE:—In nothing do more pangs of travail come to pass, than in the ministration of the gospel. The ministration of the law is a mere nothing compared with it. Evangelical preaching excludes all works accomplished in a merely outward way to which men nevertheless cleave.—"Until" points to a troublesome delay, that falls between the beginning and the accomplishment of a matter; not as if God would not at once proceed to the formation of us, but because on the side of man a bolt is interposed, and yet God does not give over.—LANGE:—Even, as in many men, especially in their outward habit, gestures, words and actions, we find such a fashion of the world, that as it were we see in them even personally the vanity, wantonness and folly of the world, and are inwardly troubled at it; so on the other hand, in believers who come to their proper vigor, the new birth from God appears in all about them, saving their yet remaining weaknesses, in such a manner, that we see in them a true form of Christ in their weakness, humility, simplicity and uprightness, and are moved to inward joy thereby.

Ver. 20. LUTHER:—The living voice is to be counted as an empress. For this can amplify or condense the matter, and suit itself to all occasions of time, place, persons and the requirement of any necessity.

Ver. 21. RIEGER:—The will has very great influence in the belief and unbelief of men. Even in falling back under the law, the will of the flesh seeks its advantage. The law is indeed the world's crafty covering, under which it slinks away from the truth of Christ; which covering must be withdrawn from it.—FRANTZ:—In the law there is contained more than the commandments; more than the ways and usages, ceremonies and ordinances enjoined in the worship of the Jews. There is also more contained therein, than many after the letter read therein. There is contained therein also a revelation of the ways of God, which God hath chosen, to carry out His everlasting purpose among men. There is contained therein a history, which has come to pass from its beginning to its accomplishment on earth, that therein, as in a mirror, should be made known the thoughts of peace and salvation, which God has towards men and which in due time He will carry into execution.

Ver. 23.—Nature assists us not to salvation, but grace alone. We are all according to our natural birth born flesh of flesh; but according to His promise hath God regenerated us through the bath of holy baptism.

Ver. 24. RIEGER:—This example serves to guard us against dealing too slightingly with the history of the Old Testament.—BERLENB. BIBLE:—All that Moses has described are figures of the inner spiritual and genuine life in Christ.—SPENER:—"Bringeth forth unto bondage." Those that will be saved by the law and its works and therefore reject the gospel, are not God's children, nor heirs of eternal life, but at their highest are only servants and therefore under sin and the curse.

Ver. 26. LUTHER:—The holy church bears and genders children continually, even to the last day, in that she exercises the ministry, that is, teaches and diffuses the gospel which is her manner of bearing. Now the gospel teaches that we are redeemed and become free from the curse of the law, from sin, death and all manner of ill, not through the law and works, but through Christ. Therefore is the holy church not subjected to the law or works, but free is she, a mother without law, without sin and death. But what she is as a mother, so are also her children.—"Free."—Even the ten commandments have no right to accuse, nor to terrify the conscience, wherein Christ rules by His grace and moreover outwardly: the civil laws of Moses concern us no longer. Yet the gospel does not therewith make us free from all other civil laws, for so long as we are in this natural life, the gospel subjects us to the civil laws which the government of each land has. But since our mortal life must forsooth have some ceremonies, we can by no means dispense with them. Therefore the gospel admits that we may make in the Christian Church some special ordinances concerning holy days, times, places, *etc.*—but not in the thought that those who observe such order, should thereby merit forgiveness of sins.

Ver. 27. Although the little flock, *i. e.*, the dear Christian Church, that receives the doctrine of the gospel, and earnestly cleaves thereto, appears altogether unfruitful, forsaken, weak and despicable, and moreover outwardly suffers persecution, and is constrained to hear herself accused of teaching heretical and seditious things, she is nevertheless alone fruitful before God, and brings forth through the ministry innumerably many children, who are heirs of eternal life.

Ver. 28. In STARKE:—Natural birth has with God no preëminence; He chooses Abel before Cain, Jacob before Esau, Ephraim before Manasses, *etc.*; whoever feareth Him and worketh righteousness, is accepted of Him, and whoever cleaves in true faith to the promise, is a child of one promise, and shall attain to the promised everlasting inheritance.—If we are like Isaac in his birth, let us also become like him in his virtues.

Ver. 29. LANGE:—Whatever church oppresses and persecutes another in matters of faith, such an one is not the true apostolic church; therefore also she neither stands in the true filial relation to God, nor has part in the inheritance of eternal life.—LUTHER:—It is ever thus, that Ishmael persecutes Isaac, but on the contrary the good Isaac leaves Ishmael in peace. Whoever will be unpersecuted by Ishmael, let him profess that he is no Christian.—SPENER:—The church's condition is in some particulars ever the same; it may always be said: As it was at that time so is it now.

Ver. 30.—SPENER:—Persecutions' harm in fact not the persecuted but the persecutors. To the persecuted there remains yet God's grace, love and heaven, but the persecutors load themselves with God's wrath.—BERLENB. BIBLE:—The whole natural man must, as a scoffer and wild man such as Ishmael was, be set aside from all righteousness of birth, and devices of his own through a renewed obedient will. And although that involves a dying and giving up, inasmuch as the false nature sinks into the death of its own desires and so becomes powerless, yet the new awakened sense makes no account of that, because it has a hatred against the old man, and renounces therefore courageously all impulses of nature, let them have as holy a seeming as they may. Thereby the scoffer becomes in his turn a scoffing before the new man.

Vers. 21–30. Two sorts of children of Abraham: to which dost thou belong? To the children of the bondwoman or of the freewoman? Law or grace? Either—or? 1. The two stand indeed in relation to each other (one Father), but yet are 2. essentially distinct (two widely different mothers). *a.* Law–Flesh (= the lawman still the carnal man), Grace — Spirit (=the carnal man has no part in it); *b.* Law–Bondage, Grace–Freedom.—Christians are children, not of the bondwoman, but of the freewoman. 1. Rejoice! 2. Consider well!—The

Jerusalem above 1. a mother, 2. a mother through promise, 3. a free mother.—The covenant of law a fruitful mother. (Many depend on it, because the natural man remains thereby natural), but yet the covenant of grace has the promise of God.—Christians are children of the Jerusalem above. 1. How? Because children of the promise. 2. What do they obtain thereby? They participate in her condition of freedom.—The Jerusalem above free: 1) not bound to the law = not held to obtaining salvation by works of the law; 2) not obnoxious to its curse. The children of the promise, *i. e.*, 1. They are members of God's people not by nature but only through promise; 2. they attain heavenly inheritance, only in consequence of promise, not by their own works.—Christians have their type in Isaac; 1. Born as he through promise (see above); 2. Persecuted like him, by Ishmael, 3. but for all that children of the freewoman and therefore alone heirs.—Who obtains the inheritance? 1) not the natural man, but the spiritual; 2) not the son of the bondwoman but of the freewoman.—Human self-will (Hagar, Ishmael), divine counsel; 1) The latter permits the former, 2) but still gains the victory.

---

**E. Admonition to perseverance in Christian freedom—with a threatening allusion to the pernicious consequences of the opposite course.**

CHAPTER IV. 31—V. 6.

31 So then [Wherefore],[1] brethren, we are not children of the [a] bondwoman, but
IV. 1 of the free. Stand fast therefore in the liberty wherewith Christ hath made us
free [Stand fast therefore in the liberty for which Christ made us free, or For freedom Christ made us free. Stand fast therefore],[2] and be not entangled again with
2 [in] the yoke of bondage. Behold, I Paul[3] say unto you, that if ye be circumcised
3 [i. e., *submit to circumcision*],[4] Christ shall [will] profit you nothing. For [Moreover, δέ continuative] I testify again to every man that is circumcised [who has him-
4 self circumcised], that he is a debtor to do the whole law. Christ is become of no
effect unto you [Ye are separated from Christ],[5] whosoever of you are justified [being
5 justified] by [in] the law; ye are fallen [fallen away] from grace. For we through
6 [by] the Spirit wait[6] for the hope of righteousness by [from] faith. For in Jesus
Christ [Christ Jesus] neither circumcision availeth any thing, nor uncircumcision;
but faith which worketh by [working through] love.

**F. Renewed lamentation over the apostasy of the Galatians. Sharp testimony against the misleading misrepresentations of his preaching on the part of the false teachers.**

CHAPTER V. 7–12.

7 Ye did run [were running] well; who did hinder[7] you that ye should not obey
8, 9 the truth?[8] This [The] persuasion *cometh* not of him that calleth you. A lit-
10 tle leaven leaveneth[9] the whole lump. I [I, for my part] have confidence in [as
regards] you through [in] the Lord, that ye will be none [in nothing] otherwise
11 minded: but he that troubleth you shall bear his judgment, whosoever he be. And
[But] I, brethren, if I yet [still] preach circumcision, why do I yet [still] suffer
persecution? then is the offence of the cross ceased [the scandal of the cross done
12 away with]. I would they were even cut off which trouble you [I would that they
who are unsettling you would even mutilate themselves, or would even cut themselves off from you].[10]

[1] Ver. 31.—א. διό. [So B. D[1]. Lachmann, Tischendorf, Meyer, Ellicott, Alford, Lightfoot. Ἄρα (Rec.) is feebly supported; as also ἡμεῖς δέ.—R.]

[2] Ver. 1.—The correct reading is probably that of Lachmann: τῇ ἐλευθερίᾳ ἡμᾶς Χριστὸς ἠλευθέρωσεν· στήκετε οὖν. So א. which also begins chap. v. with στήκετε. [This reading is supported also by A. B. C. D., and adopted by Usteri, Meyer (4th ed., Schmoller mentions the other reading as his) and Alford. Τῇ ἐλευθερίᾳ, ᾗ ἡμᾶς Χριστὸς ἠλευθέρωσεν, στήκετε οὖν is supported by D.[2 3] E. K. L., the great majority of cursives, many versions and fathers, and is adopted by Griesbach, Rückert, Tischendorf, Wieseler, Ellicott, Wordsworth, Lightfoot (who differs in punctuation however). Between these two readings the choice is very difficult. The authorities are so equally divided, and as the verbal difference is slight, the critical question resolves itself into this delicate one: whether the transcriber was more likely to have omitted or inserted ᾗ, because of ἡμᾶς immediately following. Meyer thinks it was inserted, others that it was omitted. The latter opinion

seems more probable, and the second reading is preferable on diplomatic grounds. The renderings given above are in accordance with the two readings, but minor variations in interpretation are noticed in the EXEG. NOTES.

We find besides, οὖν placed after ἐλευθερίᾳ, but this is feebly supported; it is put after στήκετε in ℵ. A. B. C. F. On this position of the particle, an argument for Lachmann's punctuation is based, though it is not decisive. Χριστός is placed before ἡμᾶς in C. K. L.; after it in ℵ. A. B. D. E. F. G.

Lightfoot not only begins a new sentence at στήκετε, but, retaining ῇ, is forced to join the first clause directly with ver. 31, and to render: we are sons "of her who is free with that freedom which Christ has given us." So Schott and Rinck. This seems forced, but Lightfoot's note on the various readings is valuable.—On the other variations from the E. V., in this verse, see EXEG. NOTES.—R.]

[3] Ver. 2.—ℵ. omits Παῦλος, inserted however by the corrector.

[4] Ver. 2.—[Both here and in ver. 3, the reference is not to the fact of having been circumcised, but now resorting to the rite as necessary.—R.]

[5] Ver. 4.—[Schmoller renders: *abgetrennt seid ihr von (der gemeinschaft mit) Christo.* The construction is pregnant, and scarcely admits of a literal translation. Vulgate: *evacuati estis a.* Alford's "annihilates from Christ" is objectionable. Ellicott's paraphrase is good: "Your union with Christ became void" (so Meyer). It seems both more lively and more exact to retain the present in English, since "the aorists (κατηργήθητε, ἐξεπέσατε) represent the consequences as instantaneous" (Lightfoot).—R.]

[6] Ver. 5.—ℵ. has ἐκδεχόμεθα, ℵ.[3] ἀπεκδεχόμεθα.

[7] Ver. 7.—[Rec. has ἀνέκοψε, but the correct reading is ἐνέκοψε (all MSS., most cursives, and modern editors).—R.]

[8] Ver. 7.—Τῇ ἀληθείᾳ μὴ πείθεσθαι is, without ground, deemed spurious by Semler and Kopp. [ℵ. A. B. Lachmann, Lightfoot, omit τῇ; retained on good authority by Tischendorf, Meyer, Ellicott.—R.]

[9] Ver. 9.—Δολοῖ is a gloss.

[10] Ver. 12.—[See EXEG. NOTES, on the meaning of this verse.—R.]

## EXEGETICAL AND CRITICAL.

Ver. 31. **Wherefore, brethren, we are not children of a bondwoman.**—Paul, after the indirect warning in vers. 29, 30, sums up the contents of vers. 22 sq. once more, in an exact form, appealing to the Christian sense of dignity =you will therefore surely not suffer yourselves to be reduced to children of the bondwoman. [Notice the omission of the article: "not of any bondwoman," Judaism or any form of heathenism (LIGHTFOOT, MEYER, ELLICOTT). This explanation is more striking and appropriate than that of ALFORD, who is disposed to think παιδίσκης is anarthrous, because emphatically prefixed to its governing noun.—R.]—**But of the free,**—therefore ourselves free. This Paul expressly states in the following sentence.

Ver. 1, refers the freedom of *Christians* to Christ; yet the main idea is no longer the fact or method of their having become free, but the end, namely: τῇ ἐλευθερίᾳ, for freedom, for being and remaining free. Then follows the admonition itself; στήκετε, used absolutely, without any modifying clause=remain firm. [Schmoller follows Lachmann, in beginning a new sentence with στήκετε; of course if a different punctuation is adopted, the verb is modified by the preceding clause, without altering its meaning however. He also takes τῇ ἐλευθερίᾳ as dative *commodi*, "for freedom," not instrumental, "with freedom" (so ALFORD). It must be remarked that this pointing makes the style very abrupt, and that since the stress in this interpretation rests on *for* freedom, the end of their being made free, so emphatic a thought would scarcely be expressed by a dative of doubtful force, for as LIGHTFOOT observes, the dative is awkward, in whatever way it is taken. Even MEYER explains the passage far more satisfactorily, on the theory that the other reading is correct. Following this reading, we render: "Stand fast therefore in the liberty for" or "with which Christ made us free." The prominent dative then denotes "the sphere in which and to which the action is limited" (ELLICOTT); and the relative ῇ is either dative *commodi* (WINER, ELLICOTT) or ablative (instrumental, LUTHER, BEZA, CALVIN). MEYER thinks this latter usage is uncommon with Paul. The former is safer. The sense is then: therefore stand fast in that liberty (which is our state as children of the freewoman, and) for which, to remain in which, Christ made us free.—R.]

**Be not entangled again.**—As Gentiles they had not formerly been under the yoke of the Mosaic law, but for all that had certainly (see iv. 8) been in bondage; having now become free from it by their faith in Christ, they ought not to allow themselves to be enslaved again by a yoke. [**In the yoke of bondage.**—"In" it, because the thought is of being ensnared; they were to stand upright, not to bow to the yoke (LIGHTFOOT); "bondage" was its predominant nature (ELLICOTT).—R.] All that preceded, doctrinal exposition and expostulation, pointed to *this* exhortation: to remain free. But just because this lies at the foundation of everything preceding, the brief, plain utterance in this verse suffices, and the Apostle at once turns to a warning menace in case the admonition should not be heeded, and the Galatians instead should go so far as to submit to circumcision.

Ver. 2. **Behold I Paul say unto you that if ye be circumcised.**—Rousing personal attention with "Behold" and with the interposition of his personal authority,* "I Paul," he warns them against the final step, not yet taken by them, which would bring them completely under the yoke of the law, namely, the receiving of circumcision. [It is highly probable that some of them had been circumcised, and that the present points to the continuance of this course of conduct among them (ALFORD, ELLICOTT). He does not mean that the fact of a man's being a circumcised man would prevent his being a Christian, but if after all this instruction and warning, they resorted to this rite as necessary to salvation, "Christ will," etc.—R.] They would then have had no advantage of Christ, because they would have sought salvation in circumcision and not of Christ.—**Will profit you nothing.**—The future is probably (as in ver. 5) to be referred to the παρουσία and the establishment of the Messianic kingdom. [So MEYER, who finds in this a reference to its nearness. But he is fond of such references. ELLICOTT with more propriety says: "it simply marks the certain *result* of such a course of practice;

* [WORDSWORTH finds here a reference to the false accusation (ver. 11) that he preached circumcision, and LIGHTFOOT thinks this is probably an indirect refutation of calumnies as well as an assertion of authority.—R.]

'Christ (as you will find) will never profit you anything.'"—R.]

Ver. 3. **Moreover I testify again.**—Paul strengthens his warning by referring to a further consequence of receiving circumcision. It obliges to the observance of the *whole* law; "for circumcision makes one a full participant in the covenant of law, a proselyte of righteousness, and the law demands of the one that is held to it its complete fulfilment (iii. 10)." MEYER. At the same time Paul gives with this a more precise explanation of "Christ will profit you nothing" so much the more certainly will this be the case, because a man by receiving circumcision becomes **a debtor to do the whole law,** and therefore is not at liberty to persuade himself, that he does not mean to erect again the law as a whole, but only to accept one point. But all, who are "of the works of the law are under the curse," iii. 10.—In view of the solemnity of the asseveration we must suppose that the false teachers designedly concealed this perilous consequence of circumcision or sought to soften it. "Again" alludes to the earlier (second) presence of the Apostle.

Ver. 4. **Ye are separated from Christ.**—"Paul by speaking asyndetically and recurring to the second person speaks so much the more emphatically and vividly."—MEYER.—The verse expresses the consequence of becoming "a debtor to do the whole law" (for ἐν νόμῳ δικαιοῦσθαι is substantially identically with this). This is the καταργ. ἀπὸ τοῦ Χριστοῦ which completes the explanation of the declaration in ver. 2.—Καταργεῖσθαι ἀπό τινος, a pregnant expression = the connection in which one stands with any one is done away, and so one is loose from him.—Justification by the law and justification for Christ's sake are mutually exclusive; whoever seeks the first falls out of fellowship with Christ. **Justified,** here of course an expression representing the view of the persons concerned, who think "through the law we shall be justified."—**Ye are fallen away from grace.**—Here he expressly names the benefit the loss of which they suffer by "being justified in the law" and the resulting separation from Christ. A cutting contrast: they think that they are being justified, but by this very means instead they are fallen away from grace, so far is an actual justification from being possible in this way.* 'Εκπίπτειν τῆς χάριτος opposed to ἑστηκέναι ἐν τῇ χάριτι (Rom. v. 2).

Ver. 5. **For we by the spirit wait for the hope of righteousness from faith.**—"A justification of the judgment passed in ver. 4 upon those that seek to be justified through the law, drawn *e contrario, i. e.*, from the entirely different manner in which Paul and those like him wish to be justified." MEYER. ["We" *i. e.* those who have not sought justification in the law, and fallen from grace; the contrast is not very strongly marked in the subject however (δέ is not used), for Paul addresses the Galatians, not as those who had fallen, but were in danger of falling, and the subject "we" may include them also.—R.] Πνεύματι is used neither of the human spirit in itself, nor of the spirit of man enlightened by the Holy Ghost, but of the Spirit of God as the objective principle of the Christian life. As it is from the Holy Spirit working in believers, that the whole Christian life proceeds, so in particular the persevering Christian hope is thus wrought, of the fulfilment of which he also gives pledge (2 Cor. i. 22; v. 5, Eph. i. 14; Rom. iii. 11–23). So WIESELER and MEYER. But of course this hope of future righteousness proceeds from the Holy Ghost only so far as it rests upon a right basis. This basis is then stated in ἐκ πίστεως, which is meant to express that Christians ground their hope of future righteousness not upon the works of the law, but precisely on faith alone, that they hope to be justified not in the law but by faith. ['Ε κ π ί σ τ ε ω ς does not therefore describe πνεύματι (LUTHER), but the latter sets forth the agent: "by the spirit," the former the origin or source (Schmoller says with less exactness, the ground) of their hope. "By faith" cannot qualify "righteousness," as the order of the E. V. seems to indicate.—R.] Δικαιοσύνη is here also of course, Righteousness before God = δικαίωσις. But this is here represented for Christians as something future; we are therefore not to understand it of that which takes place in time, but of the δικαίωσις which comes to completion only at the final judgment. But it is a difficulty that it does not simply read: ἐλπίδα δικ. ἔχομεν, but ἐλπ. ἀπεκδ. whereby the hope itself is presented in turn as an object of hope. 'Ελπίς is therefore here to be understood as the object of hope, *res sperata*, as in Col. i. 5; Tit. ii. 13, and δ ι κ α ι ο σ ύ ν η ς as genitive of apposition. 'Απεκδέχεσθαι is more precisely not = ἐλπίζειν itself, but = to wait for, to expect perseveringly (WIESELER). [This view of the passage, which is that of WIESELER, avoids the seeming pleonasm, "wait for the hope," but is open to one serious objection, viz.: that the genitive is never thus used with ἐλπίς (MEYER). Besides ἐλπίδα ἀπεκδεχόμεθα is not pleonastic, but forcible and almost poetical, the accusative being cognate (ELLICOTT). The genitive may be regarded as 1) *subjecti;* the hoped for reward of righteousness, *sc.* eternal life (so Beza, Bengel and most older commentators). This avoids the seeming difficulty of every other interpretation, viz.: making "righteousness" future, but it is not in keeping with the context, as it introduces and gives prominence to an adjunct of "righteousness," while the passage treats of "justification." 2) It seems best then to take it as genitive *objecti, i. e.* the hope of being justified (so MEYER, ELLICOTT, ALFORD, also the versions of Tyndale and Cranmer). This is strictly grammatical and in keeping with the context. The objection that it makes "righteousness" future is easily met, see below.—R.] That Paul should here speak of the (complete and final) justification, as something to be expected first in the future, is entirely accordant with the context. In ver. 4 he speaks of such as, being already justified by faith, now turn to the law and thereby suffer the loss of grace. In order to illustrate the latter, he now enforces the truth, that a Christian must remain in faith, because only then can he have

* [LIGHTFOOT renders "are driven forth, are banished with Hagar your mother," but while this meaning of ἐκπίπτειν is classical, it is not found elsewhere in New Testament and must not be pressed.—R.]

the hope of justification at the judgment; faith remains the condition of the state of grace, for even at the final judgment it is the condition of gracious acceptance. [This view contrasts Christianity with Judaism, and represents "justification as one of those divine results, which stretches into eternity, conveying with it and involving the idea of future blessedness and glorification" (ELLICOTT).—R.]

Ver. 6. He now proceeds to justify the waiting "for the hope from faith" on the part of the *Christian.* **For in Christ Jesus** = for him that is in Christ Jesus, for the Christian, **neither circumcision availeth anything** = has no influence in the attainment of justification (in the sense of ver. 5), **nor uncircumcision** (while the Galatian false teachers laid so great stress upon this distinction); **but faith working through love,** faith which shows itself operative through love.—'Ενεργεῖσθαι is always middle in the New Testament. The passive meaning given by many of the older Catholics, as BELLARMINE and ESTIUS, in the interest of the Catholic system, is therefore incorrect. Reference is made to this display of the activity of faith through love, in view of the following section ver. 13 sq., the theme of which is given in our verse. [LIGHTFOOT: "These words bridge over the gulf which seems to separate the language of St. Paul and St. James. Both assert a principle of practical energy, as opposed to a barren, inactive theory." Against the use made of this passage by modern Romanist commentators who give up the passive sense, such as WINDISCHMANN, MÖHLER, *Symbolik*, see ALFORD and DOCTRINAL NOTES below.—R.]

Ver. 7. **Ye were running well.**—Short, emotional, and therefore asyndetic propositions respecting the unhappy alterations which had taken place with the Galatians.—The comparison of the Christian walk to a race is, as is well known, a favorite one with Paul. The running well consisted in obedience to the truth, that is, in their going in the true=evangelical, way, seeking their righteousness in faith.—Paul asks in surprise: **Who did hinder you?***

Ver. 8. He here answers the last assertion to himself and them. Certainly, it is not God that has turned you away, has brought you upon this other way! The intriguing of the false teachers is represented as something ungodly. 'Η πεισμ. κ. τ. λ., therefore, is to be translated; The persuading is not from your caller=God. The calling and the persuading are opposed to each other as distinct in character; the former is divine activity, the latter not, but essentially human with human intention, art, importunity (MEYER).—In itself "persuasion" could have also a passive signification=the being persuaded, disposition to follow; and so many interpreters take it here also=obsequiousness towards the false teachers. [In favor of the latter meaning we have the support of the Greek expositors, and perhaps the paranomasia (πείθεσθαι, ver 7). But MEYER, ALFORD, ELLICOTT prefer the active meaning, both because it is better established, and because it suits the active meaning of "calleth." It seems to accord better with ver. 9 also.—R.]

Ver. 9. **A little leaven.**—It is disputed whether this refers to doctrine or persons; a little leaven of doctrine, as a few bad men, false teachers. Manifestly the former. It is not the number of the false teachers that is of account, but the influence of their teaching, not the πείθοντες but the πεισμονή. Plainly nothing else is meant by "leaven" than the immediately preceding "persuasion," for of this, "leaven" is an image. As the leaven works into the **lump,** so does the "persuasion," the persuasive, seducing word into the soul (or into a whole community): therefore=even an influence in itself apparently insignificant, may nevertheless be ruinous to the whole man (or whole community of men). [The proverb (quoted also 1 Cor. v. 6) is undoubtedly true both of doctrines and persons. To which it refers here is extremely doubtful. In support of each view the best commentators may be cited, and the context is not decisive, for while ver. 8 may favor the former reference, ver. 10 with its individualizing turn, favors the latter. Leaven is, as usually, a symbol of evil.—R.] This of course contains a warning to be on their guard, and to turn back in time, and remove the leaven.—The Apostle, in order the easier to win them to him, expresses the confidence which he still continues to have in them.

Ver. 10. **I, for my part,**—even though the false teachers believe you already won over to them.—He knows his confidence to be grounded **in the Lord.** The Lord will doubtless bring it to pass and give you the right mind—in the interest of His cause.—Οὐδὲν ἄλλο φρονήσετε is best taken absolutely=that you will not be otherwise minded than hitherto, that you will not alter your conviction, will not apostatize. It is true, a giving way had indeed already begun; but it was as yet only in its incipiency; evidently Paul deals with them throughout as those that are yet wavering, and therefore it may well be hoped of them that matters will not come to an actual ἄλλο φρονεῖν=change of conviction. Up to the present time they are only, as is immediately expressed, "troubled."—**He that troubleth you**=every one, who, &c. The supposition that the Apostle refers to a leader among his opponents well known to himself (ERASMUS, LUTHER, BENGEL and others), or even to Peter (JEROME), is supported by nothing in the Epistle. Therefore also **whosoever he be** ought to be understood as entirely general, and not referred to any eminent consideration enjoyed by the false teachers. Undoubtedly, however, Paul means to signify, that no consideration whatever could cause him to waver in this judgment.—Κρῖμα=God's sentence of condemnation (*e. g.* Mark xii. 40, Lc. xx. 47; Rom. ii. 3; xiii. 12); this is conceived as something exceedingly irksome, a burden, therefore βαστάσει.

Ver. 11. **But I, brethren, if I still preach**

*[The verb here used means "to break up a road," so as to render it impassable. It originally took the dative of the person, but in the New Testament is followed by an accusative. LIGHTFOOT seems to think ἀνέκοψεν (Rec.) would suit the metaphor of the stadium better, its meaning being "to beat back," to hinder with the further idea of thrusting back (ELLICOTT), but the other reading is too well supported. He also remarks that the transcribers seem to have taken offence at the word ἐγκόπτειν, since it is frequently altered, e. g. 1 Thess. ii. 18; Acts xxiv. 4.—R.]

**circumcision.**—Paul refutes moreover the pretence of the false teachers, invented to further their cause, that he himself elsewhere preached circumcision. They had probably appealed, in support of their charge, to the circumcision of Timothy, which had lately taken place, but which by no means took place on the ground of its necessity to salvation (Acts xvi. 3. See moreover, the explanation of ii. 4).—"Still" dates not from a period within his apostolic career itself, as though Paul as Apostle had yet at one time preached circumcision, which in view of the manner of Paul's conversion and of his whole previous course is an unpsychological and unhistorical assumption, but it dates from his conversion. **Why do I still suffer persecution.**—This second ἔτι is a logical one: what reason remains, *etc.*?—**Then is the scandal of the cross done away with.**—Apodosis of the conditional sentence, "if I still preach circumcision," for the purpose of demonstrating the nullity of the protasis: he would no longer be persecuted.—Τὸ σκάνδ. τοῦ σταυροῦ more precisely =that, which is offensive in the preceding of Christ's death on the cross, namely, that it is proclaimed as the only ground of salvation. Had Paul, with this or instead of it, still preached circumcision as necessary to salvation, the Jew would have seen his law maintained in authority, and would not have taken offence at the death on the cross, and especially the preaching of it.

Ver. 12. Ὄφελον καὶ ἀποκόψονται.—The ordinary explanation is: Would that they would even have themselves made eunuchs, for which partly the middle signification of the future ἀποκόψονται is cited, partly the connection, which is thought to point (καί) to a play of words upon περιτομή. But, as this would be a bitter turn of wit, and as the assumption, that Paul means thereby to lash the sexual intemperance of the false teachers, is arbitrary, it is not pleasant to accede to this explanation. The lexical argument, which has the most weight, is the hardest to meet; it can only be said that the passive use of the future middle, even in the classics, is by no means unknown. On the other hand the connection, which is especially adduced in support of this explanation, has not a strictly demonstrative force, as WIESELER remarks. He, it is true, lays almost too much stress on the absence of an actual paronomasia; on the fact that Paul did not at least choose ἐκτείνειν, as being a very common word among the Greeks for castration, and the paronomasia with κατατομή (Phil. iii. 23) proves at least so much as this, that Paul in opposition to such Judaizers, was not particularly tender in dealing with περιτομή, for this is a sarcastic allusion to περιτομή. On the other hand this remark of his particularly is correct, that we should then expect instead of ἀναστ. an allusion to περιτ., the more so, as in ver. 11 περιτ. is not at all alluded to in the light of a demand made by them. If we can therefore make up our minds to take ἀποκ. as passive, this would be in itself entirely suitable, especially for the final sentence: Would they were even hewn off=condemned by God (since the reference to excommunication is less congruous). Καί certainly is far from necessitating the reference to περιτ., as with either explanation it is alike a climactic particle. [It seems entirely incorrect to take the passive sense, for which there is no authority in the New Testament. ELLICOTT, preserves the middle sense, and yet avoids the seemingly coarse interpretation, which is usually given. He renders: "would even cut themselves off from you." Unfortunately καί is a climactic particle, and this view gives us an anti-climax. In fact were there no question of taste involved, scarce a doubt would arise as to the Apostle's meaning. Have we a right to adopt forced interpretations, to avoid a natural one, because it seems to us unrefined? As LIGHTFOOT remarks "If it seems strange that St. Paul should have alluded to such a practice at all, it must be remembered that as this was a recognized form of heathen self-devotion, it could not possibly be shunned in conversation, and must at times have been mentioned by a Christian preacher. The remonstrance is doubly significant as addressed to Galatians, for Pessinus, one of their chief towns, was the home of the worship of Cybele, in honor of whom these mutilations were practiced." WORDSWORTH: "There would be more hope from their *ex-cision*, than from their circumcision. For then they would be excluded from the Jewish congregation, they would feel the rigor of the law, they would be ashamed of enforcing it on you. Then there would be good hope, that they also would joyfully hail and accept the gracious liberty of the gospel, and would be joined as sound members to the Body of Christ."—R.]—Ἀναστατοῦντες, **unsettling**=to bring into tumult, stronger than ταράσσειν. WIESELER: To render seditious, namely, against the order of Christianity, or rather against its Lord and King, Christ.—[CHRYSOSTOM: "Well does he say ἀναστατοῦντες, for abandoning their country and their freedom and their kindred in heaven, they compelled them to seek a foreign and a strange land; banishing from the heavenly Jerusalem and the free, and forcing them to wander about as captives and aliens." (From LIGHTFOOT.)—R.]

## DOCTRINAL AND ETHICAL.

1. *Christian Liberty.* Respecting the idea of Freedom, which Paul in this Epistle maintains and vindicates for Christians with such decision (from iii. 25 on, substantially this, but more on its negative side; in express words in this section), we are to consider that it does not primarily mean freedom from the accusations and the curse of the law (wrath of God, etc.), but, agreeably to the whole polemics of the Apostle, means freedom from the claims (requirements) of the law, from the obligation of attaching ourselves to it, in order by works of the law to seek salvation (to seek it through these conjointly with faith, yes, essentially to seek it through these). Too precipitately and too prevailingly does Luther, for example, take this freedom, which Christ has won, in the former sense, and in this sense eulogizes it as the most precious benefit. Undoubtedly, however, freedom in this sense stands causally connected with freedom in the other; in the first place by the very fact that only he who through Christ is delivered from the curse of the law, is a Christian, and only to him does freedom from the law itself accrue (although

strictly speaking this does not belong here);—and secondly, inasmuch as only to him who does not give himself any more into bondage under the law, does freedom from its curse also remain assured, while conversely, whoever gives up the other freedom, loses also this, and thus comes into double bondage. Hence it is fully admissible to comprehend in the freedom which Paul claims for the Christian, his freedom from the curse of the law—not exegetically it is true, but at least in the practical application of the doctrine. Still more; in the reference to freedom from the curse of the law (wrath of God), an entirely just apprehension of the doctrine is involved, since Paul contends with such earnestness for the freedom of the Christians from the law, and against the imposing of the law upon them, and thus against their being brought upon the ground of the righteousness of works, for this very reason, that thereby we forfeit also our freedom from the curse of the law, and so come under this curse, losing thereby the advantage that we have in Christ, the certainty of the grace of God. His strong emphasizing of the freedom of Christians has its ground indeed not merely in an abstract pride of freedom, leading him to feel: Christians now have no longer need of allowing themselves to be held in bondage by a law, but it is grounded in the doctrinal knowledge of the loss of salvation, which would result from the giving up of that freedom.

2. *Either the law wholly, or not at all; either Christ or the law.* The Apostle presents two momentous alternatives and thereby sets himself against all half courses and their self-deceiving effect. The first is: "Either the law wholly—or not at all." Whoever once places himself in one particular on the legal ground, cannot stop short with that one. For in the first place the law, although a whole consisting of many members, is yet a whole in which one member depends on another. And secondly for this very reason the blessing of God is not promised to the observance of one or the other part of it, but only to the observance of the whole; whoever therefore will become partaker of the blessing in the way of law, must observe the whole law. But if he shrinks from undertaking the whole, either because he recognizes much of it as abolished for the Christian, or because much of it is burdensome to him, or as he thinks of the impossibility of fulfilling all aright, and of the curse which is denounced against all short comings, then let him give up the legal position altogether. This suggests then the other alternative: "Either Christ or the law." The two "do not match," i. e. whoever will be justified by works of law, thereby renounces virtually, and ought therefore to renounce formally the consolations of grace in Christ; for in so doing he does not seek his righteousness in Christ, but rejects Him. Commonly however man would be glad to take the latter with the former, would at least, without building upon it, be well content with the free grace of God, as the complement of his imperfect righteousness of works; but in vain—the sentence is: Fallen away from grace!—"This text, vers. 2 and 4, is a true touchstone, by which we may securely and certainly judge all manner of doctrines, works and ceremonies of all men. Whoever now, be they Papists, Turks, Jews, sectaries,—or whoever they may be, teach, that anything is necessary to salvation besides faith in Christ, they hear in this place the sentence of the Holy Ghost pronounced against them by the Apostle, namely, that Christ profiteth them nothing. But if St. Paul can venture to pass so terrible a judgment against the law and circumcision, which God Himself has given, what kind of judgment would he utter upon the chaff and the dross of men's ordinances? Wherefore this text is such a thunderclap, that by right the whole papal realm should be astounded and terrified thereat." LUTHER.

3. "*Waiting for the hope of righteousness.*" Justification, on one hand, is a benefit to be obtained even now, but on the other hand, that which we now obtain is not yet the whole, not yet the consummation. But the justification of the Christian in the present is not on this account in any way an illusion, nor is the joyful certainty, which faith has, of being justified in Christ, prejudiced. On the contrary the believer knows very well that at first he can only have this benefit in a measure corresponding to the imperfection of the present dispensation. The joyfulness of faith would be beclouded if the hope of consummation in eternity, in spite of all present imperfection, did not essentially appertain to faith, as *certain* hope. Hoping and waiting include, it is true, a negative element, a not yet having; but they also include essentially a positive element, the certainty that what is not yet possessed will nevertheless be attained, and this positive element is derived from nothing else than faith. Hope is grounded in faith—but never in our works; faith is therefore not only necessary in the beginning, but *remains* so perpetually; if we lose it, we lose hope also.

4. *Faith, Hope, Love.* Faith, that has hope, is the one thing that characterizes the Christian, to which is added Love. As in hope faith becomes a waiting faith, πίστις ἀπεκδεχομένη, so through love does it become an active faith, π. ἐνεργουμένη, *i. e.*, the ἐνέργεια does not first through love come into faith, but rather faith manifests in this love its own indwelling energy; had it no such ἐνέργεια in itself, there would be no such result as love, and where this energy is wanting to it, because it is a mere nominal faith, there is no such result. Even so the capacity of waiting does first come into faith, not through hope, but on the contrary, because this inheres in faith, from faith emanates hope.—The Catholic doctrine of a *fides caritate formata*, as the condition of justification, has of course not the least support in this passage; for the simple reason that "working through love" affirms something enirely different: "*non per caritatem formam suam accipere vel formari fidem, sed per caritatem operosam vel efficacem esse ap. docet.*" CALOVIUS. Nor can it be concluded from this passage that the Apostle would make love the principle of justification together with faith. See the EXEGETICAL NOTES above, but especially LUTHER, who has so truly apprehended the significance of our passage: "Paul treats not in this place of what Faith accomplishes before God, as how one becomes righteous before God; for this he has done at full length above; but he says just

here at the end, as it were for a short conclusion, what is a true Christian life; in Christ such a faith alone avails, which is no feigned, hypocritical one, but a true living faith. Now such a faith is one that exercises itself and perseveres in good works through love. For this is nothing else than to say: Whoever will be a true Christian man and in Christ's Kingdom, he must forsooth have a true faith. But now assuredly the faith is not sound, where the works of love do not follow after. Therewith he shuts out from the Kingdom of Christ all hypocrites, both on the right hand and on the left; on the right all Jews and work-saints, but on the left all slothful and secure folk, who say: If faith without works makes righteous, then God requires nothing of us than only that we believe, therefore we are permitted to do what we list."

5. *Love does not overlook perversion of doctrine.* Certain as it is that faith, active through *love*, is part of the Christian *life*, yet over against those, who destroy faith by perversion of *doctrine*, indulgence for love's sake, is not in place, but earnestness and severity (comp. the remarks of LUTHER upon this, in the HOMILETICAL NOTES, ver. 10).

### HOMILETICAL AND PRACTICAL.

Ver. 1. LUTHER:—Let us learn to count this our freedom, most noble, exalted and precious, which no emperor, no prophet, nor patriarch, no angel from heaven, but Christ, God's Son, hath obtained for us; not for this, that He might relieve us from a bodily and temporal subjection, but from a spiritual and eternal imprisonment of the cruellest tyrants, namely, the law, sin, death, devil, &c.—Those that will be secure and snore on without care, these will not keep this freedom. For Satan is to the light of the Gospel hostile above measure, *i. e.*, to the doctrine of grace, freedom, consolation and life. Therefore, where he is aware that it is about to dawn, he keeps no holiday, but sets himself speedily with all might against it. [CALVIN:—He reminds them that they ought not to despise a freedom so precious. And certainly it is an invaluable blessing, in defence of which it is our duty to fight, even to death. If men lay upon our shoulders an unjust burden, it may be borne; but if they endeavor to bring our conscience into bondage, we must resist valiantly, even to death. If men be permitted to bind our consciences, we shall be deprived of an invaluable blessing, and an insult will be, at the same time, offered to Christ, the author of our freedom.—R.]

[COWPER:—This is a liberty unsung
By poets, and by senators unpraised;
Which monarchs cannot grant, nor all the powers
Of Earth and Hell confederate take away:
A liberty which persecution, fraud,
Oppression, prisons, have no power to bind;
Which whoso tastes can be enslaved no more.
'Tis liberty of heart, derived from Heaven,
Bought with His blood who gave it to mankind.
* * * The oppressor holds
His body bound; but knows not what a range
His spirit takes, unconscious of a chain,
And that to bind him is a vain attempt,
Whom God delights in, and in whom He dwells.—R.]

Ver. 2. LUTHER:—Under the sun there is no more hurtful or poisonous thing, than the doctrine of human laws and works, that are received in the imagination of thereby obtaining forgiveness of sins. For they take away in one heap the truth of the gospel and Christ Himself.

Ver. 3. "A debtor to do the whole law." If we overlook this chance, and Moses begins in one particular to rule over us, we must thereafter be wholly and entirely subject to his power, whether we will or not. Therefore, to be brief, we cannot, yea, ought not, nor will not suffer, that any one should hang any one fraction of Moses' law [*Gesetzlein Mosis*] upon our neck.

Ver. 4. "Ye are separated from Christ."—How could one speak more powerfully against the law? What can or will any one bring up against this mighty thunderclap? It is not possible that the gospel and the law can dwell and rule in one heart at the same time with one another, but of necessity either Christ must yield to the law or the law to Christ. Therefore, when thou fanciest that Christ and confidence in the law might dwell together with one another in thy heart, thou art of a certainty to believe and know, that in thy heart not Christ, but the very devil dwells and keeps house, who under the form of Christ accuses and terrifies thee, and demands that thou through the law and thine own works shouldst make thyself righteous; for the true Christ has not that way.—Even as one that falls out of a ship, let it happen as it may, must certainly drown in the sea; even so can it not be otherwise than that whoever falls away from grace, must be condemned and lost.—If those fall away from Grace, that will be justified by the law of God, beloved, whither will those fall that will be justified through human ordinances, their vows and merits? Into the deep abyss of hell, to the devil.

Ver 5. SPENER:—Faith is not merely the beginning of our salvation, so that we must receive the first grace from God, and afterwards earn the rest ourselves, but all remaining gifts of grace and glory are alone expected and bestowed from faith.—LUTHER:—This is an admirable, noble consolation, wherewith all wretched, perplexed hearts, that feel their sin and are terrified thereat, are mightily holpen against all the fiery darts of the devil. For when the conscience has to wrestle and strive in such distress and perplexity, it becomes terrified and anxious, and the feeling of sin, of God's wrath and of death is so great that it seems as if there were neither righteousness nor salvation to hope for. Then is it time to say: Dear brother, thou wouldst be glad to have such a righteousness, as might be felt, whereof thou mightest have joy and comfort, even as sin lets itself be felt and stirs up terror and despond; now that cannot be done, but do thou labor on, that the righteousness, which thou hast in hope, and which is yet hidden, may surpass the sin which thou feelest; and know, that it is not such a righteousness as lets itself be seen or felt, but as to which one must hope that in is time it will be reached. Therefore thou art not to judge after the feeling of sin, but according to the promise and doctrine of faith, through which Christ is promised to thee, that he may be thy perfect and everlasting righteousness.—STARKE:—Waiting comprehends in it; a believing assurance of certain attainment of the thing hoped for, a high estimation of the same, a continual remembrance thereof, an ardent longing thereafter, a joy in the apprehension of future felicity, a patient expectation, an abstinence from all that stands opposed to the purity and steadfastness of such hope.—Those that will be righteous by the law have nothing more to expect of Christ but believers have yet glorious benefits to hope from him.

Ver. 6. LUTHER:—St. Paul points out here what is the fashion of the Christian life, namely, that it is nothing else than, inwardly, faith towards God and, outwardly, love and works towards our neighbor, so that a man becomes perfectly a Christian, inwardly by faith towards God, who does not need our works, and outwardly by works towards men, whom our faith can help nothing, but our works and our love.—Of faith, what it is, what its inward hidden nature, power, work and office is, has he treated above, where he says that faith makes us righteous before God. But here he conjoins it with love and works, *i. e.* he speaks of its works and office, which it outwardly and publicly accomplishes, that it is the stirrer up to good works and to love, yea not alone the stirrer up, but the true doer and workmaster of all good works.—There stands St. Paul and says outright, that faith, which worketh by love, makes a Christian, says not that cowls, fasts, distinct attire or genuflections make a Christian.—Anything else, be it called what it may, makes no one a Christian: only faith and love do so. See also above in the DOCTRINAL NOTES.

Ver. 7. In STARKE:—Running in religion is good, running well still better, to accomplish the race best of all. To a Christian life there appertains standing and walking: standing, that one may not fall, walking, that one may not stand still, which is commonly linked with a going back.—LUTHER:—These words are very comforting, for Christians have ever this temptation, to imagine that their life is an idle and sleepy matter, it seems more a creeping than a running. But so far as they remain steadfast in the wholesome doctrine, walk in the Spirit and wait on their vocation, they should in no wise trouble themselves, although it seems as if their work and doing went slowly on, and crept rather than walked. But our master, God, judges far otherwise. What seems to us slow walking, seems to Him quick and swift running, item, what we count for mournfulness, suffering, death *etc.*, that is with Him joy, laughing and blessedness.—"Who did hinder you?" And now they supposed, forsooth, that all their matters were going most prosperously and most swiftly along.—HEDINGER:—Have a care, pilgrim! on the way to heaven there are many stumbling blocks.—Hearest thou the sirens sing and the robbers whistle? Finish thou thy course with joy, let not the threatening and flattering of the world lead thee astray! The Lord is with thee!—LANGE:—Beware of all credulousness, especially in spiritual things, which concern the well-being of the soul! Let a doctrine wear ever so good a guise, it must nevertheless be tested by God's word.

Ver. 8. LUTHER:—The devil is a prince of persuaders. He can so blow up and magnify the very smallest sins, that he who is tempted, thinks nothing else than that they are so great and terrible sins, as are worthy the punishment of eternal death. Then is it high time that we comfort such a disturbed soul in such wise as St. Paul has here done, saying to it, that such persuasion is not of Christ, since it gainsays the word of the gospel, which depicts Christ to us, not as an accuser, but as meek and compassionate, a Saviour and Comforter.

Ver. 9. HEDINGER:—The least particle of evil infects, a single spark kindles a forest. Away with it! But O ye careless! is it a small thing to you, to be corrupted through idle talk and companyings, through poison of lies against Christ?

Ver. 10. LUTHER:—Has St. Paul done right in saying: I have a good confidence towards you, while yet the Holy Scripture forbids that we should have confidence in man? Answer: Faith and Love both believe, yet is the belief of the two not directed upon one thing. The faith is directed towards God, therefore it cannot be deceived: but love believes man, therefore is it often and greatly deceived. But yet the faith that love has is such a needful thing in this present life, that without it this life cannot at all continue. For if no man trusts nor believes another, what would this life upon earth become? Christians out of love believe people easier than the subtle children of the world are wont to do. For that believers trust people and expect good of them, that is beautiful fruit of the Holy Ghost and faith. But the Christian adds: In the Lord=so far do I trust you and expect good of you, as the Lord is in you and ye in Him, that is, so far as ye abide in the truth.—We must diligently distinguish doctrine from life. Doctrine is heaven, life the earth. In life there is sin, error, discord. Here love should pass by and overlook, should forbear; here should forgiveness of sins bear sway, yet so that one should not wish to uphold such sin and error. But with doctrine it is quite another thing, for it is holy, pure, ummixed, heavenly, divine; therefore can we not suffer it, that any one should distort it even in the least particular. Whoever will alter or adulterate it, against such a one there is neither love nor compassion.

Ver. 11. St. Paul holds that for a certain sign, that it is not and cannot be the true gospel, if it is preached in peace and in quietness and is not gainsayed nor persecuted. On the other hand, the world, when it sees that from the preaching of the gospel great rumors, divisions, scandal and tumults follow, holds that for a certain size that such teaching is heretical and seditious.—To murderers, thieves and other evil-doers grace is shown; on the contrary the world deems that no more evil, mischievous people are to be found than Christians; therefore it also persuades itself that they can never have punishment and torment enough inflicted on them.—As long as persecutions and suffering endure, the state of the church is good. The church must suffer persecution, if the gospel is purely preached. For the gospel goes about to preach alone God's compassion, grace, glory and praise, and on the other hand discovers the devil's craft and malice. Where the gospel comes it cannot be otherwise, there must follow the scandal of the cross; where that does not come to pass, there certainly the devil is not yet fairly hit, but only a little grazed.—May God be surety that the offence of the cross do not cease, which would soon come to pass, if we only preached, what the prince of this world with his members would be glad to hear, namely, how to be justified and saved by one's own works. [The offence of the cross. 1. It asks men to humble their pride and take salvation as a free gift; this is a great scandal. 2. It sometimes seems to cease: 3. It never does.—R.] The homiletical uses of the single verses, especially 1–9, are easily suggested by the sententious character of the greater part.

Vers. 1–6 From LISCO:—The care taken by the Christian, to stand fast in the true freedom.—Vers. 7–12. How are we to rescue those who stand in danger of apostacy? 1. By bringing to their minds their earlier life in communion with God; 2. by warning against the destruction to which they are hastening, vers. 9, 10; 3. by the testimony of our own walk and perseverance in fellowship with God through Christ, ver. 11. For vers. 1–6 at New Year. FRANTZ:—A good counsel at the New Year for all, who will strengthen their inward life: 1. Stand fast in the freedom, wherewith Christ hath made us free; 2. lose not Christ and fall not away from grace; 3. wait in the Spirit through faith for the righteousness that is to be hoped for; 4. walk in faith which worketh by love.

---

## G. Extended exhortation to the Galatians, instead of turning back from Faith to works of the Law, to give activity to their Faith (in a right understanding of Christian freedom) by ministering Love, as the best fulfilment of the Law.

CHAPTER V. 13—VI. 10.

### 1. More general—reverting to the principle of ethical opposition between Spirit and Flesh, in a discussion, partly didactic.

(Chap. v. 13–24.)

(Vers. 16–24.—*Epistle for 14th Sunday after Trinity.*)

13 For, brethren, ye have been called unto liberty [ye were called unto liberty,
brethren];[1] only *use* not liberty [or your liberty] for an occasion to the flesh, but
14 by [or by means of your] love serve one another. For all the [the whole] law is
15 fulfilled[2] in one word,[3] *even* in this; Thou shalt love thy neighbor as thyself.[4] But
if ye bite and devour one another, take heed that ye be not consumed one of an-
16 other. *This* I say then [Now I say], Walk in [by][5] the Spirit and ye shall not ful-
17 fill the lust of the flesh. For the flesh lusteth against the Spirit, and the Spirit
against the flesh: and [for][6] these are contrary [opposed] the one to the other; so that
18 ye cannot do the things that ye would [that[7] ye may not do what things ye would].
19 But if ye be led of [by] the Spirit, ye are not under the law. Now the works of the
flesh are manifest, which are *these* [of which kind are],[8] adultery [omit adultery],[9]
20 fornication, uncleanness, lasciviousness [wantonness], idolatry, witchcraft [sorcery],
hatred [hatreds], variance [strife],[10] emulations [jealousy], wrath, strife, seditions,
21 heresies [caballings, dissensions, factions], envyings, murders,[11] drunkenness, revel-
lings, and such like: of the which I tell you before, as I have also told *you* in time past
[I forewarn you as I did forewarn you], that they which do such things [as these][12]
22 shall not inherit the kingdom of God. But the fruit of the Spirit is love, joy, peace,
23 longsuffering, gentleness [benignity], goodness, faith [or trustfulness], Meekness,
24 temperance: against such [as these] there is no law. And [Now][13] they that are
Christ's have crucified the flesh with the [its] affections and lusts.

1 Ver. 13.—[It seems better to retain the Greek order, which places ἀδελφοί at the end of the clause. The aorist ἐκλήθητε may be rendered by the English perfect, but Ellicott gives the simple past tense as above.—R.]

2 Ver. 14.—Rec: πληροῦται. The correct reading is that of Lachmann, Tischendorf: πεπλήρωται. So א.[A. B. C. and modern editors.—R.]

3 Ver. 14.—Ἐν ὑμῖν before ἐν ἑνὶ λόγῳ is not sufficiently supported.

4 Ver. 14.—[Lightfoot: "The received text has ἑαυτόν which some would retain against the authority of the best MSS., on the ground that it was altered by scribes ignorant of this usage of ἑαυτοῦ for the first and second persons. The case however with respect to the New Testament seems to stand thus; that whereas (1) in the plural we always find ἑαυτῶν

*etc.*, never ἡμῶν αὐτῶν, ὑμῶν αὐτῶν *etc.*, as mere reflexives, yet (2) in the singular there is not one decisive instance of ἑαυτοῦ in the first or second persons; the authority of the best MSS. being mostly against it. See A. Buttmann, p. 99."—R.]

[5] Ver. 16.—[Πνεύματι. The normal dative (Meyer); the instrumental dative (Schmoller). In either case "by" not "in."—R.]

[6] Ver. 17.—Ταῦτα γάρ is to be preferred to ταῦτα δέ, as better attested. [The latter which is the reading of the Rec., and Lachmann is probably a correction, to avoid the repetition of γάρ. The Rec. and Lachmann also read ἀντίκ. ἀλλήλους, on insufficient authority; ℵ. K. L.: the order is reversed in most MSS. and by the best modern editors.—R.]

[7] Ver 17.—[Ἵνα is considered telic here as usually, by the best commentators. "So that" must be rejected. See Exeg. Notes.—R.]

[8] Ver. 19.—[Ἅτινα has here a *classifying* force (Ellicott).—R.]

[9] Ver. 19.—Μοιχεία of the Rec. is to be rejected with Lachmann, Tischendorf. [So ℵ. A. B. C. Meyer, Alford, Ellicott, Wordsworth, Lightfoot.—R.]

[10] Ver. 20.—Rec: ἔρεις, ζῆλοι; the singular changed into the plural, apparently on account of the neighboring plurals. ℵ. has ἔρις, ζῆλοι. [The variations are great; the best editors now adopt the singular in both these cases. On the meaning of the words in these lists of vices and virtues, see Exeg. Notes.—R.]

[11] Ver. 21.—Φόνοι is to be retained, the preponderance of authority is in its favor. [Omitted in ℵ. B. by Tischendorf, bracketted by Lachmann, Alford and Lightfoot. Retained by Meyer and Ellicott, on the authority of A. C. D. E. F. G. K., most cursives and versions. The similarity in sound to the preceding word is quite as much an argument for retaining as for rejecting it.—R.]

[12] Ver. 21.—[Τὰ τοιαῦτα. "Such things as these," "all such things." "The article with τοιοῦτος denotes a known person or thing, or the whole class of such, but not an undefined individual out of the class; as in that case τοιοῦτος is anarthrous" (Ellicott). So in ver. 23.—R.

[13] Ver. 24.—[Δέ must be rendered "now" or "but", not "and." The two classes of deeds have been set forth, and this verse is a practical application.—R.]

## EXEGETICAL AND CRITICAL.

Ver. 13. **For ye were called unto liberty, brethren.**—"For": Paul justifies the strong expression, he has used in ver. 12, against the false teachers. They deserved this rebuke, for—they seek to deprive you of your freedom, and yet—ye are called to that (by God through your conversion to Christ); therefore they strive against the counsel and will of God Himself.—To this thought: "ye were called unto liberty," Paul however now adds a restriction, a warning against misunderstanding and misuse of this liberty (which in all that precedes he had vindicated with such decision for Christians, and which he had made it their duty not to surrender): **only use not your liberty for an occasion to the flesh,** μόνον μὴ κ. τ. λ. We must supply, say τρέπετε=Turn not, use not liberty as a pretext for the flesh=let not the flesh (your sinful human nature) obtain in this freedom (from the law) an occasion to pretend that it is therefore now allowed to man to do what he will, and therefore it also may claim indulgence with its sinful lusts. This of course would be an entire perversion of Christian freedom, were the flesh thus allowed to take advantage of it. The antithesis shows distinctly, what Paul regards as the essence of the sarcical state; not by any means the corporeal nature, properly so called, but the selfish Egoism. For he exhorts: **but by your love serve one another**; love being conceived as the means of serving.—Δουλεύειν in happy antithesis to the ἐλευθερία of Christians. Christians are not to be servants to the law; in this sense they are free; but on the other hand this freedom does not exclude but includes δουλεύειν in the sense of "serving one another. [Lightfoot: "Both ἀγάπης and δουλεύετε are emphatic. St. Paul's meaning may be expressed by a paraphrase thus; 'you desire to be in bondage: I too recommend to you a bondage, the subservience of mutual *love.* Temper your liberty with this bondage, and it will not degenerate into license'."—R.]

With this verse a new section, of course, begins, but it is incorrect to begin here, as is variously done, a second or third main division. Above all it is not to be supposed that the Apostle henceforth addresses himself to those Galatian Christians who had held fast the principle of evangelical freedom; on the contrary he has throughout the whole Epistle the same individuals in mind, namely, those led astray by Judaism, and his present exhortation also is immediately connected with the leading thought of the Epistle. How nearly? This he, himself, plainly sets forth in the first place with μόνον μή: the energetic admonition to the maintenance of freedom receives its needful complement in the warning against misuse of the same, by the reference to its ethical character.—But this is unquestionably only one side, hardly more than the mere point of attachment. Paul gives his exhortation to serviceable love not merely as a precaution in case the Galatians, perceiving the inadmissibleness of the legal position, should desire to return to the freer one, but this also belongs, together with the entire explication which it receives in the following verses, to the polemics against their present erroneous view To that legalism, which he combatted, as slighting faith, and surrendering itself into false bondage, he opposes as the truth, "the fulfilling of the law" by the activity of faith in love (comp. ver. 6), where we make ourselves servants, more generally in a walk by the Spirit, in which one is free from the law in the very "fulfilling" of it (vers. 14, 18, 23). He is the more earnest in holding this up to them, because the Galatians especially, in spite of (or on account of) their legal zeal, were wanting in this fulfilment of the law through a walk by the Spirit, a fulfilment which obliges Christians also (comp., especially ver. 15). The same persons who wanted to impose the law upon themselves, were content to be lacking in that which is the heart of the law; those who wished to make themselves servants to the law, would not be servants to one another. It was therefore of moment, to exclaim to these: Behold, what you need, is not in any way to turn yourselves away from faith, as if this were too little, to the law, but simply to make faith active through a walk in the Spirit, in love. Comp. ver. 6, and also chap. vi., where the more detailed exhortations follow. We thus see plainly how impossible it is to disconnect this section from the preceding one, how on the other hand it, concurs with the entire polemics of the Apostle, nay, how these find in it their true, convincing culmination.—It is of course incorrect to oppose this section, as hortatory, to the preceding part of the Epistle, as didactic, for this reason that the preceding part also includes exhortation (especially ver. 1); this however was dogmatic, and now comes ethical exhortation. Unquestionably therefore this section might with some propriety be called the Ethical part, in distinction from the Doctrinal; but if by this were meant, as commonly, that Paul now leaves the controversy concerning the relation of the Law to Faith, and, having no longer in mind the defection of the Galatian churches, merely proceeds to exhort to a walk of Christian morality, with reference to ethical short-comings, this too must be deemed incorrect according to what has been remarked. Moreover, even if such a distinction into a dogmatic and an ethical part is not unwarranted in fact, it is at all events not exact in form; this section cannot be formally contrasted with all that precedes. For certainly the discourse proceeds without interruption; Paul is speaking hortatively to the Galatians (especially from ver. 1 on), but on the ground of the doctrinal exposition, and now he merely gives a sudden ethical turn to this exhortation, bringing, as has been remarked, the whole to an appropriate conclusion.*

Ver. 14. **For the whole law is fulfilled.**—It is not easy to determine either the meaning of this clause, or its connection with what precedes. The first explanation, which offers itself on account of ἐν ἑνὶ λόγῳ, taken πληροῦται as= ἀνακεφαλαιοῦται, *comprehenditur*, as Rom. viii. 9. [So LUTHER, CALVIN, OLSHAUSEN, *et al.*—R.] But this must be rejected as lexically untenable. Besides with the reading [now generally adopted], πεπλήρωται it becomes at once incorrect. —As little does νόμον πληρ. have here the same sense as in Matt. v. 17=to bring out, to make evident the deeper sense, the ideal substance in distinction from the literal form. Doubtless it is not a πληροῦν in the doctrine that is here in question, and in reality, if πληρ. were taken in this sense, the explanation would come back again to the one already disapproved, namely, that the commandment of love to our neighbor is the substance of ὁ πᾶς νόμος, since that which is substance, in another aspect, is also foundation. Πληροῦν is to be understood of fulfilment by deed, conformity, *satisfacere legi*. [ELLICOTT: "The perfect πεπλήρωται suitably points to the completed and permanent act."—R.] It is peculiar then, no doubt, that this is said to be **in one word,** ἐν ἑνὶ λόγῳ, and this to be regarded as an abbreviated expression for: By conformity to the one word, precept (from Lev. xix. 18), immediately follows: **Thou shalt love thy neighbor as thyself.**—[MEYER: "*Neighbor* is for the Christian, who rightly (Matt. v. 17) applies this Mosaic command to himself, his fellow-Christian (comp. ver. 13, ἀλλήλοις), as for the Jew it was fellow-Jew; but how little this is to be taken as *excluding any one* whatever, is shown by the whole spirit of Christianity, which finds its most beautiful expression in the case of the Samaritan (Luke x.); Paul himself was such a Samaritan toward Jew and Gentile."—R.] But how far does Paul declare obedience to the one commandment of love to our neighbor, an obedience to the whole law? Not in the sense in which Love is styled πλήρωμα νόμου (Rom. xiii. 8–10). Nearly related as the two passages appear to be, they must by no means be confounded. For in Rom. xiii. it is expressly stated what is to be understood by νόμος, namely, the individual commandments of the Decalogue which respect conduct towards our neighbor, and love is called the πλήρωμα of those, because, whoever has the *dispositions* of love, and in truth only such a one, will of course fulfil also the duties of love commanded by the law. But that "the whole law" in this passage is not to be arbitrarily turned into "second table of the Decalogue," nor even interpreted generally = Moral law, is plain; on the contrary, it doubtless signifies nothing else than: the whole Mosaic law. But in the second place it is also clear, that Paul cannot mean to say, that in love to our neighbor is found the pledge of the fulfilment of the whole law. For this latter Paul has not at all in mind, it is precisely the opposite that he is aiming at; his meaning is, that on him who does this there is no future requirement made in respect to observance of the law, that from this he is free. The sense of πεπλήρωται can therefore only be: He is to be regarded as if he had fulfilled the law, and therefore the law can exact nothing further of him. By no means therefore is the commandment of love to our neighbor regarded by Paul as the summary of the whole law; this would be entirely incorrect. He will rather say this, that if any one fulfils this, all the rest comes no more into account; of course, with reference to his emphatic demonstration in what precedes, that the law has lost its binding force for the believer. If the believer now does not take this faith to be a dead one, but quickens it through love, he has done all; there can be of further claims of the law upon him no mention, but he *ought* on the other side to have and exercise love, for only then can he regard himself as free from the claims of the whole land besides, only then, in fact, is he a believer.—If it is asked how Paul *could* view the whole law as fulfilled in love to our neighbor, especially without even mentioning love to God, this question is mostly raised with the understanding that he means to designate the commandment of love to our neighbor as the summary, or the fulfilment of it as the condition and principle of the fulfilment of the whole law; and if he meant it so, his assertion must unquestionably be declared unwarranted.* (Where the

*[On the division of the Epistle, see Introd. § 4. While we must guard against too formal division of the Epistle, we may distinguish it into parts without separating them or breaking the current of thought. The memory is much assisted by the convenient division of LIGHTFOOT: personal, doctrinal and practical. Whether the last named part begins with ver. 1, or here, is perhaps immaterial, since such distinction into parts involves neither the supposition that the Apostle made such formal distinction, nor an arbitrary view of the Epistle as a whole. We may mar the unity quite as much by insisting on too strict sub-division into sections.—R.]

*[Schmoller probably means to make an argument *ab impossibili* here, but the form of it is not pleasing. Certainly it were better to say: Paul could not mean this, for it is contrary to the teachings of his Master and inconsistent with his own statements elsewhere. MEYER remarks: "That, by citing only the command of love to our neighbor, Paul does not exclude the command of love to God, is self-evident to the Christian consciousness from the necessary connection of love to God and to our neighbor (comp. 1 Jno. iv. 20; 1 Cor. viii. 1–3); the context (vers. 13–15) led Paul to speak of the latter only."—R.]

former is in question, Jesus in Matt. xxii. 34 sq. places the two commandments together; and where the latter, Paul, Rom. xiii., restricts the law to the second table.) But this understanding of his proposition has been already designated as incorrect. He doubtless means to say: Of him who has love to his neighbor the law can exact nothing more. The question, rightly stated, is therefore only this: How could Paul attribute to love towards our neighbor so eminent a position, that he designates him who should fulfil it as free from all else? Must he not also, nay, above all, demand of the believer a fulfilling of the commandment of love to God, and could he, except on condition that both were found in a man, esteem it equivalent to a fulfilment of the whole law? As to this it is simply to be remarked, that (1) he conceives Faith as essentially comprehending love to God, and (2) cannot conceive love to our neighbor without love to God, and therefore in demanding the former from Christians, he of course does not mean to release them from the latter. He does not, however, mention love to God, for his exhortation has not respect to a merely inward fulfilling of the law, belonging to the disposition, but to that fulfilling of the law which comes into manifestation, and shows itself forth in the walk, to the true ethical conduct of the life, and especially of the common life, and this rests upon love to our neighbor. Therefore this only is made the subject of discourse.—If now the Apostle uses this proposition to establish the preceding exhortation (γάρ), this is not in the sense that he means thereby to represent the "serving by love" (ver. 13), as a divine duty because commanded by the law; after he has previously denied so decidedly that Christians are under the law, he cannot make the fact that it is commanded in the law a motive for the exercise of love. The principal emphasis lies rather upon πᾶς and πεπλήρ., on the circumstance that through serving love the whole law is fulfilled, in the sense given=enough has been done for the law, *i. e.*, negatively, they are therewith absolved from the rest of the law. Therefore nearly=Love one another: for therewith the whole ground of controversy, respecting the observance of the law, whether this or that precept is to be observed, is taken away. The whole sentence, therefore, serves rather to strengthen his exhortation than to give, strictly speaking, a reason for it. The commandment of love to our neighbor, although expressed by a citation from the law (Leviticus): ἀγαπήσεις τὸν πλ. κ. τ. λ, does not therefore come into consideration as *a particular commandment of the law*, as if Paul from the other commandments, as being abrogated, excepts this one as remaining in force; only the commandment to exercise love towards our neighbor remains in fact valid for the Christian (and if it is done, the law has no further claim upon him); but *to him* it is a commandment not on account of the law, but *because* he is a Christian, on account of his faith in Christ, or because (ver. 6) "in Christ" alone "faith working through love" "availeth anything." Into the question how far the faith in Christ *obliges* to love, Paul does not enter, but he then goes on to show that this love is the operation of the Spirit, which faith brings. —While the proposition serves primarily to commend the exhortation, and while such an argument must have had the more weight for this end with those zealous for the law, yet of course at the same time it deals a blow against this zeal for the law, and exhibits its emptiness; for all the rest, the many observances are, according to it, purely superfluous; with the one thing, Love to our neighbor, all is done. [MEYER: "Paul looked down from a lofty spiritual level, and saw all other commands of the law subordinated to the law of love, that whoever had fulfilled *this* command, must be treated as having fulfilled the whole." The fact that Paul chose this particular expression, "the whole law is fulfilled," places his teaching in opposition to antinomian tendencies, just as the Sermon on the Mount shows Christ's position to the law, viewed as a purely ethical rule of life. "The whole law," *i. e.*, the Mosaic law, regarded in this light, was fulfilled in the case of the believer by this love to his neighbor; for the whole law of Moses had an ethical purpose, which purpose is now fulfilled to its full extent only when the believer, because he as a believer, is living "by the Spirit" has that temper of heart to God, which enables him to obey this "one word."—Schmoller insists too strongly on the idea that "all the rest are superfluous." It is doubtful whether this is implied even in ver. 18. The DOCTRINAL NOTES show his meaning more clearly.—R.]

Ver. 15. **But if ye bite and devour one another.**—This is=if ye intend of serving one another through love, do just the opposite: bear ill will towards and hate one another, and let this come into act, plot mischief against one another, yea, seek to destroy one another; something like this is the sense of these strong expressions borrowed from ravening beasts. Then **take heed**, adds Paul with incisive words, that the result be not the opposite of what you intend, **that ye be not consumed of one another.**—Each might be disposed to supplant the other, but in the end it will come to this, all will be wasted away. The sentence thus coöperates *per contrarium* to the establishment of ver. 12. The explanation: "your Christian community will go to pieces," I am inclined to regard as too special. It is not improbable, indeed, that this influence of the Judaizers occasioned divisions among the Galatians, and threw them into controversies upon the question of the law; yet I should not be disposed to refer this δάκνειν καὶ κατεσθίειν so definitely to that, as is commonly done. For this is at least intimated nowhere else in the Epistle.

Ver. 16. **Now I say, walk by the Spirit.**—With λέγω δέ Paul conducts his exhortation to serve one another by love (agreeably to the warning already given in the first half of ver. 13.) back to a more general, fundamental exhortation to walk by the Spirit (for in the Spirit he sees the Agent that leads to love), and then designates Spirit and Flesh as the two ethical principles opposite to one another, expressing themselves in opposite workings.—Πνεύματι περιπ. Dative of instrument; properly: walk through the Spirit, so that He is (not the path in which—WIESELER, but) the power, through which they walk=πνεύματι ἀγόμενοι, ver. 18. [The dative may be instrumental, as in ver. 18, but it is better, perhaps, with MEYER, ALFORD, ELLICOTT, to consider it a normal dative, that by which, according to which they are to walk (almost =κατὰ πνεῦμα), for the reason that "Spirit" is contrasted in this passage not merely with "flesh," but also with "law," and the double contrast is best brought out thus, since under the idea of the normal dative, that of rule or direction is included. WIESELER brings out the same meaning, but takes the dative as instrumental.—R.] Πνεῦμα is here also doubtless =The Holy Ghost; it is this, that overcomes the σάρξ. He enters, it is true, into the hearts of believers, and works only by impelling and determining the walk, as He who dwells in the believers. But yet πνεῦμα is not on this account=the new disposition of the believer himself, sanctified by the Spirit, but remains ever distinct from the individual human spirit as Divine, transcending it. [MEYER adopts this view, and remarks that the absence of the article is not against it. "The distinction affirmed by HARLESS, that τὸ πνεῦμα means the *objective* Holy Ghost, πνεῦμα without the article the *subjective*, cannot be justified, since πνεῦμα has the nature of a proper name, and always, even when it dwells and reigns in the human spirit, remains *objective*, as the *Divine* πνεῦμα specifically distinct from the human (Rom. vii. 16)."—R.]

**And ye shall not fulfil the lust of the flesh.**—We are led to construe this clause, as one of result, both by grammatical considerations (καί with οὐ μή and the subjunctive or future after an imperative has this force commonly) and by the context. In "walk by the Spirit" he indicates the means of victory over "the lust of the flesh." [On the grammatical point urged above, see the note of ELLICOTT *in loco*. He claims that the clause *might* be imperative, but "as there is no distinct instance of such a construction in the New Testament, and still more as the next verses seem more naturally to supply the reasons for the assertion than for the command, it seems best to adopt the future translation." (So E. V., MEYER also in 4th ed., and above.) This future with οὐ μή is strong: "shall in no wise" (LIGHTFOOT).—On the word "flesh," see DOCTRINAL NOTE 4.—R.]

Ver. 19. **For.**—This introduces, in the first place, simply the proof of a "lust of the flesh" (ver. 16)=of such an one I speak, for **the flesh lusteth**. Paul does not stop, however, but is led further to the antagonistic idea ἐπιθυμεῖν Πνεῦμα.—**Against the Spirit, and the Spirit against the flesh.**—Each principle combats the other, and seeks to wrest the dominion from it, and on the other hand to place itself in the possession of this. [It is scarcely proper to supply the verb ἐπιθυμεῖν with Πνεῦμα, but the Apostle's meaning is obvious. LIGHTFOOT suggests "strives," "fights against."—R.] This is explained by what follows: **these are opposed the one to the other, that** ἵνα=with the design, that **ye may not do what things ye would**, bring into effect precisely the desire which you have admitted into your will. Ἃ ἂν θέλητε is neither to be restricted to the good nor to the evil will. The inquiry whether the two powers in the cases in question, attain the object desired by them or not, is not proposed here, since the only purpose is to bring vividly to view the irreconcilable antagonism of their tendencies. WIESELER. Ἵνα is therefore not at all to be understood in an ecbatic sense. [ALFORD: "The necessity of supposing an ecbatic meaning for ἵνα in theology is obviated by remembering, that with God results are all purposed.—R.] The contest moreover is by no means to be conceived as an interminable one. The context shows that on the contrary there is expected of the Christian a complete surrendering of himself in order to be actuated by the one principle, the Spirit, and a *refusal to give way* to the lust of the flesh, whose motions, it is true, must still be experienced. The passage therefore, is entirely different from Rom. vii. 17 sq. [The reference is to "the free-will in its ordinary acceptation, subject only to this necessary and obvious limitation, that this conflict must be only predicated in its full extent, of the earlier and more imperfect stages of a Christian course. The state of the true believer is conflict, but with final victory." ELLICOTT.—R.]

Ver. 18 then speaks of the *victory* of this principle: **But if ye be led by the Spirit**=if the combat becomes a victory, and that on the right side; if the ἐπιθ. of the πν. becomes an ἄγειν. [BENGEL: *ubi* vero *spiritus vincit, acie res decernitur.* The dative here is instrumental.—R.] —**Ye are not under the law.**—This is according to ver. 14; there it was only stated specially of love, here generally of the "being led by the Spirit," which correspondence makes evident, how Paul regards its relation to the exercise of love; the two are to him essentially one, that is, the former is the principle of the latter. What in ver. 14 is called somewhat enigmatically a fulfilling of the whole law, is here simply and literally described as "a not being under the law." The latter is essentially identical with the former; the sense is: The law then can exact nothing more of you; implying naturally: for you are then in the right ethical condition beseeming the Christian, even though not carrying out every detail prescribed in the law. But if you—is the thought implied—are not led by the Spirit, you are then still under obligation to the law; for you are then in fact not yet all in Christ. [MEYER: "Through the impelling power of the Spirit you find yourselves in such a moral condition of life ('newness of life,' Rom. vi. 4) that the law has no power to find fault with you, to condemn and punish you. This explanation is the only correct one according to ver. 23: and this freedom is the true *moral* freedom from the law." So ELLICOTT, who remarks: "The more obvious conclusion might have seemed, 'ye are not under the influence of the flesh,' but as the law was confessedly the principle which was ordained the influences and works of the flesh, the Apostle (in accordance with the general direction of his argument) draws his conclusion relatively rather to the principle, than to the mere state and influences against which that principle was ordained." It must be borne in mind that Paul's use of the phrase "under the law" usually regards the law as a judge and pedagogue; here the Christian is viewed as one led by the Spirit, and thus taken from "under the law," but so led according to the law, as a guide to our new life of gratitude, that of the fruit of the Spirit it is ever true "against such there is no law" (ver. 23).—R.]

Ver. 19–21. **Now the works of the flesh are manifest.**—Φανερά, evident=plainly conspicuous and therefore of course undeniable. This φανερά is the main point, and therefore placed first. For Paul wishes to furnish the Galatians inducement for being "led by the Spirit," and therefore he not only calls the works of the flesh "evident," but moreover carefully enumerates them, portrays them before their eyes (puts them in the pillory); so that every one may know, what conversely belongs to being led by the Spirit, that one may not practice such things, if he will be one led by the Spirit and not under the law. The positive side is then given ver. 22 sq.—That Paul does not mean to say that all of these things are found among the Galatians, is easily understood.—"Works of the flesh"="that which is brought to pass when the flesh, *i. e.*, the sinful human nature, and not the Holy Ghost, is the actuating principle." MEYER. Therefore naturally many sins are here enumerated, which are by no means carnal sins in the common acceptation, but rather in a very special sense sins against love, agreeably to the context. There are four classes: 1. Lust (πορν.—ἀσελγ.) 2. Idolatry (εἰδωλολ., φαρμ.), 3. Contentiousness (ἔχθραι—φόνοι). 4. Intemperance (μέθαι—κῶμοι). The third class is treated the most in detail. [While we must not regard this specification as a charge against the Galatians in particular, it is extremely improbable that the Apostle would not choose such sins as most "easily beset" his readers. LIGHTFOOT very properly observes: "From early habit and constant association a Gentile church would be exposed to sins of the first two classes. The third would be a probable consequence of their religious dissensions, inflaming the excitable temperament of a Celtic people. The fourth seems to be thrown in to give a sort of completeness to the list, though not unfitly addressed, to a nation whose Gallic descent perhaps disposed them too easily to these excesses."—R.]—**Uncleanliness**, ἀκαθ., lustful impurity in general after the special **fornication**, πορνεία; **wantonness**, ἀσελγ., lustful wantonness. [LIGHTFOOT: "The same three words occur together in a different order, 2 Cor. xii. 21. The order here is perhaps the more natural: πορνεία a special form of impurity;* ἀκαθαρσία uncleanness in whatever guise, ἀσέλγεια an open reckless contempt of propriety. A man may be ἀκάθαρτος and hide his sin; he does not become ἀσελγής until he shocks public decency." As the reference in the New Testament is usually to sensuality, "wantonness" is the best rendering, "standing as it does, by the double meaning which it has, in remarkable ethical connexion with this word" ἀσέλγεια. See TRENCH, *Syn. New Testament* § xvi.—R.]—The transition from the first class to the second is easily found in the fact that with idolatrous worship many forms of unchastity were connected; but **idolatry** is not on that account to be considered as a species of lustful indulgence. [Yet the two forms of sin are so frequently joined together in the New Testament and the latter is so common a metaphor for the former in the Old Testament, as to suggest a more intimate connection than the simple fact that sensual excesses usually accompanied idolatrous worship. This fact must be regarded as an indication of some underlying affinity.—R.]—Φαρμακεία, here apparently, in juxtaposition with idolatry=**Sorcery**, not poisoning. [LIGHTFOOT: "'Idolatry,' the open recognition of false gods, 'sorcery,' the secret tampering with the powers of evil. It is a striking coincidence, if nothing more, that φαρμακεῖαι were condemned by a very stringent canon of the council held at Ancyra, the capital of Galatia, about A. D. 314."—R.]—Third class: the substantives up to αἱρέσεις have reference to dissension, the first four as shown in individual conduct, among which however, **jealousy**, ζῆλος and **wrath**, θυμοί, refer to the inner aspect, the source. [The latter is rendered "displays of wrath" by ELLICOTT, and thus referred to outward manifestations, which seems preferable, since the plural is used, serving to denote the concrete form of the abstract sin (so too the plurals which follow); were the reference to the source the singular were more appropriate. See TRENCH, *Syn. New Testament*, § xxvii., on the precise meaning of the word.—R.] The three following, **caballings, dissensions, factions** refer to the dissension of bodies of men.—**Envyings, murders** follow these, evidently named together mainly on account of the paronomasia, since φθόνος would otherwise belong with ζῆλος; "murders," however, fittingly closes the list as the culmination of discord. Besides, the two are perhaps put in juxtaposition with reference to the concurrence of envy and murder in the first murder, comp. 1 Jno. iii. 12. [LIGHTFOOT: "A principle of order may be observed in the enumeration: 1. ἔχθραι, a general expression opposed to ἀγάπη, breaches of charity in feeling or in act; from this point onward the terms are in an ascending scale: 2. ἔρις 'strife,' not necessarily implying self-interest; 3. ζῆλος 'rivalry' in which the idea of self-assertion is prominent: 4. θυμοὶ 'wraths,' a more passionate form of ἔρις; 5. ἐριθεῖαι* 'factious cabals,' a stronger development of ζῆλος: 6, 7. hostility has reached the point where the contending parties separate; such separation is either temporary (διχοστασίαι 'divisions'), or permanent (αἱρέσεις 'sects, heresies'): 8. φθόνοι, a grosser breach of charity than any hitherto mentioned, the wish to deprive another of what he has; 9. φόνοι, the extreme form which hatred can take, the deprivation of life."—On **drunkenness, revellings**, ELLICOTT remarks: "the latter is the more generic and inclusive, to which the former was the usual accompaniment."—R.]—In order to brand still further "the works of the flesh," and to restrain from them, he points moreover to the punishment decreed against them, in words which are meant to express: that however often one might

* ["Observe the prominence always given to condemnations of this deadly sin, it being one of the things which the old pagan world deemed as merely ἀδιάφορα."—ELLICOTT.—R.]

* [WORDSWORTH:—"The word ἐρίθεια is from ἔριθος, a laborer for hire, 1. a mercenary; and 2. one who hires himself to a cabal for party purposes: and therefore signifies 3. a *venal partisan*; such as the factions of *gladiators*, and other ruffians hired by rival candidates at elections to intimidate the voters in the Roman forum. Hence ἐρίθεια signifies *venal partisanship*."—R.]

come to speak of them, he would always have to render the same judgment, and to express moreover that this judgment might be rendered in advance with perfect distinctness.—Π ρ ο in προλέγω and προεῖπον=before it comes; the preterite in προεῖπον=during my presence among you.—**Shall not inherit the kingdom of God.**—Just as in 1 Cor. vi. 9 sq.; Eph. v. 5, of course with the pre-supposition: If no conversion intervenes.

Vers. 22, 23. After the negative exposition, Paul now states explicitly in what the being led by the Spirit consists, or, more particularly, reveals itself.—**The fruit of the Spirit.**—Κ α ρ π ὸ ς τ ο ῦ π ν ε ύ μ α τ ο ς, essentially the same as ἔργα, "works," ver. 19: That which comes to pass, which is brought into effect, when the Holy Ghost is the impelling principle. But in what follows it is only qualities that are mentioned, and not works, and so of course ἔργα was not appropriate. And certainly it is not unintentional, that Paul in the first place names only the inward "fruit of the Spirit," consisting in the disposition of the soul, for the reason that the Spirit primarily and principally changes and must change the inward disposition. When this is done, there is a genuine leading by the Spirit, living by the Spirit, which then finds external manifestation also in a walking by the Spirit.—The singular καρπός also is significant, "proceeding from the conception of the inward unity and ethical continuity of all that the Spirit works." As "Spirit" in this connection is conceived as the principle from which serving love proceeds, the enumeration of precisely these virtues is easily explicable. That many things besides are effected by the Spirit, does not need to be said. At the head stands **Love**, as the most general, and at the same time the chief virtue of Christians (comp. vers. 13, 14). Χ α ρ ά, one is inclined to take as **Joy** with the brethren, opposed to ζῆλοι, φθόνοι. It is no objection that this incidental idea is not contained in the word itself; the connection might easily indicate in what particular sense χαρά is here to be taken. Yet the explanation of it as the inward joyfulness of the Christian in the consciousness of the love of God may also be justified, as this too stands in close connection with his conduct towards his brethren, and is incompatible with an unloving behavior. At all events the following words from εἰρήνη to πραΰτης belong together, as designating the fruits of "love," unselfish love; ε ἰ ρ ή ν η therefore denotes **peace** with others, μ α κ ρ ο θ υ μ ί α patience under injuries, χ ρ η σ τ. gracious, friendly character, ἀ γ α θ. is nearly related to this: Benevolence (LUTHER); not so generally as, good dispositions (the special meaning is quite frequent in the Septuagint): π ί σ τ ι ς here of course not=justifying faith, but either **trustfulness**, as opposed to mistrust, or faithfulness.—Finally, **temperance**, ἐγκράτεια, is added in antithesis particularly to the sins of lust and intemperance (vers. 19-21).—[Here again LIGHTFOOT is excellent: "The difficulty of classification in this list is still greater than in the case of the works of the flesh. Nevertheless some sort of order may be observed. The catalogue falls into three groups of three each. The first of these comprises Christian habits of mind in their more general aspect, 'love, joy, peace.' (The fabric is built up story upon story. Love is the foundation, joy the superstructure, peace the crown of all.) The second gives special qualities affecting a man's intercourse with his neighbor, 'long-suffering, kindness, beneficence.' (This triad is again arranged in an ascending scale; μακροθυμία is *passive*, 'patient endurance under injuries inflicted by others;' χρηστότης, *neutral*, 'a kindly disposition towards one's neighbors' not necessarily taking a practical form;* ἀ γ α θ ω σ ύ ν η, *active*, 'goodness, beneficence' as an energetic principle.) The third, again general in character like the first, exhibits the principles which guide a Christian's conduct."—ELLICOTT: "Ἐγκράτεια, 'temperance,' is distinguished by Diog. Laert. from σωφροσύνη as implying a control over the *stronger* passions, whereas the latter implies a self-restraint in what is less vehement."—R.]—**Against such as these there is no law.** —Τ ο ι ο ύ τ ω ν is neuter, as in ver. 21, and the sense is: Such virtues the law condemns not. This, however, implies of course: Against those that possess such qualities the law is not, and this is the same thought, only more specially conceived, as in vers. 14, 18. The law requires nothing more of them, and therefore also it can bring no accusations against them. [Or rather, because the law can find nothing to oppose or restrain in such things (which fulfil its ethical purpose), the law has no power over those who bring forth the fruit of the Spirit. Schmoller presses too strongly the implied thought. BEZA and others make a *meiosis* here: these are pleasing to God, but as MEYER remarks: Paul wishes to explain only what he has said in ver. 18 of those led by the Spirit. He sets forth the fruit of the Spirit and says: *against virtues and states such as these the law is not*, and he thus makes clear, how those led by the Spirit by virtue of their moral condition are not subject to the Mosaic law. For whoever is so circumstanced, that a law is not against him, over him it has no power.—R.]

Ver. 24. **And they that are Christ's.**—Another proposition weighty in itself, and especially also in the connection. It joins on well to what precedes, with which it is probably better to connect it, although on the other hand what follows naturally connects itself with this. That is, as Paul went back from the exhortation to the exercise of love towards our neighbor to the exhortation to a walk in the Spirit, as the principle of love, so now he goes back beyond that again, and shows how this walk in the Spirit is itself grounded in fellowship with CHRIST. As thus, in the first place he spoke of the fruit of the Spirit, and then says: Now it is those that are Christ's, who have crucified their flesh, *etc.*; who therefore have crucified the very disposition opposed to the aforesaid fruit of the Spirit, the disposition from which the works of the flesh proceed, so that the opposite disposition, the fruit of the Spirit, can find a place. [ELLICOTT: "The connection of the whole paragraph appears to be as follows:—'The Spirit and the flesh are

* [Hence well expressed by "benignity." So JEROME, who renders this and the following word respectively: *benignitas, bonitas*. See TRENCH, *Synon*. 2d series.—The remarks of LIGHTFOOT are collated; the parts included in parenthesis are taken from his comments on the separate triads.—R.]

contrary to each other; if the flesh prevail, man is given over to all sin, and excluded from the kingdom of God: if the Spirit be the leading principle, man brings forth good fruits, and is free from the curse of the law. *Now* the distinguishing feature of the true Christian is the crucifixion of the flesh; consequently, it must be obvious from what has been said, the living in and being led by the Spirit'."—R.]—**Have crucified**, *ἐσταύρωσαν*.—This is conceived as something accomplished, and is therefore apparently to be referred to an individual act, the act of becoming a Christian through faith and baptism. The meaning, to be sure, is not, that now **the flesh, with its affections and lusts**, is not any longer present at all with those that have become Christians. But yet at least a walk in the flesh *should not* any longer exist in the case of Christians; we may declare to these that such a walk is in *contradiction* to their essential character as Christians, and that a walk in the Spirit may rightly be *expected* of them; yet this is only possible because we may urge this upon them: You now have crucified the flesh. It is to be noted also, that the language is not: slain, but, crucified. The former could not so well be said, as it is conceived rather as a task of the Christian to be accomplished only by continual effort (Col. iii. 5). In "crucified," however, the simple slaying is not the main idea, but the condemning, giving sentence, surrendering to infamous death; and this has necessarily taken place in becoming Christ's. [ELLICOTT: "Though this ethical crucifixion is here designated as an act *past*, it really is and must be a continuing act as well. This however the aorist, with its usual and proper force, leaves unnoticed; it simply specifies, in the form of a general truth, the act as belonging to the past, without affirming or denying any reference to the present. In all such cases the regular reference of the tense to the past may be felt in the kind of summary way in which the action is stated,—the sort of implied dismissal of the subject, and procedure to something fresh."—R.]—'Εσταύρ. naturally alludes to the cross of Christ, and the fellowship with Christ involves a crucifixion of the flesh for the very reason that it is fellowship with Christ's death on the cross; for through this the fact that men's σάρξ deserves condemnation and is obnoxious to death, is demonstrated and set forth in a way of irresistible force; for Christ indeed has only suffered what men have deserved on account of their sinful "flesh," and therefore what this itself has deserved. Whoever therefore appropriates to himself in faith Christ's death upon the cross, regards the "flesh" in himself no longer; for him in Christ's death this has been crucified. (Comp. Rom. vi. 6.) [MEYER: "'Have crucified the flesh,' expresses: to have divested themselves of all vital fellowship with sin, whose seat the σάρξ is, so that, as Christ was objectively crucified, we, by means of the entrance into the fellowship of this death on the cross, crucify the σάρξ subjectively, in moral consciousness of faith, *i.e.*, have made it entirely lifeless and inoperative through faith as the new vital element, to which we have passed over. To Christians considered *ideally* as here, this ethical slaying of the flesh is something which *has* taken place, in *reality* however, it is also something *taking place* and *continuing*."—R.] Παθήματα are passions, aroused by the σάρξ in the sensibility; these then show themselves active in definite sinful lusts, ἐπιθυμίαι. In the παθ. the man is, as is implied in the word passive; but this passivity becomes activity in the ἐπιθυμίαι. [Comp. Col. iii. 5, and see TRENCH, *Syn. New Testament*, 2d series, § xxxvii.—R.]

### DOCTRINAL AND ETHICAL.

1. Men are pointed away from the law and to faith, first and above all, because only faith in Christ and not the keeping of the precepts of the law, or the doing of works of the law, is the way to the attaining of justification and of the divine inheritance (subjectively: to the attaining of the comfort of the forgiveness of sins, of the adoption of children and the hope of the eternal inheritance). For him who has this faith, the law loses its importance, for the reason that a *usus justificatorius* it has not, while it has already fulfilled its *usus pædagogicus*, of impelling to faith, in the case of such a one.—But nevertheless the Apostle is the farthest possible from meaning that the believer on Christ is dispensed from giving a truly moral (ethico-religious) character to his inward disposition and his life (from the doing of "good works"), and is entitled to persevere in sin, that is, to indulge the "flesh." So far is this from being true that this, despite his faith and despite the fact that faith is the condition of salvation, nevertheless excludes him from the kingdom of God and from eternal life (v. 21; vi. 8). And, indeed, this *cannot* be the opinion of the Christian, for this his faith in Christ involves not merely an impulse and power to the avoidance of sin, to the willing and doing of good, but because it is a coming into fellowship with Christ's death, it immediately involves also the arising of a hatred against sin, a condemning of the flesh (ver. 21), and because it is a receiving of Christ, it involves also the beginning of a life for God (comp. ii. 19 sq. and the DOCTRINAL NOTES on that section). The latter fact, the new life, which arises or is given with faith on Christ, receives in this section its exact expression; there begins in man a working of the Spirit (πνεῦμα), who, overcoming the flesh (ver. 16), brings forth fruit in an ethically good, God-pleasing disposition of heart and life (ver. 22 sq.). Nay, it is *only* this faith in Christ which leads to this goal, as it is only this which leads to the other goal of justification. The law cannot effect this second, and quite as little can it effect the first. On the contrary, it arouses the σάρξ (and the ἁμαρτία dwelling therein), but does not assist to the receiving of the Spirit (comp. iii. 2, and Rom. vii. 8). So little therefore does faith in Christ dispense from a disposition and course of action pleasing to God, that it is just this, nay more, only this which leads thereto. If any one is disposed to call this disposition and activity to the Christian, thus conformed to God's will, a "fulfilling of the law," he does not name it wrongly; only in doing it he is to keep in mind (1) that it is not to be understood in a formal, but only in a material relation: a doing of that which the law commands, yet not *because* the law commands it, but in the strength and on the impulse of faith, or more

properly, of the Spirit, something therefore entirely different from what Paul calls "works of the law;" it is that which he so often names ἔργα ἀγαθά, works of the Spirit, rather than of the law; (2) that in this appellation law is taken in a quite restricted sense, of the properly ethical commandments (see Rom. xiii. 8 sq., where it plainly appears *what* Paul means by the νόμος; when he speaks generally, he uses the expression ἐντολαὶ θεοῦ, 1 Cor. vii. 19). "Fulfilling of the law" will therefore always be an only partially adequate expression for a Christian life, a conformity of the life to God's will. Entirely abandoning the Old Testament point of view therefore, Paul speaks directly of an ἀναπληροῦν τὸν νόμον Χριστοῦ (vi. 2).*

2. But it is true that the "doing of good works" the making faith active in a walk and mind pleasing to God, does not come to pass, as it were, of itself (as might appear from what precedes), even with the believer (even though, as of course is pre-supposed, his faith is an actual one of inward persuasion, and not merely nominal, is actually equivalent to a τοῦ Χριστοῦ εἶναι, and therefore bears within it the energy perfectly adequate to a moral renewal of the life). Even with the believer the σάρξ has not disappeared. Therefore, although abstractly we must say: the believer *cannot* dispense himself from a genuine ethical renewal of his life, yet *in concreto* we are rather to say: He *ought* not. The "thou oughtest" comes back even to him who stands on the foundation of faith. This appears in the case of the believer, in a twofold manner. In the first place and chiefly on the side of the πνεῦμα, which he receives in faith; for this works not merely as it were physically, in the form of an energy of nature, converting the will of man into agreement with the mind of God (and the figure of the καρπός must be understood *cum grano salis:* a bare *growing up* it certainly is not); the result is brought about ethically and not physically; the πνεῦμα also approaches the will with requirements, which it is true are far more intensive, which have as it were a quite different power of bending the will from the requirements of the law or of the conscience (the law of the letter or of the conscience); for they are strengthened by the persuasion which is received along with faith into the heart, of the condemnation of sin as well as the forgiveness of it, of the holiness as well as the compassion inhering in the grace of God in Christ. But it is with an "ought," however intensive, that the πνεῦμα in the believer approaches the will of man, and seeks to *determine* it to let itself be guided by him, to determine it to the ἄγεσθαι and then also to the πνεύματι περιπατεῖν: and in doing this he meets with many hindrances on the side of the σάρξ (ver. 17).—This is the immediate, inward "ought" that has place and is needful even with the believer. But to this inward monition and impulse of the Spirit, there must be added, in order to keep it ever alive and guard it against all impure admixture, one coming from without. Of this we have in this very section the speaking proof. The Apostle sees occasion given him to *admonish* the Galatian Christians with earnest words to a disposition and course of life answerable to their faith; he approaches them with an "Ought:" "So ought it to be with Christians = *because* you *believe* in Christ!" And his admonition here and elsewhere holds good also for us; it is the testimony of the Spirit conveyed through the *word—testimonium externum* (in distinction from *internum*)—the comprehensive exposition of which is the function of New Testament ethics.

3. That even the believer is not and cannot be spared the earnestly admonishing and impelling "ought" because even with him there is not found a steady will (on account of the old Adam), is the meaning of the church doctrine of the *tertius legis usus*, the *usus legis* with the *renatus* (the *us. didact.* or *normat.*), and understood in this sense it is correct. But as it is expressed it is distorted and incorrect, and is in conflict with the indisputable Pauline doctrine, that the believer is not ὑπὸ νόμον, that he may not be placed nor place himself under it. He is indeed under a law of the Spirit, so far as the Spirit admonishes, requires, rebukes, yet the Spirit does by no means merely this, but far more; this is the very least that he does. But especially is the believer in no sense whatever under the law of the letter, the Old Testament law, the proper *lex*, and with all its generalizing of the conception of *lex*, the *Formula Concordiæ*, nevertheless, in the section touching this matter does not really go beyond the Mosaic law. It does not arrive at the conception of the law of the Spirit (the law of faith), whether this is entirely inward, or expressed also in the word of Scripture (in the New Testament word of Scripture, which for the fulfilment of the ethical requirement presupposes the faith in Christ with what it has and gives). The law of the letter (the proper *lex*), has, it is true, its great significance for the believer, but it has its place not, so to speak, *after* Faith, but only *before* the same, as *pædagogus* (see above on chap. iii. 19 sq.); and in this sense it permanently *retains* its importance, and is indispensable for faith. That is, the sinfulness and imperfection of the new life even in the believer, make it needful that the law should not once only, but ever afresh, awaken in him the knowledge of sin and the impossibility of himself attaining salvation and eternal life, and by that very means drive him to assure himself of it in *faith* in Christ; and so ever impel him anew to faith. So far, therefore, as a *usus* of the *lex*, strictly so called, can be predicated even as to the *renatus*, it falls under the *usus pædagogicus*, as *usus secundus*. But in this pedagogy its function is continually exhausting itself again; *this function only does Paul ascribe to it*, and another, the

* [Whether theologians agree about terms or not, they all must recognize the fact that in so far as any law of God has a directly ethical purpose, it must continue to be binding on those who are Christ's, not binding as a law, with condemnatory power, so as to bring us again into bondage, after Christ has made us free, nor even binding on the conscience, so far as its punitive functions are concerned, but binding us with the cords of love, the bands of a man, a rule for the loving children of a Father, a guide for the glad gratitude of those whom Christ has made free. Thus far all that was of permanent ethical purpose in the Old Testament law must remain "the law of Christ;" to admit a change in God's ethics is repugnant to our souls. How much this includes is the practical question, which the New Testament itself answers in the life of Christ and the teachings of His Apostles. That it includes the Decalogue, that each and all of those Commandments are still in force, as a law, in the sense indicated above, there can be no reasonable doubt.—R.]

function *docere, ut in vera pietate vivemus et ambulemus, we* have no right to attribute to it, especially as we thereby come into conflict with the definite assurance that the law only stirs up sin and the σάρξ, and of itself continually hinders anew the Spirit's gaining dominion and therewith the attainment of the *vera pietas.* The law contributes directly neither to justification nor to the new life, and cannot therefore be directly the means of maintaining the latter. What it can and should do, was and is, to open the way for that which does lead to justification and to the new life, namely, Faith. As this is its work at first, so is it ever after. The *accomplishment* of these two things it must then leave to faith, first as that which lays hold of God's grace—for justification, then as that which has laid hold of it and therewith receives the Spirit. This Holy Ghost now, and not the νόμος, is alone in condition as the spirit of faith to assist to ever renewed victory over the σάρξ, partly through His teaching, partly through His monition, partly through His persuasion and drawing. For if the believer did right because admonished by the law, he would only attain again to ἔργα νόμου, but not to veritable ἔργα ἀγαθά.—Only so much is true, that *in concreto* very many a Christian, because faith has been with him from the beginning or has become only a name, allows himself to be guided merely by the law of the letter, at least if he has moral earnestness of temper, and thereby accomplishes nothing more than ἔργα νόμου, as to which he simply deceives himself, in accounting them perhaps for ἔργα τοῦ πνεύματος. More or less, moreover, does he seek in these ἔργα νόμου his justification also, and his hope; half-way at least, reckoning as the other half the merit of Christ, yet more in name than in reality. [It is only necessary to remark here, that Paul uses the word νόμος as covering the whole Mosaic law. That this whole Mosaic law has not the third use, of "teaching us how we may live and walk in true piety," is very evident. So also, that the new life of the believer is only a new life, in so far as it is through the teaching, monition, persuasion and drawing of the Spirit, must be believed and felt by the Christian. Still what does that Spirit teach and admonish us to do? To "walk even as he walked," all will agree. And how did He walk, that Master whom we follow?—He fulfilled all righteousness, He obeyed the law for us. Clearly then the Spirit, which receives of the things of Christ and shows them unto us, will show us as our duty, what Christ did, the complete obedience to God's requirements, and this will include all of permanent ethical value in the Mosaic law.—That may be *but* a part, yet it *is* a part, for what was in itself *right* at Sinai's foot is right at the foot of the cross. The Spirit is the Holy Spirit, Holiness is opposed to sin, Sin is opposition to God, it expresses itself in disobedience to His moral law,—the Holy Spirit must teach, admonish, persuade and draw us to the observance of whatever has been at any time an expression of God's moral law. The law cannot have a *usus pædagogicus* still, did it not convict us of sin; it cannot convict us of sin, unless its requirements are holy, and just and good; and as such the Spirit of Holiness must teach us the *moral* law still.—The controversy about the third use of the law, between the Lutherans and Reformed, seems to be one of terms. The only practical question that can arise out of it, is one respecting the obligation to observe the Fourth Commandment.—R.]

4. *Spirit and Flesh.* Πνεῦμα and σάρξ are the two polar antithesis, as the Apostle most vividly shows in this section, ver. 17. Πνεῦμα is the Holy Ghost, the Divine principle, that enters along with faith in Christ into the man, generating in him a divine temper and divine life, and that in conflict with the σάρξ and its παθήματα and ἐπιθυμίαι. Σάρξ is in itself simply (in antithesis to the Divine principle), human nature, of course the whole because the living nature, and embraces therefore body and soul. But it is not human nature on the side of its relation to God, but on the side of its alienation from God, on which side man with relation to God draws himself back upon himself, seeks himself and takes honor to himself, withdrawing it from God; in short human nature as sinful.—The use of "flesh" to denote human nature in general, is grounded in the Hebrew idiom, according to which בָּשָׂר is used by synecdoche for the whole man, and this idiom itself is in its turn, without doubt, grounded in the experience and Scriptural doctrine of the frailty of man, which induced the sacred writers to derive the designation for man generally, from that part of man in which his frailty is most conspicuous. As this frailty again has its ground, according to Biblical teaching, in man's alienation from God, there became connected with σάρξ, the established designation of human nature, the accessory idea of alienation from God=sinfulness. This took place in the proportion in which this view into man's alienation from God even from birth, as the deepest ground of his frailty, became clear, and in the New Testament, therefore, more than in the Old.—The expression σάρξ, therefore gives us no right whatever, to think of the bodily organism more than of the soul, and (with reference to the accessory notion of sinfulness,) to find intimated in the expression either the view of the derivation of sin from the body, or an especial reference to so-called fleshly sins more than others. (Comp. WIESELER's thorough exposition of this conception.)—The essential element in the idea of the σάρξ is the turning away from God and referring ourselves to ourselves, the self-seeking, egoistic element. This is primarily in respect to God, but immediately connected with it is the fact that a man in reference to other men also seeks himself, his enjoyment or his gain. It is easily explicable therefore why love appears as the first effect of the πνεῦμα, being the temper and act opposed to selfishness. In this section the Apostle has, it is true, special occasion to exhort to the love of our neighbor, but his speaking of love is not on this account merely casual. [Comp. on σάρξ, J. MÜLLER, *Christian doctrine of sin.*—R.]

## HOMILETICAL AND PRACTICAL.

Ver. 13. LUTHER:—The natural man understands nothing of the doctrine of grace; therefore comes it, when he hears this doctrine, that he straightway draws it down to his own lust and lewdness, and concludes on this wise: If the law concerns us not and has no right to us, then will we live as we list.—How we at this time have seen in all ranks that all will fain be evangelical and enjoy the Christian liberty, and yet nevertheless the great crowd goes its own way; this one follows his avarice, the other his lewdness, the third his pride and haughtiness, *etc.*—RIEGER:—The liberty to which we are called by the gospel, is not so intended that we may tear ourselves loose from the law at our own will and please the flesh.—Into such a freedom the law can with honor dismiss man; for through Christ and the curse borne on the cross the law has its highest honor, and sin or the flesh wins thereby no advantage. For precisely that which was impossible to the law, namely, to bring to pass an inward enduring hatred against evil and an inward cleaving to good, from a willing heart, is accomplished by faith in Christ, and therefore the liberty of faith is not against the law.—HEUBNER:—By the side of the highest good stands the highest evil, by the side of freedom, lawlessness. No word has been so abused and desecrated, as Freedom.

LUTHER:—"By love serve one another." We must diligently teach in religion both sorts of doctrine, of Faith and Works; yet so that we carry neither too far. Else, where one teaches Works alone, he loses Faith, but if one teaches concerning Faith alone, forthwith gross, carnal men begin to dream that works are not necessary. Yet must the doctrine of Faith be planted first, or it cannot be understood what good works really are.—Although we have been justified, yet have we still sin in us, which rhymes as ill with good works as with faith, but draws us away from both. Besides flesh and reason is so disposed that it has by nature all its delight and pleasure in Pharisaic and superstitious works, and does those works with far greater earnestness which itself has chosen, than those which God has commanded. Therefore have rightminded preachers as much to do, in admonishing the people to genuine love and really good works, as in teaching genuine faith.—Christians must consider thus, that in their conscience they are indeed free from the curse of the law, sin and death, but as to the body they are servants, for therein should one serve another by love.

Ver. 14. It is needless for any one to trouble you with circumcision and Moses' ceremonies; see to this before all things, that you remain steadfast in the doctrine of faith. Will you after that do good works, as indeed you should, I will with a single word point out to you the noblest and greatest of all works, which ye should do, that ye may fulfil all laws: Love one another! Therefore the true, perfect doctrine and Christian theology of Faith and Love is in long and in short this: Believe on Christ, love thy neighbor as thyself! It is most short, to look upon the words, but if it is to be practical, it is broader, higher and deeper than heaven and earth.—The reason imagines it a very low thing, to say nothing of its being an act of God's service, for one to help the other by love, *i. e.*, for one to instruct and set aright a wanderer, comfort a mourner and afflicted, support the weak, for every one to help his neighbor, as he can, and make up for that which he lacks; *item*, for one to be obedient to government, hold his parents in honor, to have patience at home and bear with a whimsical, strange-tempered yoke-fellow, with ill-mannered servants, *etc.*; all which amounts to this: By love serve one another. But believe me, they are not contemptible and mean, but excellent and precious works, because God has commanded them and they please Him. It is of no concern therefore, whether the world looks upon them as mean and contemptible or not.—It is a short word, but excellently and powerfully spoken: Love thy neighbor as thyself! We cannot give any one a better, more certain and more exact example, how he should love his neighbor, than if we say to him that he should love him so as he loves himself. Nor can one have a better, nor nobler virtue than Love, and this high virtue can be directed towards nothing better than towards our neighbor.—If thou wouldst know how thou shouldst love thy neighbor, consider diligently how dear thou art to thyself, that thou wouldst gladly have help and counsel given thee, if thou wert in distress and necessity, as much as all creatures could. Therefore needest thou no book, out of which to learn how thou shouldst love thy neighbor.—RIEGER:—The call of the gospel to Christ and the grace which has come by Him, the sense of being one Spirit with Christ, brings us under the law of Christ, where in love we have all at once, and assumes also the willingness to serve one another through love. The warding off the claims of faith in the gospel with the pretext of love to man, is a critical sign of our times.

Ver. 15. STARKE:—Hatred, envy and reviling are as the teeth of snakes and lions. What shame, that among Christians there is such an evil kind of people!—What mean these wearisome, and mischievous lawsuits?—LANGE:—Each vice brings in time some punishment with it, as every virtue has in advance some recompense. For even as love does him good that cherishes it, so does hatred and contention bring nothing but disquiet and ill-content, and indeed injures the body also in health.—RIEGER:—The biting begins on good pretexts; but men easily go further, to do mischief to the property, to disparage the merits, *etc.*—ROOS:—To bite and devour one another, is not only the wont of the populace, but also the way of many learned men, whereof their learned journals, reviews, *etc.*, bear witness. And so do they devour one another mutually, *i. e.*, they destroy altogether one another's credit and the usefulness which each yet had, perhaps also a part of their life. Their *esprit* is flesh, what may then the rest be?

Vers. 16, 17. LUTHER:—Paul means by lust of the flesh not alone unchastity, but also all other sinful cravings, whereby the saints are tempted. —It is impossible that you can follow the Spirit in all things whatever and not also feel the flesh, and that you should remain unhindered by it; yea, it will hinder you and so hinder you that you will not be able to do what you gladly would do. In this all that you can do is to withstand the flesh, which quickly becomes inflamed with anger, impatience, *etc.*; murmurs, hates, bites, becomes angry against God, falls into doubting; and to follow the Spirit, which admonishes you to peace, patience, hope, faith. To know this is for believers most profitable and comforting.

When I was yet a monk, I often thought that I must be lost, when I felt an evil temptation. Then undertook I many kinds of discipline, confessed every day, and yet it all helped me nothing. For the same temptations evermore recurred; therefore tormented I myself perpetually with such thoughts: See, there you have committed such and such a sin, *etc.*, therefore there is no help for you, all your good works are come to nothing. Had I then rightly understood St. Paul's words, I would not have tormented myself so severely, but would have considered with myself, as I am now wont to do: Dear Martin, it amounts to nothing, your leading an angelical life here on earth; so long as you live in the flesh, it will not give over its way. Yet do not therefore despond, but withstand it through the Spirit, that thou mayest not fulfil its lust, and it cannot hurt thee, because thou art in Jesus Christ. —Whoever thinks that a Christian must have no fault at all in him, and yet feels that in himself there are many and manifold shortcomings, such a one must at the last be consumed of melancholy. But whoever understands it, him must such temptation of the flesh, *i. e.*, evil, serve for his best good. For when the flesh will tempt to sin, he is led with earnestness to pray, to seek forgiveness of sins through Christ, to lay hold of the righteousness of the law, after which perhaps he would never have so greatly longed.—It is to Christians profitable and good that they feel such troublesomeness of the flesh, that they may not become proud over the supposed righteousness of their works, as if they were in favor with God on account of the same.

STARKE:—The contest of the flesh and the Spirit exists alone in the regenerate. The conflict which exists in an unregenerate man, so that he does not fulfil all evil lusts that stir in him, is only a conflict of the reason with its natural impulses and gross sensual desires. This is to be carefully distinguished from the former, that one may not, because he feels within himself a struggle against sin, immediately reckon himself regenerate.—The strife of the Spirit against the flesh is an infallible token of regeneration and a state of grace, and is distinguished from the strife which is waged by the mere powers of reason in this, that the former always wins the victory.—These words are misused by the children of the world to this effect, that it is vain to strive after a holy character, because we cannot, after all, do what we would. But mark, what the regenerate, who are spoken of here, will according to the Spirit, and what according to the flesh. They are not aiming first to obtain the dominion over sin, for this they have already, but they would fain quench and be rid of everything sinful; but this, on account of the flesh cleaving to them, they cannot do. According to the flesh they would fain let sin come to dominion again, but that they do not, because the Spirit strives against it and overcomes the flesh. Therefore it follows from this, that a believer can by all means live holy, but here can arrive at no perfection.

RIEGER:—The flesh and the sin which cleaves to the same, lust and its allurements and enticements we indeed experience, nay more, there may also occur cases where it is not as plain as we could wish that the lust has not been admitted and treacherously taken the will with it. But by renewal in the spirit of the mind one may always count himself to be no debtor to the flesh, to fulfil its lusts, but may take the curse from Christ's cross and hang it upon the flesh, and from Christ's Spirit may gain the willingness to separate therefrom. Between the strivings of the Spirit and of the flesh against each other it must become evident, which way the man, after receiving sufficient strength, is bending his will, and on which side he takes his stand. If the Spirit's impulses and leadings continue with a man and if he is honestly minded to obey the Spirit and its holy opposition to the flesh, he does not indeed deny the law the right to show him his imperfections, but he is not under it, and is not at the last judged by it. Christ has taken the believer under His atoning shield against the curse of the law, and has moreover bestowed on him His spirit, which impels him as to all other good, so also to combat for this faith, although there is many a conflict and many a doubt before he can without ceasing so believe and act.

Ver. 19. LUTHER:—It is a very different thing to be tempted by the flesh, and yet not to follow its lusts, but to walk in the Spirit and strive against them, from what it is to consent to the lust of the flesh and abide therein and nevertheless to make great boast of the Spirit, and to make as though one lived Christianly. The former St. Paul comforts, in that he says: Because they are ruled by the Spirit they are not under the law; but the others he threatens with everlasting damnation, in that he declares: They that do such things shall not inherit the kingdom of heaven.—SPENER:—By works of the flesh, Paul, it is true, understands principally actual outward, outbreaking deeds, but he does not thereby exclude inward vices, which are also rightly called works of the flesh. Nay, as respects the outward sins themselves, their sinfulness consists not merely in the outward deed itself, but in the evil and prevailing inclination thereto. Therefore is one guilty of adultery, fornication, gluttony, drunkenness, quarrelsomeness, *etc.*, who allows such vices to gain the upper hand in his soul, even though from want of opportunity, or fear of infamy or trouble he restrains himself from the outward act; for God looks on the heart and its longings.

"Drunkenness, revellings." In STARKE:—The Apostle is not speaking merely of the habit and custom of drinking; therefore it is a false excuse if any one thinks that a debauch is no sin if only one does not make a business of it. The devil invented this excuse. When any one so overfills himself that he is unfit for prayer and the business of his calling, that is drunkenness; what then are we to think of the respectable world with its sinful and damnable Christian drinking bouts? and what too of this continual drinking of healths, than as of a temptation to swill down liquor? — "They which do such things." It is not said: They that do such things daily; for even though one does any such thing only now and then, on certain occasions, yea even only once, but voluntarily, he forfeits the kingdom of God, so long as he remains under the dominion of this work of the flesh. Nor is it said: They that do all this. It is not needful for a man to do all these sins or many such, to fall under the penalty, but it is enough, if a man lets one single sin rule over him, let it be what it will. Now it rules over him, not only while he is committing it, but so long as the purpose never to commit it again, is not yet fully fixed.—They shall not only not procure eternal life by their works of the flesh (as may well be supposed), but, if they set their hopes, not upon earning eternal life by their works, but receiving it as a gift to be received by faith, they will not, leading a dissolute life, inherit it any more than earn it.—He inherits not the kingdom of grace, still less the kingdom of glory, even though his funeral sermon extols him as blessed, surely, very, or even most blessed.

Ver. 22. It is not enough to flee the manifest works of the flesh, but we must bring true virtues to take their place. The Spirit of Christ must water and warm the hearts of men with His heavenly consolation, if they are to be fruitful to good works.—"Works of the flesh," said Paul, as being what comes into view and can be apprehended by reason alone, as to what they are, and that they are evil; but he does not use this term of the fruits of the Spirit as being for the most part internal, and although they express themselves in outward works, yet they cannot be comprehended and judged by the mere reason; nay, reason, should she pronounce a judgment, would be more apt to pronounce a judgment against them. Indeed, the fruits of the Spirit often exist in good measure in those, who yet in true poverty of Spirit complain of the lack of them.—Roos:—All these fruits are found in every spiritual man, although in one this, in another that fruit is more richly possessed.

Luther:—*Joy*. This means the loving discourse of the bridegroom and his bride, *i. e.*, the joyful, loving thoughts, which a believing heart has concerning Christ, the wholesome admonitions, the joyful hymns, thanksgiving psalms and songs of praise, with which Christians admonish and cheer one another. The Scripture testifieth once and again, that God had no pleasure in the sadness of the spirit, but wills, that we be joyful in Him. Therefore also He sent His Son, not to make us perturbed and mournful, but joyful. Therefore do the Prophets, Apostles and Christ Himself admonish, yea, command us, that we be glad and joyful. Where this spiritual joy is, there does the heart inwardly rejoice through faith in Christ, and moreover shows forth such joy outwardly with words and gestures; yea, it can be joyful even in the midst of affliction and death. Such joy is to the world unknown.—*Patience*. This is a virtue of such sort, that one does not alone endure and suffer waywardness, ill-luck, wrong, *etc.*, but also bears long with those that do him such evil, and waits if perchance they may at some time amend themselves. The devil has this way, that when he cannot in tempting us overcome by main force and might, he watches nevertheless with wearisome continuance, and worries us out if he can, for he knows well what weak, earthen vessels we are, that cannot at the last endure violence and repeated hard strokes; therefore he oft gains great advantage, in that he perseveres so long and diligently.—*Gentleness*.—This is: that one is so disposed, that every one gets on well with him and loves to deal with him. For Christians should not be unfriendly and cross-tempered people, but mild, courteous, friendly, such as every one loves to consort with, who bear with others' faults, are easy to give way to others, and can put up with the whim of others. Such a courteous friendly man was our Lord Jesus Christ, as we see in the Gospel from beginning to end.

In Starke:—*Goodness*—All nature is to us a mirror of kindness. For where is there a creature that does not serve and do good to man? For us the sun shines, for us the earth bears fruit, us does the heaven cover, to us does the air minister breath, everything stands at our command; should we then be the only ones not to practice kindness?—Luther:—*Faith*.—He that has this faith, such an one suspects no evil of other people, but has a loving, simple heart towards every man; and although he be deceived, he yet remains long-suffering and kind, and forbears with him that hath deceived him. *In summa*, he believes every man and yet puts his confidence in no man but alone in God.—Roos:—Against spiritual men the law is not, for although they are not without fault yet they are wholly under grace (Rom. vi. 14), and are partakers of the blessing in Christ Jesus (Gal. iii. 13, 14). There are people, who imagine themselves to have preached the gospel, when they encourage others, by a human persuasion, to let go the Jewish way of thinking, not anxiously to count this or that for a sin, and to entertain no scruple about permitted things. But although such persuasions, addressed to a natural man, may bring about a show of freedom, and such a man may then imagine that he is no longer under the law, though he really is, yet the great question remains, whether the law is not against him. The right of the law to curse him, is not an usurpation, but a well-founded, sacred right, to which there is nothing to oppose but Christ's death on the cross. Has then every one who boasts of freedom become a believer in this crucified Saviour? And has he also, by means of this faith, become spiritual, so that he exhibits the fruit of the Spirit within him? It is only against such that the law is not.

Ver. 24. "Have crucified the flesh."—Starke:—This word well expresses how sin must, little by little, be disabled and slain, for the crucified man did not die at once; he was first made fast with nails to the cross and then kept there, till, through the loss of blood and through hunger and thirst he became weaker and weaker, and finally died. In the beginning of repentance the old man is nailed to the cross, and then in conversion he is fastened to it anew, when he gets a hand or a foot free; the soul carefully avoiding all occasions whereby evil lusts can be aroused, until indwelling sin is more and more disabled by all manner of acts of repentance and devotion, which are contrary to corrupt nature, which acts must extend through the whole life. But now all power to crucify the flesh is to be derived from Christ's death on the cross.

Rieger:—They that have ceased from the

law and all endeavors to obtain life and righteousness therefrom, and on the other hand belong to Christ and accept Him as the source of their life and holiness, such keep their flesh crucified. They are and live yet in the flesh, to be sure, and so experience how close sin cleaves and how heavy it weighs; they experience the enticements of inward lust, but they have learned from the gospel the meaning of God in the cross of Christ, and have believed it, and can believe the judgment executed on the body of their Redeemer as in God's eyes in force also against their own flesh. And indeed they desire no rest for the flesh, but impose on it the curse, which through Christ's cross is imposed thereon, and behold this wearisome and painful dying with a hope gathered out of the gospel.

On vers. 13–15. Christianity and Freedom: (1) How little we have occasion, on behalf of freedom, to repent of being Christians and becoming Christians more and more; (2) how deeply we must rue that freedom which we do not establish and confirm by the power of Christ.—The Christian is free and yet a servant of all.—The right union of Freedom and Love (1) needful (2) difficult.—By love serve one another! (1) An actual (2) but also a blessed service.

On vers. 16–24: Walk in the Spirit, *etc.*, ye shall not fulfil the lust of the flesh: (1) the lust of the flesh, (2) the resisting of it in the Spirit. —The walk in the Spirit; (1) is not accomplished without conflict (ver. 17) (2) but saves from destruction (vers. 19–21), (3) leads to a glorious goal (ver. 22).—With his exhortations to walk in the Spirit (1) the Apostle places us upon a fearful battle-field (ver. 17), (2) gives us the view into a frightful abyss (ver. 19 sq.), (3) leads us into a lovely garden (ver. 22 sq.). The conflict of the flesh and the Spirit: (1) in what does it consist? (2) to what should it impel?—Temptations through the flesh must come: despond not!—but must be combatted and overcome through the Spirit: be not careless!—There is no believer so holy or strong that he does not feel his flesh, but also none so weak that he cannot withstand it.—The motions of the flesh a damper to pride, a testimony against self-devised spiritualism.—Three times three fruits of the Spirit; a lovely garland. —To have crucified the flesh a token that one is Christ's.—Who can crucify his flesh? Only he who is Christ's.—The crucifying of the flesh (1) takes place indeed, when one is Christ's, but (2) does not of itself make certain that one is Christ's.

Kapff:—Under what law is the believer? (1) Not under that of the flesh, (2) not under that of Moses, but (3) under that of the Spirit.—Rautenberg:—The crucifixion of the flesh: a token of true Christianity, a work of the Holy Ghost, a victory of Christian freedom, a progress to inward peace.—In Lisco:—The conflict of the Spirit with the flesh: (1) Where does it arise? Only where a life in the Spirit is begun. (2) Why is it necessary? *a*) On account of the inward incompatibility of flesh and Spirit, *b*) on account of the consequences, which proceed therefrom, good or evil fruits. (3) How should it end? By the Spirit's overcoming the flesh.—The walk in the Spirit: (1) It kills the works of the flesh, (2) it brings in its place the fruits of the Spirit.—Flesh or Spirit? Choose! (1) The flesh is thy destruction; (2) the Spirit creates divine life; (3) as Christians we are bound to the life of the Spirit.—(*Fast-day Sermon*): The call on Fast-day: the works of the flesh are manifest. (1) What works are works of the flesh: (2) what those have to expect, who do such works.—(*Whit-Sunday Sermon*): We are partakers of the Holy Spirit only when we do the works of the Spirit.—Genzken:—What do we yet lack of a walk in the Spirit? (1) The beginning is, that the flesh lusteth against the Spirit and the Spirit against the flesh, and many have not even advanced so far; (2) the next step is, that we no more fulfil the lusts of the flesh, and many are not even ashamed of the manifest works of the flesh; (3) the consummation is, that we bring forth the fruits of the Spirit, and from that we are all yet far distant.—Greiner:—Flesh and Spirit: (1) they are contrary one to the other; (2) their ways lead asunder in time and eternity.—Engelhard:—The life of that man, who is ruled by the Spirit of God: (1) He breaks with sin and mortifies daily the old man; (2) he is filled with the fruits of righteousness, which do not conflict with the law, but which can never be accomplished under the dominion of the law; (3) and receives accordingly the most excellent of all rewards, the inheritance of the kingdom of God.

Vers. 13–24. Frantz:—Beware that ye do not, through freedom, give a handle to the flesh, for (1) freedom in Christ is not without law; it has its law, only not in the members, but in Christ, which law is love. (2) It is not without control; but its control is exercised not by the flesh, but by the Spirit.

2. More special Admonition to the Walk in the Spirit (to serving Love), or warning against excessive self-valuation and envious selfishness.

(CHAP. v. 25, 26.—vi. 1–10.)

(*Epistle for the fifteenth Sunday after Trinity.*)

25, 26 If we live in [by][1] the Spirit, let us also walk in [by] the Spirit. Let us not
be desirous of vain-glory [become vain-glorious], provoking one another, envying
one another.

a. Warning against unloving self-exaltation above others (vi. 1-5).

VI. 1 Brethren, if [even if][3] a man be overtaken in a fault, ye which [who] are
spiritual, restore such a one in the spirit of meekness; considering thyself, lest thou
2 also [shouldst] be tempted. Bear ye one another's burdens, and so [or thus shall
3 ye] fulfil[4] the law of Christ. For if a man think himself to be something, when he
4 is nothing, he deceiveth himself. But let every [each] man prove his own work,
and then shall he have rejoicing in himself alone, and not in another [his ground of
boasting only in what concerneth himself, and not in what concerneth the other].[5]
5 For every [each] man shall bear his own load.[6]

b. Warning against envious selfishness.—Admonition to unweariedness in doing good, especially to teachers of the word (vers. 6–10).

6 Let [But let] him that is taught in the word communicate unto him that teacheth in
7 all good things. Be not deceived; God is not mocked: for whatsoever a man sow-
8 eth, that shall he also reap. For he that soweth to his [own] flesh shall of the flesh
reap corruption; but he that soweth to the Spirit shall of the Spirit reap life ever-
9 lasting And [But] let us not be weary[7] in well doing: for in due season we shall
10 reap, if we faint not. As we have therefore [Accordingly then as we have][8] oppor-
tunity, let us do good[9] unto all *men*, especially unto them who are of the household
of faith.

1 Ver. 25.—[The dative Πνεύματι has perhaps a slightly different force in each member of this verse, but "by" will express the meaning in each case, better than "in."—R.]

2 Ver. 26.—["Become vain-glorious" is both a more literal and a more correct rendering of γινώμεθα κενόδοξοι.—R.]

3 VI. 1.—["Even if" preserves the force of καί.—R.]

4 Ver. 2.—'Αναπληρώσετε is strongly supported; and is to be preferred (with Lachmann and Schott) to the reading σατε; the latter was perhaps occasioned by the preceding imperatives. It is found however in ℵ., where, singularly enough, we have the moods reversed, βαστάσετε occuring in the preceding clause. ℵ[3]. however reads βαστάζετε. [The future, ἀναπληρώσετε, is the reading of ℵ[3]. B. F. G., most versions; it is adopted by Meyer, De Wette, Mill, Ellicott, Lightfoot. The aorist imperative, σατε, is found in A. C. D. E. K., most cursives, Tischendorf (later eds.), Alford, Wordsworth. The aorist imperative is rare, and this is an argument in favor of retaining it. If it be retained, the E. V. is correct, with the other reading, it must be emended as above. The question is not easily settled, since the external authority is so nearly balanced.—R.]

5 Ver. 4.—[Ellicott paraphrases as above. The E. V. is not satisfactory. See EXEG. NOTES.—R.]

6 Ver. 5.—["Load" is a good rendering. "Burden" is open to this great objection, that it does not discriminate between φορτίον and βάρη (ver. 2).—R.]

7 Ver. 9.—['Εγκακῶμεν is the correct reading. ℵ. A. B. Lachmann, Tischendorf, Alford, Ellicott, Wordsworth, Lightfoot. It is doubtful whether ἐκκακεῖν (Rec. ἐκκακῶμεν) is a genuine word.—R.]

8 Ver. 10.—['Αρα οὖν, "accordingly then," see EXEG. NOTES.—R.]

9 Ver. 10.—'Εργαζώμεθα. The reading ἐργαζόμεθα is too weakly supported. [So all modern Editors. Lachmann at first adopted the latter reading, but soon discarded it.—R.]

## EXEGETICAL AND CRITICAL.

Paul, after the exhortation, ver. 13 (and the more general one, ver. 16), had passed on to a more didactic exposition. But from ver. 25 on, he returns to the general exhortation to "walk by the Spirit" (which, as he means it, is essentially equivalent to exercising serving love) immediately specifying it more particularly, ver. 26; vi. 1 sq.

Ver. 25. **If we live by the Spirit.**—*Ζῆν πνεύματι* means of course not the outward life, the realization in walk of this life in the Spirit, for the words "let us also walk," *etc.*, are the first in which the Apostle exhorts them to stamp the life by the Spirit upon the outward walk. Ζῆν therefore means the inner life, and the spiritual life is here referred to, as one at first entirely internal. It is not improbable that "live" is to be taken here in a pregnant sense (MEYER)=if we are living through the Spirit, *i. e.*, death occurs to the man, who is Christ's, with respect to the "flesh;" but in another respect precisely thus does Life come in; the death of the old man introduces the life of the new (comp. ii. 19, 20), and this latter is grounded upon the "Spirit." [There is some doubt as to the force of the dative *πνεύματι* here. Schmoller renders it *durch den Geist;* MEYER calls it ablatival, and ELLICOTT says it is "here adopted rather than *διά* with the accusative as thus forming a sharper antithesis to the dative which follows." ALFORD follows the E. V., but, while objecting to the ablatival dative, gives the same sense to the word. LIGHTFOOT renders "to the Spirit," after the parallel passage, Rom. vi. 2, 10: "die unto sin," *etc.* But the first view is preferable.—R.]—**Let us also walk by the Spirit,**=*περιπ. πν.* ver. 16. [Schmoller thus makes the second *πνεύματι* an instrumental dative, but it seems better to take it as a normal dative (so ver. 16) with MEYER, ELLICOTT, *et al.* The verb *στοιχεῖν* seems to imply a more studied following of a prescribed course.—The Greek order is striking: "If we live by the Spirit, by the Spirit also let us walk." "By" has both the instrumental and normal force in English.—R.] In what this walk should consist is then shown.

Ver. 26. **Let us not become vain-glorious.**—The walking by the Spirit (or walking in love) should show itself thus. Κενόδοξον εἶναι= *vanam gloriam captare,* to affect vain-glory. [Γινώμεθα, "become" vain-glorious, there being in the verb as well as in the use of the first person an intentional *mildness* as though the sin had not yet taken root (ELLICOTT).—R.] The sense appears to be: we should not seek glory by provoking one another and envying one another, for such glory is "vain," worthless.—**Provoking one another.**—Ἀλλήλους προκαλούμενοι, by vaunting in the presence of those to whom we feel ourselves superior, by pressing our superiority.—**Envying one another.**—Ἀλλήλοις φθονοῦντες, not favoring one another, enviously refusing to acknowledge the good qualities that a man possesses. (Φθονεῖν is to be taken in this sense here, see below on vers. 6, 10.)—The seeking of vain-glory naturally goes hand in hand with provoking and envious behavior. Where the former is abandoned, the latter also disappears. The warning of this verse is nothing else than the admonition to serve one another by means of love (ver. 13), somewhat more particularly defined. The Apostle now reverts to this, in order to give it a more precise application. The remark on ver. 16, that the exhortation of the Apostle may have had a direct connection with the main theme of the Epistle, since the intrusion of the false teachers might very naturally have provoked a bitter party strife in the churches, applies also to the more special application of that admonition (ver. 13) in this section. Especially is it not improbable that through the intrusion of the false teachers the relation of the individual members to their teachers had been disturbed, thus giving occasion to the earnest admonition, vi. 6 sq. Yet this conjecture is not absolutely necessary; we need only suppose that some circumstances in the churches gave him particular occasion to direct his exhortation to this point.—[The context seems to justify the close connection of what follows with this verse. It is urged, however, that "brethren" indicates a change of topic (comp. iv. 12), and also that the change from the first to the second person favors the opinion that a new paragraph begins with vi. 1. But the thoughts are too closely linked, to allow these arguments from mere forms of expression to be conclusive against the close connection which MEYER and others defend.—R.]

VI. Vers. 1–5. These verses extend the warning of v. 26, against "provoking one another." The Christian instead of using any advantage he may possess over another, or any defect he may observe in him, to exalt himself above him (and thereby to provoke him), should, as walking by the Spirit, do just the reverse, should set his neighbor right, when he sees him at fault (ver. 1) and then help him bear the burdens which oppress him (ver. 2). Ver. 3 justifies these admonitions by the remark that a man's thinking himself to be something, when he is nothing, is self-cheatery; for it is such a vain imagining that underlies the refusal to set others right (in the spirit of meekness) and to carry their burdens. As the right means to be saved from this self-deception, Paul proceeds to commend self-examination. (On this, see below, vers. 4, 5.) [ELLICOTT thinks it probable "that the teachers are mainly addressed in vers. 1–6, and the hearers and laity in vers. 6–10." But while there are points in the exhortation specially applicable to classes thus distinguished, it seems best not to discriminate thus, for it limits the force of some parts of the exhortation, and might lead to an incorrect interpretation of ver. 1.—R.]

Ver. 1. [**Brethren.**—BEZA: a whole argument lies hidden under this one word.—R.]—**Even if a man be overtaken.**—Προληφθῇ: *πρό* expresses undoubtedly the unexpectedness of the being taken=before a man is aware, or is able to offer resistance. The *ἐν* shows that the verb is here to be understood as=to entangle, so that **in a fault,** according to the frequent Biblical image, is used of the snare in which any one is caught (WIESELER). LUTHER gives the sense quite correctly: "*übereilt,*" overtaken. [The strictly temporal reference (before the arrival of the Epistle, or a recurrence of the offence) is unsatisfactory. ELLICOTT, ALFORD and LIGHTFOOT join *καί* with the verb: "if a man be even surprised," *i. e.*, caught before he can escape, *flagrante delicto;* thus implying an aggravation of the offence. But it is not necessary to connect *καί* thus, and such a meaning of the verb is rare, while the interpretation does not accord with the context so well as the common view given above. MEYER: The Apostle charitably regards the sins, which may occur among the Galatians, as *peccata precipitantiæ.*—R.]

**Ye who are spiritual.**—This refers back to ver. 25=ye who have the Holy Ghost, show your possession of it, your living by the Spirit, by such action. He thus describes "provoking one another," as something repugnant to their very character. In view of this exalted predicate, which he ascribes to them, they should now reflect, what demeanor is the becoming one for them as "spiritual." This implies that they are not now conducting themselves agreeably to this designation, or such admonitions would be unnecessary. [The general character of the exhortation forbids our finding in this phrase a reference to a party of more liberal views, who had taken his side against the Judaizers, and were not paying sufficient regard to the weaker brethren. Hence there is no irony, but he is giving a test for their spirituality. It is true those who would stand the test, who were really led by the Spirit, would necessarily be the adherents of Paul, as the representative of the freedom of the gospel, but there is no evidence that there was such a party when he wrote.—R.]—But to the validity of this claim to be "spiritual," it is necessary that, when a brother is overtaken in a fault, the πνευματικός should **restore such a one**, should bring him into his normal state, instead of turning this fall into an occasion of self-exaltation against him. [Καταρτίζετε: the verb is properly a surgical term, applied to the setting of a joint, here used in an ethical sense, the idea of amendment being more prominent than that of punishment. The figurative meaning would perhaps imply some official act of restoration, but this is forbidden by the context.—R.] This "restoring" (or the wish for it) is the main idea, and not strictly speaking, as is commonly assumed, **the spirit of meekness**; or at least not this alone. This latter phrase only states the manner in which the setting right should be performed. This spirit must attend the act, or there is no real restoration, only a seeming one, in which the irritating lust of praise still seeks its gratification. It is forced, to understand "spirit" of the Holy Spirit, whose character is meekness, or rather who bestows meekness; it signifies the human spirit disposed to meekness. The foregoing "spiritual" does not require us to understand the Holy Spirit here, comp. 1 Cor. iv. 21. [It does not mean merely "a meek spirit," but a spirit whose characterizing quality is "meekness," with an ultimate reference to the Holy Spirit. (See ELLICOTT.) As "spiritual," possessing the Holy Spirit, their spirit toward offenders should be characterized by "meekness."—R.]—**Considering thyself.**—An individualizing transition to the singular. The added clause contains a motive to "restore" (not merely to "meekness").—**Lest thou also should be tempted**—and it happen to thee to be overtaken in a fault.

Ver. 2 makes the admonition of ver. 1 more general. It is not always by setting our neighbor right, that we may do him good; another exhibition of love is to bear his burdens.—**Burdens.**—Βάρη is undoubtedly in itself quite general: whatever presses our neighbor, lies heavy upon him, so that occasion is given to the vain-glorious man to provoke him. Moral delinquencies, such as are named in ver. 1, are included; but also more grievous things, such as outward distress.—**Bear.**—*Βαστάζετε*, of course, does not mean: endure (for I do not endure what oppresses my neighbor, but only that, for example, with which he oppresses me), but simply: bear=to take upon our shoulders as our own burdens, and thereby help him to bear; this includes, in some circumstances, the lightening of them; in others, their entire removal (WIESELER).—We see that the restoring of a neighbor who has been overtaken in a fault falls under this general idea of bearing his burden.—The Apostle adds to this admonition a powerful motive for its fulfilment: **and thus shall ye fulfil the law of Christ.**—The expression "fulfil the law of Christ" is significant, and designedly chosen with reference to the zealots for the law. You will forsooth have a law, now see here is a law but "of Christ;" fulfil that! At the same time it refers back to ver. 14, where the duty of love to our neighbor has been designated as the commandment equivalent to the whole Mosaic law, but a "law of Christ," not of Moses. [Yet this "law of Christ" must necessarily include that "law." which He not only came to fulfil, but so fully illustrated and enforced in His teachings. The use of the future indicative instead of the imperative seems to imply, that the Christian needs "the law of Christ" only as a guide to grateful duty. "Thus shall ye fulfil" what your hearts would fulfil, "the law of Christ," "who died for us and rose again."—R.]

Ver. 3. **For if a man think himself to be something, when he is nothing.**—"When he is nothing" belongs to the protasis. Being nothing: not precisely in the ethical sense alone, but one, who can in truth make no claim to consideration above others, yet ambitiously assumes this. This of course involves the admission that one may be something, but such a one is least likely to assume this; it is the one that is nothing, who is most likely to lay claim to consideration above his merits.—**He deceiveth himself,** his "glory" shows itself to be "vain," [LIGHTFOOT: "φρεναπατᾷ, 'deceives by his fancies.' Comp. Tit. i. 10. More is implied by this word than by ἀπατᾶν, for it brings out the idea of *subjective fancies* and thus enforces the previous δοκεῖ. It was possibly coined by St. Paul, for it seems not to be found in any earlier writer, and at a later date occurs chiefly, if not solely in ecclesiastical authors."—R.]

Ver. 4. Paul therefore immediately after enjoins: **let each man prove his own work.** —Τὸ ἔργον: not collective=the aggregate of his actions; for it is not particularly an ethical self-examination that is referred to, but general, about equivalent to: His case, the way matters stand with him. [The view of MEYER, ALFORD, ELLICOTT, *et al.*, that τὸ ἔργον is emphatic and collective, seems on the whole preferable.—R.]—The reason why he enjoins this, is then stated with: **then shall he have his ground of boasting only in what concerneth himself and not in what concerneth the other.**—"He will then have matter of self-gratulation only it will be in reference to himself, and not to another." [See the excellent note of ELLICOTT, the results of whose exegesis are given in the above rendering. The preposition εἰς must be translated by a paraphrasis, in order to preserve the same force in both cases. Τὸν ἕτερον, "the other"—the man with whom he was comparing himself; general in its meaning, but particular in each case of comparison. (ALFORD.)—R.] Every one, in that case, directing his look as he does in self-examination only upon himself, will refer his self-praise only to himself; will only boast of such excellences as he may discover in himself; but he will not vaunt himself on the ground of the deficiencies which he finds in others. And if this results from the very *nature* of self-examination, as directing the look of the man upon himself alone, it will also be sure to come to pass from the result, which every one will find from self-examination, as this is stated in ver. 5, with which Paul gives special weight to the *οὐκ εἰς τὸν ἕτερον*. Of course not to the *εἰς ἑαυτόν*. In order to have *εἰς τὸν ἕτερον καύχημα*, *i. e.*, in order to be able to make what another lacks a ground for boasting over him, one must not only have many good qualities but a preeminence *above* the other, of which he is conscious.

Ver. 5. But this is not the case. On the contrary *ἕκαστος τὸ ἴδιον φορτίον βαστάσει*, **each man**: I as well as the other, I cannot therefore make his *φορτίον*, a ground of vaunting myself against him.—**Shall bear.**—Future, expressing the result of the self-examination, because it succeeds it (not referring to the last judgment) = it will turn out, that every one has a burden of his own to bear, [*i. e.*, now in actual life, he is appointed to bear, must bear.—R.]—**His own load.**—*Φορτίον*: although principally meaning moral imperfection, yet here it is not to be limited to this; it means imperfection of every kind, every defect which one discovers in himself. *Φορτίον* is in itself a *vox media*, it may be either heavy or light; *βάρος* can only be heavy. To this general declaration the more general word exactly suits; respecting the degree of burdensomeness Paul does not in the first instance mean to make a statement, but only to say that each one has his own *φορτίον*. It is otherwise in ver. 2: there the idea of heaviness is the main one. [CONYBEARE finds here an allusion to Æsop's fable (*πῆραι δύο*), but ELLICOTT thinks this not very plausible. LIGHTFOOT says: "*βάρη* suggests the idea of an adventitious and oppressive burden, which is not implied in *φορτίον*. The latter is the common term for a man's pack. Each Christian soldier bears his own kit." Still this does not sufficiently imply the idea of imperfection and consequent grievousness, which the context, with its injunctions to self-examination, seems to demand.—R.]—The difficulty in vers. 4 and 5 is, that the Apostle condenses together two thoughts: 1. "in what concerneth himself alone," 2. "not in what concerneth the other;" which to be sure are in one aspect identical, and yet must be distinguished, because the second is strengthened by the subsequent declaration, "for each man," *etc.*, which gives it a somewhat different sense from what it has when disjoined from this and taken with what precedes. DE WETTE takes it differently: And then will he have his joy (if he has any, which is manifestly put as doubtful) for himself alone (for his own joy) and not for others (to irritate and provoke them therewith).—Self-examination is therefore the antidote to "provoking one another;" it is to oppose this that the Apostle has enjoined it.

Vers. 6–10. This division also is a specifying of the admonition v. 26; it must, although more remotely related, still have reference to it, because it is undeniably a carrying out of the admonition to "serve one another by means of love," (v. 13,) of which, as we have seen, v. 26, only gives the negative expression. More accurately considered this division opposes the second vice named in v. 26, "envying one another." It contains admonitions to an abounding, unwearied "communication in good things," and this is the direct opposite of "envying one another"=grudgingly withholding. Only he who is unenvious will do good to all.

Ver. 6. The exhortation in this verse does not therefore come in so abruptly, as at first sight appears. Paul first opposes envious grudging in that relation in which it looks particularly ill, and yet must have occurred, in the relation of **him that is taught** in the word of God to **him that teacheth**, and in contrast with this, admonishes to **communicate** and that **in all good things.** This is of course not= in all that is morally good (MEYER), but = in all good things [*i. e.*, temporal possessions of every kind.—R.]. It is expressed with the utmost generalness, and is therefore to be understood in its broadest sense; care for temporal support is included in it, but not exclusively intended; there is to be, according to the words, a sharing of all good things, that is, in a certain sense a community of benefits; he "that is taught" is to give "him that teacheth" a share in all his advantages. This is the very strongest antithesis to "envying." [The verb means literally "go shares with." It is intransitive here, followed by the dative of the person, and the *thing* ("in all good things") governed by a preposition. There is no lexical or grammatical difficulty. Almost all commentators refer the verse to the temporal support of ministers. MEYER gives it an ethical meaning mainly to preserve the connection, and Schmoller, for the same reason, makes the meaning general, as above. But *δέ* arrests the former topic before it passes out of sight (LIGHTFOOT), and serves here to indicate the contrast between the temporal and spiritual application (ELLICOTT). As if he had said: "I spoke of bearing one another's burdens. There is one special application I would make of this rule. Provide for the temporal wants of your teachers in Christ." *Κατηχούμενος* here means simply "instructed," and is followed by an accusative of reference (*λόγον*), "in the word," *i. e.*, the gospel.—R.]

Vers. 7–10. To give weight to this admonition to him that is taught in the word that he should show a generous liberality in all things to his teacher, Paul points to the last judgment, to the law of Divine retribution as one of immutable validity. This is primarily meant to strengthen only the special admonition, ver. 6, and shows how earnestly he means it, that he attributes to it an importance which we may not in any way lessen; but still this confirmatory reference to Divine retribution is expressed with such generalness, that Paul is able immediately to deduce from it an entirely general exhortation to unwearied "well doing," which he then again specializes somewhat in ver. 10. But the main matter is still the "communicating in all good things" in opposition to "envying one another."

Ver. 7. **Be not deceived.**—Do not entertain the erroneous thought, even should it occur, or be presented to you, that **God** can be **mocked** (lit., to turn up the nose at), that is, with success. (All glory sought therein is vain.) This mocking would occur, if man might do what he would, if he could with impunity neglect a communication of good things to his teacher, who himself imparts that which is best to him. The declaration that this cannot occur, is established by **for whatsoever a man soweth, that shall he also reap.***—[Τοῦτο καί; "this and nothing else than this" (ELLICOTT).—R.] The essential correspondence between the seed sown and the fruit reaped, which takes place according to a law of nature and is therefore subject to no mutation, is a current image in other writings also (even in profane writers, *e. g.* Cicero, *de Orat.* II. 65, *ut sementem faceris, ita metes*, and others), for the exact correspondence between the retribution of God in the judgment and the moral acts of man in his earthly life.

Ver. 8. The general proposition of ver. 7 is established in this verse. **For**, never will it fail of coming to pass, that **he that soweth to his own flesh shall** therefrom **reap corruption**; and even so **he that soweth to the Spirit shall of the Spirit reap life everlasting.**—"Corruption" is therefore conceived as that which corresponds to sowing to the flesh, as the harvest to the seed, or "corruption" is essentially the crop into which the flesh when sown develops, and in like manner "life everlasting" is nothing else than the ripened fruit sown to the Spirit.—Ὁ σπείρων, it may be remarked, does not alter the figure in ver. 7b, making it the soil instead of the seed, but, as Paul has to speak of two different sorts of seeds, he only designates this difference according to the difference of the soil, on which it is sown; for seed is always chosen according to the soil that is to be sown; that which is sown upon the flesh is even thereby a different seed from that which is sown upon the Spirit. Perhaps it would be better to say: ὃ in ver. 7 is not merely tó be understood of the seed itself, but of the whole manner and method of the sowing, and so to be taken as equivalent to this: According as any one sows, even so shall he also reap; and in view of this "according as" we should have in ver. 8 to understand especially the soil which is sown, inasmuch as it is especially on this that the character of the harvest depends, as good or bad. For it is this that is treated of here. Flesh and Spirit, moreover, are figuratively represented as the soil, because they are conditioning, quickening factors, and therefore to sow upon the flesh or Spirit generically = to let one's self be determined in the act by the flesh or Spirit. Πνεῦμα of course, as in ver. 16 sq. = the Holy Ghost, and therefore lacks ἑαυτοῦ, which stands with σάρξ.† Φθορά, agreeably to the contrast with ζωὴ αἰώνιος = Destruction, Ruin, and that eternal ruin = ἀπώλεια, θάνατος, not = Transitoriness.—Ver. 8 was only a proof of ver. 7b, according to its two contrasted sides; 7b itself again was in proof of θεὸς οὐ μυκτηρίζεται. The sense of this is: One cannot neglect doing good, without being punished of God. But the thought is not expressed.

Ver. 9. Here, however, it is expressed affirmatively, agreeably to 8b, as an admonition (because it is true, as said in vers. 7 and 8, that what a man sows, he reaps) to do "well," in a certain sense to sow τὸ καλόν. That the admonition rests immediately upon what precedes, is shown by the continuance of the image, which we find at least in the second clause.—**Well doing** is to be taken in its greatest possible extension; agreeably to the signification of καλόν, about = to do what is praiseworthy, only it must not be taken so generally as no longer to fall within the sphere of unenvious exhibition of love towards our neighbor. This is the frame, within which this "well doing" also falls.—**Let us not be weary.**—["Behave cowardly, lose heart."—R.] It is possible to grow weary, because "well doing" is at first a sowing, which, according to the laws of nature, is not immediately, perhaps not till long after, followed by the harvest. It comes **in due season**, καιρῷ ἰδίῳ, not just when we wish it: at the precise time, when it can appear according to its inward law, as ordained by God. Agreeably to the eschatological expectations of the Apostle we have here to understand particularly the Parusia.—**If we faint not.**—Μὴ ἐκλυόμενοι, to be taken as conditional and to be referred to the sowing: if we do not become weary in that. This is no "languid repetition of the warning against ἐγκακεῖν" (USTERI); for it is just this not becoming weary in good which Paul wishes to emphasize, as the condition of reaping the harvest (WIESELER). [BENGEL: *ἐγκακεῖν est in velle, ἐκλύεσθαι est in posse.* The latter is a consequence of the former (LIGHTFOOT). The verse is one of mingled warning and encouragement, and the latter element appears from the promise to those who do not "faint," for one may be "weary," and not yet have fainted.—R.]

Ver. 10. [**Accordingly then as we have.**—Ἄρα οὖν, "so then," "accordingly then;" ὡς, not "while," nor "according as," nor since, but "in proportion as" (ALFORD).—R.] The mention of the "season" of the harvest reminds him to warn against wasting the καιρός, season, **opportunity**, of the sowing, because when the former is come, it will be too late for the latter. And in conclusion Paul deduces from the more general admonition (ver. 9) the more special exhortation **let us do good**, which is also to be taken in the widest possible extent, but still retaining the special idea of doing good. The generic interpretation of ἐργαζώμεθα τὸ ἀγαθόν = to do what is morally good (MEYER, as in ver. 6), is inconsistent especially with the distinction, which Paul makes with **especially**, *etc.* For to the doing of what is morally good, one is of course equally obliged towards *all* men, members of the household of faith or strangers to it (WIESELER).—**To them who are of the household of faith.**—Οἰκεῖοι τῆς πίστεως, doubt-

*[LIGHTFOOT calls attention to the fact that this proverb occurs in 2 Cor. ix. 6, in reference to the collection for the poor saints at Jerusalem, to which object the Galatians had been asked to contribute (1 Cor. xvi. 1); he therefore conjectures that this implies a general censure of their habitual niggardliness.—R.]

†[Perhaps as LIGHTFOOT suggests to bring out the idea of selfishness. It need not be made emphatic, but is best retained in English by "to his own flesh."—R.]

ress not merely=those belonging to faith, as an amplification of the simple term: Believers (MEYER), but kindred in faith, fellow-Christians, as constituting together one οἶκος τῆς πίστεως, one family of faith.* The emphasis rests upon the fact that believers are *of one family;* for this is the reason why love should be especially shown to them (WIESELER).—The expression is of course general and comprehends their fellow-Christians as a body, but yet it refers back to ver. 6; because their fellow-Christians should be so especially the objects of the "doing good," it follows from this, that those who teach should least of all be excluded therefrom. Paul in 1 Cor. xvi. 1, 2, refers to a more specific instruction concerning beneficence which he had given to the Galatians.

### DOCTRINAL AND ETHICAL.

1. *Self-exaltation and self-seeking.* In respect to the right conduct of Christians towards each other, Paul designates two vices as especially incompatible therewith: Self-exaltation and self-seeking. And indeed there is nothing which more undermines society in general than these two vices; while self-exaltation rends the inner bond of unity with our fellow-men, self-seeking rends besides this the outer bond. But now the maintaining of fellowship is the specific character of the relation of Christians to each other; they are meant to form an undivided whole. These two vices therefore stand in diametrical opposition to the very nature of the Christian life. And of course they must, for they are the immediate offspring of the "flesh," whose essence is self-seeking. But Christians should walk by the Spirit, and should prove this to each other especially by serving love.—Certain as it is therefore, that both self-exaltation and self-seeking stand opposed to the essence of Christian fellowship, and must therefore be most vigorously contended against, it is nevertheless equally certain, that they may, and do in fact, appear within the circle of Christian fellowship. For this is by no means as yet pure and free from such manifestations of the "flesh," though not thereby necessarily losing the name of Christian fellowship. On the contrary an individual or a community may really "have the Spirit," be possessed of a spiritual life, while yet in their walk the sarcical element still manifests itself in various ways, against which we must protest. Things must be rebuked which, looking at the ideal, and not at the concrete fact, might appear impossible to occur; admonitions must be given, which might from the ideal point of view appear superfluous. The admonitions given in this section are the simple proof of what was remarked on the former section, respecting the indispensableness of continual admonition, respecting the "shall" which the Spirit inwardly, as also the Word of Scripture from without, must continually present to the Christian. While therefore we must not be lax, as if every thing in the Christian life, including the fruits of the Spirit, came of itself, and while we must earnestly represent to the Christian the incongruity of every thing sarcical with his faith, we must on the other hand be very careful not to make rigoristic requirements of him, not to expect that no manifestation of the flesh should ever appear in him; we must not, in particular, imagine that among Christians every thing must, as it were, of itself, be serving love. And therefore, even when many virtues of the Christian life are yet very defective, we must not be quick to deny that one is "spiritual," to dispute the sincerity of his faith and declare him to be a hypocrite.

2. *Admonitions especially necessary for those busy about the law.* "But was it then necessary, one might here ask, that Paul should write such admonitions to people, who were already anxious about works of the law and out of conscience were submitting themselves to the Jewish ordinances? Was there not then in their case an exaggerated piety, that needed rather to be tempered? Alas, no! The world lies in wickedness and yet is busy about works of the law. It lives in contention and envy, in turbulence and lewdness, and yet forsooth will be saved by its virtue. By what sort of virtue? By a magnanimity, which from time to time, amid many evil deeds, a man may practice toward his neighbor, by wit and lively discourse, by a decent gravity, the offspring of age and function, of interest and love of honor, by the observance of political and ecclesiastical laws, yet with many exceptions. Let no one go into raptures over this virtue.—At a distance it appears great, but near by it is mean and in God's eyes naught. Do not such people need to have some one proclaim to them: Be not deceived, God is not mocked? The Galatians gave themselves up to the Jewish law, which did in fact contain the strictest moral teaching. They sought salvation earnestly, and sought it, not by vices, but by virtue and religious works; yet notwithstanding this Paul was constrained to warn them against all manner of gross sins, especially against hatred and envy, and to proclaim to them: Be not deceived, God is not mocked! How certain it is therefore, that he who does not live in faith on the Son of God, will be overmastered by sin, and in spite of his endeavors to be virtuous, will become ever more vicious! If then one does not come into the right way, he at last mocks God. And how does one mock Him? In this way, that one desperately imagines that He will at last take black for white, that He will let him reap wheat, who has sown tares, and will reward the sin, to which men have given the name of a virtue. By such principles, which to be sure, when we read them on paper, contradict the first principles of human intelligence, the whole world is ruled, and therefore is there occasion to say it: God is not mocked; what a man sows in this world, that, and nothing else, shall he reap in the next." Roos.

3. *What a man sows, that shall he also reap.* An utterance as simple, as it is true and deep. According to it, all the actions of men are a sowing, which shall have a harvest, the actions of men shall bear a fruit. This image, taken from the processes of nature, declares in the first place in general terms, that actions never stop with themselves, but that with inexorable certainty

* [ALFORD and ELLICOTT deny this reference, but any other meaning seems insipid, and might have been better expressed in some other way.—R.]

a retribution will one day follow, as certainly as the sowing is only a beginning, which according to a settled law leads at last to the harvest. This it is true does not follow at once, and therefore there is need of patience, but afterwards, when the time has come, and then without fail. And, more definitely, the seed bears a harvest, and such a harvest as corresponds exactly with itself. The actions of men therefore find a retribution fully adequate. On this account it is not so indifferent what kind of seed we sow, for the seed, that is, our acts, will bear their proper fruit, and no other. If we want then a fruit to please us, we must sow a seed that will bring it; we shall never succeed in getting a harvest that is independent of the seed; and on the contrary no one can deprive us of the harvest that answers to the seed. The harvest of our actions is nothing casual, it is that which they must produce. It rests with us, then to determine the harvest, by determining the seed. If "corruption" is the harvest of sowing to the flesh, and "life everlasting" the harvest of sowing to the Spirit, each result follows by an inward necessity. The former is only the carnal sowing come to ripeness, the latter is only the ripened seed sown to the Spirit. Thereby the character of arbitrariness and externality is removed from the Divine retribution, and objections from this side obviated. But on the other hand it must not be thought, that we can in this way set aside the positive Divine activity, and therewith retribution in a definite sense, and change it into a kind of natural process. As in the natural process of the springing of the harvest from the seed, the inner law of nature, according to which this takes place, is no other than the law of God, as it is He who gives it effect, so is it also in this spiritual harvest. His ordinance is it, that "corruption" grows up from the sowing to the flesh and the reverse. And especially is this so, in that corruption is really what it is, only as decreed by Him, as consisting in being rejected by Him, and even so, on the contrary, life everlasting; this is His gift for the sowing to the spirit, only because He gives it and gives Himself also therein. Moreover the time of harvest is in itself simply a future one for the time of sowing; when the sowing, therefore, is over, every moment may be a "due season" for the harvest, even in this world, and there are indeed many such harvests. But these are only anticipations. The proper, due season for the harvest first comes with the time appointed by God for general retribution at the consummation of the kingdom of God. Not till then will the sowing to the flesh have ripened into corruption, and the sowing of the spirit into life everlasting. Before that, the time of the sowing still continues, and it is still possible to change the character of the harvest by changing the one sort of seed for the other.

4. *Care for spiritual teachers.* The emphasis and earnestness, with which Paul admonishes against a selfish behavior of the church towards her teachers, are remarkable. This very estimate of spiritual good, as above all others, makes him the more impatient of selfishness concealing itself behind a pretended spiritual mind. "The support of teachers by their hearers is grounded on a divine institution, not only in the Old Testament (comp. Priests and Levites), but also in the New. Although now in the New Testament there is no definite prescription how much of their property hearers shall contribute to their teachers, yet it is certain from the New Testament that God requires an adequate and liberal support. This admonition was the more necessary in the Apostle's time, because there were not then, as now, yearly incomes definitely appointed. But now that there are such settled incomes the admonition to hearers has not lost its force, especially when they know that the regular income is insufficient. Christ's commandment binds them then to a subsidy. Men act to-day, as if their forefathers alone had been bound to care for the support of their teachers, and the hearers of to-day had nothing to add to this." STARKE.—LUTHER expresses himself very definitely and strongly respecting this duty towards teachers, *e. g.*: "It is indeed impossible that true Christians should endure to have their pastors pinched and in want. But because they do not only suffer this, but laugh in their sleeve at it, it is certain, that they are worse than Turks and Heathen."

### HOMILETICAL AND PRACTICAL.

Ver. 25. HEUBNER:—The internal and the external must harmonize, must be one. The outer life is the reflection and thereby the sign of the inward life.—RIEGER:—To keep the flesh crucified is the only way to give room for the spirit, whose life appears in growing strength in a spiritual walk. Although walking is a consequence inseparable from life, yet the Apostle exhorts thereto, as to a duty, on account of the danger of slothfulness creeping on, as indeed one cannot walk without taking some special thought about it.—[BROWN:—If we are spiritually alive, let us show that we are so by being spiritually active.—R.]

Ver. 26. LUTHER:—Love of vain glory is a common vice the whole world through, in all conditions. No village so small but there be one or two peasants therein, that will fain be taken for wiser and better than the rest. It is so pleasant to be pointed at with the finger and hear it said: See there is a man that is fit for anything! This vice is common, yet nowhere does it such harm, as to those who fulfil a spiritual function and service in the church.—[CALVIN:—It is not lawful for us to glory but in God alone. Every other kind of glorying is pure vanity. Mutual provocations and envyings are the daughters of ambition.—R.]—STARKE:—To seek honor with a proud spirit, is a token of a carnal man and an abomination to God. Lust of praise leads many sins together, held in one leash, as the huntsman leads hounds. Nothing is more opposite to the love of our neighbor, than high-minded self-love; wherefore it is of no use to commend the latter where the former is not eradicated.—HEUBNER:—The stoic pride of virtue also is the worst kind of vain-gloriousness.

Chap. VI. Ver. 1. LUTHER:—The forgiveness of sins belongs to those who are weak and frail in faith and life, and yet acknowledge their sins and pray for forgiveness; but to those who pervert the doctrine, it does not belong.—RIEGER:—The very words, in which the Apostle describes what behavior beseems us in regard to others' faults, are so chosen, that they insensibly incline us to the more merciful side. *A man* (how easy for a *man* to fall) is *overtaken* by the suddenness of temptation, by the concurrence of many circumstances, that have beclouded his vision. In such circumstances admonition, rebuke, persuasion, consolation, *etc.*, may do the work of *restoration*, even as a dislocated limb may be again set in place. But for this there is needed the *Spirit*, and therefore on the one hand not blind love, not a careless disparagement of the fault, and on the other hand not severity, but insight into the gospel, to draw from thence motives for forbearing admonition, such as shall advance the crucifixion of the flesh and the strengthening of the inward man.—HEDINGER:—Are we ourselves pure and blameless as angels, that our neighbor's fault drives us so quickly to arms? Was it Christ's way to break the bruised reed? Let us do as He did! The Lord is in the still small voice, although mighty winds sometimes herald his coming.—AUGUSTINE:—Rebuke administered in bitterness, profits not. *Quidquid lacerato animo dicetis, punientis est impetus, non caritas corrigentis; dilige et dic, quod voles.*—[CALVIN:—Nothing is more difficult than to bring us to examine or acknowledge our own weakness. Whatever may be our acuteness in detecting the faults of others, we do not see "the wallet that hangs behind our own back."—Whenever we have occasion to pronounce censure, let us begin with ourselves, and, remembering our own weakness, let us be indulgent to others.—R.]

Ver. 2. LUTHER:—A Christian must have strong shoulders and stout legs, in order to bear the flesh, *i. e.*, the weakness of his brethren; for they have vices that are troublesome and annoying. Therefore must love pass by and overlook, and endure much. We must learn, since we can so easily endure and overlook our own sins and faults, many of which we daily commit, to bear also other people's sin.—In STARKE:—What is our whole religion, but a burden-bearing? We have our own and also others' burden to bear. We are all on a journey; if one is like to give way, the other must refresh him; if one is likely to fall, the other must help him up.—If it is not to be answered for, that we should not help another bear his burden, how unchristian must it be, to double his burdens for him.—[WORDSWORTH:—Poverty is the load of some, and wealth is the load of others, perhaps the greater load of the two. It may weigh thee down to perdition. Bear the load of thy neighbor's poverty, and let him bear with thee the load of thy wealth. Thou lightenest thy load by lightening his.—R.]—[The law of Christ is the law of mutual love.—R.]

Ver. 3. STARKE:—Self-conceit and haughtiness have cheated many a man. Pride is the harbinger of a heavy fall. It is often a grace, when God allows the presumptuous one to fall, that he may come to a knowledge of his own nothingness.—[BROWN:—Those who in their own estimation have little to learn, have in truth learned but little.—The greater advances a man makes in true Christianity, the more humble he becomes.—R.]

Ver. 4. LUTHER:—He that faithfully discharges his function, does not inquire much what men say of him, it is all one to him, whether the world praises or reviles him, but he has his honor within himself, that is, the testimony of his conscience, and the honor before God. It will doubtless in time come to pass, that your honor, which you have within yourselves, will be acknowledged also by other people. But if you have your honor only from others, it will surely come to pass, that the shame and ignominy, which you have now inwardly concealed in your heart, will in time become manifest to other people also.—STARKE:—Daily self-examination is one of the most important of all the duties of a Christian. A Christian must always look more at himself than at others, and examine his own life more than another's; for God will judge each man according as He finds him to be in himself and before his own conscience.—RIEGER:—To seek one's glory by self-comparison with others, or even, it may be, by disparagement of others, by divulging their faults, is a perilous course, and will avail nothing, when hereafter each one shall have to give account of himself before God.

Ver. 5. HEUBNER:—Every genuine self-examination will certainly always have humiliation as its result.—[WORDSWORTH:—We cannot make the burdens of our own sins lighter by imputing a heavier burden of sins to others. Praise of ourselves, whether it proceeds from our own lips, or those of others, cannot lighten our burdens. Because we are heavy laden, Christ exhorts us to take His light burden. Thus he converts our heavy burdens into light wings. The wings of birds are their weights, which they bear and which bear them. Let thy soul have the weight of Christ's burden; it has the pinions of peace and the wings of charity, and will bear thee to heaven. Thus bear thy own weight and it will bear thee.—R.]

Vers. 6-10. The more carefully one avoids judicial severity and other unwarranted assumptions in regard to others, the more room there is to make our intercourse with one another profitable for love and good works.

Ver. 6. LUTHER:—I do not love to expound such sentences, which speak for us, that are ministers of the Word; moreover, it may look, if one is zealous to treat such texts before the people, as if he did it on account of avarice. But one must nevertheless instruct the people thereabout, that they may know what degree of honor and support they owe to their teachers. This is also good for us, that are in the ministry, to know, that we may not take our deserved recompense with uneasy conscience, and as if we had no right thereto.—RIEGER:—The Scripture has not accounted it superfluous, to put into His Word, that remains good for all time, the admonition to communicate in all good things with him who teaches. But it is to be left wholly to this same Spirit and His prompting, when he will bring the observance of this admonition so into effect, that it exercises faith and strengthens faith.—STARKE:—Between teachers and hearers there should be a lovely exchange and joyful barter. A hearer needs not to complain as though he suffered disadvantage in this exchange. Whoever will not give our Lord God a penny, gets his due, when he is forced to give the devil a dollar.—In general the world requites the very greatest benefits bestowed upon it with the very basest unthankfulness.—[CALVIN:—It is one of the tricks of Satan to defraud godly ministers of support, that the church may be deprived of their services. Paul's recommendation arose from a desire to preserve a gospel ministry.—BROWN:—It had been well for the church and for the world, had Christianity been sustained and extended solely by the voluntary exertions and the voluntary contributions of those who themselves had experienced its invaluable blessings, and who felt the obligations under which both duty and gratitude laid them to supply the temporal wants of those who ministered to their spiritual necessities. Here, as in every other case, the foolishness of God is wiser than men.*—R.]

Ver. 7. In STARKE:—Mock on: God will endure it for awhile, and will not send a thunderbolt at once; yet will He not always be silent, but early enough will hold discourse with thee in wrath.—Whoever under any manner of apparent excuses seeks to deceive his neighbor, such an one mocks the omniscient God and does himself the greatest conceivable injury.—HEUBNER:—Besotted man would fain persuade himself that God's severity, His threatenings and judgments are not to be taken so very much in earnest. God is directly mocked when He is blasphemed, indirectly, when His commandments are presumptuously neglected.

Vers. 7, 8. In STARKE:—The realm of nature has many vestiges of Divine wisdom, goodness, righteousness in it, which show forth and reveal themselves yet more gloriously in the realm of grace.—It is undoubtedly agreeable to the Divine order, as in the realm of grace so in that of nature, that every one should enjoy what he himself sows or does, whether good or evil. But whoever does evil and yet hopes for good, opposes himself to God's order in vain, and his hope is lost.—The sowing to the flesh cannot possibly be followed by anything but an evil harvest, unless such a harvest before it ripen, be uprooted by true repentance.—Our whole life is nothing but a seed-time, with which the future harvest in eternity is inevitably connected. Ah! let every one take heed that he scatter not tares and yonder be compelled to reap the curse.—Corruption does not really come from God, either directly or indirectly, but from the flesh.—RIEGER:—How slight and insignificant good and evil often appear when first sown! But how steadily they grow day and night, unnoticed by man. How late, but how infallibly do they reappear at the harvest! How irrevocable is the neglected seed time! Who can force it into being an unsown harvest?—HEUBNER:—Future and present stand in the strictest connection. Our future state will not only follow our present, but will be in the very strictest sense its product; the two will stand in as real a nexus as the seed sown and the harvest.—There is a double seed-time and harvest! Sowing to the flesh does not consist merely in a gross carnality of life, such as is followed by the most wretched want and pain, but in all living and working, even that which, materially considered, is the most beneficent and laudable, when it proceeds from an impure motive. Sowing to the Spirit is not merely the spiritual vocation, but every sowing, which is done at the leading of the Spirit.—[CALVIN:—Our liberality is restrained by the supposition that whatever passes into the hands of another is lost to ourselves, and by the alarm we feel about our own prospects in life. These views Paul meets here.—BURKITT:—The Spirit of Him that raised up Jesus from the dead, will also raise us up at the great day, and reward our present parting with the things of this life which we cannot keep, with eternal life which we shall never lose.—R.]

Ver. 9. STARKE:—This admonition is uttered as an encouragement, as a way which has the least appearance of authority assumed over others. It is a way therefore which preachers should incline to use.—Christians may become weary in the race, for they find many an assault and many a hindrance. Happy are they who encourage themselves with this word: Let us not be weary in well doing! The more laborious the seedtime has been, the richer shall the harvest be. The harvest comes hereafter; the first fruits of the present time are a small matter compared with what is to come.—Christians are not greedy for reward, and do not demand it from God on the ground of merit, but they do suffer their work to be sweetened, and themselves spurred up to activity and faithfulness by the prospect of the reward.—[Fatigue is not weariness.—In well doing we are more apt to be weary than fatigued.—Weariness may come from habits of slothfulness.—The due season is God's season.—If we work on, feeling weary, yet not fainting, we shall reap.—R.]

Ver. 10. HEUBNER:—The incalculable value of the present life consists in this, that we have opportunity to do good. The fleshly minded cannot hereafter make up the good which he had the vocation and opportunity to do, *e. g.*, the hard hearted rich man, the negligent father or pastor, *etc.*—STARKE:—One should not put off remembering the poor till death. *Quod moriens das, ideo das, quod tecum ferre non potes; da igitur, dum vivis, et mercedem habebis.*—[BROWN:—The Christian knows no limits in doing good, except those which are fixed by his power and opportunity of doing good.—For a Christian to be unkind to a Christian is not only wrong, it is monstrous.—R.]—RIEGER:—As the house of God, the church, is of two kinds, the visible and the invisible, so are also those of the household of two kinds, namely, those who belong to the visible church, and then the true believers, whose faith and sincerity of heart are invisible. From this it follows, that one owes more love to his fellow-believers, even such as are so but in profession, than to those of another religion; but most to really believing fellow-members, to whom the appellation: they of the household of faith, especially applies. In the present day it is our business to seek out those who have pressed through from the service of the letter into the life of religion, into the service of the Spirit, and to count

* [The principle of *voluntaryism* so plainly implied in the verse has found its happiest exemplification in our own country. Dr. BROWN represents one of the few European churches (United Presbyterian Church of Scotland), that has not only acted upon, but stoutly contended for this principle.—R.]

them for the members of the household of faith chiefly commended to us.—SPENER:—The more closely one, besides the general bond, is connected with any one by a special bond also, the more is he under obligation towards such a one. Thus a man is bound to his wife, parents to their children, brothers and sisters and blood relatives to one another, masters to their servants, citizens of one town or dwellers in one house to each other, in respect to works of love, more than they are to others; yet always without prejudice to the general love of our neighbor.

*On the whole Section:*—Wherein Christians' walk in the Spirit should especially show itself in their conduct towards one another: (1) In this, that no one exalts himself above others, but that one helps another up when he falls and assists him to bear his burdens; (2) in this, that no one grudgingly withholds what is his from another, but willingly lets him share in all and is unwearied in doing good (especially towards those who impart to one the bread of life in the word of God).—SARWEY:—If ye live in the Spirit, then walk in the Spirit; if ye walk in the Spirit, then walk in humility and forbearance, and in thankfulness towards your teacher and in liberality towards your brethren; and if ye walk therein ye walk in blessing.—GLÖCKLER:—Concerning the spirituality of the children of God: (1) What people are in the word of God called spiritual; (2) what their duties are towards others and those of others towards them; (3) whether it is necessary for all that wish to be saved, to be be spiritual men; (4) how and when then one is to set about becoming a spiritual man. — HENGSTENBERG: — Christian love of neighbors as a chief part of a walk in the Spirit: it shows itself: (1) in loving converse with our neighbor, and that (*a*) in unambitious humility; (*b*) in helpful long-suffering; (*c*) in enduring patience; (2) in loving activity for our neighbor's good: (*a*) in willing advancement of church and school in our own dwelling place, see ver. 6; (*b*) in ready zeal for giving and helping for the sowing of the gospel in still wider circles (vers. 7, 8); (*c*) in general, in untiring doing of good of all kinds, especially to those of the household of faith (vers. 9, 10).

On vi. 1–5: Self-exaltation. (1) Wherein it shows itself. In this, that it does not do, what is mentioned in vers. 1 and 2. (2) What secures against it: Self-examination.

The single verses of the whole section almost all afford a theme at once, especially as several have the character of apothegms.

Ver. 25. Text and theme of a *Whitsunday sermon* in NITZSCH (*Auswahl* I. p. 177): — (1) The grounds of this Whitsuntide declaration. (*a*) The spiritual life requires to be demonstrated and revealed in the walk, or it does not exist; (*b*) it requires to be maintained and augmented by the walk or it is lost. (2) The substance of this requirement: not=abandon the world and kill the body; nor yet=no longer esteem the word and violate the law; but=in the power of the atonement pursue after holiness.

Ver. 2. Suitable text for a wedding discourse; vers. 7, 8, Fast-day, or New Year's eve, or harvest text; ver. 9, also a harvest text.

---

## CONCLUSION OF THE EPISTLE.

Written by the Apostle with his own hand. He portrays himself in contrast with the False Teachers. An entreaty for future quiet out of regard to his sufferings. BENEDICTIONS.

### CHAPTER VI. 11—18.

11 Ye see how large a letter I have written [See in how large letters I have written,
12 or with what letters I write] unto you with mine own hand. As many as desire to
make a fair shew in the flesh, they constrain you to be circumcised; only lest they
13 should [that they should not][2] suffer persecution for the cross of Christ. For neither they themselves [not even do they] who are circumcised[3] keep the law [themselves]; but desire to have you circumcised, that they may glory in your flesh.
14 But God forbid that I should glory, save in the cross of our Lord Jesus Christ, by
15 whom the world is crucified unto me, and I unto the world[4]. For in Christ Jesus
[omit in Christ Jesus][5] neither circumcision availeth[6] anything, nor uncircumcision, but
16 a new creature. And as many as walk [shall walk][7] according to this rule, peace
17 *be* on them, and mercy, and upon the Israel of God. From [omit From] henceforth
let no man trouble me: for I bear in my body the marks of the Lord [omit the Lord][8]
18 Jesus. Brethren, the grace of our Lord Jesus Christ *be* with your spirit [The
grace of our Lord Jesus Christ be with your spirit, brethren]. Amen.

[1] Ver. 11.—[The E. V. is obviously incorrect both in rendering "ye see" and "how large a letter;" the two interpretations offered to our choice are given above. See EXEG. NOTES. The aorist ἔγραψα must be rendered: "I have written," if it is not an epistolary aorist; "I wrote" (Am. Bib. Un.) is verbally correct, but is not in any case a proper English dress for the Apostle's idea.—R.]

[2] Ver. 12.—[Μή is misplaced in Rec. after ἵνα. It should follow Χριστοῦ. Διώκωνται is the reading of ℵ. B. D. E.,

adopted by Griesbach, Scholz, Lachmann, Meyer, Alford, Ellicott, Lightfoot, Wordsworth. Tischendorf (with A. C. F. G. K. L.), διώκονται; an improbable solecism, arising from the frequent interchange of ω̃ and ο.—R.]

[3] Ver. 13.—Rec. περιτεμνόμενοι; the reading περιτετμημένοι is, however, recommended by Griesbach, and adopted by Lachmann and Scholz. "With right; the perfect is absolutely necessary, since the Judaistic teachers are meant. The present was introduced by the transcribers, who had just written περιτέμνεσθαι and perhaps were reminded of ver. 3." Meyer. [If the perfect be the correct reading, we must render, "who have been circumcised," or simply "the circumcised;" but the present is not only *lectio difficilior*, but is supported by preponderant external authority (א. A. C. D. E. K., many versions); it is therefore adopted by Tischendorf, Alford, Ellicott, Lightfoot, Wordsworth.—R.]

[4] Ver. 14.—Τῷ is omitted by Lachmann on important authorities. [א. A. B. *etc.*; Alford, Lightfoot omit the article. There is great room for doubt, since the omission may be readily accounted for both by the similarity of the preceding syllable and the desire to conform with the anarthrous κόσμος; Meyer, Tischendorf, Ellicott, Wordsworth retain it.—A careful examination of all the proposed emendations leaves the impression that the rendering of this verse in the E. V. ought not to be altered in the least particular.—R.]

[5] Ver. 15.—'Εν γὰρ Χριστῷ 'Ιησοῦ is probably an explanatory gloss from ver. 6, though א. has it. We should read simply: οὔτε—γάρ. [The MSS. authority for the longer reading is very great, but so many old versions follow the shorter one, and the probability of an importation from ver. 6 is so great, that Tischendorf and almost all editors adopt it.—R.]

[6] Ver. 15.—'Εστίν; Elz. and Matth. [and Rec.] have ἰσχύει (from ver. 6) against decisive authorities.

[7] Ver. 16.—Στοιχήσουσιν. The reading στοιχοῦσιν is approved by Griesbach, put in the margin by Lachmann, and adopted by Tischendorf. Meyer asks with right: "What reason could the transcribers have had for changing it into the future?" [The authorities for the future are weighty; the change to the present is more explicable; the future is slightly more difficult. Adopted by Meyer, Alford, Lightfoot, Wordsworth; hence "shall walk."—R.]

[8] Ver. 17.—Κυρίου is omitted by Lachmann and Tischendorf, [Meyer, Alford, Ellicott, Lightfoot, on the authority of A. B. C.—R.]; probably imported from ver. 18, but א. has τοῦ κυρίου 'Ιησοῦ Χριστοῦ. [Wordsworth, with his usual conservative tendencies, follows the Rec.—R.]

## EXEGETICAL AND CRITICAL.

Ver. 11. **See with what letters I write [or in what large letters I have written** (see below)—R.] **unto you with mine own hand.**—Paul as a rule dictated his Epistles; but attested them by adding at least the conclusion in his own hand (comp. 2 Thess. iii. 17). So also in this Epistle. But as it is the first letter which he has written to the Galatians, he begs them to notice* his handwriting. This is the sense of πηλίκοις γράμμασιν, which is therefore simply = with what sort of letters. 'Εγραψα, according to the familiar epistolary usage; the aorist does not therefore refer back to the portion already written, but Paul means what he is just beginning to write in conclusion. So LAURENT, *zur Kritik der Briefe des Apostles Paulus*, in the *Studien und Kritiken*, 1864 H. 4, p. 643 sq.—His interpretation seems to have more in its favor than that of WIESELER (adopted in the 1st edition of this work), who renders it: "See with how great letters," *etc.*, referring the words to the whole Epistle, in this sense, that he means to give his readers a token of his special love in having written to them in quite large, and therefore unusually legible, characters, and that, not through an amanuensis, as ordinarily, but with his own hand. Against this LAURENT remarks: How is it conceivable that immediately after so profound and earnest a discourse, the Apostle should have reviewed the characters he had already written, and have made so trivial a remark about their appearance? Besides the letters were not at all large; not much larger than ours. In Paul's day cursive writing was already in use. While therefore the amanuensis probably wrote in uncial letters, Paul himself wrote cursively[!?]†—But his purpose in adding the conclusion with his own hand was in this case not merely to attest the Epistle. For the conclusion is unusually long. Paul was also impelled to write by the desire of impressing more deeply on the minds of the Galatians a notice respecting his own person in opposition to the false teachers.

[Two questions arise in the interpretation of this verse: 1. to what does the Apostle call attention; 2. to how much does he refer. The answer to the first question turns upon the meaning of πηλίκοις γράμμασιν, that to the second mainly, though not exclusively, upon the force of ἔγραψα. 1. We may determine with comparative certainty the meaning of πηλίκοις γράμμασιν. Πηλίκος, occurring only here and in Heb. vii. 3 (where the reference is to magnitude, though in an ethical sense), is not synonymous with πόσος, "how many;" hence "how many letters"=how large a letter, is incorrect; nor does the plural γράμματα mean "letter," for which Paul invariably uses ἐπιστολή. Besides the phrase γράφειν γράμμασιν, in the sense of "write a letter," is nowhere found. Nor is πηλίκος identical with ποῖος (so Schmoller and others), "what kind;" ELLICOTT justly characterizes this interpretation as arbitrary. It means "how large," referring to the size, implying that, for some cause, what Paul himself wrote was written in larger characters than usual (or perhaps than an amanuensis was in the habit of using). There is no necessity for finding a reference to shapelessness. It is no valid objection to say that this reference was trivial, for other things that Paul has written may be thus spoken of with equal propriety (comp. 2 Tim. iv. 13). See MEYER, ALFORD, ELLICOTT, WORDSWORTH and LIGHTFOOT. 2. To how much does he refer? In other words, did Paul write the whole Epistle with his own hand, or only these concluding verses. The aorist indicates the former, unless it be an epistolary aorist. But the burden of proof rests with those who maintain this. Besides if the reference be exclusively to what follows, it seems singular that the epistolary aorist should be chosen. We cannot perhaps decide the question from this word alone, but there are other considerations which may be urged in favor of the autographic character of the whole Epistle. *a*) Attention may have been called to the size of the letters, as a proof that Paul had written the whole, not using an amanuensis, who would probably have written more rapidly, hence in smaller characters, and this would be a proof of his earnestness and affection. *b*) The Epistle is largely a personal vindication, and hence was more likely to be an autograph. *c*) ALFORD

* ["'Ιδετε is imperative; "see" not "ye see" as E. V.—R.]

† [It does not appear whether this statement is made by Schmoller, on his own authority, or that of Laurent. There seems to be no other authority for it. The very reverse is more probable.—R.]

finds a similarity, in style and in use of words, between this and the Pastoral Epistles (which he regards as autographs), see Vol. III. *New Testament Prolegg.* pp. 4, 79 sq. *d*) WORDSWORTH refers to the passage in Habakkuk cited in this Epistle, (iii. 11), and finds in the injunction to the prophet to write "the just shall live by faith" in large characters, an implication that this Epistle on the same theme was written in similar characters. (This however is not of much weight.) Although the use of *ἔγραψα* is not decisive, yet taken in connection with the meaning of *πηλίκοις*, and whatever of weight attaches to the considerations mentioned above, it is much safer to assume that Paul wrote the whole letter; the probabilities are strongly in favor of this view. (So ALFORD, ELLICOTT and WORDSWORTH most decidedly.) There is a conjecture that the size or shapelessness of the letters arose from Paul's weakness of vision, but it must be regarded as only a conjecture. Comp. iv. 15. Paul could not have been unskilful in writing Greek.—R.]

Ver. 12. **As many as desire to make a fair shew in the flesh.**—In condensed sharp language the Apostle (vers. 12, 13) characterizes the intrigues of the false teachers. They are people who want to have a good repute (*εὐπροσωπῆσαι*), but for all that live in the flesh, according to the lusts of the flesh,* and shun suffering. Therefore **they constrain you to be circumcised.**—(*Ἀναγκάζουσιν ὑμᾶς περιτέμνεσθαι*= "are busied with forcing a circumcision upon you.") For this is done **only that they should not suffer persecution for the cross of Christ.**—*Τῷ σταυρῷ* not: on account of the cross, but: by the cross; the cross of Christ is itself represented as the persecutor—a significant image for these people's fear of the cross, because it brings persecution. But the cross of Christ brings with it such persecution, *sc.* on the part of the Jews, only when it is preached and confessed as the sole condition of salvation, which is not done when circumcision is regarded as a condition of salvation. Therefore they insist upon this, in order to escape persecution. [It seems better to take *τῷ σταυρῷ* as the dative of the *ground* or occasion (so MEYER, ALFORD, ELLICOTT and many others). Schmoller actually presents this view in his explanatory remark. It cannot mean "with the sufferings of the cross" (WINER). The objection to both is that "the cross of Christ" means "the atoning death of Christ upon the cross" (BROWN), and this meaning will not admit of these interpretations.—R.]

Ver. 13. Paul immediately explains the strong *μόνον*, "only" (ver. 12). They have in this no other view than the one assigned—the purely egoistic one—they are not concerned for the law on its own account; **for not even do they who are circumcised keep the law themselves.**—Of the circumcised, or those who receive circumcision, [the reference being to the Judaizing party; the perfect would perhaps point more to the leaders, the present to the party as one which was then enforcing this rite, —R.] with all their zeal for circumcision, it might be expected that they kept the law. But their conduct is hypocritical. When **they desire to have you circumcised**, it is not in the interest of the law, but only **that they may glory in your flesh**, that they may be able to boast themselves; and it is moreover the *σάρξ* of the Galatians, that is to be the subject of their boasting: to be taken either physically, with reference to the circumcision to be performed in their flesh; or in a sense similar to ver. 12, because if the Galatians should receive circumcision, they would follow the *σάρξ* and its suggestions, would display a carnal weakness and pliability of which these men would then boast as their own work. [The latter view is preferable.—R.]

Ver. 14. **But God forbid that I should glory.**—To this sinful boasting of the false teachers, to whom the cross of Christ is more or less a scandal, and who are unwilling to suffer any persecution for its sake, Paul opposes his own boasting, whose subject is this very cross of Christ.—**Save in the cross of our Lord Jesus Christ.**—MEYER incorrectly supposes that Paul wishes to mention the subject of his official glorying over against the official vauntings of the false teachers, and hence understands "the cross of our Lord Jesus Christ" of the preaching of the cross of Christ, not of the fact itself. [In the 4th Ed. MEYER says: Only the cross of Christ should be the subject of his *καυχᾶσθαι*, *viz.*: that nothing other than the Redemption accomplished on the cross by Christ was the ground, contents and Divine assurance of his faith, life, hope, labor, *etc.*"—Surely this is not open to Schmoller's objection.—R.] WIESELER:—Paul will, in contrast with these Judaizers, not boast at all of what he is or has or does, and therefore also not of his official labors, but of the cross of Christ.—**By whom or which.**—*Δι' οὗ* is then most naturally referred to the main idea, "cross," not to "our Lord Jesus Christ." [The meaning is evidently the same, whether the relative be referred to one or the other; "by which" would mean through the cross of Christ; "by whom," through Christ crucified. Still there is much force in the suggestion, that the subject immediately preceding, "so fully and triumphantly expressed, so important and so emphasized, throws the other word into the shade." (It is not necessary to suppose that in this case we would find *ἐν ᾧ*.) Besides, the idea of sundered fellowship with the world, which follows, seems to imply here more of a fellowship with Christ than with the cross. See MEYER, ALFORD and ELLICOTT, and on the other side CALVIN, BENGEL, BROWN and LIGHTFOOT.—R.]

**The world is crucified unto me.**—By this Paul does not mean to state, for instance, why he cannot any longer boast of anything else, *viz.*, because nothing else exists for him (MEYER), but he gives in a few yet pregnant words a glimpse into the significance which the cross has for him, on account of its operation. It is of course only because the cross is for me the object of faith, because I stand by faith in inward fellowship therewith (comp. ii. 19), [or, better, with Christ Himself as the Crucified One—R.], that a crucifixion has been accomplished in my case also. Paul, however, is here speaking not simply of the fact that *he* or his old Ego has been crucified. Recognizing as he does his old Ego as one entangled with the world, and recognizing

* [Or perhaps, "make a fair shew in things which appertain to a mere fleshly life."—R.]

this entanglement with the world as its distinguishing character, he says, that the world, to which it clung, has been crucified to him, *i. e.*, the world had become in his eyes condemned, yea dead = had utterly lost all significance, all attractive power for him, and that therefore his fellowship with it had been wholly broken off. Of course Paul's fellowship of faith with the cross of Christ [or Christ crucified—R.] involved no direct action upon the world itself, but only upon it so far as it appertained to him, *i. e.*, upon his fellowship with it.—**And I to the world.**—And even so had he been crucified to the world. A crucifixion of him had naturally been the consequence of his fellowship of faith with the cross of Christ (comp. ii. 19), but calling to mind his former entanglement with the world, he declares himself crucified "to the world," says, that in its eyes also he is one dedicated to death, yea, a dead man, so that he has no longer any attraction for the world, that the world will have nothing more to do with him, that its fellowship with him is also fully dissolved. This double statement thus expresses in the strongest manner, the absolute dissolution of every bond between him and the world. To him this result appeared a gain, and he saw in this a new reason, for glorifying in the cross of Christ. The second clause, κἀγὼ τῷ κόσμῳ, appears to imply also the positive statement, that not only does the world no longer regard him as one of its own, but also hates and persecutes him, and thus does precisely that which his adversaries seek to avoid (ver. 12); yet Paul accounts it as nothing, but glories in the cross of Christ, although it brings these consequences with it; so highly does he value the gain, which he has from it.

Ver. 15. **For.**—He immediately gives the reason for his determination to boast *exclusively* of the cross of Christ (not for the δι' οὗ, MEYER).—**Neither circumcision availeth anything, nor uncircumcision, but a new creature.**—Everything depends on the last, nothing on the first. But it is the cross of Christ which leads to this new creation, and that through the operation of it described by δι' οὗ in ver. 14. This reciprocal crucifixion of the world and the old man to each other is the death of the old man and the beginning of a new one. [Καινὴ κτίσις is probably passive, the thing created, resulting from a new creation on the part of God.—R]

Ver. 16. **And as many as shall walk according to this rule.**—In ver. 15 Paul stated a principle; here he designates this as the standard, according to which one should walk. Upon all who shall thus walk (the future applies to the time from the receipt of the Epistle thenceforward; Paul hopes that the Epistle will have a converting and confirming effect upon the readers) he invokes **peace*** (see on i. 3) and **mercy**, thereby indicating the high importance of this standard. As this belongs to the conclusion, it is best to take it as a benediction: others understand it as a statement, supplying ἔσται.—The correct interpretation of **and upon the Israel of God** is the explicative one = that is [for they are the Israel of God.—R.] For there is here no reason for bringing the Jewish Christians into especial prominence; besides, the comprehensive ὅσοι does not admit of a national distinction being now first made in addition, and others named, who, it would even appear, had not to walk according to this standard. On the other hand, "the designation of all those, who walk according to this Anti-Judaistic standard, as the Israel of God, the true theocratic people, at this solemn close, is, as it were, the triumph of the whole Epistle."—MEYER. [ELLICOTT doubts whether καί can have so strong an explicative force, and prefers to take it as copulative, as if the Apostle's thought turned to his kindred according to the flesh; but the exegetical objections to this view are great, and the other interpretation is so suitable that it must be adopted.—R.]

Ver. 17. **Henceforth let no man trouble me**, *i. e.*, by still listening to the false teachers; **for I** (ἐγώ and not the persecution-shunning false teachers) **bear in my body the marks of Jesus**, the stigmata of Jesus, *i. e.*, the proofs, that I am a real servant of Jesus (στίγματα with reference to the marks which masters had branded upon their slaves), namely, in all the traces, scars, wounds, and the like, of the maltreatments and persecutions, which I have endured in my apostolic calling. ["Of Jesus," *i. e.* my Master, Captain, God, for slaves, soldiers and votaries bore such marks. See WORDSWORTH and LIGHTFOOT *in loco*.—R.]

Ver. 18. **The grace of our Lord Jesus Christ be with your spirit.**—Μετὰ τοῦ πνεύματος ὑμῶν; we are not to understand a special intention in his not writing the simple μεθ' ὑμῶν; yet we should not overlook what is significant in the expression. Grace operates and is meant to operate upon the πνεῦμα of the man; only so does it operate truly and fully, and just such a full, truly salutary operation of grace does he wish for them.—**Brethren.**—Ἀδελφοί: "The Epistle, so severe in its prevailing tone, concludes with this address, in which unaltered brotherly love expresses itself." MEYER. [BENGEL: *Ita mollitur totius epistolæ severitas.*—R.]—**Amen.**

## DOCTRINAL AND ETHICAL.

*Christ's cross is the touchstone of true Christianity.* What Paul says in this section of the Judaistic teachers, applies strikingly *mutatis mutandis*, to the great mass of nominal Christians.* They by no means wish to keep the law in its whole extent, that is much too burdensome for them; on the contrary they appeal to the fact that they forsooth believe on Christ, and therefore are free from the yoke of the law. But now on the other hand they have as little mind to believe on Christ in the whole extent of faith; what is inconvenient in this, they leave behind, and that is the cross of Christ, *i. e.*, so far as it is a means of quieting the conscience, it is willingly accepted, but so far as it includes a dying of the old man, and the entering into a fellowship of the cross with Christ, they will none of it. Instead of this men turn rather to the otherwise despised law, and arbitrarily make the law to consist in this or that particular, some practice, some abstinence,

* [WORDSWORTH remarks that this is the only place in the New Testament where εἰρήνη is placed before ἔλεος.—R.]

* [True where this commentary was written, but partially true everywhere.—R.]

and imagine themselves there to be satisfying all the severer requirements of God, while yet they are far from this utterance: The world is crucified to me and I unto the world!—Christ's cross is the touchstone of true Christianity; it is in this, that salvation and comfort is to be sought, and so far it would not be so very hard to glory in the cross of Christ, which many are willing to do. But salvation and consolation are to be sought exclusively in that, no longer in the world, no longer in one's self, everything else is to be accounted loss, and on the other hand the fellowship with the cross of Christ is to be counted no loss; in brief, there must come into being a new creature. This is the "Canon" (ver. 16) for a Christian; only he who guides himself according to this becomes and is in truth a Christian. This is hard and yet not impossible. God will help therein by the pedagogy of his law, and will lead to faith, and to faith will give the Spirit, which helps through to the new creature.—Comp. also Roos: "Paul shows, that it is not so completely indifferent, what a man thinks of Christ and His cross. Now-a-days, as many of the people say: I pray, read, hear, and am none of the worst. A clever man of the world says: I do much evil, but I have a good heart with it all, and between my evil works I also do some good ones. God will look at me on my good side. What now shall we make of Jesus of Nazareth? Here the world boggles. At last it says: Let Him pass for a good teacher, who has told us, that God is not the God of the Jews only, but also of the Gentiles, and that He loves such virtuous persons as we. Let Him be also an example for imitation. Finally, let Him be also, if one will so have it, the Redeemer, who has acquired for us freedom to hasten on a broad and easy way, with a trifle of virtue, light-mindedly to eternity, and notwithstanding our wickedness to fear no punishment. Now consider, whether this is the gospel of Paul, and whether he so preached Christ. Can such a man say that he boasts only of the cross of Christ, and that through it the world is crucified to him and he unto the world? Has he experienced a new creation? Is the culture, which age, office, intercourse with men, has given him, worthy of this lofty name? Is he in Christ Jesus? Has he the confidence, as he is, to stand before the holy God? Let him, in moments of reflection, put this question to himself and hear concerning it the answer of God and the Bible. Perhaps God will be so gracious as yet to reveal to him the gospel which Paul preached, and if this is so, he will be astonished to find that before this, he, without his knowledge, had a false religion. Mercy and peace be upon every one that is thus brought right."

## HOMILETICAL AND PRACTICAL.

Ver. 12. Rieger:—In every age there are points in which the world insists upon being yielded to, agreeing then to leave other points untouched. And whoever does not consent to this impure commingling, must not only suffer persecution, but also bear the reproach, that he himself is to blame, that he suffers only on account of his own self-will.—Hedinger:—How many thousand brethren have ye, ye clerical placemen, in Galatia? The handful of barley, the merry countenance, the assured friendliness, the favorable patron your comfort; flattery and trimming the sails, you think, will bring a man on. I do not agree with you. Moses' course and choice is the best. Christ's reproach before the purple of Egypt.—Starke:—Love must, indeed, cover and excuse a neighbor's faults, but from hypocrites and seducers one must, for a warning, tear away the mask; especially should those do it to whose office it appertains.—Spener:—The doctrine of Christ preaches Christ's cross, and brings a cross to him who preaches it.

Ver. 13. Hedinger:—To preach to others and be one's self a reprobate, to lade others with burdens, and not one's self to touch them with a finger, what hypocrisy!—Starke:—It is an attribute of false teachers and zealots for religion, who are only concerned with the outside, to proselytize a man to the religion, let him believe afterwards as he will. This is a carnal zeal with abundant craving for notoriety.

Ver. 14. Il Starke:—Christians must not be ashamed of the cross of Christ, but rather glory in being justified and saved by that alone. Faith in Christ, the Crucified One, brings commonly such a fellowship of suffering with Him, that one has to bear his cross after the Lord Christ.—As soon as the union of a soul with Christ through faith takes place, so soon is the tie which holds it to the sin prevailing in the world, loosed.—A Christian may have much which even the world esteems, but the heart must not rest upon it.—Luther:—The world is crucified to me, *i. e.*, I account, that the world is damned; and even so am I in turn crucified unto the world, *i. e.*, it accounts, that I am damned. Thus we condemn one another. I anathematize all its human righteousness, doctrine, and work, as the very devil's poison, and it in return anathematizes also my doctrine and work, counts me for a mischievous man, *etc.*

Ver. 15. Luther:—"A new creature" does not mean, that one clothes himself differently, and puts on a different air, from before, but it means the renewal of the mind, which is brought about by the Holy Ghost. From that there follows an alteration of the outer life. For where the heart through the gospel obtains a new light, there it never fails that the outward senses also are altered. The ears have there no longer pleasure, in hearing human dreams and fools' tidings, but God's word alone. The mouth no longer boasts of a man's own works, righteousness and monastic rule, but of God's compassion in Christ Jesus. This then is an alteration, which consists not in words, but in work and in power.

Ver. 16. [Burkitt:—1. Christianity is a walk: a free and voluntary motion, an uniform and even motion, a progressive motion, a constant motion. 2. This walk is a walk by rule. A Christian is not a lawless person to range up and down as fancy leads him. 3. The rule is the law of the new creature. The new creature, in the principles and workings of it, is made the ground, the pattern and direction of our obedience, and we frame and square all the actions of our lives according thereunto. 4. The blessed privileges belonging to those who thus walk:

peace and mercy. 5. Such are the true Israel: a thousand times greater privilege than to be the children of Abraham's flesh.—R.]—RIEGER:—Even if one cannot accept the ungodly peace offered by those who make a fair show in the flesh, yet one by steadfast abiding within the limits of his faith, has the enjoyment of a Divine peace, and mercy is shown us in recompense of what many a one will lay upon us with an unrighteous judgment.

Ver. 17. In STARKE:—The burdened servant of the Lord has a claim to be unmolested.—It is not necessary to be ever anew entering into argument with unprofitable chatterers in defence of the truth, especially where it has been once and again vindicated against them.—LUTHER:—Because I am Christ's servant and walk after the right rule, *i. e.*, because I publicly confess, that out of Christ no man can attain to salvation, therefore also must I wear my Lord's livery, which does not consist in marks and scars that I have inflicted in will worship as presumption on myself, like Francis, but such as are without my thanks or will inflicted on me by the world and Satan for Jesus' sake.

Ver. 18. In STARKE:—Grace is the beginning, middle and end in Paul's writings. As the beginning of religion is grace, so does its progress depend upon grace. Dost thou, O Christian, in thy solicitations from men, find neither grace nor comfort? Be not dismayed! The grace of thy Lord Jesus remains assured to thee.—Let every one see to it, that he be and remain a dear brother of Paul, *i. e.*, a true child of God; so may he also appropriate to himself the wish that God's grace may remain with him, with a believing Amen.—[BROWN:—Thus does the Apostle conclude this admirable Epistle, and show us, by his example, what it is to do all things in the name of the Lord Jesus, giving thanks to God the Father by him.—R.]

Fleeing the cross, or boasting of the cross? The decisive question in religion.—In LISCO:—The incomparable worthiness of the cross of Christ to be gloried in: 1. That a man can only refuse to acknowledge this out of unworthy motives. a) That such a refusal exists; b) why many refuse: *a*) because one will only make a fair show in the flesh, *β*) because one is not willing to be persecuted with the cross of Christ, *γ*) because one will have glorying for himself and by means of himself. 2. On what account the cross of Christ is thus solely worthy to be gloried in: a) for the sake of that, which came to pass thereon; b) for the sake of the fruit which the cross of Christ bears in the hearts and lives of His people: *a*) as respects their demeanor toward the world, *β*) as respects their temper towards others: they cherish warm love towards those of like mind; they contemn the assaults of those, that are not so minded; they wish that all may become and remain sharers in His grace.

[The Apostle had first vindicated *his* apostleship, then *his* gospel, but was it for his own glory? Nay, in one sense ver. 14 is a summing up of the whole Epistle; all this defence, this earnestness, this boldness, this tenderness, was but a glorying in the cross of our Lord Jesus Christ.—Many see the cross, some trust in it, not all of these glory in it. Why not? Because their fellowship with Christ is not yet such, that the world is crucified to them and they to the world.—Those who gloried in the cross of Christ have gotten glory to Christ and His cross.—Among the many celebrated sermons on ver. 14 may be mentioned those of Bishops ATTERBURY and BEVERIDGE, also of McLAURIN, SUMMERFIELD and McCHEYNE.—R.]